Bear Flag and Bay State
in the Civil War

Bear Flag and Bay State in the Civil War

The Californians of the Second Massachusetts Cavalry

THOMAS E. PARSON

McFarland & Company, Inc., Publishers
Jefferson, North Carolina, and London

The present work is a reprint of the illustrated case bound edition of Bear Flag and Bay State in the Civil War: The Californians of the Second Massachusetts Cavalry, *first published in 2001 by McFarland.*

LIBRARY OF CONGRESS CATALOGUING-IN-PUBLICATION DATA

Parson, Thomas E., 1960–
Bear flag and Bay State in the Civil War : the Californians of the
Second Massachusetts Cavalry / Thomas E. Parson.
p. cm.
Includes bibliographical references and index.

ISBN-13: 978-0-7864-3257-8
softcover : 50# alkaline paper ∞

1. United States. Army. Massachusetts Cavalry Regiment, 2nd (1862–1865)
2. United States. Army. California Cavalry Battalion (1862–1865)
3. Massachusetts — History — Civil War, 1861–1865 — Regimental histories.
4. California — History — Civil War, 1861–1865 — Regimental histories.
5. United States — History — Civil War, 1861–1865 — Regimental histories.
6. Soldiers — California — History — 19th century.
7. Soldiers — Massachusetts — History — 19th century.
8. Massachusetts — History — Civil War, 1861–1865 — Cavalry operations.
9. California — History — Civil War, 1861–1865 — Cavalry operations.
10. United States — History — Civil War, 1861–1865 — Cavalry operations.
I. Title.
E513.6 2nd.P37 2007   973.7'494 — dc21   2001045015

British Library cataloguing data are available

©2001 Thomas E. Parson. All rights reserved

No part of this book may be reproduced or transmitted in any form or by any means, electronic or mechanical, including photocopying or recording, or by any information storage and retrieval system, without permission in writing from the publisher.

On the cover: Guidon of Company A (*California State Capitol Museum*); Capt. James Sewall Reed, commander of the California Hundred, and the regimental band, 2nd Massachusetts Cavalry (*U.S.A.M.H.I.*)

Manufactured in the United States of America

*McFarland & Company, Inc., Publishers
Box 611, Jefferson, North Carolina 28640
www.mcfarlandpub.com*

Contents

Acknowledgments	vii
Preface	1
Prologue	3
CHAPTER ONE—"What do you mean Gentlemen, drivers of gigs?"	5
CHAPTER TWO—The California Hundred	20
CHAPTER THREE—The California Battalion	29
CHAPTER FOUR—"Take care Major, here come the Rebs"	45
CHAPTER FIVE—Northern Virginia	64
CHAPTER SIX—The Independent Cavalry Brigade	81
CHAPTER SEVEN—Dranesville	101
CHAPTER EIGHT—Jubal Early's Washington Raid	125
CHAPTER NINE—The Shenandoah Valley	140
CHAPTER TEN—"So strong a love for country"	160
CHAPTER ELEVEN—"Let them know there is a God in Israel"	176
CHAPTER TWELVE—Appomattox	186
Epilogue	202
Appendix A: Casualties at Dranesville, February 1864	203
Appendix B: Casualties at Mt. Zion Church, July 1864	206
Appendix C: Casualties at Rockville, July 1864	208
Bibliography	211
Index	215

Acknowledgments

I could not have finished this book without the assistance, advice, and friendship of Larry Rogers of Concord, CA (great-grandson of Abraham Loane, Co. A). Thank you Larry for your generosity in sharing materials and ideas. Others who helped along the journey include: Eric Wittenberg, Toledo, OH, who gave excellent direction and helped teach me patience; Dave Stephens, Benecia, CA, who stepped in and shared numerous materials; Tom Hayes, MA, for searching and supplying countless newspaper articles; Brian Pohanka, Alexandria, VA, Allan Tischler, Winchester, VA, and Ted Mahr, all of whom supplied fresh ideas and suggestions; Kenn Denn, Kenniwick, WA, my good friend and computer genius who resurrected my ailing machine the many times I thought it was dead; Bill Parson, Ventura, CA, my dad, for stepping in when my computer finally gave up the ghost; Dr. James F. Gentsch of the University of West Alabama, my cartographer and friend; Mike Graswick, Glenshaw, PA, James Lowder, New Berlin, WI, Corinne Case, Big Bear Lake, CA, Patricia Yucatoms, Tampa, FL, Gerry Chase, Concord, NH, and Mary Paynter, Madison, WI, all descendants of members of the regiment, who shared letters and photographs; Rodney Palmer, California State Capitol Museum, Sacramento, CA, who helped track down numerous old photos; Laura Parson, Ventura, CA, my sister who read the first draft with a critical eye; Richard Kaplan, Massachusetts Archives at Columbia Point, Boston, MA, who was instrumental in my "research by mail" while I was overseas; Lydia Lucas, Minnesota Historical Society, St. Paul, MN (descendent of Harry Mortimer, Co. E), for help both professional and personal; Brenda Lawson and Alyson Reichgott, Massachusetts Historical Society, Boston, MA; Ken Degroodt, Massachusetts National Guard Military Archives and Museum, Worcester, MA; Steven Hill, State House Flag Project, Boston, MA; James Fahey, Massachusetts National Guard Supply Depot; to the current members of Co. A, 2nd Massachusetts Cavalry, The California Hundred, Capt. Ron Van Meir, commanding, who every weekend keep alive a part of history that should never be allowed to be forgotten; to Earl Robinson, Wayne Sherman, Mike Sorenson, Mike Fitzpatrick, Richard K. Tibbals, Dave Stephenson, James McLean, and Julie Rach, the contributors to the webpage of the Second Massachusetts Cavalry at www.members.home.net/reunion/, all of whom have helped with materials and photographs. And finally and most especially, to my wife Nita and daughter Sarah, who put up with my endless hours at the keyboard, forays to overgrown battlefields, and pilgrimages to musty archives, libraries and historical societies. I don't know how many times they found me working at three in the morning, tired and cross, with the alarm clock about to send me off to another day in the Navy. They'd just smile and put on a fresh pot of coffee. Thank you, my ladies, for all of your love and patience.

Preface

When I first saw a reference to the Californians that fought with the 2nd Massachusetts Cavalry, I was intrigued. Being a native of the Golden State and a student of the Civil War I wanted to know more, but there was precious little I could find out about them. As more and more information turned up I realized that a complete history of the California Hundred and Battalion should be written, that all the pieces should be brought together. As the project grew, I began to understand that telling only the story of the Californians was an injustice to the other seven companies, men from not only Massachusetts, but every state in the Union, several Confederate states, and a number of foreign countries. To tell the story properly, I had to tell the history of the entire regiment.

For the benefit of the reader, the following breakdown of unit structure is provided. It should be kept in mind that sickness, wounds, death, furloughs and temporary assignments rarely left companies and regiments at full strength.

Company: 100 men.
Squadron: 2 companies.
Battalion: 4–5 companies.
Regiment: 12 companies (Infantry regiments—10 companies).
Brigade: 3–5 regiments.
Division: 2–4 brigades.
Corps: 2–3 divisions.

Prologue

The 24th of August, 1863, found the two great eastern armies menacing each other across the muddy waters of the Rapidan River. The Army of Northern Virginia still licked its wounds from its near disaster in the hills of Pennsylvania, while the Army of the Potomac, smaller now but still flushed with unaccustomed victory, looked for the elusive corner to back Robert E. Lee into. While these two great beasts maneuvered for position the war "between the lines" continued without pause.

On this sweltering day in Northern Virginia, near the village of Coyle's Tavern, 30 Confederate Partisan Rangers under the command of Major John S. Mosby waited patiently, hidden in the roadside woods. The men were silent, veterans of guerrilla warfare, and the only sound was the occasional impatient stamp of a horse's hoof. Soon their quarry could be heard, then seen riding dustily down the country road. Twenty-five Union cavalrymen bringing 100 fresh horses to their Centerville camp.

The ride from the Cavalry Depot at Alexandria had been hot and uneventful and the men were looking forward to dinner and a long night's sleep back in camp. Each man was leading three horses and riding a fourth when Mosby and his men came crashing out of the woods towards them. Burdened by the extra horses tied to their saddles, the Union troopers were compelled to dismount and find cover. Several of the men fell under the hoofs of the rearing, panic-stricken horses. The remaining men took up their pistols and began opening fire on the Confederates.

During a short lull in the shooting, Mosby's voice rang out, "If they are from New York or Michigan, do not fire." When the identity of the Yankees was discovered he shouted, "Go in boys! Fight like demons! They are Californians!"

It is very unlikely that anyone would stop in the middle of a hail of bullets to make such a statement. Undoubtedly it was a memory that had grown during the course of an old soldier's years. The historian was correct, though — they were Californians that stood up to Mosby's men, giving back as well as they took.

These men were part of the California Hundred, officially Company "A" of the Second Massachusetts Volunteer Cavalry, a regiment comprised of five companies from California and seven from Massachusetts. In an army of colorful leaders and unique regiments they stood out and then, like so many, were forgotten with the passage of time.

Chapter One

"What do you mean Gentlemen, drivers of gigs?"

In the late summer of 1862 San Francisco was just about as far as you could get from the war being fought in the east. To many this was a blessing and indeed was the very reason they resided in California. The isolation of the region from the seat of war virtually assured any part it would play in the struggle would be a small one. The majority of the young men in the west (and many of the old ones too), however, read the stories in the newspapers and longed to be part of it. To them war was still all romance and adventure and they were missing out on the fun.

These naive notions had not been dispelled, but rather strengthened, earlier in the year when the California Column had marched boldly off to war.

A Confederate army under the command of Gen. Henry H. Sibley had entered the Rio Grande Valley from the east, intent on making the west a Confederate possession. The prospect of several deep water harbors and the northern California gold mines were a tempting target. Sibley's infantry defeated the troops of Union Col. E.R.S. Canby at the battle of Valverde, New Mexico, and a company of his cavalry pressed on and occupied Tucson.

To assist Canby in resisting the invasion, Col. James H. Carleton commander of the 1st California Infantry was tasked with leading a supporting column of troops east. Along with his own regiment Carleton had the 5th California Infantry, a company of the 2nd California Cavalry, and a company of the 3rd U.S. Light Artillery.[1]

Starting out from Los Angeles the march across the desert was a logistical masterpiece. Carleton divided the troops into small detachments and staggered their departures so as not to overburden the small and scarce waterholes along the route. The force was reunited 860 miles away at Fort Yuma, without having lost a single man. After a brief rest the column pushed on to meet the Confederates.[2]

Detachments from the two forces skirmished briefly at Pichacho Pass in Arizona but a major engagement never took place. The Confederate bid for the west coast was crushed at the battle of La Glorietta Pass in New Mexico— a tactical victory for the Confederates, but a strategic victory for Canby who had been reinforced with volunteers from Colorado. A small detachment of the Union force succeeded in getting behind Sibley and burned his supply train. With the possibility of starvation looming, and the advance of the Californians, he had no choice but to retreat to Texas.³

A major side effect of this tidy little campaign was to show the boys back in California just how much fun the war could be. The brilliant plan that Carleton had meticulously devised was ignored and it appeared his troops had merely marched off into the desert with the Confederates naturally fleeing before them. The three men who had died at Pichacho Pass were heroes, martyrs for the Union, their bloody deaths in the Arizona sand made over to appear gallant and dashing.⁴

The end result of the campaign could be measured at the recruiting stations. Nearly 16,000 volunteers, approximately 4 percent of California's total population, flocked to pledge their loyalty by enlisting in the Union Army. To a man, they clamored to be sent east.⁵

The need then for troops in the east was enormous, as it was throughout the war. It was decided in the War Department, however, that those troops raised in California could best be used on the west coast. The Regular U.S. troops that had for years garrisoned the Pacific Coast had been called east to add substance to the growing volunteer army. The necessity of guarding the overland routes and keeping an eye on the Northwestern Indian tribes fell to the California volunteers. Actual involvement in the war was limited to the "California Column" and the rounding up of occasional secession minded citizens. So the boredom that had once gripped the Regulars now seized the volunteers.⁶

There were a few groups that clung to the idea that California was destined to contribute something more to the fate of the Union. On the evening of September 8, 1862, in the city of San Francisco, four men met and drafted a telegram to the War Department. The four men, William Lenter, Eugene Sullivan, William Chaplin, and M. Jessup, proposed that they could provide 1,000 men for the war and place them in Panama if the Government would cover the cost of the remainder of the passage. The following morning the telegram was sent to Secretary of War Edwin M. Stanton.⁷

The wait for an answer was not a long one and one week later the following reply was received from Washington:

WAR DEPARTMENT
Washington City, D. C., September 13, 1862

William Lenter
San Francisco, Cal.:

If 1,000 men for the war are placed in Panama, from California, passage will be provided hence for them.

By order of the Secretary of War
C.B. Buckingham Brig. Gen.
Asst Adjt Gen.⁸

Seventeen months after President Lincoln's call for troops, California would now finally respond with men for the fight. The very next day the four-man "committee" began receiving applications for the new regiment. Not only did individuals want placement but the city of Marysville, and Yuba County contacted the committee and demanded a fair showing. In the morning edition of the *Daily Alta California*, several names were mentioned in regards to the future command structure. Among them were Col. J.D. Stevenson as colonel, David Seanel the Chief Engineer of the fire department as lieutenant colonel, and the former Chief of Police James F. Curtis as major.⁹

Patriotism ran rampant through San Francisco; every man and boy vowing to be part of the contingent. It appeared that there were far too many would-be troopers wanting to be part of the regiment than there would be places for them.

Unfortunately, though, a proposal agreed to by Stanton was not the same thing as a proposal authorized by Stanton. Without the authority of the War Department actual recruitment for the regiment could not begin. As days dragged by without the needed permission, it appeared that the loyal men of California were being forgotten or ignored.

Voices continued to be raised, however, and eventually another was heard. Ira P. Rankin, the Customs House collector of the City of San Francisco, had anticipated the Washington red tape and drafted a four-page letter to Governor John A. Andrew of Massachusetts. Sent on the 15th of September, Rankin's telegram read:

> The State of California, though to a large extent as thoroughly loyal as any in the Union has not, on account of her position been called upon for any active service in the suppression of the rebellion. Last year about 6,000 troops were called for, were promptly furnished and are now in the service — some of them in garrison — some in Indian territory, some in Arizona and New Mexico, and about 1,500 have recently gone to Utah. Our men have cheerfully and loyally gone where they have been ordered, but the duty to which they have been called is not that which they would have chosen. There are thousands of our citizens who would gladly enlist, were it judged prudent to send them out of the state, if they could go to the other side and take part in the war directly.
>
> Among such persons is Captain James S. Reed, commander of a Cavalry Company in this city, and friends of his, all like himself natives of Massachusetts, who are earnestly desirous of making up a troop of cavalry of 100 men, to go immediately East and make a part of the Massachusetts contingent, this at the request of Captain Reed and his friends that I write you and offer their services. They are true men skilled as horsemen by the habits of the country as few men in the Atlantic States ever become, and if they can have an opportunity they will certainly make their mark. They propose to uniform themselves, provide saddles, sabres, revolvers, and all equipment except horses, if provision can be made for their passage by steamer from here to New York.
>
> Is it possible for you to make such provisions? If so, and it is possible for you to accept them into the service in the manner I have indicated, it would gratify large numbers of the Sons of the Old Bay State here, and I think make a pleasant and useful impression at home. Probably an arrangement can be made with the Mail Steam Ship Co. in New York by which a company can be carried through at a reduced rate of fare.
>
> Mr. Reed suggests that if the thing can be done, you notify me of the fact immediately by telegraph, and he will go to work at once — then if you will so far trust me as to send to me by mail his commission and blank commissions for first and second lieutenant, he will be immediately organized.
>
> I can manage so as to have the officers examined as to their qualifications by the Examining Board of the Army here, and the men passed by the proper Army medical officers.
>
> It is quite possible that the whole proposed plan is inadmissible, but if it is within your power, and if it should seem expedient to you to adopt it you will greatly gratify the patriotic feelings of some good and loyal men. As you will oblige.
>
> Yours very sincerely,
> Ira P. Rankin[10]

To say that Governor Andrew was interested would be an understatement. Like the other states, Massachusetts was feeling the pinch of manpower at the enlistment stations. The droves of patriotic young men that had thronged to enlist at the early days of the war were a thing of the past. Due to the rash of Confederate offensive drives and the resulting Union casualties the need for recruits was heavier than ever. Governor Andrew fairly leaped at the proposal.

The offer came at a time that Andrew was contemplating plans for a second regiment of state cavalry. The planning was still on the drawing board and not a man or officer had been selected to begin organizing. Here was the perfect command that he could use to integrate the Californians into the state forces. Being the handpicked elite of the West Coast they could provide a nucleus for the regiment to build around.

In order to give authorization for Rankin and Reed to begin recruiting, Governor Andrew had first to secure the blessing of Secretary of War Stanton. Stanton had already been handed one such proposal which he had agreed to but which had died due to lack of organization. The telegram from the four gentlemen in San Francisco apparently had no framework other than the popular support of the local citizens. Rankin's letter detailed who would organize, what would be provided, and how they could be delivered.

The only part of the proposal in question was the cost of transporting the men to the east coast. To accomplish this Andrew suggested that the Californians be used to fill the quota of troops destined to come out of Boston. The Mayor of Boston would then turn the $200 enlistment bounty per man over to an agent of the Governor to cover the transportation costs.

Armed with facts and figures this new proposal was wired to Stanton and on the 22nd of October authorization was granted. A telegram notifying Rankin was quickly dispatched along with a question about when the men would be ready to head east.[11]

As Rankin and Reed began preparations prior to recruiting, Governor Andrew pressed on to ensure the expedient raising of the rest of the regiment. For this Andrew turned to Boston financier Amos A. Lawrence, Jr.

On the 5th of October, 1862, Lawrence wrote to Col. Henry Lee, a friend on Governor Andrew's staff, offering his services to recruit a regiment of cavalry if someone who was authorized would direct him to do so. For a brief time Lawrence considered enlisting himself but a letter from a Major Gardiner, an acquaintance in the regular army, gently told him, "No man is fitted for such service after thirty years...." Lawrence, who was well past his youth if not his prime, decided to focus his strength and abilities on recruiting.[12]

Recruiting was not a new field for Lawrence. For the previous few months he and John Murray Forbes, like Lawrence a wealthy Boston businessman, had been acting as recruiting agents for the state. An effective partnership was started here that was responsible for the raising of a modest percentage of the state's troops. The high point in their efforts to enlist men for the state was assisting in the organization of the 54th Massachusetts Infantry, the first Negro regiment raised in the north.

After the initial flood of volunteers had nearly drained the state of willing young men, a more businesslike approach was needed to attract the less patriotic. Cities began offering cash bounties to recruits in order to meet the quotas set upon them by the state. The more hard-pressed a city was to meet its quota determined the ever-fluctuating amount. The actual dollar figure had to be affordable by the city, but still high enough to draw out individuals employed at high wartime wages. It was not unheard of for a recruit to receive $1,500 although most averaged between $300 and $500, still a substantial amount to a private who drew $12 per month.[13]

It was this bounty system that Lawrence and Forbes used as recruiting agents. Forbes described the particulars: "During the period Mr. Amos A. Lawrence and I were acting together, and I persuaded him to join me in what proved to be a very successful experiment. The large bounties brought into the field a great number of middle-men, whose business was to collect recruits, and who often took the largest part of the bounties for themselves. Mr. Lawrence and I, with the governor's assent, decided to become our own brokers, and got an order that any engagement of ours should be accepted by the draft officers as equivalent to men. We then engaged with the large towns, agreeing to furnish them with men at the best prices they were willing to pay; so enabling them to settle their share of the draft without supplying any more men. When we had got a considerable fund, we engaged the men directly ourselves, or through our enlisting officers, among whom George Quincy was prominent, paying them a smaller price than we received from the towns, but giving it them direct; and thus they got a great deal more benefit out of it than when they treated with brokers. In this way we filled up our regiments and had a fund, which was used to continue recruiting, for the regimental band, and for various other useful purposes, until the end of the war. My impression is we enlisted in this way over two thousand men, and had a fund of seven or eight thousand dollars left."[14]

Lawrence had already used this system to some success when he made his offer to the state. On the 27th of October, he received a letter authorizing him to recruit a battalion of four companies (to include the one coming from California), for three years' service, or the duration of the war. The necessary bounties would come from Boston upon Lawrence's assurance that the 300 men would be forthcoming.[15]

Though at first appearance it would seem that Amos Lawrence, Jr., was the driving force behind the recruitment, the real energy lay with Mr. Forbes. A highly successful businessman, John Murray Forbes had amassed a substantial fortune before the war and could have easily made another during it. Instead he launched himself wholeheartedly into the war effort with a passion rarely matched by other civilians. Before the firing at Fort Sumter he was a delegate to the Washington Peace Conference that attempted to prevent the coming struggle. When the fighting broke out, he became invaluable to Governor Andrew, assisting in putting the State on a war footing. Although his expertise was in railroads and iron making, one of his most important acts during the war was for the Navy Department—he helped in the purchase of civilian ships and their conversion into Blockaders. Also on behalf of the Navy Department he traveled to England and attempted to purchase two powerful steam rams then being built for the Confederacy by the Laird Brothers of Liverpool.[16]

Fifty years old and too old to fight himself, John Forbes now focused on the raising of the proposed cavalry force. To begin recruiting for the battalion, it was necessary for a commanding officer to be selected. Forbes suggested a young acquaintance of his then serving on the staff of Maj. Gen. George B. McClellan: Capt. Charles Russell Lowell, Jr., of the 6th U.S. Cavalry.

In Maryland in October 1862, the headquarters camp of Maj. Gen. McClellan was no longer the vibrant, energetic nerve center it had been the year before. Several times in the last year his staff had watched "Little Mac" prepare his beloved Army of the Potomac for the final battle that would destroy the Confederacy. But as each opportunity to crush his foe arose, they failed to see him use the very weapon he had created. Despite a massive advantage in numbers, McClellan had been unable to defeat Lee at the battle of Antietam the month before. In no way did this tarnish the shining figure his army regarded him as being. Unfortunately Washington saw him in a different light. After his army was pushed back from the gates of Richmond during the Peninsula campaign, and after his showing a minimum of cooperation with Maj. Gen. John Pope when that officer's army was being mauled at Second Bull Run, Antietam was all that President Lincoln could take.

Although change of the army's command was still a rumor in the field and still weeks away, all the members of the headquarters staff knew they were hitched to a falling star. Some remained utterly loyal, serving on his staff to the very end, but a few began putting out discreet feelers to their home states and political contacts letting them know of their availability for transfer. One of these was young Charles Lowell.

"When he entered college he was unusually boyish in appearance, with a ruddy countenance overflowing with health and animal spirits...." Thus a classmate remembered the young Charley Lowell. No small wonder his appearance was boyish — the day he began studies at Harvard, he was a mere 15 years old.[17]

Born in Boston on the 2nd of January, 1835, Charles was the son of cousins Charles Russell Lowell and Anna Cabot Jackson Lowell. His blood was as blue as any in Boston. "In him," recalled his cousin Henry Higginson, "the *elan* of the Russell-Lowell-Spence line was mingled with the Jackson verve and a touch of the Irish fighting spirit of his great-grandfather, Patrick Tracy." His character included the dignity of his grandfather, the Reverend Charles Lowell, as well as the heart of his poet uncle James Russell Lowell. Young Charles was the ninth generation of a family that was eminent in the social, political and economic worlds of New England.[18]

Attendance at Boston Latin School and the English High School prepared Charley for his entrance to Harvard, the youngest man of the class of 1854. A brilliant student he quickly took his place at the head of his class and held that position for the next four years. Possessing a phenomenal memory he could retain his subjects so easily it seemed he never studied.[19]

An exceptional student in all of his courses, Charley had a special love for philosophy. He was fascinated with the writings of Plato who was his constant companion and who would provide the inspiration for his favorite oath of "By Plato." Attracted to mysticism he was also, like his close friends and family, a follower of the Transcendentalist movement.[20]

Shortly after his commencement as Valedictorian he began to learn business skills working in the counting-room of John Murray Forbes. A warm friendship began between Forbes and his young protégé. Forbes later wrote an associate in England who had offered the young Charles a position with his firm in China, "One of the strange things was how he magnetized you and me at first sight. We are both practical, unsentimental, and perhaps hard, at least externally; yet he captivated me, just as he did you, and I came home and told my wife that I had fallen in love."[21]

Young Lowell could have had any job he wanted; his family's position in society assured him of that. But Charley had set out on a career path of his own choosing, one that put truth to his own words from his Valedictory speech. "Mere action is no proof of progress; we make it our boast how much we do, and thus grow blind to what we do." After six months with Mr. Forbes he moved on to the iron-mill of the Ames Company* in Chicopee, Massachusetts, where he began work as a common laborer. "Filing iron and cleaning old chains..." may have seemed an unlikely prospect for a Harvard graduate, but not

---

*The Ames company would become a leading manufacturer of artillery and swords during the coming conflict between North and South.

only was he learning the physical tasks of metal working, he was observing the people around him.[22]

Never exposed so closely to simple working men, he watched and learned and paid particular attention to their working conditions, as well as the relationships with their foremen and managers. Well-meaning, the naive young Charley attempted to organize singing groups for the men in their off duty hours, time he felt was wasted. He also sent home for books to give to the men to replace the "wretched trash" they enjoyed. However, he was not immune to the squalid working conditions and began to form the ideas he planned to put in motion when he assumed a leadership position.[23]

Never intending to stay with the Ames Company, Charley moved on in the autumn of 1855 and took a management position with the Trenton Iron Company of New Jersey. Quickly impressing his employers with his enthusiasm and intellect, Lowell felt that he had finally entered on his permanent work. All appeared well until a friend from New York found him in his room coughing up blood. Tuberculosis had threatened all the members of his immediate family, and now the atmosphere of the iron mill had allowed the deadly disease to gain a foothold in his lungs. Returning to his home in Cambridge he was attended by his uncle, Dr. James Jackson. The good doctor ordered him to avoid all strenuous activity until past the age of 30.[24]

Charles Russell Lowell, Jr., Captain, 6th U.S. Cavalry, Col. 2d Massachusetts Calvary. *Courtesy of U.S.A.M.H.I.*

At this low point in Lowell's life, John M. Forbes acted on Dr. Jackson's other recommendation that Charley travel to a warmer climate. Forbes swiftly ushered the young man onto a steamer and accompanied him on a trip to the West Indies and New Orleans. The warmth and fresh air did wonders for the ailing Charley who felt his strength and health returning, but it was obvious that a longer stay in a healthy climate was what he required. Forbes and Charley's grandmother footed the bill for an extended tour of Europe. (Though Charley's family was far from destitute, his father, Charles Sr., had managed to lose a sizeable portion of the family fortune in the panic of 1837.)[25]

For two years he made his way back and forth across the continent visiting Spain, Switzerland, Austria, Germany, Italy, and Algiers. He frequently met with family and friends on their own tours and took the time to learn the language wherever he stayed. Never an accomplished equestrian, he bought a horse and soon became such a proficient rider that he much preferred that mode of transportation to all others. In Algiers he took fencing lessons and while in Austria and France attended the maneuvers of the countries' armies. His interest at the time was for the pomp and pageantry, not for the military value, but few civilians garnered so much valuable knowledge during the prewar years. Several weeks were spent with Henry Lee Higginson, his cousin and boyhood chum. Near the end of his tour Charley and Henry were exchanging letters and toying with the idea of traveling to "Bleeding Kansas" and doing something to stop the violence there.[26]

July 1858 found a tanned and healthy Charley back in the States apparently cured but forever aware of his "weak lung." He spent a month at John Forbes' estate at Naushon coaching young Will Forbes in history and algebra, as well as spending endless hours riding, fishing, and sailing. Accepting a position as treasurer with Forbes' Burlington and Missouri Railroad, Charley was soon in Burlington, Iowa, putting all of his industry into 18-hour days. For two years he faithfully discharged his duties which not only included his financial responsibilities but also the trust of 300,000 acres of right-of-way.[27]

A man of limitless potential, Lowell could have stayed with Forbes who later said, "he was fit to be at the head of any railroad in the West...." But the iron-making business had caught him early and it was to this calling that he returned. In the autumn of 1860, again through the influence of his mentor John Forbes, Lowell secured a position as ironmaster at the Mt. Savage Iron Works in Cumberland, Maryland. He was hardly settled into his new job when the political situation of the country began to dominate his thoughts and letters. A Lincoln man and something less than an abolitionist, Lowell was acutely aware of the political struggles occurring in the border state he now called home. In December, on a business trip to New Orleans, he witnessed the unfurling of the Pelican Flag when the city received the news of South Carolina's secession. Returning to Maryland he waited, knowing that the political crisis gripping the nation was ready to explode.[28]

For Charles Lowell the explosion occurred on the 20th of April, 1861, when he learned that the day before the Sixth Massachusetts Infantry was attacked by a mob as it marched through Baltimore. Immediately resigning his position he made his way to Washington, arriving two days later ready to assist his State government in organizing its forces. Applying for a commission in the Regular Artillery, Charles put himself at the disposal of Massachusetts while he awaited a response to his application. Governor Andrew sent the young volunteer to Annapolis where he worked as a sort of unofficial state agent, tracking supplies sent from Massachusetts to her troops. It is interesting to note that Lowell made no attempt at a State commission when it is obvious that Andrew would have been quite pleased to see the young man serving Massachusetts as an officer.[29]

His appointment to the regular Army without formal military training was a long shot and he had to know it. But he believed in himself and his abilities and said so in a letter to Senator Charles Sumner:

Dear Sir, — Have you at your disposal any appointment in the Army which you would be willing to give me?

I speak and write English, French, Italian, and read German and Spanish; knew once enough of mathematics to put me at the head of my class in Harvard, though I may need a little rubbing up; am a tolerable proficient with the small sword and single-stick; and can ride a horse as far and bring him in as fresh as any other man. I am twenty-six years of age, and believe that I possess more or less of that moral courage about taking responsibility which seems at present to be found only in Southern Officers.

I scarcely know to whom to refer you, — but either Mr. J. M. Forbes, or my Uncle, James Russell Lowell, will put you in the way of hearing more about my qualifications.

If you have no appointment at your disposal, perhaps you could get me one from Iowa or even Maryland. I have been living in the latter State for a little over six months, in charge of a rolling mill at Mount Savage. I heard of the trouble at Baltimore and of the action of Governor Hicks on Saturday, and at once gave up my place and started for Washington, and was fortunate enough to get through here yesterday, after several detentions.

I am trying to get an appointment on the volunteer staff— my companion, Mr. Stewart, an Englishman, was yesterday named aide-de-camp to Colonel Stone in command of the district troops: it was a lucky hit, and I fear I shall not make as good a one.

Whether the Union stands or falls, I believe the profession of arms will henceforth be more desirable and more respected than it has been hitherto: of course I should prefer the artillery. I believe, with a week or two of preparation, I could pass the examinations.[30]

Sumner passed the letter on to Simon Cameron, Secretary of War, who called Lowell in for an interview. Charles obviously impressed the Secretary who gave the young civilian an unusual appointment as Captain in the 3rd U.S. Cavalry. Ready to do his part for the Union, Charles was vastly aware he had much to learn. "Military science I have absolutely none, — military talent I am too ignorant yet to recognize." As in his other endeavors he would prove a fast learner.[31]

Under the command of Lt. Col. William H. Emory, his first months in uniform were spent recruiting in Pennsylvania and Ohio for his regiment headquartered in Little Rock, Arkansas. The regiment, redesignated as the 6th U.S. Cavalry, had seen nearly all of its experienced officers transferred to volunteer regiments and its already thin ranks had to be filled out before it could be ready for battle. By September the regiment, 650 strong, was stationed in Bladensburg, Maryland, learning to ride and fight as a unit. December found them camped East of the Capital.[32]

After the Battle of Bull Run in July, General George McClellan was placed in command of the Army of the Potomac. As part of the reorganization of the army all of the Regular cavalry regiments were brigaded under Brig. Gen. Philip St. George Cooke and kept to the north side of the Potomac. The cold winter rain turned the cavalry camp into a muddy mess that Lowell described in a letter to his father. "It is particularly hard on cavalry, encamped on a clay bank — the horse splashed with wet clay after three hours drill is not a cheerful spectacle to the recruit who has to clean him — it opens his eyes to some of the advantages of the infantry." The regiment was finally called to service when the Army of the Potomac was transferred from its camps around the Capital to the fields surrounding Fort Monroe, Virginia, for the offensive that would become the Peninsula campaign. It was about this time that Col. Emory, who had come to look upon Lowell as "the best officer appointed from civilian life he had ever known" gave the young captain command of a squadron, or two companies.[33]

The siege of Yorktown provided no opportunities for the cavalry to distinguish themselves. Action was delayed until the Confederate army retreated from Yorktown and began making its way up the Peninsula. The cavalry was used extensively, as the retreat took the Union command by surprise and no contingency existed for a rapid pursuit. All of Chief of Cavalry Gen. George Stoneman's available cavalry as well as four batteries of horse artillery were ordered to close with the Confederates. In support were two divisions of infantry from the III and IV Corps.

Lowell's orderly, Frank Robbins, recorded his memories of his captain after the war had ended. On the other hand, Charles, a prolific letter writer, rarely if ever mentioned his participation in battle. Robbins' recollections of skirmishes and battles tend to run together making it difficult to determine which fight on which date he refers to. The particulars, however, were not as important to Robbins as testifying to the courage of Charles Lowell.

"Our Regiment was advance-guard from Yorktown to Williamsburg." At Fort Magruder, "Gen. Stoneman ordered us to draw in line and charge ... [but] the Rebs' cavalry charged us first. We fell back, and as we were crossing a swamp the Rebs overtook us. Capt. Lowell had charge of Companies K and E. The Rebs charged Company E first, and the Captain joined that Company with our Company K, and fought them with the sabre for about 10 minutes—then we retreated out of the swamp. Our Captain ordered six men to go out as skirmishers from the right of the first platoon. I was one of the six that was sent out, and Sergeant R. was ordered to take charge of us. The Sergt. had been drinking too freely, and he said that *every one of us that didn't charge and kill 20 Rebs, he would put in the guard-house*. Our Capt. told R. he could go to the rear and consider himself under arrest; then he said he would lead us himself. When we got to the swamp, he ordered two of us to dismount and take saddles off the dead horses, while he and the other men skirmished. He laughed at us for dodging when we heard the shells whistle past: he said there was no use to dodge after we heard it whistle.... After the battle [of Williamsburg] we were advance-guard ... Major Williams ordered our Capt. to go through a path that led through a pine forest, with his two companies and see what he could see. When we come out of the woods, the Rebs were formed in a line. One squadron of the Rebs fired on us and one squadron charged us with the sabre. Before they got down where we were our Capt. charged us on another squadron of theirs and charged five times until we made the big road. Our Capt. was the first man through the rebel lines every time we charged through them that day."[34]

James Lowell heard of his brother's action at Slatersville (New Kent Court-House) on May 9 and relayed the events in a letter, "I heard yesterday of a narrow escape which Charley had. He was charging and came upon a man who aimed a double-barrelled carbine at him. C---- called out to him, '*Drop that!*' and he lowered it enough to blow to pieces C----'s coat, which was strapped on his horse behind him."[35]

Captain Lowell brought further attention to himself during a reconnaissance on the 15th of May and again on the 27th during a fight at Hanover Court-House. Though not mentioned in dispatches, his bravery and coolness under fire was officially recognized when he was recommended for the brevet of major, "For distinguished services at Williamsburg and Slatersville."[36]

The 26th of June, 1862, opened the campaign known as the Seven Days. On the second day of battle Gen. Stoneman's cavalry was cut off from the main army and forced to retreat down the Peninsula to avoid capture. The 6th U.S. Cavalry made camp at Harrison's Landing on the James River and sat out the battle that raged to the northwest. Though not involved in the fighting, Capt. Lowell was deeply hurt when he learned of the death of his brother James in the battle near Glendale. A first lieutenant in the 20th Massachusetts Infantry, James Jackson Lowell was mortally wounded during the fighting on the 30th and lingered until July 4, dying in enemy hands. Charles made an attempt to reach his brother when he learned of the wounding, as did their sister Anna, a nurse on a hospital steamer anchored at Harrison's Bar. But the battlefield was in Confederate hands and James died in a farmhouse pressed into use as a hospital.[37]

Charles' recommendation for promotion eventually made its way to Gen. McClellan who on the 10th of July selected the captain to join his staff as an aide-de-camp. The young officer had little chance to distinguish himself in action but made himself invaluable during the logistical nightmare of moving the Army of the Potomac back to Washington.[38]

Lowell liked his staff duties though he was quick to admit he preferred his job as a line officer. He also liked working for the general but had reservations which he confided to Henry Higginson. "He is a great strategist, and the men have faith in him. He makes his plans admirably, makes all preparations so as to be ready for any emergency, just as the Duke of Wellington did, but unlike the Duke of Wellington, when he comes to strike he doesn't strike in a determined fashion; that is, he prepares very well, and then doesn't do the best thing—strike hard." A week later at the battle of Antietam, Charles' words would ring true and he would be placed in a position to test his own mettle.[39]

Capt. Lowell was tasked during the morning of September 17th to deliver dispatches to Sedgwick's Division of Sumner's Corps, heavily engaged on the Union right. Arriving on the field he came upon a part of the line falling back in a near rout. At once he was in the midst of the men, riding from point to point, cussing and calling the men back to the fight. Something about the scrappy little captain made the men stop and rally around him. Reforming the line he coolly rode to the front and led them back into the fray at the West Woods, near the Dunker Church. An officer on the field saw Lowell and later recorded his memory of the event. "I shall never forget the effect of his appearance. He seemed a part of his horse.... After I was wounded, one of my first anxieties was to know what became of him; for it seemed to me that no mounted man could have lived through the storm of bullets that swept the wood just after I saw him enter it."[40]

His horse was struck twice, one of the bullets shattering his scabbard, while a third bullet pierced the overcoat tied to his saddle. When the line appeared stable, he walked his bloody horse away and continued with his staff duties. He arrived with the dispatches to Gen. Sedgwick in time to be on hand when the general was wounded. A short time later he was tasked with delivering orders to Gen. Ambrose Burnside to take the bridge that forever carries his name.[41]

Of his part in the battle Lowell hardly said a word. To his mother he mentioned, "We had a severe fight day before yesterday.... None of General McClellan's aides were hit." He mentions a few friends that were wounded but nothing about the part he played. To John Forbes he wrote, " I have had my usual good luck, but shall have to buy a new sabre and shall have one horse the less to ride for a month or two."[42]

Silent as he was about his deeds during the day, they did not go unnoticed.

Thirty-nine Confederate battle flags had been captured and Gen. McClellan selected Capt. Lowell for the honor of taking the trophies to Washington and presenting them to the president. McClellan later said of his aide, "[Lowell] served me with great gallantry and devotion ... ever ready to execute any service, no matter how dangerous, difficult, or fatiguing."[43]

However, now that Gen. McClellan was to be replaced, several members of the headquarters staff, including Lowell, began to seek new assignments. Charles had actually begun hinting for a command as early as July 1862, shortly after his assignment as aide-de-camp to Gen. McClellan. He had led a squadron of cavalry during the Peninsula Campaign and believed that line command was what he was best suited for. He wrote to his friend Henry Lee Higginson, Jr., an aide of the governor, that he had no doubt he could get permission from the War Department to take a Massachusetts regiment if offered, and would apply so at once if his friend felt there was not someone more qualified.

It was suggested to him in August to spend the winter months at home in Boston recruiting a "Regiment of Gentlemen." Although it was becoming clear that Lowell desired a command of his own this was not what he had in mind.

"Gentlemen?" he scoffed. "What do you mean Gentlemen, drivers of gigs?"[44]

The subject of his own command did not come up again until Forbes and Lawrence offered him command of the newly authorized battalion. In fact Forbes had painted such a sterling portrait of Lowell that Lawrence offered him the battalion two days before the governor authorized him to raise it. His offer read as follows:

Boston, October 25, 1862

Dear Sir,
    I am authorized to assure you that if you should think favorably of the proposition to take command of a battalion of cavalry to be raised in this State for three years service, his excellency the Governor will issue to you a commission as Major. In this case your presence will be required here at once to assist in the organization of the battalion.
    It is the intention to appoint Captains who are now in active service; gentlemen with whom you are probably acquainted.

Your obedient servant
A.A.L.[45]

This was very close to what Lowell was looking for but the situation was too improper for him, coming as it had through irregular channels. He voiced his hesitation in a letter to his close friend and confidant, John M. Forbes.

Berlin, Maryland, Oct 30, 1862

My Dear Mr. Forbes,
    I hardly know what to say to your plan: if the question were simply, Will you take the Colonelcy of the Second Massachusetts Cavalry, a regiment to be raised on same terms and in the same way as the First Massachusetts?—I should have no hesitation in saying yes: but Mr. Lawrence's offer I hardly see my way clear to accept.
    1st. The Battalion, as an independent organization, is not recognized by the War Department: if I get permission to take command of such an organization it can be only through improper influence and in defiance of General Orders, and I do not care to attempt it:—leave of absence to take command of a regiment is authorized, and I should not hesitate to apply for it.
    2nd. I have always thought I was more useful on General McClellan's staff than I would be serving with my own regiment (the 6th U.S. Cavalry)—but with my own regiment as Captain, I should now almost always have command of a BATTALION: were I then to accept Mr. Lawrence's offer, I should merely be exchanging active service for at least a temporary inaction, for the sake of getting rank and pay of Major. I want to keep my military record cleaner than that.

3rd. (A Boston gentleman) speaks of Mr. L's battalion as, " a battalion for home use — i.e. the militia." Does he really mean for home use when we are so short of cavalry in the army — or does he merely mean that it is composed of nine months men? My honest opinion is that it is an injustice to the government to raise any cavalry for so short a period; still, if it is decided to do so, that would not make me decline a command. Two months drill in the field under a good commanding officer will make a regiment of some account — but I would not take any command which was meant for home use.

4th. Mr. L. has the principal voice in naming the officers — would any influence afterwards be used to keep in position officers proved incompetent, and for whose removal all proper military steps had been taken?

You will see from the above that while I should like very much to take command of a Second Massachusetts Cavalry, — I am unwilling to say "yes" to the present offer, unless (or until) the affair assumes such shape that the Governor can ask of me, from the War Department, leave of absence to take command of a REGIMENT.

I have been very much obliged to you for several letters, but I have never answered your questions. Only, if General McClellan silently shoulders all the errors of his subordinate generals, is it not fair to give him credit for their success? I have never been more annoyed than, when in Washington a month ago, to see the avidity with which people gathered up and believed Hooker's criticisms on the General. I did not care to open my lips against them: personally I like Hooker very much, but I fear he will do us a mischief if he ever gets a large command. He has got his head in the clouds.[46]

This letter gives an excellent insight into the character of Charles Lowell. Despite craving a command of his own, he balked at accepting one when there was a chance of impropriety that might mar an otherwise respectable record. When another type of officer would have leaped at the chance for the promotion, not to mention the possibility of the safety of being attached to the home guard, he preferred the lower rank with duty at the front. The last paragraph also shows one instance of his uncanny ability to assess members of the high command.

Even if the four conditions were corrected to his satisfaction, Lowell knew that he must still refuse the offer given by Lawrence and Forbes. State commissions came from one man and one man only: Governor Andrew. If the two agents wanted Capt. Lowell, the proper channels had to be followed and his letter made that perfectly clear. Rather than allowing an ordeal of bureaucratic red tape, the governor was quick to agree and sent off the necessary telegrams to the War Department.[47]

There was no secret to the governor's willingness to give command to a captain only 27 years old. Undoubtedly he knew the young officer socially, but was also aware of his service to the state prior to being commissioned. Governor Andrew was more than willing to have Lowell command his new cavalry — not a battalion, but a full regiment.

A telegram to Secretary Stanton on the 3rd of November from the governor was soon returned giving Andrew and the young captain just what they both wanted.

Nov. 4th 1862

Capt. Charles R. Lowell
On Genl. McClellans Staff
Head Quarters
Army of the Potomac
via Washington D.C.

If General McClellan will permit — Secretary Stanton consents to your absence to recruit a regiment of Three Years Cavalry here as Colonel. We wish to begin forthwith. Colonelcy must be settled first and his presence had while forming roster and recruiting.

John Andrew
Gov. Massachusetts[48]

Here it all was in one simple, tidy

package. An offer from the governor, backed by the Secretary of War, to Lowell to become colonel of a three-year cavalry regiment. The endorsement by Stanton would cover any problems arising from Lowell's transfer to the volunteers from the regular army. His reply was not long in coming. His acceptance telegram reached Boston that night, and stated that he had secured the general's permission and would soon be in Boston to begin recruiting.

Notes

1. Josephy, *The Civil War in the American West*, p. 90; *The Official Records of the War of the Rebellion*, L, Pt. 1, p. 137: hereafter cited as *OR*.
2. Josephy, *The Civil War in the American West*, p. 272; *OR*, L, Pt.1, pp. 136–146.
3. Faust, *Historical Times Illustrated Encyclopedia of the Civil War*, pp. 442–23: hereafter cited as *Encyclopedia*; Josephy, *The Civil War in the American West*, p. 90.
4. Kirsch and Perry, *West of the West*, pp. 366–374.
5. Lavender, *California; A Bicentennial History*, p. 102.
6. Lavender, *California; A Bicentennial History*, pp. 102–103.
7. *OR*, L, Pt. 1, p. 112.
8. *OR*, L, Pt. 1, p. 117.
9. *Daily Alta California*, Sept. 14, 1863.
10. Executive Letters Collection, Massachusetts State Archives, Vol. 19, pp. 226–229: hereafter cited as Exec. Letters.
11. Letters Official Collection, Massachusetts State Archives, Vol. 19, p. 409: hereafter cited as Letters Official.
12. Lawrence, *Life and Letters of Amos A. Lawrence with Extracts from His Diary and Correspondence*, p. 184. Hereafter cited as Lawrence.
13. Faust, *Encyclopedia*, pp. 72–73.
14. Forbes, *Letters and Recollections of John Murray Forbes*, Vol. 1, pp. 333–334.
15. Letters Official, V. 20, p. 26.
16. Humphreys, *Field, Camp, Hospital, and Prison*, p 328: hereafter cited as *Field and Camp*; Emerson, *Life and Letters of Charles Russell Lowell, Jr.*, p. 425: hereafter cited as *Life and Letters*.
17. Higginson, "Charles Russell Lowell" *Harvard Memorial Biographies*, Vol. 1, p. 297: hereafter cited as "Lowell."
18. Greenslet, *The Lowells and Their Seven Worlds*, p. 237; Higginson, "Lowell" p. 296.
19. Greenslet, *The Lowells and Their Seven Worlds*, p. 238; Higginson, "Lowell" p. 297.
20. Greenslet, *The Lowells and Their Seven Worlds*, p. 238; Higginson, "Lowell" p. 298.
21. Emerson, *Life and Letters*, pp. 398–99; Greenslet, *The Lowells and Their Seven Worlds*, p. 238.
22. Emerson, *Life and Letters*, pp. 12–13; Higginson, "Lowell," pp. 300–301.
23. Greenslet, *The Lowells and Their Seven Worlds*, p. 239.
24. Emerson, *Life and Letters*, pp. 14–15; Greenslet, *The Lowells and Their Seven Worlds*, p. 240; Higginson, "Lowell," p. 303.
25. Emerson, *Life and Letters*, pp. 386–387; Greenslet, *The Lowells and Their Seven Worlds*, p. 240.
26. Greenslet, *The Lowells and Their Seven Worlds*, pp. 240–241; Higginson, "Lowell," p. 304.
27. Emerson, *Life and Letters*, p. 19; Greenslet, *The Lowells and Their Seven Worlds*, p. 241; Higginson, "Lowell," p. 305.
28. Greenslet, *The Lowells and Their Seven Worlds*, p. 242; Higginson, "Lowell," p. 305.
29. Higginson, "Lowell," pp. 306–307; Higginson, *Massachusetts in the Army and Navy*, Vol. I, p. 16, Vol. II, p.187.
30. Emerson, *Life and Letters*, pp. 201–202.
31. Emerson, *Life and Letters*, p. 207.
32. Emerson, *Life and Letters*, pp. 21, 218.
33. Emerson, *Life and Letters*, pp. 220, 408.
34. Emerson, *Life and Letters*, pp. 22–24.
35. Emerson, *Life and Letters*, p. 373.
36. Emerson, *Life and Letters*, p. 27; Higginson, "Lowell," p. 310.
37. Emerson, *Life and Letters*, pp. 26, 408; Greenslet, *The Lowells and Their Seven Worlds*, p. 246.
38. Higginson, "Lowell," p. 311; Sears, *George McClellan: The Young Napoleon*, p. 237.
39. Emerson, *Life and Letters*, p. 421; Greenslet, *The Lowells and Their Seven Worlds*, p. 246.

40. Emerson, *Life and Letters*, p. 410; Higginson, "Lowell," p. 311.
41. Emerson, *Life and Letters*, p. 472.
42. Emerson, *Life and Letters*, pp. 224–225; Greenslet, *The Lowells and Their Seven Worlds*, p. 248.
43. Emerson, *Life and Letters*, pp. 27–29; Higginson, "Lowell," p. 312; *Massachusetts in the Army and Navy*, p. 187.
44. Emerson, *Life and Letters*, p. 30.
45. Lawrence, *Lawrence*, p. 185.
46. Emerson, *Life and Letters*, pp. 229–231.
47. *OR*, III, p. 334.
48. Letters Official, Vol. 20, p 139.

Chapter Two

The California Hundred

As the command structure for the regiment was being organized in Boston, San Francisco was a hive of activity as recruitment began for the authorized company. When authority to recruit the company was received on the 22nd of October, 1862, the focus of the project shifted from Ira Rankin, who had carried on the correspondence with Boston, to Capt. J. Sewall Reed.

James Sewall Reed, a native of Milton, Massachusetts, was only 17 years old when he joined the rush to the California gold mines in 1849. Part-time miner, part-time rancher, Reed was also involved with California's prewar militia. In 1852 he signed on with the Eureka Light Horse Guards and later as Captain of the 1st Light Dragoons. Selected as captain of Company B in the Citizens Dragoons he was also active during the state's vigilante movement in 1856.[1]

Capt. Reed was hardly prepared for the sight that greeted him as he approached the junction of Post and Kearny streets on the morning of October 28th. Assembly Hall had been selected as the recruiting station, and on this cool, fall morning, a line of men stretched down the street and around the corner. Reed soon found himself in a position few recruiting officers ever did: the position to be selective. There were only 100 spots to be filled and over 500 men would end up applying.

First to present himself was 19-year-old Henry H. Fillebrown who had stood in line throughout the night waiting to enlist. Fillebrown was one of the lucky few that day; he was enrolled as a private. Young Henry was chosen for a specific talent that he possessed, one that all the recruits were required to have in order to be considered. They all had to be able to ride. The company was destined to be cavalry and if a man couldn't ride he was politely shown the door. Of the dozens of hopefuls that showed up that first morning only ten were signed up.[2]

The men that were selected during the initial recruitment were given a physical examination to ensure they could withstand the vigorous life of a soldier. One volunteer described the exam as "laughable; a dozen men entirely naked going through a gymnastic performance...." George Towle, one of the hopeful selectees recalled shivering in the cold hall waiting his turn to jump over a table. "Fortunately the man ahead of me had jumped on top of it and broken the table down, so that my jump was easy. I was put through all the exercises and tests that the medical

BATTLE SCENES

Received by Steamer.

1800 LATEST BATTLE SCENES; 10 different designs Union Paper and Envelopes; 1100 Latest Song Books; Military Handbooks; Dream Books; Letter Writers, and latest Novels, &c., received and for sale at the very lowest rates.

D. E. APPLETON & CO.,
oc28-7 508 Montgomery street.

Cavalry Company for the East.

THE UNDERSIGNED HAS BEEN authorized by the Secretary of War to raise a Company of Cavalry for service in the East to make a part of the Massachusetts quota.

A Roll of the Company is at Assembly Hall, corner Post and Kearny streets where persons desirous of joining can enroll their names.

No one need apply who is not a good horseman and in good health. Men from the country preferred. The Roll will be kept open a reasonable time before selections are made.

All expenses will be paid as soon as accepted.

Further particulars apply to Office, corner Post and Kearny street.

oc28-2ptf **J. SEWALL REED.**

DAVID HENRIQUES,
Member of the
SAN FRANCISCO STOCK AND EXCHANGE BOARD
and
REAL ESTATE AGENT.
Office 422 Montgomery street.
oc28-1m2p Between Sacramento and California sts.

MONEY TO LOAN!

MONEY TO LOAN—IN SUMS TO SUIT at Low Rates of Interest.

DAVID HENRIQUES,
Real Estate and Stock Broker,
422 Montgomery street,
oc28-1m2p Bet. Sacramento and California sts.

Ex Kingfisher.

40 BARRELS ZANTE CURRANTS;
25 hhds Porto Rico Sugar;
25 ½ pipes Pure Spirits;
10 tcs Brazil Nuts;
25 bbls Peanuts;
15 cases Prunes;
5 frails Dates;
2 cases Citron;
2 cases Orange and Lemon Peel.

For sale by
oc23-2p7 **GEO. F. BRAGG & CO.**

STATE OF CALIFORNIA, CITY AND County of San Francisco. In Probate Court In the matter of the Estate of ELIAS S. COOPER, deceased:

Pursuant to an order of said Court, made on the twenty-seventh day of October, A. D. 1862, notice is hereby given, that MONDAY, the 10th day of NOVEMBER, A. D. 1862, at eleven o'clock A. M. of said day, and the Court room of said Court, at the City Hall, in the City and County of San Francisco, have been appointed as the time and place for proving the Will of said Elias S. Cooper, deceased, and for hearing the application of Levi C. Lane and Joseph W. Reay, for the issuance to the said petitioners of letters testamentary, when and where any person interested may appear and contest the same.

GRAIN SACKS.
Flour Bags.

20 BALES, 30-INCH BROWN SHIRTING, suitable for FLOUR or GRAIN SACKS, just received and for sale by
GOLDSTEIN, RYAN & CO.
oc14-2ptf Corner Front and Sacramento sts.

WOODEN WARE,
Willow Ware,
BRUSHES,
Twines,
Rope, and
Housekeeping Articles.

THE LARGEST AND FINEST ASSORTMENT on the Pacific Coast.

For sale, wholesale and retail, by
ELAM & HOWES,
oc1-2ptf Nos. 310 and 312 Clay street.

U. S. Legal Tender Notes

BOUGHT AND SOLD AT CURRENT RATES.

By **F. H. WOODS,**
BROKER,
S. W. corner of Montgomery and Clay streets.
se16-2p

AUGUST KOEHLER,
MANUFACTURER OF TRUSSES
No. 659 Washington street.
oc1-2px

A. C. WIGHTMAN. JOHN A. MITCHELL.
WIGHTMAN & MITCHELL,
Commission and Stock Brokers.
No. 84 C street, Virginia City, N. T.
Orders solicited, and promptly attended to.
se24-2p1m*

GUNS, RIFLES, PISTOLS,
Sporting Articles,
MATERIALS
For Guns, Rifles and Pistols.
Indian Goods, Beads, &c.,
IVORY HANDLE TABLE CUTLERY.
WOSTENHOLM & SONS' IXL
AND
JOSEPH RODGERS & SONS'
CELEBRATED

Daily Alta California of October 28, 1862.

officer required, and was there upon pronounced physically fit."[3]

The early requirements that kept scores of men from being selected were relaxed somewhat when the high standards were found to be too strict and were actually disqualifying men who by all other means were fit to serve. A notice in the *Daily Alta California* requested an additional 25 men for the company and several men who had been considered too light, too young, or were not so proficient on horseback were allowed to sign up.[4]

As the men were selected they were quartered in Assembly Hall and were tasked with a heavy training regimen of company maneuvers and sabre exercises. Issued uniforms, blankets and sabres their remaining equipment would be distributed when they arrived in the East. Private Towle recalled receiving his equipment: "The blankets which we received at San Francisco were made at the Mission Woolen Mills as also I think was the material for our uniforms; both of which we found when we got East, were of much better quality than was supplied to the troops there. Our uniform and an overcoat with long cape light blue in color; jacket reaching to the hips; dark blue in color, fatigue blouse, dark blue in color; trousers light blue in color and dark blue cap with a sloping visor. The jacket profusely ornamented with yellow worsted braid around the collar and cuffs and down each seam at the back and along the edges of the jacket in front; but we discarded the yellow braid."[5]

For five weeks the scene at the enlistment station repeated itself until the last name was selected and placed on the muster roll. Later Massachusetts would claim the majority of the men were Bay Staters returning to serve their home state, and to a large extent this was true; but only one man claimed Massachusetts as home when enlisting. No matter where the men were from before, they now considered themselves Californians, an identity that would provide them with an esprit de corps that the rest of the regiment would never achieve.[6]

As November came to a close and the day for departure drew near, the City of San Francisco opened its hearts and doors to the men that would soon represent them in the east. Capt. Reed was the guest of honor at the Armory of the 1st Light Dragoons on the 26th. His old command, now led by Capt. C.L. Taylor, presented him with a magnificent set of pistols and a saddle with bridle and blanket. The gifts were presented during a formal ceremony that

Capt. James Sewall Reed, Commander of Company A, the California Hundred. Killed in action February 22, 1864, at Dranesville, Virginia. *Courtesy of U.S.A.M.H.I.*

was followed by toasts and camaraderie late into the night. During another night of festivities more presentations were made, this time to the entire company. The captain of the Sumner Light Guard (Co. I, First Regiment California Militia) presented a check of $100 to "The California Rangers to aid in their outfit."[7]

On the 3rd of December, Capt. Reed's company of cavalry, now numbering 85 men, was mustered into Federal service by Lt. Col. George Ringgold. The ceremony was brief, and to the civilians watching, rather boring, as it lacked the pomp and ceremony that the public and press thrived on. The people wanted a parade to cheer their heroes and a parade was what they got. Three days later the company, now 100 strong, marched in ranks down Montgomery Street to the Plaza where they were reviewed by General George Wright, commander of the Department of the Pacific. They made a favorable impression on Gen. Wright and were nearly deafened by the cheering crowds.[8]

The company assembled again that afternoon for their evening drill at Assembly Hall. *The Daily Alta* described the scene. "When they were going through their evolutions the First Lieutenant was called out and presented with a magnificent sword and paraphernalia, all of the latest style and most exquisite workmanship ... a massive gold plate on the scabbard bears the following inscription: Presented to Archibald McKendry by his friends, December 6th, 1862." Before the war was over 1st Lt. McKendry, "Old Badgers" to his men, would be promoted several times and eventually became a brevet colonel, in command of the 2nd Massachusetts Cavalry.[9]

Three days later, on the 9th of December, the company was given an ovation at Platt's Hall. A committee of prominent citizens had planned an evening of speeches, music, and dancing and the hall had been colorfully decorated with flags and streamers. The evening was marred somewhat by a cold winter rain that unfortunately kept many of the ladies at home. The festivities began with the band of the 9th California Infantry playing while the Hundred marched in and performed a series of evolutions under the call of Capt. Reed.

Mr. E.H. Washburne, the evening's master of ceremonies, called the crowded room to order and blasted out a lengthy oration reminding "the picked men of California" to remember that the eyes of the civilized world would be upon them. Two more speakers held the floor before Mr. Washburne returned and read a letter from the Reverend Thomas Starr King who considered the Hundred his "pets." The letter read:

> To the committee of arrangements for the festival in Honor of the California Rangers Gentlemen—I regret to inform you that a duty which I cannot postpone will prevent my attendance at the entertainment this evening in honor of the Cavalry Company, until an hour that, will be too late for speaking. As for the soldiers, they speak for themselves to every American who has an eye for noble symmetry and strength. Never was Patriotism more worthily embodied. If the Government desires to see them fitly mounted for duty, it should provide for them a hundred full blooded Black Hawks—horses such as Shakespeare describes, "that bound from the earth as if their entrails were hairs; horses that trot the air; horses that make the earth sing when they touch it; horses whose neighing is like the bidding of a monarch."* Wherever these men serve the country's cause—whether in Texas or in Virginia—may heaven's blessings attend them, and invigorate their hearts and arms and steel against the enemies of the hope and honor of the American Republic!

**Shakespeare,* Henry V, *Act III, Scene VII.*

The festivities lasted late into the night with the Hundred occasionally performing close order drill for the crowd, and then dancing with the few ladies who had braved the cold and rain.[10]

At the next morning's muster three privates were called out of ranks and presented with sergeants chevrons. Hugh Armstrong was made the company first sergeant, James Wheat became quartermaster sergeant and Henry Burlingham was detailed as acting commissary sergeant. More promotions awaited the trio. At war's end, all three would be captains: Armstrong in command of the remnants of the Hundred.[11]

Time was running out for the company; their ship was pier side and would soon sail. In the final days the San Francisco public couldn't get enough of them. The next afternoon they were paraded again and reviewed at the Plaza by Mayor Teschemacher and other "prominent citizens." During the review the Hundred were presented with a guidon by Mr. Daniel Norcross. A beautiful swallow-tailed banner, the silk flag was red and white with U.S. in gold letters above a California grizzly bear. Attached to the staff was a small silver plate that read, "Presented to the California Hundred by Daniel Norcross of San Francisco, December 1, 1862." With their new flag flapping in the breeze, the company marched back to their barracks to begin the task of packing for their voyage.[12]

That evening the last man was enlisted into the company. Twenty-two-year-old James Watson, "a compact man, with big hands and a large boned face he

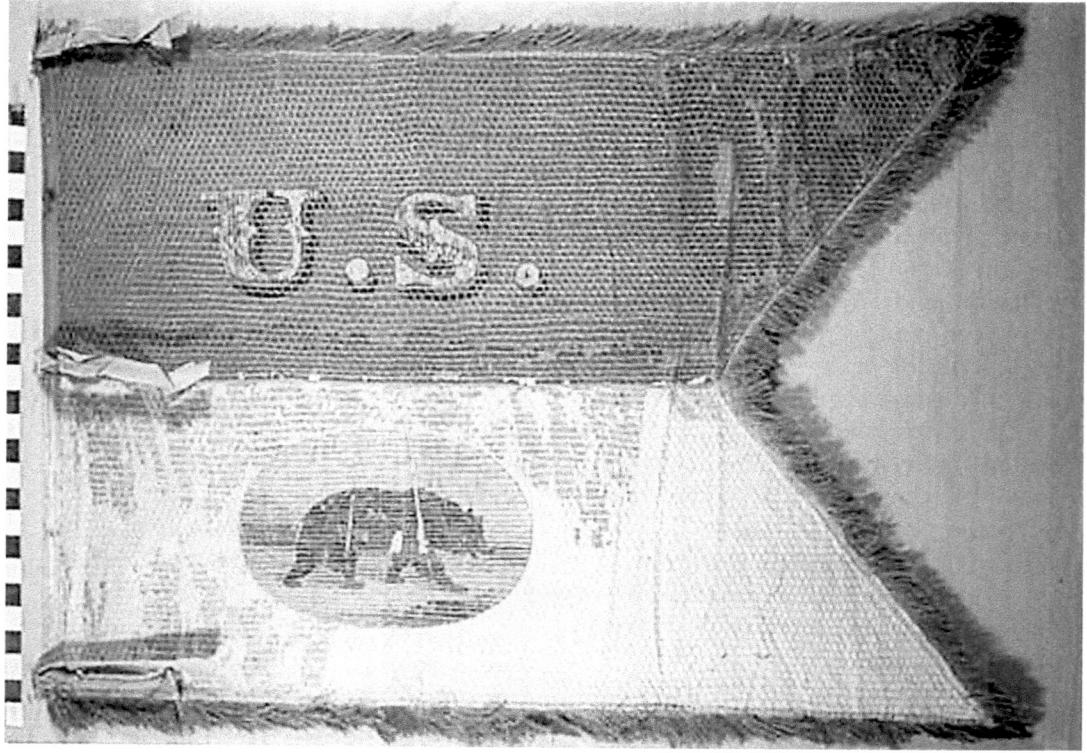

Guidon of Company A, the California Hundred. Presented to the company on December 10, 1862, in San Francisco by Mr. Daniel Norcross. *Courtesy of California State Capitol Museum.*

had inherited from his mother...," was a skilled blacksmith and horseman. One of the men already mustered in returned to the barracks drunk, and though the company was departing in the morning, he was stripped of his uniform and told to leave. Private Watson became the 101st man on the roll and would proudly claim the title of being the only native-born Californian to fight in the East. Among his few personal possessions Watson carried his lasso; "he only wants to get a turn of it round Jeff Davis' neck."[13]

"Our company," recalled Pvt. Charles Briggs, "consists of 1 Captain, 2 Lieutenants and 101 privates, two of the 104 are married men. Captain Reed and one Private who has a wife in Massachusetts. What a commotion it will create among the Boston gals to have 103 bachelors and widowers to arrive at once among them."*[14]

The predawn hours of the 11th of December were cold and cloudy as the Hundred rose from their slumber and began what would be for some of them, their last day in the Golden State. After stowing their gear in freight wagons that set out to the docks before them, they donned their new uniforms and marched to the "Lick House" where the owners provided a free breakfast for the men.[15]

The largest parade yet was planned and despite the dreary weather all of San Francisco turned out to see them off. The procession was led by Kidd's 20 piece brass band playing "Hail Columbia." The musicians were followed by six companies of honor guard consisting of the Vallejo Rifles, detachments from the Light Dragoons, the Black Hussars, Ellsworth Rifles, Light Guards, and the Old California Guard with two pieces of artillery. The Hundred fell into the place of honor at the end of the column and started off for the wharf.[16]

The streets they marched through were packed shoulder to shoulder with crowds that shouted themselves hoarse as the heroes marched by. Women waved handkerchiefs from the windows and children darted back and forth through the crowd, setting off firecrackers. The arrival at the docks was even more chaotic. Thousands had gathered, ignoring the light rain, to cheer a final farewell. Marching down the Folsom Street Wharf they boarded the ship and were drawn up at parade-rest on the upper deck. The Old Guard fired its two field pieces in salute and the crowd sang "The Star Spangled Banner," "Auld Lang Syne," and "Home Sweet Home," as the steamer *Golden Age*, "A good stout ship of 3000 tons burthen with a single engine of 1400 horse power," slipped out of her berth and headed for the Golden Gate.[17]

When the steamer cleared the bay and entered the Pacific, the waves set it into a slow roll which caused many of the men to part with their free breakfasts. Plunging through stormy seas for three days, few passengers were able to attend meals in the galley, where it was said more dishes were broken in two days than in 12 previous trips. Assigned as steerage passengers, the soldiers quickly roped off a section of the saloon deck which they appropriated for themselves and set guards to maintain their claim. The food served to those in steerage was of poor quality and the men made purchases from the ships' steward to augment their meals. The cattle that were to provide fresh beef during the voyage were swept overboard in a storm off the tip of Baja California.[18]

A break in the monotonous fare was provided when the *Golden Age* pulled into Acapulco, Mexico, on the 16th of December. Samuel Bond, a passenger onboard, recalled that several boys swam out to the

---

*There were actually two enlisted men who were married: Joseph B. Burdick, and James Watson, who kept his marriage a secret from friends and family.

ship: "these were the divers and the passengers threw over into the water a large number of dimes, not one of which did they fail to get before the shiny pieces reached bottom." While the sailors took on coal the soldiers bought fresh fruit and swam in the clear bay. The holiday ended late in the day when the ship weighed anchor and continued the journey south. Four days' sailing found them off the Isthmus of Panama where the troops loaded their baggage on the railroad cars which took them to Aspinwall on the Atlantic side.[19]

It was here in Aspinwall that the soldiers took full advantage of their first real meal since San Francisco. "We had all been half starved on the Golden Age," recalled Pvt. Briggs, "and all were crazy for good cheer. I did not eat so much as some: only one large steak, two boiled eggs, ham, kidney stew, two cups of tea, half a loaf of warm bread, two plates of apple sauce, some turnips, and began to look around for some pie, but could not discover none, and so concluded to pay my dollar and vamoose."[20]

Waiting to take them on the rest of their voyage was the *Ocean Queen*. The hope that the days of poor food were past was dashed. "It may be safely said," Towle recalled, "that on the Ocean Queen there was not a single item of the fare that was fit for food. Before you could eat the hard bread you must rattle the vermin out of it. The corned beef, so called, was rotten, rice wormy, and with us it soon became a question of starvation." This poor fare was consumed at the "steerage table" which was nothing more than a wide board loosely attached to iron rods connected to the deck above. The table swung with the motion of the ship and as there were no chairs the men were compelled to stand shoulder to shoulder and sway with their table.[21]

The complaints about the food came to a head one morning. "[T]he pans of beef were thrown overboard, the scouse, a stew mixture of rotten beef and wormy hard bread, etc., was emptied out of the pans along the swinging table and the pans thrown overboard, the rice was strewn along on top of the scouse, the molasses emptied on top of those, the pans of mustard, supplied for the rotten 'salt horse', emptied on top of it all." The ship's captain arrived at the scene of the rebellion and was very forceful in his criticism of their conduct (he cussed a blue streak), threatening to put the offenders in irons. Someone pointed out to the captain that this was unlikely as there were more soldiers onboard than crew. The soldiers informed the captain, "we propose to have something to eat and if you do not furnish it we will proceed to take it." Knowing he could not force his will, Captain Tenkelpaugh angrily backed down; but to his credit, the food for the company immediately improved. Fresh provisions were taken on along with coal in Key West, Florida, and the men settled in for the remainder of their voyage.[22]

The 104 men sailing on the *Ocean Queen* were destined to be part of the only organized group of Californians to fight in the east. They were not, however, the first to claim this honor.

In June 1861, Senator Edward C. Baker of Oregon began recruiting a regiment of infantry in Pennsylvania. Senator Baker had been a prominent lawyer in San Francisco before representing Oregon and had such a high regard for his old home that he proposed the regiment be designated the 1st California Infantry. The regiment would be credited to California's quota with the recruits coming from the farms and factories of Pennsylvania and New York. Everyone thought it was an excellent idea with the exception of California, who refused to recognize the regiment. Any body of troops that would bear the name retain his seat in the Senate *and* remain in command of his regiment.[24]

The colonel was typical of the politically appointed officers at the start of the war; thoroughly charged with patriotism and possessed of the will to see the Union saved, he was utterly void of any military ability. This lack of military training led to tragic results on the 21st of October, 1861, when Baker, leading a brigade in the division of Brig. Gen. Charles P. Stone, was ordered to make a demonstration against the Confederates at Leesburg, Virginia.[25]

The result of this movement was the Battle of Ball's Bluff, a humiliating defeat for the Union and the only battle for Col. Baker who fell dead to a Confederate sharpshooter. The 71st Pennsylvania/1st California took heavy casualties during their first baptism of fire. Despite the mauling they received they retained their organization and fought again at Antietam, Gettysburg, and Cold Harbor. A monument to their bravery stands in "the angle" at Gettysburg proudly displaying the names of their two states.[26]

Far to the west, California had more than her share of men who wanted to fight these battles themselves. On the 24th of September, 1862, just 15 days after the committee in San Francisco made their offer to the War Department, the 3rd California Infantry made another proposal. The commanding officer of the 3rd California, Col. P. Edward Conner, with his regiment in Nevada Territory, sent the following telegram to the General in Chief in Washington:

Pvt. William H.H. Hussey, later first sergeant, second lieutenant and first lieutenant of Company I. Brass cap badge reads "CAL 100." *Courtesy of Michael Fitzpatrick.*

of California would be Californians! Colonel Baker's regiment made its returns to the War Department until finally Gov. Andrew G. Curtin accepted the troops and designated them the 71st Pennsylvania Infantry. To honor Col. Baker, the regiment continued to call themselves the 1st California.[23]

Soon after organizing the regiment, Col. Baker, a close friend of Lincoln's, was offered the rank of brigadier, and later major general, both of which he refused. If he had accepted either promotion he would have been compelled to give up his seat in the Senate. By refusing a rank above field grade, the senator-soldier was able to

> Ruby Valley, Nev. Ter. Sept. 24, 1862
> Major General Halleck,
> Washington D.C.
>
> The Third Infantry California Volunteers has been in service one year and marched 600 miles; it is well officered and thoroughly drilled; it is of no service on the Overland Mail Route, as there is cavalry sufficient for its protection in Utah

District. The regiment will authorize the paymaster to withhold $30,000 of pay now due if the Government will order it east, and it pledges General Halleck never to disgrace the flag, himself, or California. The men enlisted to fight traitors, and can do so more effectually than raw recruits, and ask they may at least be put on the same footing in regard to transportation east. If the above sum is insufficient we will pay our own passage from San Francisco to Panama.

By order of the regiment:
P. Edw. Conner[27]

Conner may have thought this telegram just a bit too wordy for a few hours later he sent a briefer version of the same offer. Conner and his 3rd California were willing but Gen. Halleck was not, and this group of Californians stayed west. For the time being California would have to rely on the 104 men of company A to represent her.[28]

Notes

1. Morison, *Dying for Our Country: A Sermon on the Death of Capt. J. Sewall Reed and Rev. Thomas Starr King*, pp. 20–28.
2. Backus, "Californians in the Field: Historical Sketch of the Organization and Services of the California 'Hundred' and 'Battalion' 2d Massachusetts Cavalry," p. 6., *California Commandry Military Order of the Loyal Legion of the United States, War Paper No. 4*: hereafter cited as "Californians in the Field," *MOLLUS*.; Bond, *Journal of an Expedition*, p. 219; Kirsh and Perry, *West of the West*, p. 376; *Massachusetts Soldiers, Sailors, and Marines*, Vol. 6, pp. 228–328.
3. Towle, *Personal Recollections*, p. 1.
4. *Daily Alta California*, Nov. 26, 1862.
5. Towle, *Personal Recollections*, pp. 1–2.
6. *Massachusetts Soldiers, Sailors, and Marines*, Vol. 6, pp. 230–238.
7. *Daily Alta California*, Nov. 27, Dec. 4, 1862.
8. National Archives, Record Group 94, Co. A Order Book, Special Order #1, 1 Dec., 1862.
9. *Daily Alta California*, Dec. 7, 1862.
10. *Daily Alta California*, Dec. 10, 1862.
11. National Archives, Record group 94, Co. A Order Book, Special Order # 3, 10 Dec., 1862.
12. Hunt, *The Army of the Pacific*, p. 284; *Daily Alta California*, Dec. 11, 1862.
13. Stanley, "From San Rafael to the Civil War and Back Again," *Marin County History*, p. 2; *Boston Journal*, Feb. 4, 1863.
14. *Napa County Reporter*, Jan 24, 1863.
15. Corbett, *Diary*, 11 Dec., 1862; National Archives, Record group 94, Co. A Order Book, Special Order #5.
16. Hunt, *Army of the Pacific*, p. 284n; *Daily Alta California*, Dec. 12, 1862.
17. Bond, *Journal of an Expedition*, p. 220; *Daily Alta California*, Dec. 12, 1862.
18. Bond, *Journal of an Expedition*, pp. 221–222; Corbett, *Diary*, Dec. 14, 1862; *Napa County Reporter*, 24 Jan., 1863.
19. Bond, *Journal of an Expedition*, pp. 220, 228; Corbett, *Diary*, Dec. 16, 1862.
20. *Napa County Reporter*, Feb. 7, 1863.
21. Towle, *Personal Recollections*, p. 2.
22. Towle, *Personal Recollections*, p. 2.
23. Warner, *Generals in Blue*, p. 16; Farwell, *Ball's Bluff*, p. 17.
24. Farwell, *Ball's Bluff*, p. 18.
25. Faust, *Encyclopedia*, p. 34.
26. Faust, *Encyclopedia*, p. 34, 36–37; Fisher, "The Union's Bear Flag Defenders," p. 44, *America's Civil War*, January 1990.
27. OR, L, Pt.1, p. 133.
28. OR, L, Pt.1, p. 133.

Chapter Three

The California Battalion

As the Hundred were completing their preparations to sail, activity had increased in the east to prepare for their arrival and to fill out the rest of the regiment. A headquarters office was set up in Boston, and under the guidance of Amos A. Lawrence and John M. Forbes, the difficult job of recruiting got under way.

Difficult is an understatement. The quality and availability of recruits in and around Boston were dismal and it quickly became necessary to appoint more officers to the regiment. It would be their task to reach further into the state for new men. On the 25th of November ten officers and sergeants from various Massachusetts regiments were authorized to join the 2nd Massachusetts Cavalry and assist in recruiting. With the exception of one, all the officers accepted transfer to the regiment and were soon scouring the state for recruits.[1]

The one officer who refused the offer is worthy of mention. Refusing for the same reasons as did Lowell when first offered the rank of major, Captain Robert Gould Shaw of the 2nd Massachusetts Infantry saw no benefit in his taking command of a company in another regiment. When the offer was refused Lowell sent another, stating that Shaw would be given a squadron captaincy, which would place him in command of two companies. Shaw was very interested and confided to his mother,

> Cousin John Forbes wrote the other day, and asked me what I thought of the cavalry regiment. I have not answered yet, because I am waiting until Harry comes, to know what his intentions about it are. I shan't accept any position below that of 4th Captain (the rank I hold here), and I can't believe they can guarantee that to me.... In a new regiment, especially cavalry, I shouldn't find myself so pleasantly situated, as I should not start fair with those who have already served in that arm. Besides, the feeling all the old officers have for this regiment would make it a very melancholy affair to leave it. Nevertheless, when I see Harry, and hear more particulars of the other, I may decide for that. I have heard that Charles Lowell is to command the regiment, and Casper Crowninshield to be Senior Major. The fact of these two and Will Forbes being in it, makes it very tempting to me.*[2]

---

*Harry is Henry S. Russell who accepted the lieutenant colonelcy of the 2nd Massachusetts Cavalry. Russell and William H. Forbes (John M. Forbes' son) were both cousins of Shaw. Crowninshield had been his roommate at Harvard.

The decision was not an easy one for Robert. He wrote several letters to his sisters, mother, John Forbes, Harry Russell, and Henry Lee Higginson asking advice and trying to explain his reasoning on the matter. Even Governor Andrew became involved and was curious as to why he did not accept the position. Lowell and Shaw were friends and for a time it appeared that he would accept the post until a new offer was made to him. Declining to join the 2nd Massachusetts Cavalry, Shaw accepted Governor Andrew's later offer of the colonelcy of the 54th Massachusetts Infantry, the first Negro regiment to be raised in the north. The two friends would not lose touch, however, as their regiments were encamped next to each other during training, and Shaw's sister Josephine happened to be Charley Lowell's fiancée.[3]

As stated earlier, recruiting in the north during the fall and winter of 1862 was not an easy task. The recruiting officers went to every corner of the state to seek out eligible men and entice them into enlisting. Boston and its environs provided the bulk of the men but there were representatives of nearly every city throughout the state. A number of the men enlisting were from other states and signed up for the cash bounty. Every northern state but Delaware was represented. Several recruits claimed the south as home and the muster rolls show men from Virginia, Florida, Texas, Georgia, Tennessee, and Louisiana. There was also a sizable number of foreigners in the ranks with Canada providing the most and ten different European nations being claimed as well.[4]

The previous employment of the men was as different as their origins. Nearly every conceivable occupation was represented in the regiment, the most common being farmers, laborers, and sailors. The regimental chaplain mentioned a few in his reminiscences. "Some told of hairbreadth escapes in fights with Indians on the border; others of adventures among the wild islanders of the South Seas. There were trappers from the Rocky Mountains, who had had bears for pets; tall lumbermen from Maine, who had dared the foaming rapids and the raging torrent; old sailors who had played with the sea lion and sported with the storm; rough-bearded miners, who knew all the tricks of the gambler, and were familiar with the code of the duelist."[5]

Although it appears at first glance that men flocked from everywhere to join the regiment, this is hardly the case. The men did come from diverse locations, but it was the cash bounty that brought them to the recruiting office. All too often the lure of money brought forth an element that had no intention of serving longer than it took to get their hands on the cash. A large number of the men enlisted, were mustered in, received their cash bounty, and then deserted on the first moonless night.

These were the bounty jumpers, an expensive nuisance that plagued every regiment then recruiting in the north. These men would travel from state to state enlisting for bounties and deserting as soon as was practical. Lowell was bothered by this type of con man from nearly the first day. Some of the deserters from the 2nd Cavalry were found to be in Providence, Rhode Island, where they had enlisted for another bounty in the 5th Rhode Island Infantry. This problem caused the actual ranks to fill very slowly and with an extreme amount of effort.[6]

Company B mustered 91 men for duty on the 13th of January and within a month 45 had left camp with their bounty money. Company C was hit the hardest with 43 bounty jumpers out of 76, leaving only 33 men available for duty. Where so many regiments had been whittled down in battle, the 2nd Massachusetts Cavalry was being decimated by deserters before it could even begin training.*[7]

Recruiting under these conditions was not only difficult but occasionally dangerous. Lowell experienced the following on what he thought was a quiet morning:

> Stepping out as usual, at eight o'clock one morning at the recruiting station, he found the small squad of new recruits who were to be transferred that day to camp at Readville in a state of mutiny. Hearing the noise on his arrival, he descended at once to the basement, and the sergeant in command explained that he had ordered a man to be handcuffed, that the others had said it was unjust and should not be done, and had resisted. Colonel Lowell at once said, "The order must be obeyed." "No! No!" shouted the men. He continued: "After it is obeyed, I will hear what you have to say, and will decide the case on its merits, but it MUST be obeyed FIRST. God knows, my men, I don't want to kill any of you, but I shall shoot the first man that resists. Sergeant, iron your man." As the sergeant stepped forward with the irons, the men made a rush, and Colonel Lowell shot the leader, who fell at once. The men succumbed immediately, some bursting into tears, such was their excitement.

Lowell holstered his smoking pistol and immediately made his way to the Governor's office. Upon entering he formally saluted and said, "I have to report to you, sir, that in the discharge of my duty, I have shot a man." Again he saluted, performed an about face, and left the office. The Governor turned to a bystander and stated, "I need nothing more, Colonel Lowell is as humane as he is brave."†[8]

Despite the setbacks that plagued the raising of the Massachusetts companies, they continued to grow and some solid Massachusetts men enlisted to swell the ranks. Among them were the three Duley brothers, Eastman, Charles, and George, of Ashland. Farmers by trade, they all enlisted when the first bugle blew, George and Charles in the 13th Massachusetts, Eastman in the 16th Massachusetts. Eastman carried a bullet in his chest, a memento of Malvern Hill, Virginia, for which he had received a medical discharge. Eastman survived the war, as did Charles who was also wounded. George would be captured and he died in the prison stockade at Andersonville, Georgia.[9]

As the men were recruited they were sent to a regimental barracks at Camp Meigs, near Readville, about nine miles by rail from Boston. The wooden barracks were large, airy structures, difficult to heat in the cold Massachusetts winter; the drilling ground was a flat expanse of mud. It was here that they began to receive their first military instruction.[10]

On the 3rd of January, while watching the afternoon drill, Lowell received a telegram announcing the arrival of the California Hundred in New York. Capt. Reed and his men had endured an uneventful voyage from Panama aboard the

---

*At the end of the war the 2nd Massachusetts Cavalry had the distinction of having the highest desertion rate of any unit from Massachusetts. Of the 2,267 names on the regimental roll an incredible 614 had deserted. Of the 504 members from California only 24 were listed as deserters. Mortimer, The California 100 and Battalion, pp. 116–119.

†The ringleader, a former regular soldier by the name of William Pendergast, had his name left off the muster rolls. Two of the mutineers, privates William Johnson and Daniel Riley, were found innocent by a court-martial and served through the war with the 2nd Massachusetts Cavalry. The remaining three muntineers were imprisoned at Fort Independence in Boston Harbor. Pvt. Sylvester Riley "died" at the fort on the 12th of April, 1863. Pvt. William Lynch was executed for his deeds on the 16th of June. The third man, 16-year-old Francis Dew was sentenced to be shot but had his sentence commuted by President Lincoln to "imprisonment and hard labor for the duration of the war." He was dishonorably discharged on July 24, 1865. All of the men were members of Company G. Randolph Transcript and Norfolk Advertiser, April 11, 1863; Saturday Evening Express, June 28, 1863.

S.S. *Ocean Queen*. Arriving at 2 A.M. they now stood on the city docks ready to complete their journey. Any thought the men might have entertained about being given a hearty welcome were dashed by the early hour of their arrival.[11]

Shouldering their packs and blankets, the Hundred marched from the wharf to the Battery Barracks where they were given a "soldier's breakfast." Around noon the men marched to the New England Soldiers' Relief Association, many finding their sea legs to be a little wobbly on dry ground. Upon arriving the men were given a warm welcome and a fine meal which they ate to the sound of flattering speeches from some local dignitaries. After weeks of "steamboat grub" the troopers ignored the speakers and attacked the food. A quick march to City Hall Park after dinner and there they found the celebration they had been expecting. A large crowd cheered the Hundred as they filed into the park under their fluttering grizzly bear guidon. The mayor reviewed the troops, while the 53rd Massachusetts Infantry and an accompanying band stood by to escort them to the Stonington Ferry.[12]

The next day found the Hundred at Camp Meigs where they were designated as company A, and along with companies B, C, and D the first battalion began drill as a unit. The battalion was quartered in barracks, the cold Massachusetts winter making the use of tents impractical. Shortly after arriving Capt. Reed purchased 100 pairs of heavy cavalry boots using money in the company fund. The boots were badly needed but many found the stiff leather wrinkles at the ankles "...a source of torture..." To aid in breaking in the new boots the men spent endless hours marching through company and squadron drill and practicing with their new sabres.[13]

During these first days in camp the Californians, "...procured metal letters C.A.L. and figures making 100 and placed them in a semi circle on the top of our caps," recalled Pvt. Towle, "and those letters on occasion when we visited Boston, which was about 8 or 9 miles distant, were as serviceable as a regulation pass."[14]

Though the Californians and the Bay Staters worked well enough together on the drill field, there was no love lost between east and west. "There are about five hundred men in this camp besides ourselves," wrote Pvt. Briggs, "and they can't be trusted out of sight, for some that drink get so drunk that they forget to come back ... the other companies are red-hot with jealousy, we are so much better dressed; more uniform in size; more particular in our dress on duty..." The attention that the Californians received from the public did not help matters.[15]

On the 13th of January, after a hard day's drilling, the California Hundred was surprised at their barracks by several hundred citizens bearing baskets of hot food. While the soldiers ate, no less than ten speakers took the floor and entertained the crowd with patriotic speeches.

The final speaker of the evening was Miss Abbie Lord, a dressmaker from Charlestown. As the Bunker Hill Baptist Church choir sang "Stand By the Flag," Miss Lord unfurled a large United States flag and presented it to the Hundred. The honor of presenting the gift was given to Miss Lord for she had paid for the material, and sewn the flag herself. A small silver plate on the staff read: "Presented to the California Hundred, Captain J. Sewall Reed, by Miss Abbie Lord."[16]

At the evening's end, when the guests had all gone home, the men furled their new flag carefully and stowed it away. Large and too heavy to be carried on horseback, the flag would remain furled for over a year, and the day it was finally unfurled was one of the darkest in the company's history.

Two days later the California Hundred

were taken into Boston on a special train. They were met at the station by a battalion of state militia, the National Lancers and the Light Dragoons, who escorted the company to the City Government rooms. Upon arriving the Californians and their escorts formed a hollow square around the perimeter of the room and were entertained by a band which preceded the speeches.

First to speak was Boston's ex-mayor Wightman who had been closely involved with the Governor during the initial planning and talks that resulted in the Hundred's acceptance by Massachusetts. His speech was directed to Mayor Lincoln.

"In addition to the duties of my municipal office during the last year," he began, "I had the honor of being a general recruiting officer for furnishing some seven or eight thousand men for the United States Army. While engaged in this work, I received through Judge Russell a communication from His Excellency the Governor, stating that he had received from the State of California, the tender of a company of Massachusetts and other loyal citizens of that State, who were desirous of sharing the dangers of the field, and uniting their fortunes with those of Boston and Massachusetts soldiers. To this communication I had the pleasure of giving, through Judge Russell, an affirmative answer. I had the pleasure to say that Boston would give a fraternal grasp of the hand to the soldiers of California, even though they might come here to fight the battles not simply as Boston soldiers, nor as Massachusetts soldiers, but as soldiers of the United States—to fight under our glorious National banner and to shed, if it were necessary, their life-blood upon the altar of our common country.

"This sir is the result. California has not on this occasion sent her gold to the North, but she has sent that which is dearer and more precious to her and to us—the true and brave hearts and stout arms of her sons, that she, too, may worthily stand beside her loyal sister States, and pay her offering with theirs on the altar of our common country.

"Let us receive them with that friendly greeting and fraternal grasp of brotherhood to which they are so justly entitled; and, sir, permit me to surrender to you, the official representative of the citizens of Boston, the agreeable privilege of tendering a cordial, generous welcome to our city and its hospitalities, Captain Reed and his company of Californians, whom I have now the honor and pleasure to present to you."

After the applause and cheering died down Mayor Lincoln replied, "It gives me much satisfaction, sir, as the representative of the city of Boston, to receive from you, my predecessor, this introduction to Captain Reed and the company from California. The circumstances are very peculiar. Brave and gallant men from the shores of the Pacific, desirous to do their share in putting down this rebellion, offer their services to you and the Commonwealth, and desire to put their destiny and their fortunes with our brave Massachusetts men. It has been your fortune and you have had the honor and the official action to make these men a part and portion of the quota of Boston. It seems to me, sir, one of the pleasantest things of your administration. When you shall see their gallant deeds in action, more than ever will you be proud that your labors put them into the service. I return to you my thanks in behalf of the city of Boston."

Turning to Capt. Reed, the mayor continued, "To you, Captain Reed, let me in behalf of the city of Boston tender you a most hearty welcome. You and your command have all volunteered to place your selves in the service of the United States, desiring to form a part of the quota of Boston, thus enlisting our warmest sympathies in behalf of our beloved Commonwealth and making as it were our Boston soldiers your brothers in arms.

"The service to which you were called is one of danger and peril. I believe that the cavalry service is one of the most important in military organizations. They do not fight behind the intrenchments and in forts, but they meet the enemy in personal conflict. The greatest battles in the past have been achieved in a great measure by the cavalry arm. This is true from the time of Alexander the Great, who always led in person his Macedonian cohorts, and it is true also in the times of Cromwell. At Marston Moor and Naseby, those great battles were achieved, it is said, by cavalry. It has been said by military men that the misfortunes of the great Napoleon were owing in a considerable degree to the fact that he had not sufficient skill in the disposition of his cavalry force. And I would say also in our own times, in this present war, it has been said that if our loyal troops had in their forces a much larger number of cavalry, our successes would have been greater in many of the most important engagements and our great victories more complete.

"Captain Reed, we welcome you. You are to share in the sympathies of Bostonians. We are proud that you represent Boston and Massachusetts."

Taking his turn before the crowd, Capt. Reed replied, "Mayor Lincoln; I bring you one hundred Californians. We come not as citizens of California, neither as citizens of Massachusetts. We come as citizens of the United States, and we are proud to enroll ourselves under the quota of Boston." The short reply was interrupted twice by the cheering crowd and followed by the band rendering the "Star-Spangled Banner."

At the conclusion of the ceremony the men reformed their ranks and marched to the State house where they were formally presented to the Governor. Once again the men formed a hollow square, with the Governor, Amos Lawrence, and other prominent state politicians in the center. Bowing to the cheers of the crowd the Governor turned to Capt. Reed.

"Captain, it gives me the most unalloyed satisfaction, and it fills my heart with pride as well as joy I cannot express to have the high honor, both officially and personally, of greeting you soldiers of the Union who have passed from the distant shores of the Pacific that you may number yourselves upon the Atlantic shores with the soldiers of Massachusetts who are guarding and defending the rights, the honor, and the perpetuity of our common Union.

"Who shall dare to hesitate to doubt in the quiet of his peaceful home when men act like you soldiers, citizens like these, deserting the golden mines of that far distant State that you may hurry to our defense. I am proud, Captain and soldiers, that it is given to us to have the honor of numbering you with our own contingent, that your names are to be recorded upon the same rolls which bear the dear names of Massachusetts men. But no longer any more of Massachusetts, of New York, of Illinois, of Missouri, of Texas, of California, do we think or remember when a common hope, a common pride, a common joy, and an interest common to us all stands imperiled. That flag is the symbol by which we all swear; it is the standard which our fathers erected; it is the flag for which every good citizen will even dare to die.

"It will give you, Captain, satisfaction to know that I have this morning received assurance from Washington that the tender of a whole battalion of Californians has been permitted to me to accept. The offer of a battalion of your friends and neighbors of California was proudly accepted so far as it lay in my own power officially to do so. This morning from Washington I have the authority which I hesitate not to act upon without delay, and I dare say the winged messenger has now ditted over the wires, and I trust that now in San Francisco it is already known that this battalion will be counted a part of the Massachusetts contingent, and I also venture to declare that the message will find the California Company beneath the dome of the Capital of Massachusetts.

"The history of this war, captain, has revealed to us a changeful scene, now a momentary defeat, now a glorious triumph; but it has also revealed to us what is much more to be proud of before men, and thank I the Almighty God, that the love of country, the firmness of heroic hearts, the devotion to duty on the part of the citizen soldiers of the Union, was not, never has been, and never can be doubtful, hesitating, momentary or spasmodic.

"We have set in for a storm as long as it may please God to allow it to last. Disaster can only be the trial of our metal, delay can only be the test of our patience, and victory is only worthy when it has been fairly won.

"I doubt not, sir, I doubt not, soldiers, that you have served your own hearts and strengthened your own purposes by a high contemplation of a high idea of duty, in having left behind you all the attractions of your own homes that you might share in the hardships as well as the honors of the field.

"In committing to you, sir, a commission, and commissions to your fellow-officers in arms, giving an opportunity of service under the white flag of Massachusetts as well as the starry banner of the Union, I have done so not only with pride and gratification already feebly attempted to be expressed, but with the utmost confidence that our cause will be faithfully served, the honor of us all nobly protected, and the flag which you bear will never be surrendered to any foe.

"Unnumbered as are the fields on which the soldiers of Massachusetts have shed their blood, laid down their lives, no flag yet borne in Massachusetts hands has ever been torn from the standard bearer's grasp to grace the godless triumph of the enemy.

"These banners are committed to your care with more than ordinary confidence, and with more than ordinary solemnity of a personal and official charge, that you shall be faithful to the cause which it symbolizes, and you will baptize it, if need be, with the last drop of your heart's best blood."

The governor was then introduced to the company officers and the reception was over. The troops gratefully returned to their Readville barracks, bearing their new State colors with them.[17]

Most of the Californians had relatives in the New England states and as proper drilling could not proceed until the horses arrived, the entire company was given a ten-day furlough. Private Towle spent his furlough in Bangor, Maine, but upon his return was shocked to learn that eight men had deserted the company. Eight desertions was minor compared to the numbers seen in the Massachusetts companies, but "from shear shame" Towle was unable to tell anyone about it for years. One of the deserters, Pvt. Charles Balke, turned himself in to the Provost Guard in October and was returned to the regiment where he served honorably and was discharged at war's end as a corporal.[18]

The 1st of February was a noteworthy day for the 2nd Massachusetts Cavalry; the men were issued saddles, blankets, bridles, and other kit, and drew lots for their horses. Most of the Californians and a few of the Eastern men were familiar with riding but for the majority of the battalion the horse was an unknown quality.

The results of these first meetings were an assortment of bumps, bruises, and broken bones. The former sailors, clerks, and cabinetmakers quickly learned the dangers of walking too close behind a half tame (half wild!) horse or getting within reach of a strong set of teeth. Once firmly astride their mounts the men were taught the intricacies of getting the beasts to move. It was a frequent scene in these first weeks to see a sergeant sadly shaking his head or screaming in fury as riderless horses thundered across the parade ground and mud-covered recruits swore in frustration. Many of the curses were meant for Lowell who kept the men in the saddle for endless hours. Already accomplished riders, the Californians were vastly amused by the daily entertainment, though even they suffered from the unruly mounts. Pvt. Henry Tubbs was thrown from his horse breaking both bones of his right forearm. Most of the Westerners spent their free time trying to make their mounts bridle wise, a trait the horses did not have. This was accomplished by teaching the horse to respond to the gentlest touch of the reins on their necks by quickly turning, starting, or stopping.[19]

The troopers had mastered their drill dismounted but apparently had to relearn it when in the saddle. Pvt. Towle recalled the training. "...[W]e were quite constantly drilled mounted and as we were all green and few of us not very good riders, the horses [also being] green, when the Company would be ordered into platoon or company front formation the tendency of the horses on the flanks to crowd toward the center would sometimes subject the limbs of those near the center to a pressure which was far from pleasant, especially if the soldiers knee happened at the time to be next to the curry comb and brush in the saddle bag of the one next him. At times the pressure would nearly raise horse and rider off the ground."[20]

The governor had told the Californians that a full battalion of troopers from California had been authorized and would soon join them. The difficulty in raising sufficient numbers of troops from the Boston area had prompted Governor Andrew to ask Ira Rankin in San Francisco if he could furnish more troops. On the 13th of December, 1862, only two days after the Hundred had sailed east, Andrew telegraphed that he would accept 300 more men and Massachusetts would provide the officers.[21]

Rankin's reply offered a battalion of 400 men by the first of April. In his short return telegram he made a point of stressing that they would be led by their own major and should be officered by their own men as well. The terms of recruitment would be the same as those used with the Hundred.[22]

The thought of waiting till spring for the men seemed too long to suit the governor. His reply on the 18th requested Rankin to estimate the time needed to furnish only one company. Fully aware of the difficulties being faced in the east in regards to recruiting, Rankin knew he could hold out for a full battalion if he compromised with Andrew. Stating that no one was willing to raise a single company he offered that the battalion might be ready to sail as soon as the 1st of February. Knowing that Andrew might doubt this extremely optimistic time frame, Rankin tried to bait the Governor with his choice for the man who would be major of the battalion.[23]

He proposed the battalion be raised by Colonel DeWitt C. Thompson, formerly a resident of Massachusetts, and once a member of the staff of General in Chief, Henry W. Halleck. If General Halleck would give his approval, Col. Thompson would leave his current post as Chief of Staff to General Allen, Commander of the State Militia.[24]

The offer was very enticing to the governor but the available funds to transport the troops were becoming scarce. Before committing what funds he had earmarked, Andrew wired Gen. Halleck concerning Col. Thompson's abilities. Halleck's full endorsement persuaded Andrew to telegraph Rankin on Christmas Eve that, with the War Department's blessing, he would accept the battalion. The telegram did not mention any delivery date, but Andrew had to have misgivings about Rankin's ability to meet his own time estimate.[25]

While awaiting permission from the War Department, the availability of funds became even worse. Andrew requested Rankin to notify him what the effects of receiving only $125 per man, vice $200, would have on organizing. Rankin replied that with $200 he could ensure the men had uniforms, transportation, and a portion of their arms; $125 would only cover transportation and organization. Either way Thompson would provide four companies of officers and men and would report with them in New York 60 days after receipt of acceptance. He went on to suggest that if only $125 per man were available, they could be mustered in and uniformed by Gen. Wright, commander of the Department of the Pacific.

By the time the message was received by Governor Andrew, the available funds had plummeted to only $75 per man. Of that, $20 would be sent to Rankin for organizing purposes and the remainder used to cover transportation.[26]

On the 7th, 8th, and 9th of January, 1863, Governor Andrew wired Secretary Stanton seeking acceptance of the battalion. On the 10th, due to the lack of response by Washington, he dispatched Col. Lowell to personally travel to the War Department and resolve the matter. Lowell carried a personal appeal from the Governor to the Secretary. Their meeting, though no record was made of it, was a success. On the 13th of January, Lowell wired to the Governor and Forbes that the battalion had been authorized.[27]

As the telegram sped north to Boston another was dispatched by Brig. Gen. Ketchum of the War Department. Addressed to Gen. Wright in San Francisco it read: "The Secretary of War directs that Thompson's four cavalry companies be mustered into service — with from sixty to seventy eight privates each. Clothe and subsist them. The State of Massachusetts will transport them to Boston where they will be armed and equipped."[28]

Receiving the authorization the next morning, Thompson went to work with a fury. A six-foot, black-haired native of Berkshire County, Massachusetts, Thompson had ventured west during the gold rush. He returned briefly to his home state three years later to marry Miss Marion Brown of Hinsdale, then returned with his bride to his adopted state. On the 16th of January Thompson was commissioned a second lieutenant, though he carried the anticipated rank of major, and recruiting began. As was the case with the Hundred there was no shortage of volunteers for the four companies. The *Daily Alta California* warned, "Only those able to ride, and sober men, will be received."[29]

Although the citizens as a whole embraced the chance to send their men east, there were some who were carried along with noted reluctance. Among these was California Governor Leland Stanford. In a letter to Gen. Wright on the 25th of January, Governor Stanford stated that "The proceedings under and by force which these troops are to be raised are clearly irregular, and in violation of the rights of the state...." He went on to question the authority in Washington that would allow Massachusetts to recruit among his constituents. He chose not to interfere with the raising of the four companies provided a precedence was not set and more men taken. The *Alta California*, a great supporter of the project, reported, "...very serious doubts are expressed by true and loyal men as to the policy and propriety of sending away more men of the State, in view of the probable or possible interruptions of amicable relations with foreign powers."[30]

The four companies were designated A, B, C, and D, though upon reaching Massachusetts they would become E, L, M, and F respectively. Company officers were quickly selected for Company A, to prepare for the horde of recruits that were expected. Appointed as captain was Charles S. Eigenbrodt, a former supervisor of Alameda County, and currently a major on the staff of Brig. Gen. Ellis. A 37-year-old native of New York, Eigenbrodt was expecting to draw in a number of young men from the surrounding agricultural counties. It was thought that the men there were more daring and skilled in horsemanship.[31]

Company A, or the California Cossacks, as they were first called, also had 2nd Lt. Henry H. Crocker to aid in organizing. Crocker, a 23-year-old bartender and immigrant from Connecticut, was a sergeant in the Oakland Home Guard. He would be one of two men in the regiment who would eventually receive the Medal of Honor for "valor on the field of battle."[32]

The other three companies were led by men who would also distinguish themselves before their military service was through. Zabdiel B. Adams, a capable 29-year-old son of Massachusetts was selected as Captain of Company B. Company C was led by Captain George Manning who had been discharged from Company F of the 2nd California Cavalry, the Sacramento Rangers, where he had been serving as First Sergeant of the Provost

Capt. Charles S. Eigenbrodt. Killed in action August 25, 1864, near Halltown, Virginia. *Courtesy of U.S.A.M.H.I.*

Captain Zabdiel B. Adams, Company L, California Battalion, 2nd Massachusetts Cavalry. *Courtesy of U.S.A.M.H.I.*

Guard of San Francisco. David D. DeMerritt, also of the 2nd California Cavalry (Captain of Company F), was commissioned Captain of Company D.[33]

The recruitment of the battalion was conducted in the same fashion as was the Hundred. Once again there were far fewer places to fill than there were men to fill them. The fact that the battalion did not leave the state until fully seven weeks past Rankin's estimated date of February 3 was not due to difficulty in locating volunteers, but rather in finding men that met the strict criteria for joining the battalion. A man had to be young, in good health, and able to ride before he was even considered. If a man did manage to garner the approval of the recruiting officers, he was given a thorough medical exam by a regular army physician, Dr. Christian, and then sworn into Federal service.[34]

The new recruits' training began immediately upon their reaching the troop barracks at Platts Hall. Drill was held in the morning and afternoon, both sessions lasting two to three hours each. As the men would not perform in mounted drill until reaching the east they marched through the formations on foot. When the poor San Francisco weather prevented the men from drilling they stayed in the barracks and spent hours practicing with their sabres. In charge of military instruction was Captain Von Voast, a West Point man from the Ninth Infantry, on special assignment from Gen. Wright.[35]

Though the daily routine was full, what with drilling, policing the barracks, and guard duty, the men did find time to enjoy the sights of the city. Late afternoon often found many of them dining in one of the city's restaurants rather than submit to army chow. Evenings were frequently spent enjoying local entertainment such as Gilbert's Melodian or the What-Cheer House. If a man was running short on cash he had to spend his evenings in the barracks, not a depressing or boring spot by any means; "...all the boys felt gay acting up all the time in quarters."[36]

Like the Hundred, the recruiting of the battalion aroused the patriotism of the people of San Francisco. With a population made up of so many former residents of the east and midwest, it was no wonder that the troopers received so much attention. The Hundred and battalion would carry the fight that was in every man that wanted to, but could not, go himself.

Washington's birthday was celebrated with a "Grand Military Parade and Review" where 150 of the battalion made a "...very showy and elegant appearance." Another review was held on the Plaza on the 11th of March. Brig. Gen. John S. Ellis and his staff inspected Thompson's troops who "…acquitted themselves excellently well, for men so short a time under arms." For the benefit of the crowd watching the review, a drill was held to add to the pageantry.[37]

Presentations of swords and speeches were in abundance and a special church service was administered by the Reverend Thomas Starr King. A lavish farewell dinner was planned and Platts Hall was once again chosen as the site. This time the weather was perfect and the ladies of San Francisco attended in force. There were speeches and toasts to honor, but the battalion would remember longer the ladies and the dancing that lasted to the early hours.[38]

The next morning companies A, B, C, and a portion of D prepared themselves for their departure. The remainder of Captain DeMerritt's company was scheduled to leave at a later date. The press reported that the delay in departure was due to the difficulty in obtaining a full complement of men. By the 21st of March, the day the bulk of the battalion sailed, only 34 men had been enlisted in Company D. This was a direct result of those high standards that the recruiting officers demanded.[39]

The parade to the docks began early that morning with a large escort standing by to ensure the troopers left in style. At exactly 8 A.M. the First California Infantry Regiment began the march to the Folsom Street Wharf, followed by the Pioneer Guard under the command of Capt. Isaac Bluxone. The California Battalion, minus Capt. DeMerritt's company, brought up the rear, attended by the American Brass Band. Two guns of the California Guard artillery waited on the wharf to fire a final salute. Flags flew in abundance and the crowds cheered as the troopers filed up the gangway of the steamer *Constitution*.[40]

The crowd was enormous, eclipsing the throng at the farewell to the California Hundred in December. The *Daily Alta* reported, "The decks of the *Sierra Nevada*, which lay alongside, and the various sailing craft in the vicinity presented dense masses of spectators. Hundreds of row boats and sailing craft might also be seen flying up and down the Bay in the immediate neighborhood of the wharf. The adjoining piers and Market Street outside the pier gate, were blocked with persons of both sexes, some on foot, and many in vehicles. On no previous occasion have we seen so many live humans congregated on Folsom Street Wharf."[41]

While the cannons of the guard thundered their farewell, the 295 men manned the rails, many waving till the wharf was out of sight. Four days later the Californians sustained their first casualty. Private Hiram Townsend, a 36-year-old farmer turned cavalier, was unable to find his sea legs. Becoming seasick hours after the ship left port, Townsend spent most of the time leaning over the rail. A gale blew up on the 25th and the rolling seas gave him no rest. As he staggered once again to the rail a wave crashed against the side of the ship and in an instant Private Townsend was swept away. He was heard to call out twice but the heavy wool overcoat dragged him under before the ship could be stopped and a small boat sent out. His comrades were devastated by the loss and were furious with the crew who they felt "…made but a trifling search."[42]

The trip south was otherwise uneventful, and the cavalrymen spent day after day dealing with the boredom of life at sea. A short port visit to Manzanillo, Mexico, allowed a few of the men to go ashore and purchase food to supplement the poor shipboard fare. As the ship neared Panama another fierce storm struck causing a widespread outbreak of seasickness. While the storm grew in fury, many became increasingly concerned with ever seeing dry land again. Several of the female passengers onboard cried, and prayers were offered, while from the soldiers' berthing several ex-sailors cheered and whooped every time the ship took a roll.[43]

Eventually the trip south came to an end and the anchor was dropped off the coast of Panama. Wasting little time the troopers made their way to shore and boarded the Panama Railroad for the short trip to Aspinwall. There they found the S.S. *Ocean Queen* waiting to transport them to New York.

While leaving the harbor the *Queen* passed the British mail packet *Trent* of Mason and Slidell fame. As the two ships passed the Californians cheered three times in honor of Capt. Charles Wilkes of the U.S.S. *San Jacinto*. The British sailors mistook the cheers for themselves and were quite pleased until the true meaning was made known to them.*[44]

From Panama to Cuba the *Ocean Queen* was escorted by the U.S.S. *Connecticut* due to rumors that Capt. Raphael Semmes and his dreaded C.S.S. *Alabama* were lying in wait for them. The rebel raider was never sighted and the trip was pleasant with the possible exception of the food. If the troopers thought the *Constitution* had poor fare they were in for even worse treatment on the *Queen*. One of the men recalled: "Of our trip from Aspinwall to New York, suffice it to say that we were treated worse than dogs should be: crowded into steerage, the atmosphere of which was enough to kill ordinary men: the food consisted of 'salt horse,' salt pork ditto, and musty, hard bread. It was unfit for human beings to eat, and would have turned the stomach of a starved Digger Indian. You may form some idea of the feeling of our soldiers when I assure you that so driven to exasperation were they, that had the pirate Alabama hove into sight she would have been welcomed with cheers."[45]

The arrival of the troops in New York City was a bit of a let-down for the excited soldiers. The welcoming committee on the pier consisted of a sheriff with a writ of Habeas Corpus for Major Thompson, and a few old apple women.† The battalion marched to the Park Barracks where they were more warmly received and given a supper, "…which was relished with gusto by our half starved fellows." That evening the entire battalion was given free tickets to the New Bowery Theater.[46]

The next morning started with a march to the Park where they were formed in dress parade and addressed by Governor J.W. Nye, of Nevada Territory. At the conclusion of the governor's speech they marched through the city to the Battery where they boarded a ferry for the trip to Boston.[47]

While the three companies slowly made their transit from coast to coast, recruitment continued for Capt. DeMerritt's company back in San Francisco. The extra time taken in raising the company allowed Charles Roberts, a Californian working in Empire City, Nevada, to make a decision that changed the course of his life. Roberts had begun making entries at the beginning of the year in a small leather covered diary.

On November 7, 1861, the British mail steamer Trent *was en route from Havana, Cuba, to the British West Indies. Onboard were James Mason and John Slidell, the Confederate commissioners to England and France. The* Trent *was stopped on the high seas by the U.S.S.* San Jacinto, *commanded by Capt. Charles Wilkes, who took the two Confederates captive. The incident nearly brought the United States to war with Great Britain.*

†*Just before the departure from San Francisco, 18-year-old Isaac Golinsky changed his mind about becoming a soldier. To prevent his departure on the* Constitution, *Golinsky's brother received a writ of Habeas Corpus from a San Francisco judge, but he was too late and young Isaac sailed with the others. Upon arrival in New York, the writ was served and Isaac returned home to California. Mace,* Massachusetts Cavalry from California, *p. 38.*

His entries through the 7th of April describe the weather and little else. His entry on the 8th was his longest to that point and the most important.

"At work. Blowing and snowing. Have a great notion of going East with the Cavalry that goes from San Francisco. Got a letter from an old [friend] in San Francisco, he has joined the Battalion and thinks there is a good chance for me. Am studying very deep the question, I will be leaving a situation here to go, but that's nothing to what's at stake."[48]

Roberts' "situation" was his well-paying job as a butcher's assistant. By early the next morning, though, he had made up his mind and was on his way by foot to Carson City. By foot, stagecoach, and river boat, Roberts made his way to San Francisco, arriving on the 11th.[49]

Presenting himself to Capt. DeMerritt at first light, he and four other would-be troopers were soon before a medical examiner. One of the men was deemed unfit for service, but the remaining men, Roberts included, were soon sworn into the service of the United States. No time was wasted in putting the new men into training with the other recruits. "Done my first drilling afternoon, it comes very awkerd at first."[50]

For the next 11 days Roberts and the men of company D were given the daily routine of drill once or twice a day for two to three hours at a stretch. Plenty of time was given to the men to go into the city each day to visit family and friends. DeMerritt took a short furlough to say good-bye to his family in Sacramento, and in his absence the company was drilled by 1st Lt. Alvin Stone of Company C. For some reason, probably to assist in recruiting, Stone had not sailed with his own company, and now joined in the training of Company D. The actual first lieutenant for Company D was 26-year-old Rufus Smith, with the second lieutenant post filled by Horace B. Welch.[51]

The send-off from the pier on the 24th of April was void of the fanfare that had marked the departure of the previous companies, there being only 49 men, the last to be recruited. "There was no unusual crowd present more than some military men of San Francisco...," noted Roberts in his diary. The newspapers did not even make mention of the event. The only crowd present were the family and friends of the soldiers and the civilian passengers onboard and they could not raise their spirits enough for a parting cheer. Pulling quietly away from the dock, the S.S. *Sonora* made her way smoothly across the bay and through the Golden Gate.[52]

Roberts kept a careful record of the voyage south to Panama, noting daily the latitude and longitude, as well as the miles covered. The ship was only hours under way when four stowaways were found onboard. The stowaways were from the San Francisco Provost Guard, and had hidden out to join the company.[53]

The trip was uneventful, the days being passed by reading, card playing, and singing. As always the shipboard food did not sit well with the men. "We all eat very hearty of bean soup for dinner, this being the only meal we get during the day fit to eat, unless we buy it and pay steamboat prices." The rations were supplemented twice with fresh fruit when the ship pulled into the Mexican ports of Manzanillo and Acapulco. Twice during the trip south the passengers and crew were saddened by the death of small children. The men of Company D fared well, facing little more than the occasional dose of seasickness. Private Norman B. Payne lay tossing for days in a fever, his bunkmates taking turns sitting up with him until the fever passed.[54]

Arriving off the coast of the Isthmus on the 7th of May, the company took a late night train to the Atlantic coast where they found the S.S. *Ocean Queen* waiting to take them to New York. If the men did not know that the *Queen* was the same vessel that had ferried the other three companies north, they would soon learn why the others had grown to hate her. The first day out it was noted, "We don't get as good as grub as we did on the other side...," followed the next day by, "Our food is outrageously bad...." Decent food would have to wait till land fall in New York.[55]

To protect the steamer from Confederate privateers that prowled the gulf, the U.S.S. *Connecticut*, once again, was tasked with escorting the *Queen* to New York. The trip was without incident and as before the soldiers were faced with nothing more dangerous than boredom. Distraction was provided when another stowaway was discovered, and unable to pay his passage and refusing to work, was placed in irons for the remainder of the journey.[56]

Early on the morning of the 16th, the *Ocean Queen* pulled into New York harbor and fired two guns to call for a pilot. Lost among the throng of people at the docks, the single company made their way unnoticed into the city. Stopping long enough for a meal and to drop off the deserters from the Provost Guard, DeMerritt's company quickly boarded the ferry and were at Camp Meigs by 6 A.M.[57]

Notes

1. Massachusetts State Archives, extract from Special Orders No. 363.
2. Duncan, *Blue Eyed Child of Fortune*, pp. 256–57; Executive Letters, Vol. 74, p. 22.
3. Duncan, *Blue Eyed Child of Fortune*, pp. 258–65; Letters Official, Vol. 25, P. 64.
4. *Massachusetts Soldiers, Sailors, and Marines*, Vol. 6, pp. 230–316.
5. Humphreys, *Field and Camp*, p. 8; *Massachusetts Soldiers, Sailors, and Marines*, Vol. 6, pp. 230–316.
6. Executive letters, Vol. 24, p. 449.
7. *Massachusetts Soldiers, Sailors, and Marines*, Vol. 6, pp. 230–316.
8. Emerson, *Life and Letters*, pp. 374–75; Higginson, "Lowell," p. 318; Greenslet, *The Lowells and Their Seven Worlds*, p. 250.
9. National Archives, Record Group 94, Pension files of Eastman, Charles, and George Duley.
10. Emilio, *A Brave Black Regiment*, p. 24.
11. Letters Official, Vol. 24, p. 274.
12. Corbett, *Diary*, Jan. 3, 1863.
13. Towle, *Recollections*, p. 3.
14. Towle, *Recollections*, p. 3.
15. *Napa County Reporter*, Feb. 7, 1863.
16. Hunt, *Army of the Pacific*, p. 286; *Boston Herald*, Jan. 14, 1863.
17. *Boston Journal*, 14 Jan., 1863.
18. Towle, *Recollections*, p. 3.
19. Towle, *Recollections*, p. 3; National Archives, Record group 94, Pension Record of Henry Tubbs.
20. Towle, *Recollections*, p. 3.
21. Letters Official, Vol. 23, p. 115.
22. Letters Official, Vol. 23, p. 175.
23. Letters Official, Vol. 23, pp. 201, 312.
24. Mace, *Massachusetts Cavalry from California*, p. 33.
25. Letters Official, Vol. 23, p. 442.
26. Letters Official, Vol. 24, pp. 195, 245.
27. Letters Official, Vol. 24, pp. 348, 359, 363; Executive Letters, Vol. 74, p. 167.
28. Executive Letters, Vol. 74, p. 17.
29. National Archives, Record Group 94, Pension Record of DeWitt C. Thompson; *Daily Alta California*, Jan. 19, 1863.
30. *Daily Alta California*, Jan. 23, 1863; OR L, Pt. 1, pp. 292–93.
31. *Daily Alta California*, Jan. 21, 1863.
32. Tibbals, "Thirty Years Later," *Civil War Times Illustrated*, Apr. 1986, Vol. XXV, No. 2, p. 34.
33. Mortimer, *California Hundred and Battalion*, p. 80; *National Tribune*, Aug. 18, 1910.
34. *Daily Alta California*, Jan. 19, 1863.
35. *Daily Alta California*, Feb. 10, 1863.
36. Roberts, *Diary*, Apr. 16–22, 1863.
37. *Daily Alta California*, Feb. 24, Mar. 12, 1863.
38. Backus, "Californians in the Field," *MOLLUS*, p.8.
39. Orton, *Records of California Troops in the Civil War*, pp. 861–63; *Massachusetts Soldiers, Sailors, and Marines*, pp. 267–73.
40. *Daily Alta California*, Mar. 24, 1863.
41. *Daily Alta California*, Mar. 24, 1863.
42. *Daily Alta California*, Apr. 20, 1863.
43. *Daily Alta California*, Apr. 30, 1863; Hunt, *Army of the Pacific*, p. 289.

44. *Daily Alta California*, May 30, 1863.
45. *Daily Alta California*, May 30, 1863.
46. Hunt, *Army of the Pacific*, p. 290.
47. *Daily Alta California*, May 30, 1863; *New York Times*, Apr. 16, 1863.
48. Roberts, *Diary*, Apr. 8, 1863.
49. Roberts, *Diary*, Apr. 9–11, 1863.
50. Roberts, *Diary*, Apr. 13, 1863.
51. National Archives, Record Group 94, Co. F muster roll, enrollment to June 30, 1863; Roberts, *Diary*, Apr. 14–21, 1863.
52. Roberts, *Diary*, Apr. 23, 1863; National Archives, Record Group 94, Company F Muster Roll, enrollment to June 30, 1863.
53. Roberts, *Diary*, Apr. 24, 1863.
54. Roberts, *Diary*, Apr. 25 to May 2, 1863.
55. Roberts, *Diary*, May 7–8, 1863.
56. Roberts, *Diary*, May 9–11, 1863.
57. Roberts, *Diary*, May 16, 1863.

Chapter Four

"Take care Major, here come the Rebs"

During the months of recruitment and training of the California Battalion back in San Francisco, the Hundred, or Company A, had nearly completed its own training at Camp Meigs. The Hundred, along with companies B, C, and D, had been designated the first battalion. The four companies that comprised the California Battalion would be broken up upon their arrival in Massachusetts, two being placed in the Second Battalion, and the remaining two becoming part of the Third.

It was Col. Lowell's decision to split up the Californians, and considering the quality of the troops raised in Massachusetts, it was a sound one. It was hoped that the superior riding abilities and high morale of the westerners would act as a leaven for the other seven companies. Time would show the wisdom of this movement as the entire 2nd Massachusetts Cavalry, and not just the Californians, would become a force to be reckoned with. Unfortunately the move fostered a bitterness against Col. Lowell by the Californians that was a long time in passing.

Lowell may have had his troubles with the training and discipline of his Massachusetts recruits but he had solid officers to whip them into shape. Among them was his second in command, Lt. Col. Henry Sturgis Russell. Russell had been captain of Company G, 2nd Massachusetts Infantry when he was contacted to help raise the 2nd Massachusetts Cavalry. Twenty-four years old and battle tested, he proved instrumental in the training and organizing of the regiment, but never joined it in the field. In March of 1864 he was promoted to colonel and placed in command of the 5th Massachusetts Cavalry.

Lt. Col. Russell was married to the former Mary Forbes, daughter of John M. Forbes who was still actively involved in recruiting for the regiment. Forbes' son William, a 22-year-old officer in Company E, 1st Massachusetts Cavalry, joined his brother-in-law in training the men and became Captain of Company B of the 2nd Cavalry. In time he would acquire the nom de guerre, "Lowell's Fighting Major."

One of the most important additions to the regiment was 25-year-old Caspar Crowninshield, captain of the same Company E, 1st Massachusetts Cavalry that had produced young Will Forbes. Crowninshield

had seen a year's service in the mounted branch and had begun the war as a captain in the 20th Massachusetts Infantry. Appointed senior major in command of the First Battalion, the veteran Crowninshield would later become the leader of the regiment and eventually earn the shoulder straps of a brigadier.

The officers who made up the First Battalion (not including the Californians) were a fairly tight-knit group due to their past associations. The 1st Massachusetts Cavalry, which had sent Crowninshield and Forbes, also provided Francis Washburn and Warren Ball, now captain and second lieutenant of Company D, as well as 1st Lt. Louis Cabot of B Company. The officers of the Hundred fit well into this group of disciplined men and the battalion quickly became a functioning unit ready for action.[1]

Due to the length of time in raising the regiment, let alone training it, the first battalion was prepared for active operations long before the other two. In fact the first battalion had its marching orders a week before Thompson's battalion sailed from the West coast. As the first battalion was now nearly ready to move to the front, the question was raised as to which front they would actually go to. The first indication of their future destination had come from Governor Andrew in a telegram to Ira Rankin. In it he had stated that the cavalry, "Will join Banks' Texas expedition at Galveston." A day later, on the 3rd of November, Andrew again stated his intention to send the regiment to Maj. Gen. Banks, this time in a letter to Secretary Stanton.[2]

Banks, the former governor of Massachusetts, used his political influence to convince the city government of Boston to appropriate large sums of time and money for the raising of the 2nd Massachusetts Cavalry. Without his assistance the great plan of uniting the East and the West in a single regiment might never have transpired.

In a stream of letters to Gen. Halleck in Washington, Banks asked, pleaded, and demanded the regiment be sent to him. His final request in August 1863, turned nearly poetic at times as he stressed the now missed opportunity of having California assist in opening the Mississippi River. He also went to great length in expounding on his personal efforts in raising the regiment. "But for my personal exertions," he stated, "it would not and could not have been organized at the time it was placed in the field." When rumors began to circulate about the pending orders, John M. Forbes jumped into Banks' corner, writing the Governor and stressing the need to contact Stanton and confirm the regiment was bound for Texas.[3]

Another claim to the 2nd Massachusetts Cavalry came when Maj. Gen. William Rosecrans bypassed the War Department and requested Andrew to send the regiment to his Army of the Cumberland in Tennessee. Catching wind of this maneuver, Stanton telegraphed the Governor and made it clear that he wanted Lowell's first battalion sent to Fort Monroe as soon as possible.[4]

With their orders now confirmed the First Battalion, consisting of companies A, B, C, D, and K, under the command of Major Crowninshield, set out on the 12th of February for Fort Monroe on the Virginia Peninsula. After months of training and traveling, this final leg of their journey brought to many a touch of nervous anticipation as to what lay ahead. It wasn't fear, but rather that unknown quality each man carries, wondering how he would react under fire. The Californians looked

Opposite: Major William H. Forbes, "Lowell's Fighting Major," 2nd Massachusetts Cavalry. Captured July 6, 1864, near Aldie, Virginia. *Courtesy of U.S.A.M.H.I.*

to Capt. Reed, their tall husky commander, but he too had yet to hear his first shot fired in anger. Inspiration for some came in the form of Major Crowninshield.

Born in Boston in 1837, Caspar Crowninshield came from impressive stock. His grandfather, Benjamin W. Crowninshield, had served as Secretary of the Navy under presidents Madison and Monroe. Benjamin's brother Jacob had been nominated for the same position by Thomas Jefferson but had declined to remain in the House of Representatives. To be quite honest, these men were rather lackluster politicos and the real strength of the family would always be tied to the sea. In shipping, ship building and privateering, the name Crowninshield had always been a pace-setter in the maritime world of Salem, Massachusetts. George Crowninshield, Benjamin and Jacob's brother, described as a "swell and a dandy," built the racing sloop *Jefferson* which he later sailed as a licensed privateer during the War of 1812. After the war he built *Cleopatra's Barge*, the largest racing yacht of her time and the eventual royal yacht of King Kamehameha II. Jacob himself had once captained his own ship, the *America*, on which in 1797 he imported the first elephant to North America. Because water was in short supply during the voyage, the beast was fed, and learned to enjoy, dark beer. Never one to pass up a profit, Jacob charged spectators 25 cents for the thrill of seeing the huge animal and to watch it uncork and drink bottles of beer. The animal did its part during the performance by picking pockets with its trunk.

The patriarch of the Crowninshield family was a physician, Johannes Kaspar Richter von Kronensheldt, who came to Massachusetts in 1684, fleeing Leipzig where he had slain an adversary in a duel. He married Elizabeth Allen, anglicized his name, and became a highly respected citizen. Nearly two centuries later, the name Crowninshield had become so well regarded when Caspar's sister, Fanny, was proposed to by John Quincey Adams, Jr., her mother hinted that it might be a step down for the family to join with the Adamses. Fanny was one of the most sought-after belles in New England. Despite her mother's apprehensions the couple did wed.[5]

Caspar was educated in Boston schools and was tutored by Rev. William C. Tenny in preparation for his entrance to Harvard in 1856. Noted for his athletic abilities as well as his book work, Crowninshield was an accomplished oarsman and football player. His roommate at this time was the young Robert G. Shaw, also of the class of 1860.

In the short time between graduation and the war, Crowninshield worked briefly in the family business. Putting this aside when the first shots were fired, he accepted a captaincy in the 20th Massachusetts Infantry. Known as one of the Harvard Regiments (the other being the 2nd Massachusetts Infantry), its officers were virtually a who's who of the young Boston elite. Names such as Abbot, Putnam, Hallowell and Cabot were found on the roster as well as Oliver Wendell Holmes, Jr., and James Jackson Lowell, brother of Charles Lowell. In October the young Caspar was baptized under fire at Ball's Bluff. During the retreat from that deadly field, Crowninshield somehow located a small boat and loaded his wounded men into it. After shoving the craft from the bank, according to Oliver Wendell Holmes, Jr., "Crownie had swum over in his uniform, carrying his watch in his mouth. Bullets hit the water all around him, but it was getting dark and the Rebs missed." On the other side of the river he saw that his men were attended to and then calmly gathered up the remnants of

Opposite: Col. Caspar Crowninshield, 2nd, Massachusetts Cavalry. *Courtesy of Roger J. Hunt Collection, U.S.A.M.H.I.*

his company, clad only in his drawers and a blanket. The Major had seen the elephant and was prepared to do so again.[6]

The trip down from Readville was anything but smooth and orderly. Leaving the camp by rail the battalion passed through Providence and Hartford to New York. From there it was by steamer to Elizabeth Port, New Jersey, arriving on the evening of the 13th where they were put in the cars again for the trip to Baltimore.* The battalion arrived in Baltimore, or rather, parts of the battalion straggled in, and a good number of the men immediately deserted. "With the exception of the Californians the men are a disgrace to the name of soldier and to the State that sent them," fumed Crowninshield. A guard was posted over the men and horses to prevent any further attempts at desertion, but this idea failed when the guards promptly quit their posts and headed for the nearest tavern. The remainder of the night was spent gathering up the drunken troopers, some of whom had taken to fighting each other in the streets with their sabres. Eventually the Major secured a storm house to quarter the men as they were recaptured and began the painful process of sobering up.[7]

The battalion was forced to wait in Baltimore for transportation to Fort Monroe. Maj. Gen. William F. Smith's XI Corps had recently passed through on its own trip to the peninsula, and had taken all of the available steamers. During the wait the men were moved out of the storm house and into the much more comfortable Coleman's Eutaw House. On the afternoon of Tuesday, the 18th of February, the men were loaded onto the steamers *Kenebec* and *Express* which took them down the Chesapeake Bay to Fort Monroe. The *Kenebec* arrived at the fort first and Capt. Holman of K company, the senior officer onboard, reported to Maj. Gen. John Dix, the Department Commander. Dix assigned the battalion to the 4th Corps under Erasmus B. Keyes at Yorktown. Keyes then sent the battalion across the York River to Gloucester Point with orders to report to Brig. Gen. Richard Busteed in command of the forces in the Yorktown-Gloucester Point area. Busteed in turn sent them on to Col. Arthur H. Grimshaw of the 4th Delaware Infantry, commanding the post at Gloucester Point. The men pitched their tents near Fort Keyes, or as Crowninshield described it, "…a mud bank with four 12 pounders posted on it." A correspondent to the *Boston Journal* calling himself Cadet, saw the point in a favorable light describing "…a beautiful spot, a sandy plain thirty feet above the river."[8]

The tents were soon set up and it was then that it was discovered that the stoves for the tents had been left behind. The stoves were a pure luxury item and they were sorely missed, for the next day a snow storm blew in making the new arrivals believe they were back in Massachusetts. Some of the men, including their major, attempted to build fires inside the tents, resulting in their being smoked out into the storm. The storm lasted for two days, leaving in its wake seven horses dead from exposure and many of the men sick. For two weeks Pvt. Sam Corbett lay in the brigade hospital sweating out a bout of typhoid fever, finally being released "hungry as a bear."[9]

The camp, officially Camp Grimshaw in honor of the brigade commander, was made up of tents described in detail by Pvt. Thomas Barnstead. "The tents which we occupy are what are called here the Sibley tent; but the pole is different from those

---

The severely under strength Company B arrived in Baltimore with 23 men and one second lieutenant and arrived at Gloucester Point with only the officer and 12 men. National Archives, Co. B muster rolls, Enlistment to February 28, 1863.

which you have seen. At the bottom of these poles there is an iron-tripod, the legs of which are some four feet long, and on the top of this tripod there is a socket, into which a common upright tent pole is fitted, and, with this contrivance a tent can be stretched to its utmost capacity. The tents are occupied by from fifteen to twenty men each, and with the bottom spread with pine foliage, we get along very comfortably indeed." The tents were placed in straight lines by company with the horses attached to a picket line stretched the length of each "street," the horses given no shelter. Very close to the post was a camp of Negro refugees, escaped slaves, that had put together a small community known as Slab Richmond. "There were great quantities of large oysters in the river," Towle recalled, "which we could have by raking them up, or the Negroes would supply them shelled for ten cents a quart." Private Briggs was also impressed with the tasty shellfish, writing, "I wish in my heart I could send you some of our York River oysters— the best in the world. They are of the most delicate flavor, and four of them will cover the bottom of the largest dinner plate. I have just bought half a gallon right out of the shell, for ten cents." It would appear Briggs got the better deal.[10]

The battalion was assigned to picket and outpost duty and the men quickly fell into the routine of life at the front. The pickets were sent out in groups of 20 with an officer in charge of the detail. The cavalry camp at Gloucester Point was fairly small and the outer pickets were a mere 500 yards out. One of the lines ran along Sarah's Creek and the other along the edge of a swamp, leaving only one point where cavalry could leave or enter the camp. Aside from their own camps, a picket line extended in front of Fort Keyes and the infantry at Camp Gilpin.[11]

Major Crowninshield quickly saw problems with the way that the pickets were being used and preferred charges against several officers and men for their conduct. He stated that the men were negligent in their duty, and that most of them went to sleep while on their post. Gen. Keyes deferred to the major who implemented stronger guidelines that resulted in a more efficient and diligent picket force that now extended two miles from camp. The pickets were issued rockets to signal the alarm, and all men in the camps were expected to turn out, ready for action within three minutes of the alarm being given.[12]

The fact that Crowninshield reported these relatively minor occurrences to his corps commander instead of Gen. Busteed gives an indication of the esteem that the major held for the brigade commander. In a letter to his mother, Crowninshield held nothing back in his description of the brigadier. "Gen. Busteed was formerly a sharp New York lawyer, one of the tricky kind so I am told. He is a vulgar man, a very vulgar looking man, no pretensions about being a gentlemen, and has about as much military knowledge and ability as you would expect a pettifogging lawyer to have." His thoughts on Gen. Keyes were hardly better, "…from what I saw of him I should think his friends had better secure him gilt rooms in some lunatic asylum."[13]

The cold Virginia winter of '63 slowly passed into spring and with it came the spring rains and mud. Virginia mud was an old adversary of the men in blue. It had slowed McClellan on his campaign up the peninsula, and immobilized Gen. Burnside after the battle of Fredericksburg during his infamous "Mud March." The mud at Gloucester Point was thick and deep and the men began to search for wood planks to floor their tents.

Captains Washburne and Holman

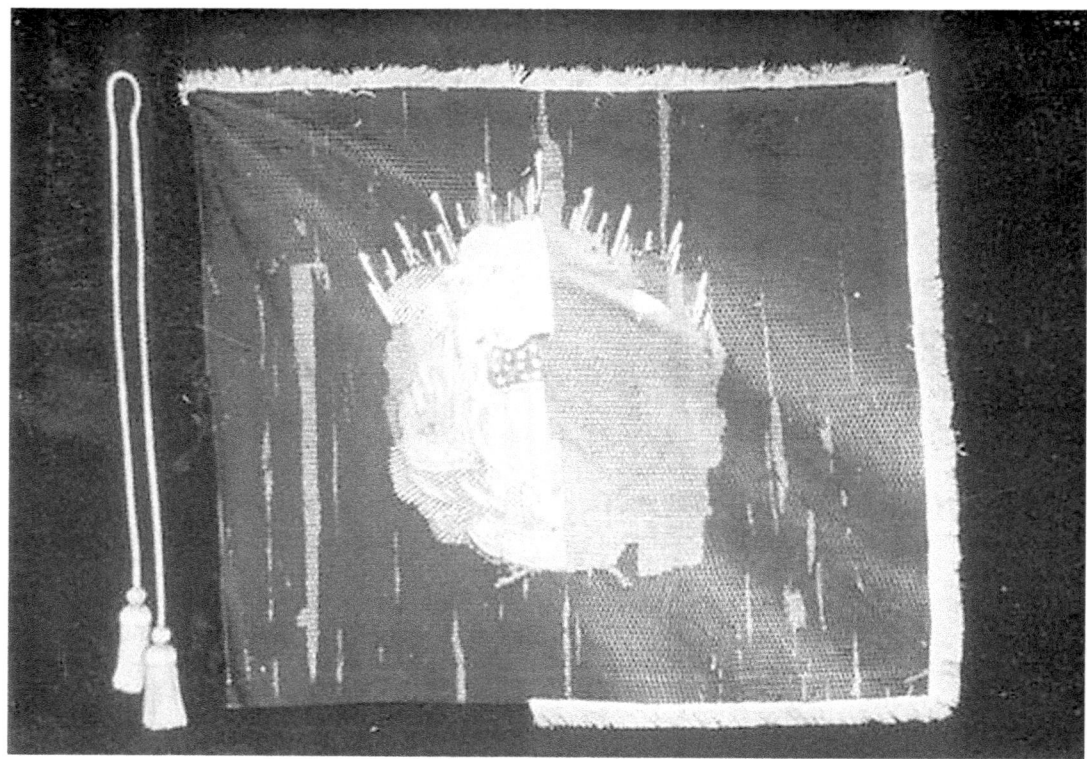

Massachusetts State Colors, 2nd Massachusetts Cavalry. *Courtesy of Massachusetts State House.*

learned of some boards that could be obtained about two miles past their lines. A wagon and several men, themselves eager for the planks, were gathered and Major Crowninshield was invited to enjoy the ride and the fine day.

The small party set out at a leisurely pace and were soon at the location of the lumber. The men stayed to load the wagon while the officers chose to ride further down the road and take in the fresh spring air. They weren't overly cautious as detachments of men had been riding daily through the area with no sign of Confederates. As a precaution Lt. Payson and 12 men were told to follow about 600 yards behind.

After riding two miles or so, a lone Confederate on horseback was seen ahead in the middle of the road. The three officers immediately gave chase as the Rebel cavalryman "…ran like smoke." The road narrowed as it entered a dense wood and the officers slowed, the fleeing horseman now being out of sight. Hearing voices, Capt. Washburne called out, "Take care Major, here come the Rebs." Immediately shots rang out and the three men quickly turned their horses and drove in their spurs. The Confederates, about 15 men, let loose a broadside miraculously missing the three officers only 20 feet away. Now the chase was reversed as the Rebels charged down the road after the three Yankees.

Lt. Payson and his men, following behind, heard the firing and saw the officers charging down the road. Three or four of Payson's men immediately lost their nerve and fled back towards camp. The remaining men charged to support the officers who had stopped to make a stand.

The addition of several new mounted Yanks surprised the Rebels who now felt they were outnumbered. Once again the charge reversed and the Confederates pounded back for the tree line. Major Crowninshield, knowing he was outnumbered and several miles from the Union lines, belatedly decided that caution was in order and directed a return to the Point. The Major and his men returned to camp with their boards and a story to tell.[14]

"It was a vary narrow escape," ran a piece in the *Boston Journal*, "in fact they were cut off and got away again. The negroes say there were twenty or thirty rebels armed with double barreled shot guns. An old barn on the side of the road opposite the lane, and in direct range, is filled with buck-shot; so are the fences all along the road. The battalion has reason to be thankful that our Major is still with us, and companies D and K that their Captains are not in Richmond. All three officers have seen much service, but they all call this their narrowest escape."[15]

Another duty for the men at Gloucester Point, now that the roads were drying up, was to patrol the area around their encampment for Rebel activity. The first of many scouts (not counting board collecting) began on the 15th of March. The foray that pushed ten miles into enemy territory produced nothing. Not a Rebel was seen.

Though no enemy were seen Gen. Busteed was convinced that an attack on his command was imminent. Alarms were given frequently but nothing developed from them. "The General who commands this post is an alarmist," fumed Crowninshield, "[if someone] says there are Rebels just outside the lines, he at once thinks there is to be an attack & turns out the infantry, Cavalry & artillery & makes a grand rumpus. Yesterday there was an alarm & also a very severe snow storm. We were kept out 4 hours in it & nearly froze to death waiting for an imaginary foe."[16]

Busteed considered leading a raid himself, telling a captain of the 2nd Massachusetts, "Why sir I'll come over here some day and take this cavalry and make a raid which shall be a matter of history hereafter." This claim drove Crowninshield to distraction, noting in a letter home, "Just fancy the old fool who hardly knows the difference between cavalry and artillery making a historical raid! oh I get so sick and disgusted of these men, these generals, that after I feel like resigning and going home, it seems to me wicked to put men under such grossly incompetent officers, surely we must have better men in the country and in the Army. To say that a man is a Brig. Gen. is almost equivalent to saying he is an ignoramus."[17]

The mild weather allowed Crowninshield to put the men through long hours of training and drill. Lt. Goodwin Stone of Company K wrote to Amos Lawrence about camp life at the point. "We are very pleasantly situated here, as you have doubtless heard already, and we are becoming as proficient in the tactics as constant drilling can make us—an occasional foray into the enemy's country keeps us supplied with pigs and poultry that have been giving 'aid & comfort' to the rebels, so that our life here is not altogether without interest." The sentiment was shared by Pvt. Barnstead: "As for me, I like a soldiers life first-rate—it being surrounded with plenty of excitement and very little to care for, with a great deal to be seen and a great deal to be learned...." Rations, the source of most soldiers complaints, were surprisingly good for the enlisted men. "Our food consists of fresh beef every other day, alternating with pork and beans, and sometimes rice; one loaf of fresh bread per day, and coffee morning and evening, sweetened with sugar."[18]

The first week of April found the battalion participating in daily scouts that were rarely more than pleasant rides. On

Unknown private, Company A, California Hundred, 2nd Massachusetts Cavalry. *Courtesy of Richard K. Tibbals Collection, U.S.A.M.H.I.*

the 9th the troopers rode out again, this time for 20 miles, but once again returned having seen nothing. On this scout, however, the enemy was there and followed the unwitting Yankees back toward their camp. The Union cavalry bedded down in their tents unaware of the Rebels who waited till daybreak to make their presence known.

It was a small cavalry detachment, some 200 men, led by Col. D.J. Godwin, formerly of the 9th Virginia Infantry, now commanding the cavalry forces of Gen. Arnold Elzey, who attempted to fool the Yankees into believing they faced a superior number of troops. He marched his troops back and forth, both mounted and dismounted, and conducted some demonstrations against the picket force. He claimed to have killed one and captured two of the enemy while sustaining two wounded himself. His attempts must have been conducted against the infantry camp as Crowninshield, who sent any news of interest home, failed to mention it in any of his letters. Godwin and his men remained in the vicinity for three days, but being unable to attack the larger force, returned to his own camp at King and Queen Courthouse.

Aside from the occasional fire of the pickets there was little to disturb the Virginia countryside. On the 19th of April the men of the First Battalion, hearing thunder, looked across the York River for the clouds. The thunder they heard was not from clouds, but rather was of the man made variety, from the artillery of Confederate Lt. Gen. James Longstreet. Longstreet with the divisions of major generals George Pickett and John B. Hood, were engaged in an assault on Suffolk on the far side of the James River. The firing produced a rash of rumors and arguments between the men at Gloucester Point, but with a shift of the wind, the thunder faded and the excitement and possibilities soon ended.[19]

Later the same day a detachment of 100 men saddled up and headed down to the York to be transported across to the peninsula. Under the command of Capt. Reed, all the able bodied men from the Hundred and Company B were detailed for picket duty at Camp West (though Company A called it Camp California), between Fort Magruder and Williamsburg. The 5th Pennsylvania Cavalry, already at Williamsburg, were impressed with the discipline and conduct of the newcomers. Major Crowninshield's training was becoming evident.[20]

This move brought the squadron very close to the enemy as the Confederates still occupied Williamsburg. The April 22nd entry in Pvt. Corbett's diary stated, "Went on picket, Rebel picket 500 yards in my front. Rebs at one end of town, Yanks at the other watching operations." The standoff over Williamsburg had been in progress for several weeks, starting in late March when an attempt was made to take the town and nearby Fort Magruder. Fort Magruder was the key to Gen. Dix's defense of his forces on the peninsula. If the fort fell, Confederates would be able to operate freely with light artillery and long-range rifles against Yorktown, necessitating a fallback to Fort Monroe at the tip of the peninsula.[21]

The attempt in March had failed to gain Williamsburg or the fort, but Gen. Busteed was certain that the good citizens had been too helpful to the Confederates, supplying information on troop strengths and placements, and requested permission to burn the historic city to the ground. Luckily Gen. Keyes had a cooler head and refused. On the 11th of April the Confederates made another go at the fort but were again repulsed by Col. West. The Confederates drew back to the north of Williamsburg, but the standoff did not last long. Soon they moved up the peninsula leaving the city to the enemy, but keeping their pickets close.

"However," recalled Pvt. Briggs, "as the rebels left, the picket line extended to where it is at present. While one of our company was standing on picket one night, three rebels crawled upon him, and the cowardly scoundrels fired upon him, killing his horse at the first shot but not injuring him any. Finding they had not killed him they advanced upon him, and he broke for a fence, from behind which he delivered three shots at them from his revolver, when they stopped, one spunky man proving too much for three of the dastardly cowards. So much for their brag of one of them being equal to three of us.

"It is the worst kind of murder to kill a man stationed on picket, and none but the most cowardly, pusillanimous rebels would attempt such a thing. The step from a traitor to a murderer seems to be easily taken, and quite natural; and all rebels caught lurking around picket stations, with arms upon them, ought to be hung from the nearest tree. Woe be to the one that should be caught by us!"[22]

Companies C, D, and K, remained at the cavalry camp at Gloucester Point and continued to be called out almost nightly for alarms that were more often than not false. On the 27th of April, the three companies went on a short expedition with a detachment of the 4th Delaware Volunteers, beyond Hickory Falls where they found a cache of Rebel supplies. The troopers destroyed a large amount of stores including, "...grain, cotton, bacon, flour, salt, coffee, sulphur, powder, flints, percussion caps, and quinine; also collected and drove within the lines 57 head of horned cattle, 260 sheep, and 8 horse and mules." The men returned that afternoon and polished and shined their gear for a review the next morning by Secretary of State William H. Seward.[23]

During this relatively quiet time in the Tidewater region, the two main armies to the north were maneuvering in what would culminate in the battle of Chancellorsville. Major General Joe Hooker had replaced Burnside in command of the Army of the Potomac and had quickly initiated plans for the demise of Lee's army. Hooker began his bold movement by advancing the newly formed Cavalry Corps under Maj. Gen. George Stoneman.

Stoneman was to lead 10,000 horsemen, nearly all of the army's cavalry, on a raid against Lee's supply lines. The cavalry was scheduled to begin their march on the 13th of April, which was immediately postponed for two weeks due to the swollen Rappahannock River.[24]

Moving again on the 29th, the Corps split into two columns, crossed the river and headed southward. Hoping to break the Orange and Alexandria Railroad near Gordonsville, and especially, the Richmond, Fredericksburg and Potomac Railroad, the raid was a complete failure. The first column, under Brig. Gen. William Averell, made it as far as Rapidan Station where they halted and ended their advance due to the unfounded belief they were about to be attacked. Unable or unwilling to complete his task, Averell was ordered back within the lines on the 2nd of May.

The main column under Brig. Gen. John Buford, accompanied by Stoneman, tore up a sizable amount of track, and a portion of the command advanced to within sight of Richmond. But the Confederates were able to repair or replace the damage nearly as fast as the Yankees could tear it up, and the second column had to abandon their attempts and make their way back to the army.

On the 6th of May, Gen. Keyes ordered Major Crowninshield to take a detachment and head for the Mattapony River where some of Stoneman's cavalry was thought to be. Taking 80 men and two days rations the Massachusetts men started off with a Negro guide who claimed to know the country. The cavalrymen pressed hard and finally dismounted at one in the morning, still vigilant for bushwhackers that plagued the area. Giving the horses a two hour rest the men mounted again and pushed on for the Mattapony. Approaching the river, they met 500 of Stoneman's cavalry, lost, and expecting to be attacked.

Having found the lost cavalrymen, Crowninshield turned the force of nearly 600 men, and began the return to Gloucester Point. Along the way a large force of the enemy cavalry pursued them but declined to make an attack. Capturing one of the enemy and losing one in return, the Union troopers made their way back to the camp at the Point without further incident.[25]

The quiet countryside around Yorktown and Gloucester Point was again undisturbed by the trappings of war, and the three companies in camp enjoyed a week of leisure. Far to the north, Col. Lowell and the remainder of the regiment were leaving Readville, headed for Washington, D.C. Major Crowninshield was tasked with presiding over the court-martial of a soldier (not of the 2nd Massachusetts Cavalry) accused of murder.[26]

During mid–May (the 14th), companies A and B returned from their stay in Williamsburg, while the next day, companies C, D, and K, under the command of Capt. Washburn, moved up the York River to West Point to serve as pickets. Both sides, however, just appeared to be going through the motions, as the heat of the area seemed to dissuade any real movements by the two forces. Both sides conducted half-hearted scouts, but nothing came of them, or was really expected from them.

"Yesterday," 2nd Lt. Henry Alvord (K) wrote on the 24th of May, "as our daily mail boat, the *Swan* from Yorktown was coming up here, just as she turned a point in the south side of the river three miles from here, a rebel battery of four guns opened a very rapid fire on her. I happened to be where I could see both boat and battery.... Every House within two miles was set on fire — about ten in all. One elegant private mansion of brick and stone furnished in the most expensive and luxurious manner was found just abandoned — tea table all set, etc., etc. That shared the same fate. The Gunboat went down with the mail boat this morning. This is no doubt but the first of a series of attacks with which we will be favored now."[27]

Crowninshield made occasional trips up the river to check on his men at West Point, many of whom were sick with fever. So many were eventually stricken that on the 1st of June the place was abandoned and the First Battalion was united again at Gloucester Point. The fever was also active at Yorktown, but Gloucester was for the most part untouched, and the health of the men soon returned.[28]

The loss of Hooker's army to Lee at Chancellorsville put a damper on the troops at the Point. None of the men placed any blame on the fighting men of the Army of the Potomac, but rather on the abilities of Gen. Hooker. Crowninshield went further and allowed the blame to be shared with the 11th Corps, the corps that first met the wrath of "Stonewall" Jackson's infamous flanking maneuver.

"The 11th Corps disgraced themselves," he wrote, "but what can you expect from Germans, or from a corps that has been so long commanded by that great humbug Siegel. Such men as Freemont, Banks, & Siegel are much better at home than in the field. Banks is doing well now because he has no one to fight against.... [H]e will be beaten sure as fate. With all his talent he is a miserable general & time will prove it to the satisfaction even of those who now regard him as one of the best generals we have." Very interesting comments about the German-American soldiers from a man whose family name was once von Kronensheldt.[29]

Day after day of picket duty and camp life eventually instilled a sense of boredom in the Californians, and, as bored soldiers often will, they began to grumble and complain. The grumbling was mostly concerning their fate that had led them to a backwater of the war rather than with the Army of the Potomac. Some of the idle talk concerned having the whole company just up and leave and join the army to the north, even going so far as to have those interested sign a petition. One of the soldiers, unsympathetic to the idea, went to Capt. Reed and told all. Reed immediately took the information to Major Crowninshield who reacted quickly and decisively. Having seen the other four companies of his battalion reduced to a mere corporal's guard by desertion he was not taking any such chances with his Californians. At midnight company A was rudely awakened.[30]

"We were told to turn out without arms, and on striking a light saw bayonets sticking through all the holes of the stockade, and when we stepped out in front found a double line of infantry there drawn up with bayonets fixed." Two pieces of artillery were employed in covering the "mutineers" as the enlisted men were led to the guardhouse and a watch was placed over the quarters of the officers, sergeants, and corporals. For four days the company was kept under arrest until the Major was convinced that the "loose talk" was not a serious threat to his command.[31]

Later the incident made its way to the California papers and to quell the reports that the "Hundred" had really intended to desert, several members wrote to the papers explaining their version of what had happened and why. As they told it, several of the soldiers were unhappy with the way in which Capt. Reed was handling the company fund, believing he had embezzled or was planning to embezzle the money. Knowing who the snitch was they purposely made up the rumor of the desertion in front of him, convinced that he would take the story to the captain. This version prompted several other men in the company to write the newspapers in defense of Capt. Reed who they assured the readers had never been anything but honest and honorable.[32]

Eventually blame for the "mutiny" was placed on Major Crowninshield who had, in many eyes, overreacted by having all of the company arrested. But even the major had defenders in the press who stated,"...not being able to make exceptions where a few had excited many to desertion, did his duty and had all arrested." It is doubtful that the major took the incident as seriously as indicated. In his letters home, where he informed his mother of any goings on of interest, he doesn't even mention that it occurred. His letters of May 30th and June 3rd (written on the same slip of paper) reveals his concern for the health of the three companies at West Point and thanks her for sending him whisky and cigars.

Col. Lowell made brief mention of the affair in a letter to his fiancée. "I have not seen the letters in the California papers and do not think I care to. Reed is a very good officer, takes the greatest pride in his company, and, since that trouble, has done well by them; his fellows have been under fire since those letters were written, and I feel sure that now the feeling is changed. I think the men in all the battalions are beginning to feel that their officers know more than the officers of any regiment they are thrown with; and this feeling, of course, has a healthy effect on their morale." What the men needed was a break in the routine.

On the 19th of June, Lt. Col. Hasbrook Davis of the 12th Illinois led a detachment from his regiment, along with Crowninshield's battalion, on an expedition to King and Queen and Middlesex Counties, "...and were eminently successful. The result was the capture of several prisoners, rebel cavalrymen, one hundred good horses and mules, thirty fire arms (including a lot of new blockade-run Colt's revolvers,) three mails direct from Richmond, a number of wagons, &c, &c. The command was away from camp but sixty hours, during which they marched over one hundred and forty miles."[33]

As Robert E. Lee's Army of Northern Virginia began to march northward through the Shenandoah Valley, the Union troops left on the peninsula began to stir. Hooker, reacting to Lee's movements, maneuvered to keep the Army of the Potomac between the Confederate general and Washington. As the Confederate forces penetrated farther and farther north, Hooker initially felt that a swift movement *south* would put the capital at Richmond in his hands. Lee's army and its proximity to the Northern capital were disregarded by Hooker who believed that Lee would halt his invasion in order to protect Richmond.

It might have worked. It may not have. At any rate, the proposal was quickly squelched by the administration, although the plan to advance on Richmond did have some merit. A demonstration against Richmond would prevent Confederate reinforcements from joining Lee, and any damage done to the Confederate rail system would disrupt the very long and thin line of supply.[34]

Maj. Gen. John A. Dix, commander of the Department of Virginia, headquartered at Yorktown, was given orders to make such a demonstration. A column of infantry under Gen. Keyes was dispatched for a rapid movement on Richmond, while the department's cavalry was sent on a raid to the north of the city to burn the bridges of the Virginia Central Railroad.

Dix believed that the division of Confederate Maj. Gen. George Pickett was at the junction between the North and South Anna Rivers. Picket was in fact across the Potomac in Maryland. Not overly optimistic about results, Dix sent out a mixture of mounted troops on a reconnaissance of the crossings of the two rivers.

Major Crowninshield and the five companies of his battalion were combined with parts of the 12th Illinois Cavalry and the 2nd New York Cavalry under command of Lt. Col. Davis of the 12th Delaware Cavalry: in all some 250 men. They were placed under the overall command of Col. Samuel P. Spear who led the 800 men of his own 11th Pennsylvania Cavalry. The entire force amounted to 1,050 men.

On the night of the 24th of June, the men led their mounts down to the York River and boarded transports. The transports *Hero* and *City of Albany* carrying Crowninshield's battalion landed early in the morning at White House Landing, surprising a company of enemy cavalry that beat a hasty retreat. Several earthwork redoubts covered the area and in one was discovered a railroad turntable that was to be used with artillery mounted on cars as a "railroad monitor." Completing the destruction of the turntable and 200 yards of track, the Union force formed in line of battle, with the 2nd Massachusetts Cavalry taking the advance. At Tunstalls Station a small Confederate picket force of 12 cavalry was overrun with one man captured, but the larger prize of a train of cars escaped before the men could reach it. Col. Spear ordered several buildings fired, including a sutlers store, as well as the telegraph lines cut.[35]

The march continued to within 16 miles of Richmond, where a halt was called for the night. Early in the morning, after a few hours' sleep in a driving rain, the march was resumed. At Nelson's Farm Major Crowninshield was tasked with leaving a squadron to guard the bridge over the Pamunkey River while the remainder of the battalion continued on with the main force up the south side of the Pamunkey to Hanover Courthouse. Here a Confederate baggage train of 35 wagons fell prey to the troopers, as well as over 200 mules. The wagons and harness were burned, along with a blacksmith's and a wheelwright's shop. The office, books, and paper of the depot were added to the flames, but the contents of a large safe remained untouched, despite all efforts to open it.

The line of march followed the Central Railroad to the bridge crossing the South Anna River where they found a Confederate force drawn up behind breastworks. Opposing the Federals was company A of the 44th North Carolina Infantry.

At the start of the Gettysburg campaign, the 44th North Carolina, of Brig. Gen. James J. Pettigrew's brigade, was detached and tasked with defending the railroad communications centered at Hanover Junction. Companies were posted at Hanover Junction and at the four bridges that spanned the South Anna and Little Rivers. Smaller detachments were posted at the numerous fords along the waterways. Tasked with covering the crossing of the Central Railroad over the South Anna was Company A. In command was Lt. Col. Taswell L. Hargrove of Granville County, with 50 men.[36]

Hargrove had his men behind a breastwork on the south side of the river, but seeing the size of the opposing force, quickly abandoned it and withdrew his men to the north bank. Dispatching a courier on foot for reinforcements, Hargrove posted his men behind a hasty defensive line that consisted of a smaller earthwork, a watchman's hut, the rail bed, and a stack of crossties. The position was about 300 yards north of the river. Several attempts to burn the bridge failed, achieving only a few wounded troopers, and forcing the need for an assault.[37]

Col. Spear started the attack by bringing up his two guns and lobbing shells across the river. The artillery was ineffective, so a dismounted assault by a small detachment was ordered. The defenders threw up such a stiff defense that Spear recalled his men and opted for a combined frontal assault and flank attack. Two squadrons of the 11th Pennsylvania Cavalry located a ford about half a mile above the bridge while Crowninshield's A and C companies, under Capt. Reed and lieutenants Rummery, Richards, and Sim, as well as 50 Pennsylvanians, crossed a small footbridge. "The footlogs supported one man at a time and only if he moved quickly...." Once across the footbridge the men scrambled up the steep rocky banks and waited under cover of the thick brush and trees that lined both shores of the river.[38]

In the hour it took Spear's troopers to cross the river, Hargrove was reinforced by the 40 men of Company G, 44th North Carolina, under Capt. Robert Bingham. Bingham and his men had double-timed from the Little River Bridge at Taylorsville (approximately four miles) and had arrived just in time for Spear's assault.

Confederate accounts of the battle, written long after the war, describe a heroic defense that drove back wave after wave of assaulting Yankees, resulting in scores of enemy casualties. The accounts of Spear and Major Crowninshield both record a vicious but quick assault. Crowninshield described the action: "My men were dismounted and ordered to charge the works on foot, while a squadron of Penn. Cavalry charged them in the flank. After some preliminary fighting we all charged & carried the works. I lost one man killed & one wounded, my men were first in the works & behaved first rate."[39]

Thirteen Confederates were killed and eight so severely wounded they were paroled and left at the scene of the fight. The remaining 60 defenders were captured, the enlisted men eventually being exchanged at Fort Monroe, and the officers being imprisoned at Fort Norfolk. Pvt. Barnstead of Company A took the time to talk to one of the prisoners. "I asked one of them if he knew what he was fighting for, and he said he did not; that he was a poor, uneducated white man, had been forced into the army, and fought because he was compelled."[40]

The number of Union casualties is very vague. In his report on June 28, Spear details Confederate casualties but fails to mention any of his own. Crowninshield, who had two of his five companies engaged, reported one man killed and one wounded. Private Samuel Corbett noted in his diary that the attackers suffered three killed and five wounded. The dozens of casualties recalled years later by Confederate veterans had apparently grown with the years.[41]

The two casualties from the 2nd Massachusetts Cavalry were both from the California Hundred. Twenty-nine-year-old Pvt. Joseph B. Burdick (A), San Francisco, was killed in the assault and Richard S. Ellet (A), San Francisco, a 19-year-old private was severely wounded. Ellet was wounded before the assault when he stepped beyond the cover at the river's bank and was shot through both thighs. He recovered from his wounds and was later promoted to lieutenant in the First Battalion Mississippi Marine Brigade.[42]

While the wounded men were being cared for, Spear ordered a detail to burn the bridge which was done so efficiently, the remains fell into the river. He then prepared his command for the return trip to the White House, stating it was impossible to continue the raid due to "...loss of ammunition, and my fatigued command...."[43]

The return to Union lines followed the initial path of the raid until reaching

Hanover Ferry. While at the ferry site, now serviced by a bridge, Col. Spear received information that he would be intercepted by troops under Confederate General Wise if he continued on the same route. Removing the planks from the bridge, the march continued passing through Hanover Courthouse. Here Gen. W.H.F. Lee, son of Gen. Robert E. Lee, was found recuperating from wounds received at the battle at Brandy Station. Gen. Lee was examined and determined to be fit enough for travel. Placed in a carriage, he joined the column as it continued its trek to the White House. A familiar face rode up to the captured general in the form of former classmate Caspar Crowninshield. A Harvard graduate, Lee had known Crowninshield well and had roomed with Caspar's cousin Ben. "Rooney" Lee, cold and aloof to the other Yankees, chatted about old times and old friends. Crowninshield offered to help him in any way he could.[44]

The column returned to White House late the next afternoon, Lee bidding goodbye to his friend and moving on towards the prison that would hold him for the next nine months. The First Battalion of the 2nd Massachusetts Cavalry went into camp alongside the 20,000 infantry of Gen. Dix.[45]

Little time was given to the men to mourn Pvt. Burdick, or even to rest their tired mounts. They had hardly reached the White House when they were drawing rations for another raid on the bridges over the North and South Annas. Having been able to burn only one of the bridges on the last raid, the entire force of 1,050 men, augmented by another 150 troopers, set out again, this time followed by Maj. Gen. George Getty's entire Second division. This immense raiding force was focused solely on the destruction of the Richmond and Potomac rail crossing of the South Anna. The raid was an utter failure.

On the 1st of July the advance set out under a hot summer sun, followed by the main body of infantry and artillery, and trailed by a lengthy wagon train. "The heat and dust were intolerable..." Getty reported, and dozens of men fell out along the line of march. As the objective grew closer, Getty began detaching troops to ensure he had an open line of retreat. It was not regiments he left behind, but entire brigades. The Second Brigade was left at Taylorsville with two batteries of artillery, the troopers of the 2nd Massachusetts Cavalry, and the exhausted soldiers that had fallen behind. The Third Brigade was left at the bridge over the Pamunkey, while the First Brigade secured Hanover Courthouse. The column was now reduced to the remaining cavalry under Col. Spear, two brigades of infantry and a single battery of artillery. Brig. Gen. Robert S. Foster led this scaled-down force to the final objective.

The cavalry pushed in several pickets as the bridge was approached on the fourth day of the raid. Spear advanced to within 100 yards of the bridge before coming under rifle and artillery fire. A battery of guns under the command of Capt. P.A. Davis of the 7th Massachusetts Artillery was called forward and brought into position. The guns were about to open fire when Foster arrived on the scene and ordered the guns to a new position.

While the gunners brought their horses up, Foster had more time to review the situation and was not pleased with what he faced. Three pieces of artillery continued to fire from the enemy's works and it appeared that there was strong infantry support. With cavalry poised to attack and infantry and artillery standing by, Foster declined to attack and soon the entire force withdrew to the far side of the Pamunky.[46]

Gen. Getty claimed the raid a success, for although he had failed to reach the South Anna, he had burned several ferry boats on the Pamunky, and torn up two sections of the Richmond and Potomac

Railroad. Although this raid, like the first, was purely diversionary, it had the potential to inflict some damage on the Confederate rail system. It took a truly optimistic commander to claim success with such meager results. The operation was best summarized by Confederate Gen. D.H. Hill who referred to it as "not a feint but a faint."[47]

This last raid to the South Anna ended the 2nd Massachusetts Cavalry's movements from the White House and the entire battalion returned to their camp at Gloucester Point. Rumors had been running wild for some time that the battalion would soon be joining the regiment in the northern part of the state. But days came and went with no orders, and hope began to fail. There was little to keep the men occupied other than camp duties and drill. Standing picket and stable guard were a welcome distraction rather than extra duty to be cursed.[48]

Early on the morning of the 25th of July, the battalion saddled up and led the advance to Gloucester Courthouse for a detachment of infantry. The gunboat *Commodore Jones* slowly cruised down the waters of the York to protect their right flank. Pvt. Towle recalled an incident of this raid in his memoirs. "It was amusing on this expedition for one in the advance to sight a Negro at work plowing in the field, for when he would see the Yankee soldiers coming he would leave his mules standing and strike across the field as though satan was after him. This we later learned was because Negroes in that section had been told that Yankees were cannibals having but one eye, which was red and situated in the middle of their foreheads." The expedition returned that evening, having seen no Rebels, guerrillas, or bushwhackers. Walking their horses into camp, the 1st battalion suddenly came back to life as the word was passed from man to man. The orders were in, they were to break camp and meet the rest of the regiment at Centerville.[49]

Notes

1. Crowninshield, Benjamin, *The History of the First Regiment of Massachusetts Volunteers*, pp. 88–89.
2. Letters Official, Vol. 20, p. 91; V. 25, p. 410.
3. *OR*, XV, pp. 257–59, 646–47, 693–94, 702–03, XXVI, Pt. 2, pp. 700, 720; Executive Letters, Vol. 74, p. 39.
4. Executive Letters, Vol. 74, p. 38.
5. Ferguson, David L., *Cleopatra's Barge: The Crowninshield Story*, p. 39; Nagel, *Descent from Glory*, pp. 213–14.
6. Bowen, *Yankee from Olympus*, p. 158; Letter from Major Crowninshield to his mother dated Feb. 18, 1863. Crowninshield-Mangus Collection: hereafter cited as Crowninshield; Humphreys, *Camp and Field*, pp. 321–24; Schouler, *Annual Report of the Adjutant General of Massachusetts for the Year Ending 1863* (Jan. 1864), pp. 932–33.
7. Crowninshield, Feb. 28, 1863; *Boston Journal*, Feb. 28, 1863.
8. Executive Letters, Vol. 74, p. 52; Crowninshield, Feb. 28, 1863; *Boston Journal*, Feb. 28, 1863; National Archives, Record Group 94, Co. K muster roll, enlistment to Feb. 28, 1863.
9. Corbett, *Diary*, Mar. 11, 1863; Crowninshield, Feb. 28, 1863.
10. Towle, *Recollections*, p. 4; *Daily Alta California*, Apr. 19, 1863; *Napa County Reporter*, May 23, 1863.
11. *Boston Journal*, Mar. 26, 1863; *Daily Alta California*, Apr. 26, 1863.
12. Crowninshield, Mar. 20, 23, 1863; *Daily Alta California*, Apr. 19, 1863.
13. Crowninshield, Feb. 28, Mar. 23, 1863.
14. Crowninshield, Mar. 31, 1863.
15. *Boston Journal*, Apr. 5, 1863.
16. Crowninshield, Apr. 5, 1863.
17. Crowninshield, Mar. 23, 1863.
18. *Daily Alta California*, Apr. 19, 26, 1863; Massachusetts Historical Society, A.A. Lawrence Papers, Box 117, G.A. Stone to Lawrence, Mar. 9, 1863.
19. Crowninshield, Apr. 19, 1863; *Napa County Reporter*, May 23, 1863.
20. Crowninshield, Apr. 28, 1863;

Schouler, *Annual Report of the Adjutant General of Massachusetts for the Year Ending 1863* (Jan 1864), p. 934; *OR*, XVIII, p. 629; *Daily Alta California*, June 10, 1863.

21. Corbett, *Diary*, Apr. 22, 1863.
22. *Daily Alta California*, June 10, 1863.
23. Crowninshield, Apr. 28, 1863; *OR*, XVIII, p. 343.
24. Faust, *Encyclopedia*, p. 721.
25. Crowninshield, May 10, 1863.
26. Crowninshield, May 10, 1863.
27. Sherman, "A New England Boy in the Civil War," *The New England Quarterly*, p. 321.
28. Crowninshield, May 19, May 30, 1863.
29. Crowninshield, May 19, 1863.
30. *Napa County Reporter*, June 27, 1863.
31. Corbett, *Diary*, May 25, 29, 1863; Towle, *Recollections*, p. 5.
32. *Evening Bulletin*, Sept. 16, 1863.
33. Schouler, *Annual Report of the Adjutant General of Massachusetts for the Year Ending 1863*, p. 934.
34. *OR*, XVII, Pt. 2, p. 820.
35. *Daily Alta California*, Aug. 10, 1863; National Archives, Record Group 94, Company K muster roll, Apr. 30 to July 15, 1863.
36. Peace, "Fighting at Great Odds," *Confederate Veteran*, Vol. XXXIV, pp. 360–71; Southern Historical Society Papers, Vol. XXV, p. 337.
37. Devine, "Defense of the South Anna Bridge," *Confederate Veteran*, Vol. XL, pp. 178–82.
38. Towle, *Diary*, p. 6; *Daily Alta California*, Aug. 10, 1863.
39. Crowninshield, July 14, 1863.
40. Bingham, "North Carolinians at South Anna Bridge," *Confederate Veteran*, Vol. XXXIV, pp. 455–58; *Daily Alta California*, Aug. 10, 1863.
41. Crowninshield, July 12, July 14, 1863; *OR*, XVII, Pt. 2, pp. 794–99.
42. Corbett, *Diary*, June 26, 1863; Towle, *Recollections*, p. 6; National Archives, Record Group 94, Co. A muster roll, Apr. 30 to June 30, 1863.
43. *OR*, XXVII, Pt. 2, pp. 794–99.
44. Crowninshield, July 2, 14, 1863; *OR*, Vol. XXVII, Pt. 2, p. 799.
45. Corbett, *Diary*, June 27, 1863.
46. *OR*, XVII, Pt. 2, pp. 852, 857–58.
47. *OR*, XVII. Pt. 2, pp. 837–39.
48. National Archives, Record Group 94, Co. A muster roll, June 30 to Aug. 30, 1863.
49. Towle, *Recollections*, p. 7; *OR*, XVII, Pt. 2, pp. 978–79; National Archives, Record Group 94, 2nd Massachusetts Cavalry Regimental records box, Special Order #322, July 15, 1863.

Chapter Five

Northern Virginia

The history of the regiment during its first seven months does not follow a single chronological line. The recruiting in Massachusetts lasted a full seven months. By the time the California Battalion (minus the stragglers from Company F) arrived in the Bay State, the First Battalion was already at Gloucester Point. Company F arrived in Boston to find an empty camp and the other two battalions gone to Washington. To give a complete history requires the narrative to go back to the 15th of May, the day the first three companies of the California Battalion arrived at Camp Meigs.

Situated about nine miles from Boston, the camp at Readville was set on the line of the Providence Railroad. The camp itself, though pleasant with a small creek bordering it, was too small for large cavalry drills. Training of the horsemen began when the men entered the camp, and continued till their final days in the state. The daily routine rarely varied. Dress Parade at 8:00 A.M., four hours of mounted drill each day, and inspection of arms each evening at 6:00 P.M. Along with that came stable duty, fatigue duty, camp guard, and the all important care of the horses.[1]

The government issue horses were a sight. Most often received in poor condition, only a fraction were fit for active service. The healthy horses were usually only half broken, the men referring to them as Massachusetts Mustangs. They were hell on the eastern boys who'd never ridden before, and often unmanageable to the saddle-wise Californians. Sgt. Gilbert R. Merritt received a vicious kick from one mount that left a broken leg and eventually led to a discharge for disability. Cpl. Alfred McLean of Company L was bucked off during drill and received a dislocated ankle for his trouble.[2]

The men worked morning and afternoon at company, squadron, and battalion drill. Divided into two battalions, they were commanded by two competent and highly regarded officers. The Second Battalion (the first being with Crowninshield in Virginia) was commanded by Will Forbes, the original captain from Company B, now wearing a major's oak leaves on his shoulders. Major Thompson, of the California Battalion led the Third Battalion.

Col. Lowell was in camp nearly every day, leaving the ongoing recruiting to Lt. Col. Russell in Boston. Lowell was staying at Mrs. Crehore's Boardinghouse about a half mile from camp. Staying at the same house was Col. Robert G. Shaw, and their fiancées, Miss Annie Haggerty and Josephine Shaw, Robert's sister.[3]

Shaw's 54th Massachusetts Infantry was in camp with the 2nd Cavalry at Camp Meigs. There was some initial concern how the black regiment would be accepted by the white cavalrymen, but a few days in camp proved the worries to be groundless. Many of the 2nd would stroll over in the evening, after the day's drill and visit with their new neighbors. Of course there were exceptions. Thomas H. Merry, a private of Company L., was a correspondent for the *Alta California* and wrote some very brutal and erroneous words about the 54th that ended up in the San Francisco press.[4]

There was still a lot of work to be done in forging the men into a unit, when orders came for Lowell to report with his command to Washington. Far from being filled out, recruiting continued for the skeleton Massachusetts companies. (H and I were so small that, for the time being, they acted as one company.) First Lieutenant Archibald McKendry of the California Hundred was left behind when the First Battalion climbed aboard the cars that would take them south. Promoted to captain and given command of Company G, McKendry was appealing to "returned Californians" in Boston to join the company. An advertisement stressed he wanted "...active, patriotic young men. None others need apply." On the 11th of May, 427 men and officers, and 437 horses, left camp and marched to the city docks. The horses were loaded into a cramped

James H. Eby, Company M, 2nd Regiment, Massachusetts Volunteer Cavalry. *Courtesy of Richard K. Tibbals Collection, U.S.A.M.H.I.*

area on the ferry built for half their number. At noon the 54th Massachusetts formed in great haste to escort the cavalry, but learned too late that they had already left.[5]

The Californians were more than pleased to be leaving Massachusetts and most harbored ill will toward the state as a

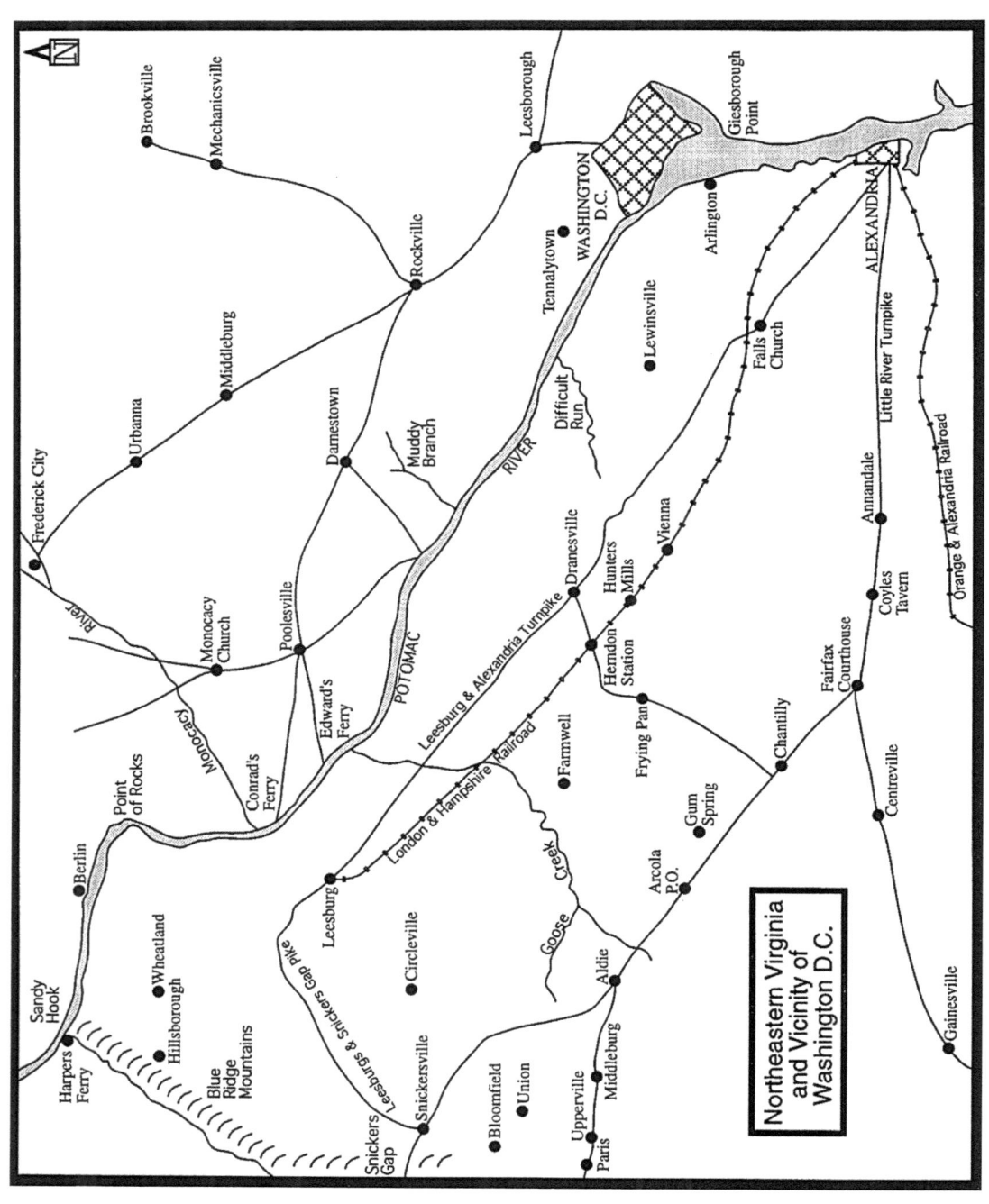

whole and Boston in particular. Arriving from the west coast with a bit of a "prima donna" attitude, they were sorely disappointed with what they considered the cold New England hospitality. Having traveled thousands of miles they were expecting a warm welcome and public ovations. Instead they were ignored by a war weary public and were outraged by the comments and opinions of the Massachusetts recruits. "[F]or it is a fact which cannot be denied, that the war feeling, or general enthusiasm for the war and the Union is *much* greater in San Francisco and throughout California than it is here in Massachusetts or New York. The Massachusetts soldiers here in camp talk as our California Secessionists do.... When speaking of the condition of the country they sigh and say 'It is no use; the war has lasted long enough.'"6

Traveling by ferry and train, the men arrived in Philadelphia where they were treated to a fine meal by the staff at the "Volunteer Refreshment Room." At the completion of the meal Major Thompson proposed three cheers for the generous citizens of Philadelphia for their hospitality. At the last cheer some wag suggested they give three groans for Massachusetts. Continuing by rail the troopers arrived in Washington on the 16th, their numbers shorter by 11 deserters and one dead horse. Their new camp was located to the east of the capital, and before long the troops were unloading their baggage wagons. The tents were set up in three rows, the two companies of a squadron being on a line, the horses of each squadron to the right of the tents. Close to the suburbs and having a fine view of the Potomac, the site was very pleasant.7

Without a delay Col. Lowell put the daily drill and training back in motion. Although the men were improving, there was still a long way to go and time was getting scarce. The regiment, minus the absent First Battalion, was assigned to the Provisional Brigade commanded by Maj. Gen. Silas Casey, formerly a division commander in the Army of the Potomac. The brigade was part of the 22nd Corps of Maj. Gen. Samuel P. Heintzelman, tasked with the defense of the capital.

The daily routine rarely varied, as Pvt. Thomas Merry explained in a letter to the *Daily Alta California*. "At 5:30 A.M., the bugle awakens us from our slumber and breaks the spell of our pleasant dreams of loved ones far away, and calls us to arise and resume the daily duty of soldiers. In a moment we are up and dressed, blankets are rolled up, tents put in order, and we sally forth to answer roll call. This over, the horses are led to water, fed, cleaned, and inspected. The bugle now sounds the breakfast call; the 'boys' give vent to their delight as they rush off after their tin cup and plate, and go to the company kitchen to receive their scanty breakfast—scanty because Uncle Sam has to fatten so many army contractors at the expense of his soldiers that his rations have become rather short. At 8 A.M., mounted and fully armed, we go to dress parade, and thence to drill, until 10:30, when we are recalled to camp. One hour of rest intervenes, and then the horses are once again watered and fed. At noon the dinner call is sounded, and with appetites sharpened by the morning exercise, we rush to our dinner. Here allow me to remark *en passant*, that our surgeon has 'shut down' on beans for us; says that they are not healthy, and our California 'Boys' are wrathy threat, for being deprived of one of the staples of food. We drill again at 2 P.M. till 4 P.M., return to camp and feed our horses, get supper, answer to our names at 'retreat' and then our day's work is done. Two hours follow, and we are again called up to roll call at 'tattoo'; at 9 P.M. 'taps' are sounded, the lights put out all over the camp, and we stretch ourselves on the ground, with a rubber and saddle blanket under us and our bed blanket over us, and sleep as soundly till morning as if we were reposing on the softest and most luxuriant couch."[8]

Lowell had barely got his men into camp when an order came from General Casey to prepare for a review. The six companies prepared their horses and uniforms, and Lowell rehearsed them for two days to walk their horses at a slow solemn pace. During the review Casey nodded approvingly, then asked to see them at a trot, and, to Lowell's horror, at a gallop! Lowell described the scene to Miss Shaw. "I smiled, — I knew I was well mounted and could keep ahead of my command, — I knew I could take round most of my horses and perhaps a few of my men, — I smiled, for I thought of Casey's probable fate, — one Major-General less, dead of a review, ridden over by wild horses. When I made the last turn, I glanced backward, the column was half a mile wide where I could last see it and seemed to stretch AD-INFINITUM. When I reformed my line, there were a dozen riderless horses, but straight in front in the old place was troublesome Casey, smiling and satisfied as ever."[9]

Despite his amusing narrative, Lowell was pleased with his regiment's performance as was General Casey. The colonel increased the training of his men while awaiting the order from Casey to take to the field.

While awaiting these orders Lowell was summoned to the War Department for a visit with Secretary of War Edwin Stanton. The Secretary questioned him about his regiment and let Lowell know he expected a great deal from it. He explained to the Colonel that he wanted to make the 2nd an "Ironsides Regiment." Lowell pointed out that more could be done by his regiment if his other battalion could be returned from Gloucester Point. Stanton agreed to bring them up, promised to have all his requisitions filled by preference, and, when the other battalion had arrived, to send the regiment where they could meet the enemy, where he would give them the "place of honor."[10]

Soon after this informal meeting, Casey requested Lowell to report officially on how soon his battalions could take the field. He replied that two hours' notice would be sufficient, but would like to continue training until the 20th of June. This would also allow time for the straggling members of Company F to reach the regiment before active operation started.[11]

On the 31st of May, Lowell was given orders to move camp and the next afternoon found men and horses at Camp Brightwood, Maryland, about four miles north of Washington. Situated near Fort Stephens, the camp was on very rough ground, thick with dust and oak stumps. The move went well though Lowell was somewhat annoyed with the amount of baggage that was carried by the companies: "...no end of bag and baggage certainly ten or twelve times as much as there should have been...." This must have put him in a mood to clean house, for two weeks later he was able to write, "I wish you could see how my Battalion will turn out tomorrow morning; not an extra gew-gaw, nothing for ornament. If they want ornamental troops around Washington, they'll let me go, — indeed, I have dropped some things which have generally been counted necessaries; two of my companies go without any blankets but those under their saddles. This is pretty well for recruits."[12]

Tasked with picketing a stretch of 15 miles, the troopers were called to alarm every night by Gen. Heintzelman. This was Heintzelman's plan for training and it infuriated Lowell who had his own ideas of how training should be conducted. Working around the general as much as possible, he continued to drill his men relentlessly on horseback and with their sabres.[13]

On the 17th of May, Capt. DeMerritt's Company F finally arrived at Camp Meigs, now populated by only a few new recruits. The men were issued their arms and sabres, and began a light routine of drill and camp duty. Pvt. Roberts and a few others went visiting the camp of the 54th Massachusetts that first night: "Visited some colored soldiers that are recruiting near us they are stout looking fellows..." The next day the 54th received their colors from Governor Andrew and their new friends were along to observe; "Some of our boys were over to see & hear the ceremonies.... They made a grand display..." The men were delayed in meeting up with the regiment while they awaited the arrival of their horses. The horses, green and wild like the others, arrived on the 30th of May and the company left six days later for Maryland. The trip, made with only one company vice six, went quickly, and the men arrived at Camp Brightwood on the 7th of June.[14]

It had been months since the battalion had last been together back in San Francisco, and there was a great deal of backslapping and storytelling. On the second day in camp Captain DeMerritt's horse reared and fell over him, badly breaking his leg. This was the first incident in a string of bad luck for the captain of F Company.[15]

While drilling on the 10th of June the men were recalled to camp, issued three days' rations and were soon trotting off in search of the enemy. Earlier that morning the newly organized Forty-Third Battalion Virginia Cavalry had splashed across the Potomac into Maryland. The Confederate force was led by Major John S. Mosby, a man who as much as Col. Lowell would dictate the activities of the regiment for the next year.[16]

A lawyer by trade, rail thin, and "hatchet faced," John Singleton Mosby didn't look the part of a dashing Confederate raider. "He was rather a slouchy rider, and did not seem to take any interest in military duties," recalled a fellow soldier from his first days in uniform. Never an advocate of slavery, Mosby was a solid Union man until Lincoln's call for volunteers drove Virginia to secession. "Virginia is my mother, God bless her. I can't fight against my mother, can I?"[17]

Enlisting as a private in the 1st Virginia Cavalry, Mosby quickly showed an aptitude for scouting. A brief stint as adjutant gave him an officer's commission, but he had such a distaste for the paperwork that he resigned within weeks. While serving as adjutant Mosby was noticed by Gen. J.E.B. Stuart, the new cavalry commander for the Confederate Army. Gen. Stuart placed Mosby on his staff with the rank of lieutenant, and put him in a position to make the most of his talents. Mosby would look back at the appointment as the turning point in his career and referred to Stuart as, "The best friend I ever had." Employed as a courier and scout, Mosby was sent on a reconnaissance of the Federal forces gathering around Richmond in June 1862. Learning that the Federal right flank was exposed, the young scout relayed the information to Stuart, and soon found himself in the advance of a 1,200 man column that brashly rode around the entire Yankee army.[18]

Pleased with his young lieutenant's performance, Stuart dispatched Mosby to the Shenandoah Valley to serve under Gen. Thomas "Stonewall" Jackson. En route to his new command, Mosby was captured by Federal cavalry, but was quickly exchanged and sent back to his post with Stuart. Serving through the summer and fall campaigns, Mosby dreaded the oncoming inactivity as the army went into winter quarters. On New Year's Eve, 1862, he made a request to Stuart to be given a detail of nine men to conduct guerrilla activities in Northern Virginia. The re-

Col. John S. Mosby, 43rd Battalion, Virginia Cavalry. *Courtesy of U.S.A.M.H.I.*

quest was granted, and ten days later Mosby made his first strike, against the Yankee pickets at Herndon Station.[19]

Due to the success of this first raid, Stuart gave Mosby a new detachment of 15 men, the men who would become the nucleus for his Rangers. Picking up recruits here and there, Mosby's band grew as he led his men on a series of attacks against pickets and vedettes. Federal attempts to stop the annoying strikes were fruitless, and the Federal commander in the area, Col. Percy Wyndham, became so exasperated he threatened to burn Middleburg, which he thought was Mosby's base of operations.[20]

Mosby was incensed that Wyndham would target a civilian community in an effort to stop his actions, and hit upon a daring plan to snatch the Federal commander from his own headquarters. Before dawn on the 9th of March, Mosby led 30 of his men into the sleepy village of Fairfax, seeking out their quarry. Luckily for Wyndham he had chosen to spend the night in the capital; but luck was not with Gen. Edwin Stoughton, commander of the Vermont Infantry Brigade, who also had his headquarters in Fairfax. The general was roused out of his warm bed and, with 32 other prisoners, was soon on his way south to captivity. Nine days later Mosby was a captain, and within two weeks promoted to major.[21]

The morning of the 10th of June, Mosby's men had routed two companies of the 6th Michigan Cavalry at their camp near Seneca Mills, killing seven and capturing 23 before burning the tents and crossing back into Virginia. The 2nd Massachusetts Cavalry rode the ten miles from Brightwood to Seneca Creek finding four dead Confederates and a trail that led into the Potomac. Rather than crossing in pursuit, Lowell led his men up the river several more miles before bedding down near Poolesville.[22]

Lowell believed that Mosby would follow the river in the direction of Leesburg before moving south towards Middleburg. Resting his men and horses for four hours, Lowell then led them across the Potomac at White's Ford hoping to find Mosby near Ball's Mill. The Federals scoured the area for signs of the Rangers and eventually found their track headed south on Goose Creek. The track led to the Little River Turnpike near Aldie where Lowell made preparation to run down his foe at Middleburg. Before this movement could be made 400 troopers of the 5th New York Cavalry rode in from the direction of Middleburg claiming all to be quiet in that area.[23]

Mosby had disbanded his men hours before and now it was quite impossible to tell who was a peaceful farmer and who was one of Mosby's men. This tactic of melting into the countryside and disbanding was one of the Rangers' most valuable maneuvers and was in large part responsible for the unit's low casualty rate and their ability to remain organized for so long in close proximity to the Union capital.[24]

With nothing to show for their rapid movement through Virginia and Maryland, Lowell's troops mounted their horses and began the ride back to camp via the Chain Bridge. The 150 mile chase was an education for the 2nd Massachusetts Cavalry. Aside from the First Battalion down on the York River, this was the first excursion into "enemy territory" for the men.

The men were astounded by the desolate looking country that was Northern Virginia. The fences were all down (long since used as firewood) and numerous houses stood vacant. The townsfolk they saw were full of hostility to the Union horsemen and made a show of slamming their doors and letting down their window shades.[25]

Back in camp at Brightwood, the tired troopers enjoyed a few days' rest. Drill, inspections, picket duty, and patrols kept them occupied, but they were soon longing for another chance to go riding in search of Rebs. On the 21st of June the men heard some cannon off in the direction of the Potomac unaware it was a major engagement between General J.E.B. Stuart and the Union cavalry of Gen. Alfred Pleasanton. The two forces were fighting near the town of Upperville and an artillery duel between Battery C of the 3rd U.S. Artillery and the Washington (South Carolina) Artillery had opened the battle. A caisson of the Washington Artillery took a direct hit, and the resulting explosion, heard for miles, was probably responsible for catching the 2nd Massachusetts Cavalry's attention.[26]

As the men lazed in the warm June sun and gorged themselves on cherries, they were completely unaware of the movements of the two main armies. Both armies were in motion and would soon meet near the southern Pennsylvania town of Gettysburg. Though the military input the regiment would contribute to the campaign was minimal, it would play a major part in the events that led to the change of the commanding general of the Army of the Potomac.

On the 23rd of June, the two battalions of the 2nd Massachusetts Cavalry were given orders to strike their tents, pack two days' rations, and report to their new camp in Poolesville, Maryland. A warm rain fell on the men as they set up their tents the next morning about half a mile from the town. A continual string of soldiers moved past their camp, first the 3rd Corps followed by their lengthy wagon train. In the morning the troopers began their new duties of picketing the Potomac from the mouth of the Monocacy River to Great Falls.[27]

On the 26th, Col. Lowell received an order from Maj. Gen. Hooker, in command of the Army of the Potomac, instructing him to take his battalions to Knoxville, Maryland, and report to Gen. Slocum and his XII Corps. Drawing in his pickets and patrols from an area of over 30 miles, Lowell telegraphed Gen. Heintzelman the next morning that he was headed for Knoxville as ordered. This movement left open the fords along a stretch of the Potomac, in particular Rowser's Ford where Stuart and his cavalry crossed just hours after Lowell removed his pickets.[28]

Arriving in Knoxville the evening of the 27th, Lowell was greeted with a pair of telegrams bearing conflicting orders. "...[A]bout 11 came two dispatches from General Heintzelman, one ordering me to remain at Poolesville, or to return if I had left, the other notifying me that General Halleck sent the same order. I was considerably disturbed, and telegraphed at once to General Hooker and to General Heintzelman and notified General Slocum. In the morning, 4 o'clock, I got order from General Hooker to report to General French (at Harpers Ferry), and from French to report immediately; also orders from Heintzelman to take no orders that did not come through his, Heintzelman's, Headquarters." Hooker was furious that this young colonel was refusing his orders and complained to Halleck. Halleck shot back that Lowell's cavalry was the only force for scouts in the Department and could not be taken from Heintzelman's command.[29]

This relatively minor incident occurring while so many major events were unfolding was merely the tip of the iceberg. Hooker had complained bitterly when Brig. Gen. John P. Slough had refused to follow Hooker's order to release the Second Brigade of the Pennsylvania Reserve Corps for duty with the Army of the Potomac. Hooker complained to Halleck, "You will find, I fear, when it is too late, that the effort to preserve departmental lines will be fatal to the cause of the country." The final straw came when Hooker ordered the removal of the Federal forces from Harpers Ferry. When Halleck countermanded Hooker's order, Hooker submitted his resignation which was readily accepted.[30]

Lowell, unaware of the part he had played in army politics, wished to stay with the Army of the Potomac but returned to

Poolesville only to find that Stuart had crossed in his absence. Feeling he would be made a scapegoat for Stuart's unchallenged crossing, he hurriedly passed out rations and set off in pursuit. Lowell's novice troopers didn't stand a chance of catching Stuart's veterans with their sizable headstart. After two days and nights of riding the 2nd Massachusetts Cavalry was able to close with the stragglers from Stuart's rear guard. During the early morning of the 1st of July in Brookville, a Confederate lieutenant and four privates were captured by the advance under 1st Lt. William C. Manning, "...as brave, dashing and gallant a young officer as can be found in the Union army." Lowell had sent a stream of telegrams to Heintzelman as he chased Stuart, and at Brookville a dispatch reached him ordering him back to Poolesville. Still worried that he would be blamed for Stuart's crossing into Maryland, the message from Heintzelman was filled with praise for his movements of the last two days.[31]

Making their way slowly back to camp, the 2nd was completely unaware of the battle raging to the north of them. A few days later when word of the great struggle reached them, the men chaffed at having missed the fight. Back in Poolesville the regiment returned to their picket duties along the Potomac. The days were spent foraging and fishing as all the rations had given out but the hardtack and coffee. The fishing in the Potomac and the Chesapeake and Ohio canal was poor, but there was still plenty of berries and an occasional pig to be found.[32]

On the 9th of July, the regiment was ordered back to Camp Brightwood but the stay was short. The next morning Col. Lowell received orders to report to Col. Percy Wyndham in Alexandria from whom he would receive further orders.[33]

Col. Sir Percy Wyndham, an English soldier of fortune, was currently in command of the cavalry remount depot at Giesboro Point while recovering from a wound taken at Brandy Station. A veteran of service in the English, French, Austrian, and Italian armies, Wyndham had been given special authority to raise the 1st New Jersey Cavalry. Foppish in appearance and sporting an enormous mustache he was nonetheless extremely aggressive on horseback and had risen to command a brigade in Pleasanton's Cavalry Corps. Convalescing from his wounds, Sir Percy was attempting to remount 3,000 of Pleasanton's troopers.[34]

Lowell's orders were to take all of the available mounted troops from Wyndham (60 men) and with his own regiment make a reconnaissance to the Shenandoah Valley to determine the number of Confederates east of the Blue Ridge. Gen. Meade's army, slow to pursue Lee from the field at Gettysburg, was in contact with the rear of the Army of Northern Virginia but the location of its head was currently a mystery.[35]

The ride out the Little River Turnpike through the barren Virginia countryside was uneventful. The column stopped for the night near Aldie where Stuart and Pleasanton had clashed on the 17th of June. Several wounded men still lay in a nearby farmhouse serving as a hospital. Pushing back a few Confederate pickets from the hills above Aldie the 2nd Massachusetts Cavalry had a fireless night sleeping with their reins in their hands.[36]

Continuing in the morning, the column rode west towards Ashby's Gap in the Blue Ridge Mountains. A few platoons of enemy cavalry met them in the hamlet of Paris at the foot of the mountains but quickly retreated up the gap without a fight. At the summit a mixed force of dismounted Confederate cavalry fired on them from behind stone walls and thick brush. Lowell sent out two companies to flank the defenders from the left and after some sharp skirmishing the rebels were soon forced from their position and compelled to retreat into the valley.[37]

All of the casualties were from the Californian Battalion. Killed in the fight were privates Walter S. Barnes (E), Bloomington, Maryland, and Henry P. Irving (E), San Francisco. Pvt. Irving was shot in the chest during the fight, and thinking he was dead, a rebel attempted to take his carbine and revolver. With the last of his strength, Irving lifted his pistol to kill the Confederate, but his life was ebbing fast and the pistol was falling from his hand as the startled rebel shot him a second time. Pvt. Barnes took a bullet that passed through his body shoulder to shoulder. He lived for about four hours, dying in an ambulance, conscious to the end. Wounded were Richard Brickley (E), New York City, who was discharged for his wounds on June 15, 1864; Sgt. William DeForest (M), Schenectady, New York, who was shot in the right temple just above the eye and discharged for wounds September 4, 1864; Bugler James Hawkins (L), California, discharged for disability from hospital in Alexandria, Virginia, June 20, 1865; Maurice Joy (E), Lynn, Massachusetts, recovered and returned to duty; William Moore (E), Gardiner, Maine, recovered and returned to duty, only to be wounded again in March of 1865; Pvt. John Smith (E), Sterling, Illinois, recovered and returned to duty; and David (Daniel) Terry (E), California, was discharged for disability on August 21, 1863. Captured were, Thomas Garrity (E), California, released on October 19, 1864, and returned to duty; 2nd Lt. John Norcross (M), California, escaped from prison in March of 1865; Roswell Smith (L), California, died December 14, 1863, as a prisoner of war in Richmond, Virginia; DeWitt Van Vleet (M), Michigan, paroled and deserted from Parole Camp, Maryland, September 17, 1864; and Hiram Vennum (E), Iroquois, County, Illinois, who died Christmas Day, 1863, as a prisoner of war at Richmond, Virginia.[38]

The day was very hazy making it difficult for the party to determine if there was any large force of Confederates in the valley. The advance guard followed the Shenandoah River south for a few miles but again saw no camps or wagon trains. A small Confederate force picketing the west bank of the river peppered the men with rifle fire but to no effect.[39]

Gathering his dead and wounded from the fight in the gap, Lowell led his men back through the mountains and north along the eastern slope of the Blue Ridge. Riding till midnight in the rain, then spending another night along the roadside with no fires, left the men cold and itching for a fight.[40]

At dawn the troopers set out again and soon charged into Leesburg hoping to surprise some enemy cavalry, but their information was flawed and a search of the town uncovered merely an officer and two privates. Pushing on through the rainy afternoon the men's spirits rose somewhat when they stopped for the evening near a milkhouse. They emptied it of fresh milk and butter, and afterward Col. Lowell posted a guard over the now empty building.[41]

The next morning the march continued, later passing "...a humble, but neat looking cottage by the road side, a lady — God bless her! — stood in the door, smiling and waving her white kerchief to us. It presented such a contrast to the frowning looks of the women, and cowardly, sneaking looks of the men we had met with in Virginia, that we felt inclined to stop and thank her; but not being able to do this, we contented ourselves by thanking God that, at least there was one Union woman in Virginia." Crossing the Potomac by way of the Chain Bridge the men gratefully returned to their tents at Brightwood, pleased with themselves but more than willing to get in out of the rain. Col. Lowell reported the absence of troops east of the Blue Ridge and of the meager results of the scout: 13 prisoners (a lieutenant and a private of the 6th Virginia Cavalry, six privates from a North Carolina cavalry regiment, a captain and his aide from Gen. Rodes' staff, and three civilians who had been helping the rebels at Ashby's gap), one of whom had been taken in Paris trying to disguise himself in women's clothes.[42]

Taking one day off to dry out and rest their mounts, the 2nd Massachusetts left their camp again on the 16th of July riding through the capital and across the Long Bridge to Alexandria. The men spent two soggy days camping a few miles west of the city waiting for orders. There was an abundance of women and small boys who passed through the camps selling apple cakes and pies to the few that had money.[43]

During this pause the 2nd Massachusetts Cavalry was attached to a small division under the command of Brig. Gen. Rufus King, consisting of two brigades of infantry, a battery of New York Artillery, and the 2nd Massachusetts Cavalry strengthened by a detachment from the 6th New York Cavalry. Gen. King was to march his command down the line of the Orange and Alexandria Railroad, taking possession of the road and repairing the burned-out bridges along the way.[44]

The thought of "joining the Infantry" was distasteful to Lowell, the blue-blooded cavalier, and he leaped at the chance on the 19th to ride to the Occoquan Creek where a Confederate conscription was said to be taking place. All local men under the age of 45 were to meet at Bentsville, about six miles southwest of Manassas Junction, where they would be drafted into Confederate service. Taking three squadrons, Lowell found no conscripts but did capture the lieutenant colonel who had ordered the draft, a few uniformed enlisted men, and a messenger of Gen. J.E.B. Stuart who was carrying a message detailing where Lowell's force was. With prisoners in tow the Federals headed north to Centerville where they made camp overlooking the field fortifications erected by Beauregard early in the war.[45]

Men and horses rested the next day in their Centerville camp. There was an abundance of blackberries nearby, and as the men were out of rations they spent the day feasting on berries and lying in the shade. Lowell wrote to Josephine about his memories of Interlaken and a view of the Jungfrau. For him, it was a lazy day with the troopers dozing under apple trees on the grassy slopes.[46]

On the 21st of July, two years to the day after the first clash at Bull Run, the 2nd Massachusetts Cavalry passed over the battlefield while starting out on another raid. The area was still littered with the wreckage of war: human skulls, bones, cannonballs, pieces of shells, and scores of lead bullets. Amidst these reminders of carnage grew a profusion of white morning-glories. Col. Lowell picked one for Miss Shaw, but on second thought threw it away. "...The association was not a pleasant one."[47]

The march passed through New Market and Greenwich without incident. Approaching Warrenton a dozen mounted Confederates were spotted, prompting Lowell to order the column to a gallop. Hoping to catch the Rebels in town, the troopers found only one crippled young veteran, sitting defiantly in his gray uniform on a hotel porch.[48]

Spending a quiet night at Bristow Station the column pushed on the next morning to Manassas Junction. As Lowell's troops entered the town they passed Brig. Gen. David Gregg's 2nd Cavalry Division of the Army of the Potomac. During a brief conversation Gregg informed Lowell that he had applied to have the 2nd Massachusetts Cavalry attached to his division and that he had a brigade of five regiments that he intended to have him lead. With a promise that he would continue to make requests for his regiment, Gregg bid Lowell good-bye and followed his division south on its scout of Gen. Lee's position.*[49]

Returning to Centerville, Lowell's troops entered into a regular routine of scouting and camp duty. On the 29th of July a court-martial was convened comprised of Major Forbes, Capt. Charles Eigenbrodt (E) and 1st Lt. Rufus Smith (A). The defendant was Capt. Zebdiel Adams of Company L as well as squadron commander for L and F, who was accused of "Habitual violation of the third paragraph of Army Regulations." The charges specified that during the last scout, while the column was halted near Centerville, Capt. Adams came up to the men of Company F yelling, "Keep your horses in line God damn you, or I will chop your heads off." Three corporals and three privates were called to testify that they had heard the captain make the threat and that he had frequently been abusive in the past. The only witness for the defense was Capt. George Blagden (K) who testified he had never known Adams to be abusive to his men.

There wasn't a chance the hard-riding Adams would be found guilty. With two fellow Californians on the court and a brother officer speaking in his defense, Lowell stacked the deck heavily in Adams' favor. After Blagden's testimony the court deliberated and brought forth the expected not guilty verdict.[50]

No longer tied to infantry and repair crews along the line of the railroad, the small cavalry post now sent out regular patrols of one or two squadrons looking for "bushwhackers." The bushwhackers were Mosby's partisan rangers who were doing all in their power to harass the rear of the Army of the Potomac.

The assignment was difficult due to Mosby's hit and run tactics and the Rangers' abilities to disappear individually into the woods when pursued. Being so familiar with the area the Confederate raiders knew every house, barn and corn crib to hide in. The local population, having no love for the Union troops, hid and fed the Rangers and confessed ignorance of their whereabouts when questioned. Searching outbuildings and homes was a task that Lowell did not relish. "I don't at all fancy the duty here, — serving against bushwhackers; it brings me in contact with too many citizens, — and sometimes with mothers and children." One night a young Confederate soldier, returning from a visit with his family, was captured by Lowell's pickets. The next morning his mother came to the camp to see him off to a Yankee prison camp. She repacked his bundle and gave him some money but never cried or asked for his release. A day later a 16-year-old boy was captured. He had joined the Rangers to avoid conscription and was more than willing to tell all he knew to Lowell, "…but he was such a babe that it seemed mean to me to question him."[51]

The patrols set a routine for the camp in Centerville and something akin to normal camp life began for the 2nd Massachusetts Cavalry. One memorable day the men were treated to fresh beef, a rare treat after days of berries and stewed apples. Time was available for mending uniforms, washing horses, and writing letters. A rumor went through the camp that the California Hundred and the rest of the First Battalion would be returning to the regiment soon. Lowell wrote to family and friends expressing his shock and grief over the death of Robert Gould Shaw at

---

*General Gregg and Lowell had been acquaintances since the early days of the war when they had served together as captains in the 6th U.S. Cavalry.

the attack on Battery Wagner near Charleston.[52]

On the evening of the 30th of July, Mosby and about 30 of his men captured 30 sutler wagons camped near Fairfax Court House. The sutlers were not soldiers but rather private businessmen who sold their merchandise in the camps. The wagons were loaded with boots, food, newspapers, illegal alcohol, and dozens of other items. Tempted by the rich cargo, Mosby elected to try and haul off the entire wagon train, a bold move considering the proximity of enemy cavalry seven miles away in Centerville. Forcing the unwilling sutlers to mount their wagons, the Rangers slowly began moving the train west along the Little River Turnpike.[53]

In command at Centerville was Brig. Gen. Rufus King. Gen. King had been court-martialed for disobedience and errors in judgment during the Second Bull Run campaign (Gen. Pope accused him of being drunk) and had since been given minor postings. Somehow King learned of Mosby's raid at Fairfax and immediately notified Lowell. The colonel made a snap decision and dispatched a number of ambulances with an escort of 20 men under the command of Lt. Goodwin Stone. These ambulances would be bait for his trap. With 150 troopers Lowell rode up the Old Road toward Aldie striking the Turnpike ahead of Mosby. Another detachment of 20 men, under Lt. Manning, was left to picket the three roads that led north to Gum Springs in the hopes of cutting off any retreat Mosby might make in this direction. Lowell and the rest of the column continued on to Aldie where they remained until dawn.[54]

Lowell's men, ready and waiting for the advancing Confederates, were surprised the next morning by gunfire from back down the Pike. As Mosby and his wagons advanced up the Turnpike Lowell's ambulances were spotted ahead of them. Intent on adding this new booty to the column, the Rangers were preparing to capture the wagons when they passed one of the roads picketed by Lt. Manning's men. Posted too close to the road or drawn by the sound of the wagons, the pickets were discovered by Mosby's men. Having been spotted by the superior

Pvt. William Cunningham, Company A, California Hundred, 2nd Massachusetts Cavalry. *Courtesy of Vallejo Naval and Historical Museum.*

force of Confederates the six-man picket force drew sabres and charged. The startled Rangers managed to cut down two of the troopers and wounded two others before they burst through the Confederate ranks and continued headlong up the Turnpike. The Confederates raced after them leaving half of their force to guard the wagons.[55]

Having heard the shots, Lowell ordered ten men to follow him while the balance of the command followed in platoons. When the pursuing Confederates saw Lowell and his column charging toward them they beat a very hasty retreat and became the pursued. Abandoning the wagons the Rangers took to the fields and once again eluded the Northern horsemen. In short order the recaptured wagons and the ambulances were turned around and under guard began the trip to Centerville. The sutlers, understandably relieved at being liberated, freely gave their rescuers cigars and cakes and other delicacies from their stock.[56]

Pvt. Charles Roberts, the California diarist, was placed in charge of a detail assigned to dig graves for the two fallen men. Hazen D. Little (L) a 28-year-old printer, and 25-year-old mason Peter Renard or Reynard (L) both from the California Battalion, were laid to rest under a locust tree in the front yard of a nearby home. The owner was civil enough to the men who had to carry out this unpleasant chore, bringing them milk and bread and allowing them to take pears off his trees.*[57]

With the wagons safely on their way back down the Pike, Lowell and his men rode westward hoping to pick up the trail of the Rangers as they headed back into "Mosby's Confederacy." Once again Lowell's instincts were correct and Mosby's trail was struck running up into the Bull Run Mountains. Gathering all his men with carbines to the front, the colonel led them over the crest of the ridge and discovered five of Mosby's men resting under a tree with nine prisoners. The Confederates ignored their prisoners and took to the woods, again saved by their knowledge of the terrain. The troopers fired a few shots and gave chase but had no chance of catching them that day.[58]

A golden opportunity to capture or kill Mosby had been missed as a result of the misfortune of Lt. Manning's men being spotted before the trap could be sprung. But the pursuit could be deemed a success as all the wagons were recaptured and Mosby was forced to flee. Lowell reported two men killed and two wounded; the two men captured early in the fight were liberated, as were seven men from a Pennsylvania cavalry regiment. He claimed to have wounded five of the enemy though the Confederates recorded only one.[59]

The two casualties of the 2nd Massachusetts were Pvt. James Bard (L), California, who quickly recovered from his wound, and Pvt. Chauncey Hull (L), California, who took a bullet in the right arm and soon saw it amputated. He was discharged for his wound on February 13, 1864, in Alexandria, Virginia.[60]

After the war Mosby recalled part of the engagement for a newspaper article. "At one time I captured a lot of loaded wagons in a sutlers train. I thought first of burning them, but finally concluded to carry them off. It was about twelve miles to a place of safety in the mountains and while on the way we met a part of the Second Massachusetts Cavalry. The California

---

*At the end of the war the grave marker was found citing that H.B. Little and Charles Raymond of the 2nd Massachusetts Cavalry had been killed July 31, 1863. There is no Charles Raymond on the 2nd's roster and it is quite possible that the grave diggers from Company F, unsure of his real name, carved what they thought the dead man's name was. Evans and Moore, Mosby's Confederacy, pp. 118–119.

Hundred and Battalion was part of the regiment we came against. They were a fine body of men and the most cheerful fighters I ever met. Well, I was obliged to leave the wagons behind and the sutlers got them back again."[61]

Lowell related the capture of the wagons to his Effie. "...[W]e retook them all, but didn't take Mosby, who is an old rat, and has a great many holes.... I dislike to have men killed in such 'inglorious warfare' as Cousin John calls it,—but it's not a warfare of my choosing, and it's all in a day's work."[62]

Notes

1. *Daily Alta California*, June 17, 1863.
2. *Daily Alta California*, May 30, 1863.
3. Emerson, *Life and Letters*, p. 416.
4. *Daily Alta California*, May 30, 1863.
5. Emerson, *Life and Letters*, p. 237; *Boston Transcript*, Feb. 10, 1863.
6. *Daily Alta California*, May 30, 1863.
7. Emerson, *Life and Letters*, p. 238; *Daily Alta California*, June 17, 1863.
8. *Daily Alta California*, July 17, 1863.
9. Emerson, *Life and Letters*, pp. 240–41.
10. Emerson, *Life and Letters*, p. 245.
11. National Archives, Record Group 94, 2nd Massachusetts Cavalry Regimental records box, letter dated May 29, 1863, Casey to Lowell.
12. Emerson, *Life and Letters*, pp. 251, 257.
13. Emerson, *Life and Letters*, pp. 251–52.
14. Roberts, *Diary*, May 18, 1863.
15. Roberts, *Diary*, June 9, 1863.
16. Roberts, *Diary*, June 10, 1863.
17. Jones, *Ranger Mosby*, p. 35; Wert, *Mosby's Rangers*, p. 28.
18. Wert, *Mosby's Rangers*, pp. 28–30.
19. Jones, *Ranger Mosby*, p. 68; Siepel, *Rebel: The Life and Times of John Singleton Mosby*, pp. 58–59, 67–68.
20. Wert, *Mosby's Rangers*, p. 41.
21. Jones, *Gray Ghosts and Rebel Raiders*, pp. 131–38; Sifakis, *Who Was Who in the Civil War*, p. 460.
22. Roberts, *Diary*, June 10, 1863; *OR*, XVII, p. 74; *Daily Alta California*, July 17, 1863.
23. Roberts, *Diary*, June 12, 1863.
24. *OR*, XVII, P. 75.
25. Roberts, *Diary*, June 13, 1863.
26. Roberts, *Diary*, June 21, 1863.
27. Roberts, *Diary*, June 23–24, 1863; *OR*, XVII, p. 324.
28. *OR*, XVII, pp. 63, 354–55, 380.
29. Emerson, *Life and Letters*, pp. 268–70, 428; *OR*, XVII, pp. 56, 60–70.
30. Coddington, *The Gettysburg Campaign*, p. 130; *OR*, XVII, p. 56.
31. Roberts, *Diary*, June 29, 1863; *OR*, XVII, pp. 65, 66, 404, 428; *Daily Alta California*, Aug. 2, 1863.
32. Roberts, *Diary*, July 2–4, 1863.
33. *OR*, XVII, p. 623.
34. Longacre, *The Cavalry at Gettysburg*, p. 54.
35. *OR*, XVII, p. 1039.
36. Roberts, *Diary*, July 11, 1863; *OR*, XVII, p. 1039.
37. Roberts, *Diary*, July 12, 1863; *OR*, XVII, p. 1039.
38. *Massachusetts Soldiers, Sailors, and Marines*, Vol. VI., pp. 228–328; *The Medical and Surgical History of the Civil War*, Vol. VII, p. 185.
39. *OR*, XVII, p. 1039.
40. *OR*, XVII, p. 1039.
41. Roberts, *Diary*, July 12, 1863.
42. Roberts, *Diary*, July 12, 1863; *OR*, XVII, pp. 704, 1039–40; *Daily Alta California*, Aug. 13, 1863.
43. Roberts, *Diary*, July 18, 1863.
44. *OR*, XVII, pp. 706, 717.
45. Emerson, *Life and Letters*, pp. 276–77; Roberts, *Diary*, July 19, 1863; *OR*, XVII, p. 747.
46. Emerson, *Life and Letters*, p. 277; Roberts, *Diary*, July 20, 1863.
47. Emerson, *Life and Letters*, p. 278; Roberts, *Diary*, July 21, 1863.
48. Roberts, *Diary*, July 21, 1863.
49. Emerson, *Life and Letters*, p. 279; Roberts, *Diary*, July 22, 1863.
50. National Archives, Record Group 94, 2nd Massachusetts Cavalry Regimental records box, General Order #28 dated July 29, 1863.
51. Emerson, *Life and Letters*, p. 283.
52. Emerson, *Life and Letters*, p. 284–89.
53. Williamson, *Mosby's Rangers*, p. 85.
54. Sifakis, *Who Was Who in the Civil War*, pp. 364–65; *OR*, XVII, pp. 988–90.
55. Roberts, *Diary*, July 31, 1863; *OR*, XVII, p. 991.
56. Roberts, *Diary*, July 13, 1863; Scott,

Partisan Life with Col. John S. Mosby, p. 116; OR, XVII, p. 991.

57. Roberts, *Diary*, July 31, 1863.
58. Roberts, *Diary*, July 31, 1863; OR, XVII, pp. 990–91.
59. OR, XVII, pp. 990–92.
60. *Medical and Surgical History of the Civil War*, X, p. 944; *Massachusetts Soldiers, Sailors, and Marines*, Vol. VI, pp. 305–06.
61. Backus, "Californians in the Field," MOLLUS., pp. 9–10.
62. Greenslet, *The Lowells and Their Seven Worlds*, p. 253n.

Chapter Six

The Independent Cavalry Brigade

On the 1st of August, 1863, Col. Lowell checked into Willard's Hotel in Washington and later that evening reported to the War Department for orders. The young colonel had attracted considerable attention in the last month and was placed in command of a small independent brigade and tasked with continuing his operations against the Confederate guerrillas in Northern Virginia. Consisting of his own 2nd Massachusetts Cavalry, as well as the 13th and 16th New York Cavalry commanded by Lt. Col. Henry S. Ganesvoort and Colonel Henry Lazelle, Lowell would be reenforced again on the 6th when detachments of his First Battalion joined the command at Centerville. (Some were left at Fort Ethan Allen for picket duty.)[1]

Considerable confusion was generated when the regiment was strung out in line during a march. Pvt. Samuel Backus of Company L explained, "While we were comparatively recruits, marching past other troops, whenever the question was asked, 'what regiment is that?' the answer would come from one part of the line 'California Hundred,' and from another 'California Battalion,' and from still another 'Second Massachusetts Cavalry.' No wonder the questioners were often puzzled to know who we really were. We soon however overcame this folly, and to say we belonged to the Second Massachusetts was honor enough in our minds. We however indulged ourselves in the thought that the Californians really did constitute the regiment, and with this idea we felt satisfied that we would not completely lose our identity."[2]

The addition of the New York troops was neither welcome nor unwelcome among the 2nd Massachusetts; it was looked upon with indifference. "The personnel of those regiments," Towle recalled, "was largely German or Dutch, and when details from either or both formed a part of a scouting expedition we always regarded them as not only of no assistance but as so much 'baggage' to be taken care of. If Mosebey [*sic*] took one of them prisoner he would strip the soldier of what he wanted and turn him loose, with a direction to go to a camp and get more."[3]

Doubtful as it may sound the theory was put to the test when Sergeant Gustavus Doane was captured during a scout.

"Cheney" Doane, a 23-year-old graduate of the University of the Pacific at Santa Clara, who had trekked across the Oregon trail with his family when he was five, was no stranger to excitement. "On one occasion when a scouting expedition had halted on the road he and two or three others went off to a farm house for something to eat. When the command returned to camp Doane was missing, and those who had been with him at the farm house reported that when they left he had in front of him a very large loaf of bread and a crock of butter which they had no idea he would leave until it was all consumed. The next day Doane came into camp and reported that after returning from the farm house to the road he found that the command had moved on, and that while following to overtake it he was intercepted by some of Mosebey's [sic] men and taken prisoner. They asked what regiment he belonged [to] and in as good a German accent as he could command told them that he belonged to the 16th New York, whereupon they took his horse and equipment and gave him a kick and told him to go to camp and get more." Soon after this event Sgt. Doane became Pvt. Doane.*[4]

The large force of the brigade was needed for Mosby and was seldom idle during the month of August. On the 5th, a sutlers wagon fell prey to a dozen Rangers. The next day the Confederates seized several more but these were soon retaken by the 2nd Massachusetts Cavalry. Once again the men gorged themselves on the recaptured plunder. The sutlers were only too happy to share their goods with their saviors and the men enjoyed pickles, cheese, cakes, wine, and clothes. Pvt. Roberts recorded in his diary that he was pleased to receive a new cap, while Pvt. Barnstead recorded, "A soldier has no pity at all for the misfortune of a sutler, as they are in the habit of charging soldiers an extortionate price for everything they sell to them, and when a chance offers to make up this extortion, it is gladly taken advantage of."[5]

The attention given to the sutler trains was noted by Gen. Robert E. Lee. On the 4th of August, Lee sent a message to Gen. Stuart stating, "I greatly commend Major Mosby for his boldness and good management. I fear he exercises but little control over his men. He has latterly carried but too few on his expeditions, and his attention has been more directed toward the capture of wagons than military damage to the enemy." In another communication on the 18th, Gen. Lee advised Stuart that, "The capture and destruction of wagon trains is advantageous, but the supply of the Federal Army is carried on by the railroad. If that should be injured, it would cause him to detach largely for its security, and thus weaken his main army."[6]

On the 11th Mosby struck again, capturing wagons on the Little River Turnpike between Fairfax Court House and Annandale. Lowell sent detachments to scour the back roads in the area bordered by Fairfax Courthouse, Annandale, Falls Church, and Vienna. Somehow Mosby and his men managed to disappear with 19 captured wagons. Unable to capture any of the raiders the Northern horsemen did bring in 116 horses, mostly recaptured Union horses, which were sent to the Cavalry Depot outside Washington.[7]

Col. Lowell took out a patrol on the evening of the 15th of August, pushing the men through the night in the direction of Leesburg. Resting for a few hours before

---

*In March 1864, Doane was promoted to first lieutenant in the Mississippi Marine Brigade. After the war he served as the first reconstruction mayor of Yazoo, Mississippi, then resigned the position for a commission in the 2nd U.S. Cavalry to fight Indians. Bonney, Battledrums and Geysers, pp. 8–15.

dawn, the command was divided into three columns and sent to scout the area between Leesburg, Dranesville and Aldie. A prisoner was taken near Gum Springs who told them that Mosby and White had joined forces, but the lone rebel turned out to be the only Confederate seen that day. Regrouping his command the next morning, Lowell turned towards Aldie sending Capt. DeMerritt's Company F to scout ahead. Cresting a hill the advance column spotted 20 rebels in the road and in a flash the chase was on. Across a creek and through a strip of woods, the enemy was finally brought to bay against a fence where they turned and loosed a volley at the Yankees. As the distance closed between the two forces, the Confederates scattered in every direction, several jumping the fence, others charging up a nearby hill where a small wood offered a chance for escape. Pvt. Roberts was charging up the slope in pursuit when his horse gave out forcing him to dismount and continue on foot. Two men were captured on the hill, a third in a barn, and six horses filled out the day's haul of prisoners. For all the gunfire, no one was hit on either side.[8]

Camping the night on a small farm, the men fed their horses freely from the barn, but Col. Lowell placed a guard over the family milkhouse. An attempt was made to flank the milkhouse by digging under the foundation, but it turned out to be too much like work, and the thirsty troopers called it a night.[9]

Two more days of crisscrossing the area and probing the gaps in the Bull Run Mountains netted another six prisoners. A column of approaching cavalry provided a few tense moments as the men deployed in line of battle, but the mounted men turned out to be the rest of the brigade under Major Thompson. Nine prisoners, six horses, and no casualties—fair results for five days in the saddle.[10]

The frequent losses of sutler wagons led Col. Lowell to suggest an alternative to his superiors. "With your approbation, I propose to establish a regular escort of 30 to 50 men over the pike from Centerville to some position near Alexandria, once each way at irregular hours, all sutlers and stray wagons to be halted and compelled to come with this escort. This will be less fatiguing to my horses, and will, I think, with the detachments going to the front, afford all necessary protection to the sutlers"—a sensible idea but one which was not acted upon.[11]

With Lowell leading the brigade, command of the regiment was turned over to Major Crowninshield (command of his battalion was given to Capt. Reed of the California Hundred). Accustomed to leading a battalion at Gloucester Point, the major was quickly thrust into the active position of regimental commander. He described his first days in command in a letter to his mother. "I have been unable to write you for the last two weeks on account of the audacious Mosby.... We have just returned from a long tramp after Mosby, we caught 8 of his men but did not succeed in capturing him. Had two slight skirmishes and plenty of hard marching. I am as I told you in command of the Regt and am having hard work I don't find the Regt in as good condition as I expected to, in regard to drill & discipline. Disputes and jealousy among officers, and a very general feeling of dissatisfaction, which requires no small amount of patience and tact to arrange. As a fighting Regt I don't believe there is a better one in the service, and if it has a chance I'm sure will distinguish itself." The regiment soon had a chance when a detachment met with Mosby again during the last week of August.[12]

The campaigning of the previous weeks had been hard on the men but more so on the horses. Several were broken down and would be of little or no use for some time to come. A detail of 25 men, mostly Californians, was formed to take the condemned horses to the Cavalry Depot at Washington. The trip north was uneventful.

Returning to Centerville on the 24th of August, the men brought a total of 102 fresh horses. Each man was responsible for four horses, riding one and leading three. It was very hot and dusty as they made their way down the Little River Turnpike. Midway through the trip they stopped to water the horses at Billy Gooding's (Coyle's) Tavern.

Unknown to the Californians their approach to Billy Gooding's was observed by Mosby and 35 of his men. Out on a scout they had come up quietly behind the Yankees and carefully planned a trap. Mosby divided his command sending Lt. Tom Turner with half the men to attack from the other side. Mosby gave what he thought was sufficient time for Turner to get in position then gave the order to attack. With a shout the Confederates converged from both directions. A California newspaper later quoted that Mosby shouted, "If they are from New York or Michigan, do not fire." With the identity of the Californians recognized, Mosby said, "Go in boys! Fight like demons! They are Californians!" However unlikely it is that Mosby made the quote, his men did just what he demanded, and the rebel yell split the air.[13]

The instant confusion caused several of the new horses to rear and plunge. As each man had three horses tied to his saddle he was completely unable to defend himself or retreat, let alone counter attack. More than one man was pitched to the ground by the terrified horses and was faced with 16 plunging, kicking hoofs. Realizing the disadvantage of holding the horses, the men let them go, dismounted, and began firing at the enemy with their revolvers. Privates John Cain and Levi Turner of Company E took cover behind a fence and began to return fire when Confederate Lt. Norman Smith and a companion rode up and ordered them to surrender. They answered with their guns, the lieutenant falling dead and the other escaping with a wound.[14]

Sgt. Joseph Varnum, in command of the detachment, having shot the last round from his revolver grabbed a Reb by the throat and was beating him over the head when another Confederate rode up to him and putting a revolver to his head, killed him instantly. A few of the men opened fire from one of the buildings but were surrounded and forced to surrender when their ammunition ran out. (Each man carried two revolvers, but for some reason no extra ammunition had been carried.) The remaining Californians were still fighting gamely when either Pvt. William Short of Company F or Pvt. Charles "Carlos" Jenkins, Company E, fired a pistol and put a bullet into the side of John Singleton Mosby. Mosby managed to stay in the saddle but led his horse back into the shelter of the trees, his men mistaking this for a signal to break off the engagement.[15]

The Confederates rounded up the scattered horses and melted into the woods with their prisoners. Two Rangers lay dead and besides Mosby, at least two others were wounded.[16]

The Union casualties are not as easily explained. Ten different accounts of the skirmish give ten different casualty tallies. (None were even able to agree on how many horses were taken.) Pvt. John McCarty (A), San Francisco, and Sgt. Joseph Varnum (M), California, were killed on the field. Pvt. George Verrick (A), San Francisco, was shot out of the saddle, falling against Pvt. Nathan Beach (A), San Francisco, whose horse fell, injuring Beach severely. Verrick died of his wounds a week later. Pvt. John McKinney (L), California, was seriously wounded but recovered and served with the regiment throughout the war. Eight men were captured: Cyrus Demsey (A), San Francisco, paroled in November 1864, and returned to duty; Cpl. Charles Jenkins (E), Los Angeles, paroled November 20, 1864, returned to duty; William Manker (E), Griggsville, Illinois, paroled November 26, 1864, returned to duty; William Morris (E), Minersville, California, paroled in April 1864, returned to duty; Peter Hanson (F), unknown, was paroled and died November 29, 1864, on the U.S. Transport *Baltic* off Hilton Head, South Carolina; John Hurley (G), Boston, paroled November 19, 1864, and returned to duty; James Hayford (M), Canton, Maine, paroled and returned to duty; and Cpl. John Owen (A), who was captured but escaped later that day. The ten different accounts also conflict on the size of the opposing forces. The Californians reported an enemy force of 90 to 100, while the Confederates were convinced that they faced a detail of over 60. The Confederates also claim to have taken over a hundred horses but the figure was probably about 75.[17]

Fortunately for Major Mosby his surgeon Dr. Dunn was along on the raid and began to immediately administer aid to his stricken commander. Dr. Dunn made the decision that Mosby should be taken to Amherst County, the home of the major's parents. Two or three men, including the doctor, stayed with Mosby while the others led by Capt. Chapman took their spoils to Upperville.[18]

When news of the skirmish reached the cavalry camp at Centerville, Col. Lowell sent a force out in pursuit but it was unable to catch up to Chapman with his sizeable lead. Returning to camp, the horsemen found Cpl. John Owen of Company A who had been captured in the skirmish but managed to escape. The return to camp was without event for the men but gave a few tense moments for Major Mosby and Dr. Dunn who crouched in the brush a few yards from the road as the Yankees rode by.[19]

As the men approached camp, Captain DeMerritt of Company F was suddenly overcome by the heat or the pressures of the last several weeks. "On our way back to camp one of my Capts. suddenly became crazy, & thought we were going to hang him," recalled Crowninshield. "All of a sudden he darted into the woods & got away from us. We hunted two hours for him but could not find him." Capt. DeMerritt returned to camp of his own accord the next morning, his broken leg refractured, and "...still crazy as a coot."[20]

News of the skirmish and the loss of the horses quickly spread and nearly all the information that went to cavalry headquarters and to the press was wrong. Brig. Gen. King was told by an "eyewitness" sutler that the 13th New York Cavalry had been attacked by "200 of Stuart's cavalry." The *Boston Journal* reported that a herd of horses with a small escort had been captured but at the last minute the 8th Pennsylvania Cavalry saved the day and recaptured most of the horses. The *New York Tribune* reported that the 13th New York lost the horses, but the 2nd Massachusetts Cavalry took most of them back. Even Secretary of War Stanton had incorrect information when he ordered Gen. Stoneman to conduct a board of inquiry about how the 13th New York lost their horses.[21]

When Lowell heard of the board he wrote the secretary of war and informed him that it was his regiment that had lost the horses and if there was any blame it should be placed on him. Secretary Stanton's high regard for Col. Lowell has already been stated, and it was matched by that of Gen. Stoneman, president of the court of inquiry. After a preliminary gathering of the facts the court recommended Lowell be more careful in the future and mentioned two points where he seemed careless; one, specifically, said that he did not properly instruct the officer in charge of the detachment, who had remained in Washington and so missed the ambush. Lowell later wrote to Josephine Shaw, "I was not careless, as [Major] Will [Forbes] or any of my officers will tell you, — I was not at all to blame. I was particularly careful on one of the points where I am blamed, — but I am perfectly willing to shoulder the blame, — prefer to, in fact, — for I think a commanding officer is to blame for everything that goes wrong under him."[22]

Three days after the fight at Billy Gooding's Tavern, a funeral was held in camp for 29-year-old Pvt. John McCarty. The service was attended by the men of Company A and all of the field and staff officers of the regiment. Conducting the ceremony was Charles A. Humphreys, the newly arrived regimental chaplain.[23]

Humphreys, a student at the Harvard Divinity School, had been recruited by his classmate Lt. Col. Russell in April 1863 to become the chaplain of the 2nd Massachusetts Cavalry. Ordained on the 14th of July, the young chaplain had only arrived in camp six days before. The day after the funeral he was tasked with taking Capt. DeMerritt to the Seminary Hospital in Georgetown. Still suffering from the effects of his breakdown as well as a broken leg, the captain had to be literally carried on Humphreys' shoulders during parts of the journey. Apparently broken in mind and body, the luckless officer would recover and eventually return to the regiment where more ill fate awaited him. For the present, his loss was a particular blow to Col. Lowell who considered the Californian, "…one of my best fellows…."[24]

With the wounding of Mosby the frequency of Confederate raids was greatly reduced. The regiment, along with the rest of the brigade, began a routine of short expeditions and picket duty. This lull in raids and counter raids allowed Major Crowninshield the time he wanted: "The Regt. needs drill & discipline and if I could have one month of leisure I could make a splendid Regt. of it…." One afternoon several of the officers met with Crowninshield and informed him that if Col. Lowell was made brigadier general that all of the officers had determined to send a petition to Governor Andrew asking that Crowninshield be made colonel. "I was very much pleased to find that they liked me as an officer, for Comdg Officers are not apt to be liked, particularly if he happens to be younger than most of his officers, as is my case. However I thanked them and determined that I prefer things to take their own course."[25]

The major's relationship with his colonel was strong in outward appearance but he held reservations about Lowell's ability. In letters to his mother, Crowninshield revealed his feelings. "The Colonel and I get on very well together. He is a very brilliant man, but is too hasty in his judgements of men & things. And is so very ambitious, that he sacrifices everything for advancement"; and, "…he is very unpopular with the regt. & every[one] prays that he may be made a Brigadier Gen. so that we may get rid of him. I get on with him very well I think he likes me & as a companion he is very pleasant but I don't consider him much of a soldier although I do consider him to be the most talented young man I ever met with and he is as brave a little fellow as ever lived but is hasty inconsiderate and has not very good judgement. He has however a more unbounded confidence in his own ability…." Crowninshield, like many of the men, would change his tune when he saw the fearless little colonel in action. Lowell did not record or disclose his feelings about the young major.[26]

Others in the regiment made note of their new commanding officer and not always favorably. Towle recalled that Crowninshield "...was a very nice and easy going and good dispositioned man who would have made a first rate private soldier, but who as an officer wasn't worth the powder to kill him." In all honesty, Crowninshield was a competent leader, but the constant presence of Col. Lowell in camp prevented him from fully assuming the role of a regimental commander.[27]

At the Centerville camp Crowninshield began forming the regiment in his fashion with a light drill schedule and a reorganization of some of the company officers. A death of one of the officers at the Georgetown Hospital and the resignation of another due to poor health required that numerous individuals be promoted to fill the empty billets. When 1st Lt. William Rumery was promoted out of the California Hundred to captain of Company D, his position had to be filled by promoting a second lieutenant. The second lieutenant's position required that a sergeant be advanced and likewise a corporal and a private. This formula had to be followed every time a vacancy was created in the command. Crowninshield's own position as battalion commander had to be filled and Capt. J. Sewall Reed was selected to carry out the duties. This placed two of the three battalions in command of Californians. Reed's spot as commander of the California Hundred was filled by Capt. Francis Washburn of Lancaster; "...a Massachusetts man, is now our Captain, and, so far, is liked very well...."[28]

The new chaplain held his first Sunday service in camp on the 3rd of September. He had called for singers to assist him in the barn where the faithful were to meet and he was pleased when 19 men answered his call. Accompanied by the regiment's 12-piece brass band, his first meeting was a success though he himself admitted he was a poor speaker. "I rely more on the little kindnesses, attentions, and words of cheer of every day than on Sunday preaching...."[29]

After his Sunday service Chaplain Humphreys would go to the brigade hospital and hold abbreviated services in each of the three regimental wings. The sick and wounded were always pleased to see him, for along with his kind words and sympathetic ear he brought books, games, puzzles, and pillows stuffed with milkweed down. He would write letters for those unable to and would notify family and friends of their condition.[30]

In camp he performed similar duties, as well as acting as the regimental postmaster. His tent was always open to the men but he rarely went to the enlisted men's, feeling that their privacy was one of their few treasures. When a man was short on money he knew he could rely on the chaplain for a small loan till payday. "...[T]he loan of a few dollars would frequently relieve distress and always make the men more contented with their lot. I used to have several hundred dollars thus floating around in the regiment, and though much of it got water-logged and sunk never to return, I felt that it had done good service."[31]

A former first bass in the Harvard Glee Club, the chaplain brought his love of song to Centerville and formed a camp quartet. Capt. Reed sang first tenor, backed up by Major Forbes, second tenor. 1st Lt. Goodwin Stone filled out the group as second bass. Often during the late summer evenings the men's voices could be heard from one of the tents "...resounding with laughter and song."[32]

One of the few things that stressed the young chaplain was the frequency of profane language in camp. It distressed him to a degree that he made a point of noting this shocking behavior to Col. Lowell. "I today had to call attention," Lowell wrote Miss Shaw, "...in a general order to the prevalence of profanity in the command,

and at the same time to add that perhaps I had not set them a good example in this respect. I don't swear very much or very deep, — but I do swear, more often at officers than men, and there is a great deal of swearing in the regiment which I wish to check: of course, I shall stop it myself entirely; I shall enforce the Articles of War if necessary...." Apparently the colonel's will was weak, for a few short months later the chaplain wrote a report of the moral and religious condition of the regiment. "I cannot pass down any company street without hearing the name of God either taken lightly in sport or irreverently in a curse. I cannot even sit long in my tent without hearing loudly shouted some imprecation with the name of God thoughtlessly added." If the colonel took the message to heart personally he definitely lost it in the heat of battle. Towle recalled that during a fight in the Shenandoah the next summer, he was acting as an orderly to Lowell who gave him an order to have Lt. Col. Crowninshield move his men into action. The movement was not made to Lowell's satisfaction and he sent Towle back with the message, "god damn you get out of the road."[33]

Pvt. Abraham Loane, Company A, 2nd Massachusetts Cavalry. *Courtesy of Vallejo Naval and Historical Museum.*

During this quiet time at the first week of September, the men were mustered to meet with the paymaster. As always an inspection was held. Major Forbes, in reviewing the men of Company D, was examining a pistol. As he held it up for inspection and cocked it he put his finger on the trigger and the weapon went off. The ball passed through his cap visor. After the initial shock had worn off and it was determined that the major was not shot, he had to deal with the snickering and banter that followed.[34]

Though the pace was significantly slower than in the previous month, scouts and expeditions were still sent out at regular intervals. On the 6th of September, Capt. Rice (who had replaced the luckless DeMerritt of Company F) led out a 45-

man scout northward toward the Potomac. The troopers expected to find some of Major White's men and have some "fun." Major Elijah V. White was the commander of the 35th Virginia Cavalry Battalion nicknamed the "Comanches." A partisan band like Mosby's, White's poorly disciplined men nearly mutinied when they were assigned to a regular cavalry brigade. They were still given frequent opportunities for separate raids, though, and had stepped up their activity in the surrounding area.[35]

Learning from a Negro that White and 12 men were in Leesburg the column rode quietly through town as the inhabitants were coming out of church. Three rebels spotted the cavalry and galloped out of town at a furious rate. The captain held his men back from pursuing, anticipating a trap; but there was no danger, and further down the road they came upon one of the Confederates lying drunk under a tree.[36]

With their inebriated prisoner in tow, the scout pushed on to the Potomac and crossed over to White's Island where they spent the night. The next day was spent riding down the river checking all of the islands for contraband. Stopping for the night at the canal lock at Seneca Falls several of the men acquired some whiskey and picked a fight with a local civilian.[37]

On the third and final day of the trip the column followed the river down to Chain Bridge and crossed back over to the Virginia side. A story passed through the ranks that Lt. Frank Williams of Mosby's command with 20 or 30 men were lying in wait up the road. But the rumor was false and the men returned to Centerville without incident.[38]

On the 10th of September, the long-awaited visit by the paymaster finally occurred. The men had to drill twice before being allowed to line up for their pay and then it took hours before the last man had received his money. By then the gambling was in full swing and in the morning several of the men were already broke. For others cash money meant a trip to the sutler and a break from "army grub." Chaplain Humphreys made it a custom on payday to take money into the city and send it to the men's wives and families.[39]

A few days later there was a commotion in camp that led to the court-martial of Pvt. Michael Keefe (H), Milford. During the proceedings Keefe was unable to justify why he had slung a rock at his sergeant and then compounded his problems by threatening to hit an officer of the 13th New York who intervened. He was also unable to explain why he called the same officer a "son of a bitch," and, as the officer put it, "...[Keefe said] that it was none of my business and that if I meddled with him he would shoot me." Found guilty, Keefe was sentenced to hard labor for the remainder of his term, "...*and to wear a fourteen pound ball with a four foot chain attached to his left leg during the first sixty days of his confinement.*"[40]

Another break in the routine came on the 15th when companies C, F, G, and I were detached for picket duty at Muddy Branch, Maryland, about 20 miles up the Potomac from Washington. In command of the detachment was Capt. Reed who led the men across the Long Bridge through Washington to the government stables. After turning in some broken-down horses, the captain allowed the men to go where they pleased as long as they were back by eight o'clock in the morning. Big mistake. The next morning was spent gathering up drunken troopers, many of whom were so tight they couldn't stay on their horses. Eventually all the men were accounted for and Capt. Reed pushed them on to their new camp along the Chesapeake and Ohio Canal near the mouth of Muddy Branch. After a few days Major Thompson arrived with the regimental doctor, Major DeWolf, and set up battalion headquarters. Tasked with picketing the Potomac from Muddy Branch to the mouth of the Monocacy the men once again fell into a quiet pattern of picket, patrol and camp duty. Having completed his job of setting up the camp, Reed returned to his battalion in Centerville.[41]

It was during this time that problems began to resurface concerning the morale of the Californians. A general feeling of dissatisfaction had been growing in the California companies, a condition that had started from their first days in the east. The California Hundred had been treated well during training at Readville but the battalion had been given the cold shoulder, eclipsed by the popularity of the 54th Massachusetts. The second blow to the morale of the westerners was Lowell's decision to spread the California companies through the three battalions rather than keeping them together. Earlier, in May 1863, the colonel had further alienated his Californians with the issue of his General Order No. 8 which read in part: "Company commanders will see the men wear on the forage cap only the insignia of the corp, and the number and the letter all made by regulations all other letters must be removed before the next parade or inspection, and not again worn either in or out of camp." This directive was aimed specifically at the unique cap badges worn by the Californians.[42]

The officers of the California companies also had their complaints. The four captains of the California Battalion had not been mustered into service until their companies had been recruited to their maximum strength. The Massachusetts officers on the other hand had been commissioned when their companies had obtained minimum allowable strength. Under these conditions all of the California officers (excluding the commander of Company A) were at the bottom of the list for seniority purposes and therefore behind their Massachusetts counterparts in regards to promotions.

Bigger problems were brewing with the senior Californian, Major Thompson. By far the oldest officer among the field and staff and the key player in the raising of the California Battalion, the major had expected a prominent spot in the regimental leadership. With Lt. Col. Russell remaining in Boston till his transfer to the 5th Massachusetts Cavalry there was a gap in the chain of command that should have been filled with one of the three majors. But with one battalion detached at the time to Gloucester Point, Lowell was able to handle the regiment ably without needing to pass on responsibility to a subordinate. When Lowell was appointed to brigade command, leadership of the regiment naturally passed to the senior major, 26-year-old Caspar Crowninshield, much to the dissatisfaction of the older Thompson. The two officers were on such poor terms that when the order to send a battalion to Muddy Branch was received it took little imagination to figure out who would command the detachment. Thompson considered the assignment "banishment" and the California men in the ranks saw this as yet another insult to their pride.

The "mutiny" among the California Hundred back at Gloucester Point had occurred when the men were relatively idle, and those grumblings had ceased when the men were busied with raids and skirmishes. As the regiment fell into a routine of picket and patrols, the Californians once again had ample time to consider their situation. They had volunteered to fight and had expected at the very least to be attached to one of the campaigning armies, not a post searching for bushwhackers and horse thieves. Their distaste for serving with Massachusetts officers and seeing their own major sent off to Maryland led the small core of grumblers to rehash the idea of transferring to another regiment.

Thompson had recently sent his own request to Secretary Stanton, requesting permission to return to California to raise a regiment that would be brought east with himself in command. This was not the first attempt Thompson made to transfer out of the 2nd Massachusetts, having sent the following letter to his friend Lafayette C. Baker, of the 1st D.C. Cavalry.

     Hd Qrs Cav Forces Dept Wash
     Centerville Aug 20th 1863

Col L.C. Baker
Washington

 Colonel
  I see by the papers that there has been some secession troubles in California, and it is reported here that a force of regular troops has been sent there. If this is the case it would be against the interest of California to try to raise troops there to come here, on the contrary the five companies which I have helped raise, now here, should be sent there first, as they intend to return there when discharged, and are ardently devoted to the interest and safety of that State. They were all enlisted there, and are entitled by army regulations to be discharged there, and transportation provided to San Francisco, so the Government would gain by sending them in preference to other troops. A large portion of these companies are composed of the most intelligent, and patriotic young men in California, and would make good officers and non-commissioned officers for new regiments if more should be raised. They have now been in the service about seven months, and came on here intending to do their best for the cause of the country, but if California which they all love so well, is in any danger from rebels within or foreign foes without they would much prefer to go back and fight there, one half of the efficiency of the California Companies has been destroyed by being attached to the 2d Ms Cavalry which is controlled by a small clique of young Boston Aristocracy, who to advance their own personal interests have already broken the agreement, pledges, good faith and honorable obligations of the State of Massachusetts made to us before coming here. The Governor accepted the Battalion as a representative force from California in the war at the East, to remain intact, and be officered and filled by Californians. This Battalion has been broken up by Colonel Lowell, against the protest and wishes of all, two companies remaining with me, and one assigned to each of the other Battalions, whose commanders are personal friends of his, for the purpose of giving them a respectable command, which they had not, and could not get otherwise. There are about four hundred and fifty of our Californians with fourteen officers in the Regiment, while there are about one hundred and fifty Massachusetts soldiers, with some thirty officers including all the Field and Staff but myself, and the officers of seven skeleton companies. All the fighting and important service has been done by the Californians, but Col Lowell and the 2d Ms Cavalry have all the public and official credit given the regiment. As we are doing our country service we do not mind this, but we do not wish to be used and treated by the officers, and in a regiment, of another State, like hirelings for the purpose of making promotions and reputations for officers which we have all become to hate, and despise. It is very hard for the officers and men of these fine companies, who come from California with such high hopes of doing good service for the cause of the Union, and at the same time making a reputation for themselves and their State, to be used as machines to accomplish the aggrandizement of a few officers who do nothing or care nothing for them, or their State, and who have tried to order out and crush out every thing Californian about them. If the War Department could detach these companies from the 2d Ms Cavalry and send them to California where they are anxious to go if there is war in that State, or let them act here as a California Cavalry Battalion which they were raised for I know they would do much more and better service than as they are now, and at the same time an act of justice, and I might say humanity, would be done to a fine and brave body of men and soldiers as ever formed under our Flag. If troops should not be wanted in California seven new companies

could be raised there and join these five and make a splendid regiment here, or they could go there and help form one. The California Companies are designated in the 2d Ms Cavalry as Cos. A, E, F, L and M and any changes should include all officers, and men enrolled, and mustered in California.

Please submit these matters to the Secretary of War and try to do something for us. Every man in California would be glad to see us out of our unfortunate position.

I am Colonel
Most Respt Yours
D.W.C. Thompson
Maj. Cal Cav Batt
2Ms Cav[43]

Knowing that Thompson had sowed some of the seeds of discord among the Californians, Lowell was ready to get rid of his troublesome major. Rather than making an issue of the insubordination, Lowell sent a glowing letter of endorsement to Gen. Halleck supporting Thompson's plan to return to the west (without the five companies) and raise his own regiment; "I am convinced no one could undertake the recruiting of such a regiment with better chance of success than he...." The major's plan was not accepted, but now that Lowell was made aware of the problems festering among the heart of his regiment he made changes to improve their morale.[44]

Despite the ill feelings from some of the Californians, Lowell and Crowninshield had a very high regard for their westerners. When Crowninshield was appointed to lead the regiment his battalion was turned over to Capt. Reed who had earned the respect of all the regimental officers with his competence and bravery. Crowninshield considered him a great friend and Lowell said of him, "Reed is a very good officer, takes the greatest pride in his company...." The other California officers were also highly thought of, prompting Lowell to request that, "In justice to the Captains of the California Battalion of my regiment..." the commissioning dates of Captains Eigenbrodt, Adams and DeMerritt be changed, and so put them in their proper place in the seniority of the regiment's captains. As for the enlisted men, Lowell described them as "...of the class of which our first Eastern regiments were made up — all young, vigorous and zealous — all hating a rebel ... worth three of the ordinary recruits now picked up in our Eastern Cities."[45]

As Lowell and Crowninshield subtly let the Californians know they were appreciated, the grumblings became fainter. Thompson was given free reign as the Commander, Cavalry Forces, Muddy Branch, which consisted of his battalion and 210 men of "Scott's 900."* Far from pleased with the arrangement, Thompson bided his time through the winter waiting for an opportunity to take what he felt was his proper place in the regiment. To his credit, Major Thompson did a competent job in establishing the pickets along a stretch of the Potomac. Pickets were posted from Muddy Branch to the Monocacy with details at the all fords in between. In addition, regular patrols were sent out as far as Great Falls and Chick's Ford.[46]

The bulk of the regiment stayed active out of the Centerville camp. With Mosby recuperating there was little action with the partisan rangers. Raids and scouts now focused on bringing to bay the "Comanches" of the 35th Virginia Cavalry Battalion.

On the 17th of September, Crowninshield set out on a four day raid after White that netted four captured and one rebel drowned. The Yankee commander almost drowned himself — "...while in hot pursuit of the rebs, rolled head over heels in a deep brook. I was not hurt, but slightly moistened."[47]

---

*11th New York Cavalry.

The regiment moved on the 6th of October from Centerville to Fairfax Courthouse, then three days later to Vienna. The camp at Vienna was chosen by Col. Lowell for several reasons: it was easily picketed, there was plenty of fresh water (a must for cavalry), and it could readily be supplied by the Loudoun and Hampshire railroad. Early in the war, the bridge crossing the creek known as Difficult Run was burned, making Vienna the terminus of the line. Though Fairfax County was staunchly secessionist, Vienna was a pocket of Union support due to the large percentage of former New Yorkers who lived throughout the community. During the state referendum on the decision to secede, the vote in Vienna was 78 to 44 in favor of rejecting the ordinance.[48]

Originally settled about 1767 by John Hunter of County Ayr, Scotland, the first building of the community was his home known as Ayr Hill. As other planters settled nearby, the name Ayr Hill was applied to the community as a whole. In the mid–1850s, Peter Hendrick of Vienna, New York, arrived in the area, purchasing over 1,000 acres and quickly becoming one of the largest landowners in the neighborhood. As his hometown in New York was changing its name to Phelps, he used his influence to have Ayr Hill changed to Vienna.[49]

Among the prominent buildings in Vienna was Lydecker's Store, standing adjacent to the railroad and used throughout the war (by both armies) as a stable, officers' quarters, and by Lowell as the brigade hospital. By the time the brigade set up camp, the village had changed hands four times and been camp to ten different Union and Confederate regiments. The 2nd Massachusetts set up its tents on the site of John Hunter's original farm, Col. Lowell establishing his headquarters in Ayr Hill, overlooking the camp. The sibley tents were pitched in their orderly rows, with the lines of stables set between and uncomfortably close to the tents. Majors Crowninshield and Forbes, as well as Capt. Reed and the chaplain, set up their tents on a low ridge at the end of the company streets. The downhill slope of the camp, bordered by the railroad, was eventually protected by an abatis and a wooden stockade.[50]

The First and Second battalions continued the frequent raids after White and Mosby but were also tasked with providing pickets at numerous and ever-changing positions. Raids on the 12th and 18th of October resulted in the capture of a few prisoners that revealed that Mosby had recovered from his wounds and was again actively raiding in Meade's rear.[51]

When Mosby's increased activity was noted, Lowell was ordered to take harsh measures against the inhabitants of Mosby's Confederacy. The orders came from Maj. Gen. Christopher C. Augur, the newly appointed commander of the XXII Corps and the Department of Washington, and instructed Lowell to burn the houses of all persons actively assisting Mosby or White. In the next month Lowell burned a total of one house and two mills. The owner of the house was captured wearing the Confederate uniform but was a known murderer and thief. The duty of burning houses was distasteful to Lowell and the incident compelled him to write his foe. "I wrote Mosby saying that it was not the intention to burn the houses of any men for simply belonging to his command.... I shall probably have to burn other houses, but it will be done with all possible consideration." Never an advocate of total war, the philosophical Lowell was one of a dying breed of romantic cavaliers, though he would never see it in himself. He had the authority to put the torch to the area but the tactic was so unsavory it probably never occurred to him to use it as more than an occasional warning. An honorable man in an inglorious job, Lowell managed to see similar traits in his adversary. "... Mosby is an honorable foe, and should be treated as such." Mosby, however, saw himself in a completely different light, which explains why he so often prevailed against Lowell. "In one respect the charge that I did not fight fair is true. I fought for success, and not for display. There was no man in the Confederate Army who had less of the Spirit of Knighthood in him or who took a more practical view of war than I did." But Col. Lowell's chivalrous actions and constant patrols made a lasting impression on Mosby, who later wrote, "I have often said that, of all the Federal commanders opposed to me, I had the highest respect for Colonel Lowell, both as an officer and a gentleman."[52]

On the 22nd of October, Capt. Charles Eigenbrodt of Company E took a detachment of his men and joined with a small force of the 1st D.C. Cavalry for a raid. Along the Little River Turnpike near Fairfax Courthouse the force was tipped off by a civilian that a small band of Rangers was planning to steal some Federal horses from a nearby camp. Approaching quietly through a heavy thicket, the Union soldiers were within 50 yards of the five rebels before they were discovered. The Confederates fled but their exhausted horses were quickly run down. The fight was over in moments. The guerrilla Charles Mason was killed outright and three others were captured. Lt. Frank Williams, though wounded, managed to ride his horse alongside a fence and spring from the saddle to the dense cover on the other side. Despite a search by the Yankees he managed to evade them and escape on foot.[53]

One of the prisoners, Robert Harrover of Company D, was taken to Washington where a military commission found him guilty of desertion and sentenced him to be shot. His sentence was commuted to ten years by the president, but Harrover had no intention of languishing in a Federal prison. Shortly before his scheduled transfer to the Albany Penitentiary, he and another prisoner tied blankets together and lowered themselves out of a second story window to the street below. Unnoticed by the patrolling guards the two disappeared into the night, and with the assistance of friends in the city were soon back with their comrades in Virginia.[54]

The last week of October was quiet enough for Lowell to take a short leave from his brigade. On the 31st, Charles Lowell and Josephine Shaw were married at Staten Island, New York. There was not time for a honeymoon and in a matter of days the newlyweds had set up their home in Ayr Hill adjoining the cavalry camp. Not one to sit quietly waiting for her husband to return each evening, Mrs. Lowell was constantly busy helping in the brigade hospital or around the camp. She was a great help to Chaplain Humphreys who recorded, "With the foreigners in the hospital, I was greatly assisted by the wife of the commander, who visited the patients very frequently. She delighted the Frenchmen, Italians, and Germans, by conversing with them in their own languages, that so vividly recalled their early homes. She often assisted in writing letters for the disabled soldiers, and when I sought to give comfort to the dying, her presence soothed the pangs of parting, with a restful consciousness of woman's faithful watching and a mother's tenderness."[55]

Forty years after the war, one of the colonel's troopers wrote Mrs. Lowell, fondly recalling her presence in camp. "I remember you well, when you came to Camp at Vienna the bride of our gallant Colonel. I see you to-day in my mind's eye, making your daily trip to the hospital, in wet weather equipped in a waterproof and little gum boots; the boys appreciated that and it was fully commented on in quarters."[56]

Private Charlie Binns was drunk the night he had a falling out with Mosby, and rather than wait for his punishment he slipped out of camp and deserted to the enemy. Binns had no intention of landing in a Yankee prison camp and offered to lead the 2nd Massachusetts Cavalry against his old comrades in exchange for his freedom. Col. Lowell accepted Binns' services, and on the 18th of November a raid set out with Binns and Alexander "Yankee" Davis as guides. (Davis, a known Union man, had a farm on the Little River Turnpike near Aldie.)

Capt. William Rumery, a 39-year-old former bricklayer from California, led the 100-man detachment toward the Blue Ridge Mountains. Seventy-five of the men marched dismounted, keeping off the roads and moving only at night, while the remaining 25 rode only during the day, scouting out the farms and houses along the way. It was questionable whether Binns was helping the Yankees or leading them into a trap. Pvt. Wells West, along with privates Valorus Dearborn, and "Bray," were detailed to keep an eye on Binns, with orders to shoot him if he betrayed them.

The march set off in a westerly direction avoiding the main roads. Capt. Rumery hit upon the idea that Binns might be a little more talkative if he had some whiskey to loosen his tongue. The result was that the captain had a much lower tol-

Captain William M. Rumery, Company D, 2nd Massachusetts Cavalry. *Courtesy of U.S.A.M.H.I.*

erance for alcohol than Binns and was soon feeling the effects. Binns was playing it straight, however, and began pointing out homes where he knew Rangers were staying. Details were detached to each house in turn but no Rangers were found. Unfortunately Mosby had called his men together for a raid against the Orange and Alexandria Railroad and 75 men had answered his call. At midnight Rumery, now thoroughly drunk, called a halt and the dismounted troopers bedded down for the night. Rumery passed out under a tree and was soon joined by Binns who had managed to consume a good deal of liquor himself. Pvt. West recalled the scene years later. "It was nip and tuck which could carry the biggest load of booze, the captain or Bins [sic]. Bray also liked his dram. All three of them went to sleep soon after we went into camp. Then Dearborn and I got the whiskey bottle and smashed it."[57]

The next evening the dismounted men set off again and spent the night marching and searching homes, again with no success. On the third night the tactics began to pay off. "We captured our first prisoners—five of Mosby's men," recalled West. "They were in the attic of a cabin occupied by one woman. All were armed with revolvers. Rummery concluded that Bins was all right and we were relieved from guarding him but were given another task. We marched two abreast: two of our men, then a man with a prisoner—the man holding the prisoner's right hand with his left, with his revolver in his right hand." By morning Rumery had 23 prisoners.[58]

After three nights of searching, the word had finally gotten out what the Yankees were up to and small parties of Rangers began to skirmish with the force but declined to attack them outright. The fighting resulted in the death of one of the Rangers. Later that morning a rendezvous was made near Rector's Cross Roads with Col. Lowell who led 150 men from the 2nd Massachusetts and the 16th New York Cavalry. Rumery passed on all he had learned during the march and the colonel divided his force into four detachments to scour the area in all directions. By midnight the forces met up again near Mount Zion Church, ending the raid. Lowell was able to claim 18 uniformed prisoners who claimed to be Mosby's men, seven "notorious smugglers and horse-thieves," 35 horses, and one dead Confederate. There were no Union casualties. Colonel Lowell was pleased with the results of the raid, giving praise to Rumery in his official report and sought to have Binns recognized as a scout entitled to full pay.[59]

Anxious to get back to his wife at camp, Lowell, with the advance guard as escort, put his horse to a hard gallop and kept the pace for nearly the entire 30-mile, 3½ hour ride. The main body, with prisoners in tow, arrived in camp the next night, waiting till the next morning to take the captured to Washington. "A sad accident happened to one of our men detailed to guard the prisoners," recalled Pvt. Barnstead, "the night they remained in our camp. Wilson was his name, and was a member of Company L, California Battalion. Standing in the doorway of the loghouse in which the prisoners were confined, resting the butt of the carbine on the door sill, (a log a foot through,) and leaning his breast upon the muzzle, the carbine slipped from the sill, striking the hammer as it went, exploding the cap, and the charge entered his breast, just over the heart, coming out under the shoulder blade, on the back, causing his death in a few moments."*[60]

Moved to Muddy Branch, Maryland, in September, Major Thompson continued to stay under the skin of Col. Lowell through the efforts of Pvt. Thomas M. Merry, a correspondent for the *Daily Alta California*. Beginning in May, Merry's letters list a stream of grievances against Massachusetts, the regiment, and frequently, the military abilities of Col. Lowell. His initial complaints dealt with the use of State bounty money to finance the battalion's transportation east. His hint of

---

*Frederick Wilson (L), California.

financial scamming between Amos Lawrence and Ira Rankin drew a sharp retort by Rankin in the *Evening Bulletin*, and led Merry to amend his complaints and focus on the Massachusetts officers, especially Col. Lowell. When expressing his thoughts that Mosby's men should be fought like Indians, he adds, "...but Col. Lowell will never do it, for all the knowledge he possesses of fighting Indians or guerrillas has been acquired by reading Sylvanius Cobb's stories in the *New York Ledger*, while burning the 'midnight oil' at Harvard, but what is difficult in this, he more than makes up in his knowledge of dress parades and policing camps." He also writes, "We have just reason to complain of the Colonel that the State chose to command the regiment. Col. Lowell has done all in his power to spite us, both officers and men...."[61]

At the same time that Merry's insubordination was reaching its height in the western press, reports came to Lowell's attention that Thompson's camp was in a terrible state of neglect. On the 9th of November, Major Thompson was ordered to Vienna to make a full explanation of the state of his command. Capt. Holman was dispatched to inspect the camp at Muddy Branch, and Major Forbes, temporarily replacing Thompson, took the opportunity to inspect the camp of the detachment from the 11th New York Cavalry. Both reports condemned conditions at Muddy Branch, Forbes writing, "...that the det. from 'Scott's Nine Hundred' were in a very demoralized and undisciplined state.... Capt. Ellsworth in command of the Battalion frequently intoxicated and always neglecting his duties."[62]

Thompson was able to explain to Lowell's satisfaction that all was well in Maryland, and three days later was back at work at his post. One incident resulting from the inquiries was the revelation that Merry was responsible for the articles in the *Daily Alta*.[63]

On the 13th, as Thompson was returning to Maryland, Merry was ordered by Crowninshield to return for duty to his company at Vienna. Thompson immediately protested to Col. Lowell stating, "...no other soldier can be well spared for such duty who is competent." Crowninshield retorted that Merry "...be ordered to his company at Vienna as he has availed himself of opportunities to disturb the good order of the Regt & his continuance on Det. Ser. is undesirable." That afternoon Merry crossed the Potomac and resumed his duties with Company L.[64]

As all of these events transpired around them, starting with the transfer of Thompson's battalion to Maryland, the die-hard core of grumblers within the California contingent attempted to take matters into their own hands. A petition was drafted requesting the five companies from San Francisco be transferred to "Col. Baker's Rangers" (the 1st D.C. Cavalry), and sent off to the secretary of war. The petition made its way to Governor Andrew, who in turn sent it to Lowell requesting he investigate. Naturally Thompson was questioned about the matter and was ordered to reply as to his knowledge of the event.

> Headquarters Cav. Forces Nr. Potomac
> Muddy Branch Dec 3rd 1863
>
> Col. C.R. Lowell
> 2d Ms Cavalry
>
> Colonel
> In compliance with your request that I should furnish you a statement in writing of what information I had in relation to certain petitions from the men in five Cal companies in 2d Ms Cavalry to be transferred to Col Bakers Rangers I have the honor to report that the first I heard of them was on the 27 of Nov when I was in Washington by order of Maj. Gen Augur to make arrangements in relation to the Maryland election. On that day I met Sergeant Williams of Co. E on the sidewalk. He was on his way to Baltimore to

vote. I asked him what the Cavalry forces at Vienna were doing and how the Cal companies were. He told me generally then informed me that the Cal companies had sent petitions to the Secretary of War to be transferred to Col Bakers Rangers. I asked him if the officers had signed them and he told me no that it was intended that they should not join the men in the matter, and had not been consulted about the petition or words to that effect. On the 5th Nov Capt Eigenbrodt had returned from the election at Clarksburg with his company he informed me that the Cal men had sent petitions to the Secretary of War to be transferred to Col Bakers Rangers and I think he said that the officers had not taken in part in the matter.
About the same time my orderly private White of Co. E informed me that some of the men had told him that the Californians had petitioned the Secretary of War to be transferred to Col Bakers Rangers. This was told him when he was in Washington with me on the 2 Nov or at my camp by men who came over from your camp during election about the 4th or 5th of Nov. I don't know which. One of the Cal companies (Co. "F") is attached to my command but I did not see or here of any such petition being signed in my camp and did not know of any such having been signed or sent to the Secretary of War until Capt Washburn came to my camp to investigate the matter unless I inferred it from the general information I have received that the Cal companies had sent such petitions. I was not informed or consulted in relation to the petitions and gave them little thought as I was constantly engaged with my military duties and supposed they had been sent to the Secretary of War he would either approve or reject them and that would end the matter.

I am Colonel
Most Respt Yours
D.W.C. Thompson
Maj. 2 Ms Cav
Comdg Post[65]

Interesting letter. At one point he says he knew of the petition on the 2nd of November and at another claims he is unaware until the 27th. Informed of the action by three different subordinates he at no time thinks to pass on the information to his commanding officer, but sat on it in hope that Secretary Stanton would agree to the transfer. As critical as Major Thompson had been of the Massachusetts clique, his own actions as a subordinate (including his letter to Col. Baker back in August) were rebellious and bordered on being seditious. But there was more to come from the troublesome major.

Regimental problems aside, the task at hand was to deal with guerrillas, and this went on without pause. During the next few weeks Lowell continued to send out dismounted patrols but the Rangers were not to be tricked again so soon, and the raids netted little. The Rangers on the other hand had begun to systematically attack the brigade's pickets in an effort to replace their own run down horses. On the 13th the picket at Germantown (men of the 13th or 16th New York Cavalry), was surprised by a force of some 20 guerrillas. Two pickets were mortally wounded and five horses captured, the Confederates disappearing into the night. A week later Col. Lowell reported that a force of 20 or 30 guerrillas attacked one of his picket posts wounding four men and carrying off four horses. The same night an officer and an enlisted man were set upon and wounded by the Rangers. "One of the wounded men, near Hunter's Mill, was shot a second time through the body by a guerrilla, after he had surrendered and given up his pistol." The wounded man, Pvt. Oscar Burnap (E), New York, was shot through the chest but miraculously survived. Another Californian wounded that night was Pvt. Seth Cooper (M), Iowa Hills, California, who took a bullet that entered above his left ear, ricocheted off his skull, through his neck and lodged above the left lung. Cooper survived and refusing a discharge, made the grade for the Veteran Reserve Corps.[66]

With several men killed or wounded a change was made to the routine governing the pickets. Pvt. Towle who frequently stood picket recalled, "During the winter at Vienna those not detailed on scouting expeditions were usually detailed on either camp guard, picket duty or patrol duty every other day and night and our pickets were very frequently bushwhacked at night by men of the confederate cavalry who had lost their mount and took that means of securing a horse. Because of that the picket was required to stand dismounted, the horses of the first detail so being returned to camp and after the pickets relieved would ride them back to camp. It was very cold much of the time and because of that the men on picket were often relieved every hour. As a result of this continuous duty I, on one occasion, was very much in need of a good nights sleep. In order to secure that I applied for a pass to Washington, and after securing that I went to my tent and went to sleep. In the afternoon the orderly sergeant wanted to detail me on picket duty, but I showed him the pass and convinced him that I was in Washington and so escaped such detail. That was the only time that I ever maneuvered to escape duty."

Despite the lack of results with the dismounted raids, Col. Lowell continued to send them out and in the last week of December his persistence paid off. A raid through White Plains, Middleburg, Philomont and Dranesville netted a few prisoners but the real success came during a skirmish with a squad of Rangers that resulted in several Confederates captured and one killed. Another fight, this time with what Lowell believed was a company of the Black Horse Cavalry, added to the haul of prisoners. The colonel was able to report, "We captured a lieutenant and several of the men from it. We have brought in 1 captain, 1 lieutenant, 17 privates (10 of them being Mosby's men, the others of the Fourth, Eighth, and Twelfth Virginia Cavalry); also 10 citizens and 1 rebel forage contractor, all connected to be with Mosby or with the Fourth Virginia.... I have to report 1 man of the Second Massachusetts Cavalry wounded (not seriously), and 1 man captured carrying a dispatch."[67]

Notes

1. OR, XXVII, Pt. 2, p. 989; *Daily Alta California*, Sept. 28, 1863.
2. Backus, "Californians in the Field," *MOLLUS.*, p. 9; Emerson, *Life and Letters*, p. 416.
3. Towle, *Recollections*, p. 10.
4. Bonney, *Battledrums and Geysers*, pp. 8–15.
5. Roberts, *Diary*, Aug. 7, 1863; *Daily Alta California*, Sept. 28, 1863.
6. OR, XXVII, Pt. 2, p. 992.
7. OR, XXIX, Pt. 2, pp. 968–69.
8. Roberts, *Diary*, Aug. 15–18, 1863; OR, XXIX, Pt. 1, pp. 75–76.
9. Roberts, *Diary*, Aug. 18, 1863.
10. Roberts, *Diary*, Aug. 19, 1863.
11. OR, XXIX, Pt. 2, p. 969.
12. Crowninshield, Aug. 21, 1863.
13. Crawford, *Mosby and His Men*, pp. 99–100; Scott, *Partisan Life with Mosby*, p. 121.
14. *Boston Journal*, Sept. 4, 1863.
15. Hunt, *Army of the Pacific*, p. 293; *National Tribune*, Oct. 1, 1883.
16. Wert, *Mosby's Rangers*, p. 96; *Daily Alta California*, Sept. 28, 1863.
17. Corbett, *Diary*, Aug. 24, 1863; Crawford, *Mosby and His Men*, pp. 99–101; Hunt, *Army of the Pacific*, p. 294; Kirsch and Murphy, *West of the West*, p. 383; *Massachusetts Soldiers, Sailors, and Marines*, Vol. VI, pp. 238–328; Orton, *Record of California Men in the War of the Rebellion 1861–1867*, p. 849; Scott, *Partisan Life with Mosby*, pp. 120–21; Wert, *Mosby's Rangers*, pp. 95–96; Williamson, *Mosby's Rangers*, pp. 87–89; OR, XXIX, Pt. 2, pp. 80–81; National Archives, Record Group 94, Co. A muster roll, June 30 to Aug. 30, 1863, Pension Record of Nathan Beach; *Boston Saturday Evening Gazette*, Aug. 29, 1863; *Daily Alta California*, Sep. 28, Oct. 4, 1863; *National Tribune*, Oct. 4, Nov. 8, 1883.
18. Crawford, *Mosby and His Men*, p. 101.
19. Roberts, *Diary*, Aug. 25, 1863; Williamson, *Mosby's Rangers*, p. 90.
20. Crowninshield, Aug. 25, 1863; National Archives, Record Group 94, DeMerritt Service Record; Roberts, *Diary*, Aug. 25, 1863.

21. Emerson, *Life and Letters*, p. 441; *OR*, XXIX, Pt. 2, pp. 98–99; *Boston Journal*, Aug. 21, 1863; *New York Tribune*, Sept. 1, 1863.
22. National Archives, Record Group 94, 2nd Massachusetts Cavalry Regimental record box, Special Order #380, War Dept., Adjutant Gen. Office, Aug. 25, 1863.
23. Humphreys, *Field and Camp*, p. 371.
24. Emerson, *Life and Letters*, p. 229; Humphreys, *Field and Camp*, pp. 369, 371–72.
25. Crowninshield, Aug. 25, 1863.
26. Crowninshield, Aug. 25, 1863.
27. Towle, *Recollections*, p. 5.
28. *Daily Alta California*, Sept. 28, 1863.
29. Humphreys, *Field and Camp*, pp. 16, 372.
30. Humphreys, *Field and Camp*, pp. 10, 14.
31. Humphreys, *Field and Camp*, p. 6.
32. Humphreys, *Field and Camp*, pp. 4, 303.
33. Emerson, *Life and Letters*, p. 301; Humphreys, *Field and Camp*, pp. 385–89; Towle, *Recollections*, p. 17.
34. Roberts, *Diary*, Aug. 31, 1863.
35. Roberts, *Diary*, Sept. 6, 1863.
36. Roberts, *Diary*, Sept. 6, 1863.
37. Roberts, *Diary*, Sept. 7, 1863.
38. Roberts, *Diary*, Sept. 8, 1863.
39. Humphreys, *Field and Camp*, p. 6; Roberts, *Diary*, Sept. 10, 1863.
40. National Archives, Records Group No. 94, Independent Cavalry Brigade records, Dept. of Washington, Court Martial proceedings of Pvt. Michael Keefe.
41. Roberts, *Diary*, Sept. 16–17, 1863; National Archives, Record Group 94, Independent Cavalry Brigade records, Dept. of Washington, Special Orders #30.
42. National Archives, Record group 94, Co. A Order Book, General Order #8, May 23, 1863.
43. National Archives, Record group 393, Thompson to Baker, Aug. 20, 1863.
44. National Archives, Record Group 94, Lowell to Halleck, Aug. 22, 1863.
45. Emerson, *Life and Letters*, p. 290; National Archives, Record Group 94, 2nd Massachusetts Cavalry Regimental records box, Lowell to Halleck Aug. 27, 1863, Lowell to Thomas Sept. 7, 1863.
46. National Archives, Record group 94, Report of Capt. Charles Horton, Oct. 18, 1863; Thompson to Lowell, Dec. 14, 1863.
47. Crowninshield, Sept. 23, 1863.
48. Stuntz, *This Was Vienna, Virginia*, pp. 94, 105, 117; National Archives, Record Group 94, Lowell to Taylor, 2 Oct., 1863.
49. Stuntz, *This Was Vienna, Virginia*, pp. 20, 103.
50. Harrison, "The Sojourn of the Second Massachusetts Cavalry in Vienna," *Northern Virginia Heritage*, June 1985, p. 11; Stuntz, *This Was Vienna, Virginia*, p. 107.
51. Crowninshield, Oct. 14, 1863; *OR*, XXIX, Pt. 2, pp. 350, 480–81.
52. Emerson, *Life and Letters*, pp. 312–13, 437; Higginson, "Lowell," p. 314.
53. Williamson, *Mosby's Rangers*, pp. 100–01; *OR*, XXIX, p. 494; National Archives, Record Group 94, Co. E muster roll, Aug. 31 to Oct. 31, 1863.
54. Williamson, *Mosby's Rangers*, p. 101.
55. Emerson, *Life and Letters*, p. 445; Greenslet, *The Lowells and Their Seven Worlds*, p. 251.
56. Greenslet, *The Lowells and Their Seven Worlds*, p. 252.
57. West, Autobiography of Wells Wallace West, p. 6: hereafter cited as West, Autobiography.
58. West, Autobiography, p. 6; *OR*, XXIX, Pt. 2, p. 658.
59. *Daily Alta California*, Dec. 29, 1863.
60. *Boston Journal*, Nov. 28, 1863; *Daily Alta California*, Dec. 29, 1863.
61. *Daily Alta California*, May 30 and Oct. 4, 1863.
62. National Archives, Record Group 94, Independent Cavalry Brigade, Dept. of Wash., Special Orders #51 and 52; Letters Received, Cavalry Camp, Dept. of Wash., 16 Nov, 1863, Report of Major Forbes.
63. National Archives, Record Group 94, Independent Cavalry Brigade, Dept. of Wash., Special Order #54.
64. National Archives, Record Group 94, Letters received, Cavalry Camp, Dept. of Wash., Nov. 13, 1863, Major Crowninshield; Nov. 14, 1863, Major Thompson; Nov. 20, 1863, Major Crowninshield.
65. National Archives, Record Group 94, 2nd Massachusetts Cavalry Regimental record box, letter dated 3 Dec., 1863, Thompson to Lowell.
66. Corbett, *Diary*, Dec. 20, 1863; Emerson, *Life and Letters*, p. 447; *OR*, XXIX, Pt. 2, pp. 471, 652; *Medical and Surgical History of the Civil War*, Vol. VIII, pp. 585–86.
67. Emerson, *Life and Letters*, p. 448; *OR*, XXIX, Pt. 2, pp. 994–95; National Archives, Record Group 94, Company A muster roll, Oct. 31 to Dec. 31, 1863.

Chapter Seven

Dranesville

"Again has another year commenced to join its ages with the past and the record of the old year is written with all its joys and sorrows." So began the first entry in the 1864 diary of Pvt. Valorus Dearborn. Dearborn kept a very precise diary, always starting his entries with his expenditures and any income followed by a weather report. Next would come camp news, gossip, and mention of letters received and written. Valorus had a girl back home in San Francisco named Sue and her letters brought happiness to a very lonely man. At least they did until Sue's letters turned cold. The reader can feel his heart breaking each time he received a letter that did not hold the words of reconciliation that he longed for. Dearborn would never make amends with his lady. His diary ends suddenly in September; his last entry was the 11th of September, the day before he was killed in the Shenandoah Valley.[1]

Pvt. Samuel J. Corbett made no special New Year's entry in his diary. His first entry wasn't until the 10th of January and it heralded the arrival of Mr. Henry Fries, a Boston musician who was to be the leader of the regimental band. Back in October Corbett wrote in his diary, "Was presented with an E flat Alto Horn, with the request that I should join a Regimental Band the Officers are getting up." The band consisted of about 15 men who built their own quarters and stables, and slept together in stockaded sibley tents. The band played for Chaplain Humphreys' services and occasionally would serenade before the tents of the brigade officers.[2]

The first few weeks of January were bitterly cold and were especially hard on the pickets, several of who had hands and feet frozen. The severe weather curtailed any scouts or raids, and for a few brief weeks the men enjoyed winter quarters. Planks were scavenged from nearby homes (to the dismay of their owners) and used to floor and stockade the tents. Dearborn had been a carpenter before the war and his services were frequently sought out by the officers. He helped Capt. Reed, Chaplain Humphreys, and Lt. Meader with their quarters, and then passed the time making saber knots which he gave away to the men.[3]

During this lull in activity several men and officers were transferred out of the command for commissions in other Massachusetts regiments. Eleven officers of the 5th Massachusetts Cavalry (colored) came from the 2nd Massachusetts Cavalry including their new colonel, Harry Russell, who had been the lieutenant colonel of

Officers of 2nd Regiment, Massachusetts Volunteer Cavalry (l. to r.): unknown private, Capt. Francis Washburne, Surgeon Oscar De Wolf, Capt. Louis Cabot, Capt. Lewis Dabney, Capt. John T. Richards, Col. Caspar Crowninshield, Lt. Col. Henry S. Russell, Col. Charles R. Lowell, Capt. Charles E. Rice, Capt. Goodwin A. Stone, Major William H. Forbes, unknown private, 1st Lt. Charles Payson. *Courtesy of Richard K. Tibbals Collection, U.S.A.M.H.I.*

the 2nd. Of the four officers sent to the 4th Massachusetts Cavalry, Lt. Col. Francis Washburn would receive a promotion to brigadier general for his service at the High Bridge on April 6th, 1865, where he was mortally wounded. In all some 36 men transferred out of the 2nd Massachusetts Cavalry for commissions in other commands, 25 of them to Negro regiments.[4]

By the 12th, the weather had abated enough to send out a small scout. They returned the next day with four prisoners in tow and soon another detail was sent out in search of rebels. By the 15th, details were coming and going, dispatched in all directions. "It is easy to give in detail the movements of an infantry regiment," wrote Capt. Henry Alvord, "but with a regiment of cavalry it is impossible. Besides the regular picket and patrol duty, there are every-day escorts and scouting parties sent out, differing in strength and for different lengths of time. These details and expeditions, of different kinds, make up the work of a cavalry regiment; and it would be an endless task to speak of them all."[5]

On one of the many scouts, William Ormsby, a 24-year-old private from Company E, met a young Southern woman and was smitten. Unable to see her again he contemplated deserting in order to be with her. Ormsby felt he had every reason to go and no reason to stay. One of the original Company E members from San Francisco, "Pony," so called for his previous days as a Pony Express rider, had a grudge against his regiment and his officers.*[6]

In November, Ormsby had been court-martialed for selling his horse while on a pass and returning to camp on a

---

*Though several accounts credit his being a rider, rosters of the Pony Express riders do not include a William Ormsby. Either he rode under an alias or quite possibly rode for a smaller local service.

"...worthless animal entirely unfit for service...." Several witnesses were called for the defense and the prosecution, testifying to the condition of the animals and the practice of trading horses within the company. Though claiming innocence, Ormsby was found guilty of the charges and ordered to forfeit $6.50 of pay per month for four months.[7]

On another occasion Ormsby supposedly captured two Rebels singlehandedly, and when bringing them back to the command one of the prisoners was able to escape. Ormsby was accused of taking a bribe from the escaped prisoner and though no charges were actually filed he spent the next month in the guardhouse.[8]

"Oppressed, goaded, and life made a torment by Wm. C. Manning 1st Lieut of the company," recalled Pvt. Mortimer, "punished and kept in the Guard House a large potion of the time on slight pretexts, he having at one time been orderly to this officer and in several ways incurred his enmity and he hounded him to his death." Mortimer and Ormsby, both small and slight of stature, were known as "the little fellows" of the company.[9]

On the 24th of January, while standing picket at Lewinsville, Ormsby convinced himself it was time to leave and deserted, taking with him his carbine, equipment and horse. Not only did he commit the sin of desertion, he compounded it by joining up with Mosby's Rangers. He didn't actually enlist with the Rangers but to prevent being sent to a prison camp, he agreed to act as a guide against the local federal troops.[10]

Two weeks after he deserted, Ormsby, wearing a Confederate uniform, led a detachment of Mosby's men on a raid against what he thought was the 13th or 16th New York but was actually his own regiment. A column of the 2nd Massachusetts was passing through Aldie when the Confederates charged with Ormsby in the front rank. The attack was quickly beaten back with no casualties on either side. The guerrillas left Ormsby to his own devices as they melted away into the woods.[11]

Ormsby fled on foot closely pursued by a squad of horsemen. He attempted to escape by jumping across a small stream but was tackled roughly from behind. The surprise and shame must have washed over his face when he found it was members of his own company that had taken him down. The fight gone from him, Ormsby was bound and put on a horse for the return to the Vienna camp.

The column arrived early the next morning and before evening a drumhead court-martial had been convened. Ormsby requested that Chaplain Humphreys speak in his defense. The chaplain agreed but knew it was little more than a gesture to the man; the crime was unforgivable and everyone involved knew it. Serving as prosecutor was Capt. Lewis Dabney of Company D, a Harvard law student and future leader of the Boston bar. The chaplain made his plea stressing Ormsby's youth and the beauty of the Southern belle that tempted him. A sentence of death was inevitable, and soon the verdict was delivered; the condemned man was then led to the guardhouse to await his fate.[12]

At eleven the next morning the brigade was formed on three sides of a hollow square to witness the execution. The band played a funeral dirge, marching at a solemn pace, followed by four men carrying the coffin. Next came the firing squad of 12 men, and, last of all, Ormsby. When all were in their proper places the chaplain offered up a prayer and the condemned man was asked if he had anything to say. Chaplain Humphreys recalled his words. "Comrades! I want to acknowledge that I am guilty and that my punishment is just. But I want also that you should know that I did not desert because I lost faith in our cause. I believe we are on the right side, and I think it will succeed. But take warning from my example, and whatever comes do not desert the old flag for which I am proud to die." Turning to Col. Lowell he asked his forgiveness, then turned to the firing squad, put his hand on his chest and said, "Boys, I hope you will fire well." The chaplain tied a handkerchief around his eyes, shook his hand and sat him on the end of his coffin. Eleven loaded carbines pointed at his chest fired in a volley sending Ormsby to his maker. The 12th carbine had a blank cartridge, allowing each of the riflemen the chance to believe he had not fired one of the fatal rounds.[13]

It was an unusual move for Lowell to call the drumhead court-martial considering how close he was to his departmental commander in Washington. The drumhead was only to be used in cases of emergency when a subordinate officer was not in communication with his superiors. The colonel reported his actions, after the fact, to Gen. Augur who in turn reported them to Secretary Stanton. Expecting to be reprimanded, Lowell never heard an official word about the matter. The 2nd Massachusetts was still taking losses from bounty jumpers and Lowell had sent out the strongest message on what would happen to deserters from his brigade. President Lincoln had a tendency to pardon condemned men; the young colonel knew this and never gave him the chance. The silence from Stanton and Augur was a sign of their approval.[14]

The first week of February brought a welcome break to the weather and for a few weeks it seemed as though spring had come. Though the Yankee patrols continued, there were no raids or attacks by the Confederates. "We are very quiet here now no alarms & no Mosby," wrote Crowninshield. It was so quiet that Gen. Augur ordered Lowell to take command of the Cavalry Depot at Giesboro Point. To the southeast of Washington, just across the Eastern Branch of the Potomac, the depot supplied the remounts for all of the Eastern departments. While Lowell was detached, command of the Brigade passed to Col. Lazelle of the 16th New York Cavalry.[15]

The scouts and patrols were becoming routine and there was no reason to suspect anything out of the ordinary when Capt. Reed led a detachment of 128 men out on a scout through Loudoun County. The 2nd Massachusetts Cavalry provided 111 of the men, mostly from companies B, E, and M with the 16th New York providing a detachment of 17 troopers under Lt. Cannon of that regiment. Reed led his men out the Little River Turnpike to Middleburg, north to Leesburg, and planned to return to camp down the Leesburg and Alexandria or Dranesville Pike.[16]

On the 21st, Mosby learned of Reed's scout while preparing a report of his recent actions. About 160 Rangers had gathered at Piedmont for the funeral of one of their own, a Pvt. McCobb, and were quickly in the saddle ready to pursue the Yankees. Mosby sent a few men in advance to ascertain Reed's location while the remainder of the men rode to Middleburg with the intention of striking the Federals before they returned to their Vienna camp. At Middleburg, Mosby learned the enemy had pressed on down the Dranesville Pike and gone into camp for the night at a farm just east of Goose Creek. The Rangers quietly closed the gap between the forces and set plans for an ambush.[17]

During the night a 150 man scout from the 16th New York joined Reed's men in their roadside bivouac, and in the morning Major Frazier's column rode with Reed in his march down the pike. Mosby had posted his men to the north of Dranesville near Anker's (or Anchor's) blacksmith shop. To the west of his position, where the Pike crosses Broad Run, there was a fork in the road, the other road leading south to Guilford Station. Knowing the combined column was too big to attack, he could only watch and wait. When the Federals reached the fork Major Frazier led the New Yorkers down the "country road" while Reed with his 128 men continued down the Pike toward Dranesville.[18]

Riding in their normal marching formation the 2nd Massachusetts was led by an advance of four men, followed 100 paces behind by a sergeant with 14 men, then by the remainder of the column 300 paces behind. The formation was a good one for scouting the roads, but was flawed if an attack came from either flank. Mosby's scouts had observed the Yankee marching order the day before and had planned accordingly.[19]

About two miles before Dranesville, near a small creek known as Sugarland Run, a thick stand of pines ran along the Pike. Mosby posted his men inside the cover of the trees and placed them in positions to hit Reed in the front, rear, and flank simultaneously. The signal to charge was left with Ranger Richard Mountjoy in the center of the line with 15 dismounted men armed with carbines. The Rangers held their breath as Reed's men walked their horses right into the trap.[20]

Mosby had posted three men in the road to act as bait, hopefully causing the advance guard to charge, thus leading the van into the jaws of the trap. As it happened, when the advance guard saw the Confederates in the road they did not charge but halted and were calling back to the column that enemy riders were in sight. The column was riding down a gentle slope and came to a halt when the advance guard sighted the Confederates. The Yankee column had stopped just short of the perfect position for Mosby to launch his attack. The decision to attack or to wait for the Federals to fully enter the trap couldn't be delayed, with every moment increasing the possibility of Mosby's men being discovered.[21]

Before Mosby could decide, Mountjoy's carbines tore into the front of the column and Capt. Frank Williams and Capt. William Chapman charged their companies, "...with a terrific yell..." into the front and center of Reed's column. "At first the Federals made a hot fight, but, unable to withstand the impetuosity of our charge, they broke and fled in every direction...." Mosby himself described the action. "Surprised and confounded, with no time to form, they made but feeble resistance...."[22]

Reed had no chance to form his men and the only response was in small isolated pockets. The end of the Federal column was actually on Chapman's flank and made a tough fight for a few minutes. "[Reed's] Californians, especially notoriously good fighters, were standing up to the rack like men, dealing out to us the best they had. They rallied at every call on them and went down with banners flying." But too much of the command had fled and Mosby's superior numbers were showing. Some of the men fled back in the direction of Leesburg while others raced north toward the Potomac, the only direction free of Rangers. The Rebels later claimed that several Yankees were driven into the river and drowned, though actually Lt. Dabney led 25 men to safety by swimming their horses across the water.[23]

Among Mosby's men was Baron Robert Von Massow, a Prussian army officer who had joined the Rangers with a letter of introduction from Heros Von Borcke of General Stuart's staff. In the heat of the fight Von Massow charged toward Capt. Reed waving his sword, and believing he saw Reed make a gesture of surrender rode past him into the thick of the fight. Reed had no intention of surrendering, and shot Von Massow out of the saddle as he thundered by. Capt. Chapman, riding behind Von Massow, saw the exchange and leveled his pistol at Reed and at a distance of less than three feet put a fatal bullet through his left lung. Pvt. Munson of the Rangers recalled, "I was near enough to see him hit, and remember he tried to raise his weapon for another shot, found his strength going, and plunged forward on his face...." Moments later Munson fell with a Yankee bullet in his body.[24]

Capt. George Manning, now in command, ordered his brother William, 1st lieutenant of Company E, to have his men take down the rail fence for a stand in the field. The order was hardly out of his mouth when he was hit in the left leg with a shotgun blast, followed moments later by a shot that dropped his horse. "My horse went down on the hard pike, falling on my leg, which caused me such excruciating pain that I nearly fainted. My horse arose to his feet again, made a lunge sidewise, and we both rolled into the ditch by the side of the pike, and I was lost to the world for awhile."[25]

Within minutes the fight was over, the field covered with the bodies of men and horses. A pursuit of the fleeing Federals resulted in a haul of 57 prisoners, at least seven of whom were wounded. Ten men including Capt. Reed were left dead on the field. Two dozen had been driven headlong into the Potomac. Mosby's rout was complete. His own casualties amounted to one killed and four wounded.[26]

Anticipating a pursuit from the bulk of the 2nd Massachusetts Cavalry at Vienna, Mosby quickly rounded up his prisoners and captured horses and headed west. Californians George Manning, captain of M Company, and his brother 1st Lt. William Manning of L Company were the only officers taken and spent the rest of the war in a prison camp. The bulk of the enlisted men were sent to Andersonville, the remainder imprisoned in Savannah. Of the 55 enlisted men sent to Southern prisons 31 died there, three were exchanged that fall, and the remainder waited patiently until freed with the collapse of the Confederacy. Pvt. Joseph Kemp of B Company was not content to wait for death or parole and joined the 10th Tennessee Infantry. Captured at Egypt Station, Mississippi, in December, he was imprisoned for four months before putting the blue suit back on and enlisting in the 8th U.S. Infantry. Cpl. William Lawrence, one of the few enlisted men imprisoned at Danville, Virginia, escaped from the prison pen there. Pvt. Alfred Roe of the 9th New York Heavy Artillery described the breakout: "The only escapes from our prison were effected by two men, one a member of the Second Massachusetts Cavalry, though he was a Californian, who let themselves down into a sink, wrenched off the grate leading into the narrow sewer, and at the imminent peril of suffocation, through indescribable filth, made their way out to the river and eventual liberty."[27]

News of Mosby's victory reached the camp at Vienna that evening and Major Crowninshield immediately set out with 250 men. By the time they arrived in Dranesville the Confederates had a 12-hour head start with no chance of being caught. The dead were gathered up from the road and 17 wounded men were accounted for and attended to, they having been left or overlooked by the Confederates. Capt. Reed was found lying in the road stripped to his undershirt and drawers. Privates Richard Powers and Stephen Spooner, both Massachusetts farmers, had only recently joined the regiment, enlisting in Boston in mid–September. Four of the dead had made the long trip from California. The tally of killed increased to 11

Opposite: **Captain George F. Manning, Company M, California Battalion, 2nd Massachusetts Cavalry. Taken prisoner February 22, 1864, at Dranesville, Virginia.** *Courtesy of U.S.A.M.H.I.*

Brigade Hospital of the 2nd Massachusetts and 13th and 16th New York Cavalry, Vienna, Virginia. *Courtesy of U.S.A.M.H.I.*

when 19-year-old John Hayden (B), Boston, died of his wounds.*[28]

The return back to camp was a nightmare ordeal for the wounded. "Some of the wounded had broken legs, and screamed with agony as we lifted them into the wagons. These farm wagons were without springs, and as we wended our way home over the rough roads the cries of the wounded were excruciating." Chaplain Humphreys rode in ahead of the returning column to break the news of Reed's death to his wife, in camp for a visit. "She knew better than I did that he was a man without reproach, but I could tell her that he was a soldier without fear, and faithful to every duty, and much loved by his men." The men of the California Hundred shared in the cost of having Reed's body embalmed in Washington and sent to Dorchester where he was to be buried. In his report of the action Brig. Gen. Tyler noted that Reed was "...a brave and noble soldier." Crowninshield wrote home, "I miss poor Capt. Reed very much (he was acting as Major of the 2d Bat.) he was honest & brave & a great friend of mine."[29]

Capt. Reed's funeral was held in the Second Congregational Church, the same church he had been married in five years before. Buried with military honors, Reed's coffin was shrouded with the American flag presented to the company by Abbie Lord; too big to be carried on horseback, the flag had remained furled until used at the funeral. Back in San Francisco, the Tiger Engine Company, of which Capt. Reed was one of the founders, flew its flag at half mast in a token of mourning.[30]

Two days after the fight, Company A returned to the battlefield looking for more of the regiment's killed and wounded. The

*For a detailed list of casualties see Appendix A.

scout was unable to proceed past Dranesville due to a strong force of 700 Confederate infantry and cavalry occupying the town. Too weak to attack the rebels the detail returned to camp. Shortly after their arrival 25 of the men, missing since the fight, showed up in camp, having escaped the rebels by swimming the Potomac. On the 25th, Colonel Lazelle, commanding the brigade, ordered Major Crowninshield to take the balance of the brigade then in camp and attack the enemy forces near Dranesville — 200 men of the 2nd Massachusetts, 200 of the 16th New York, and 125 of the 13th New York, for a total of 525 troopers. Two pieces of artillery were provided for the action but Crowninshield chose to leave them behind. A thorough sweep of the area as far as Leesburg found the Rebel troops gone and the countryside once again quiet.[31]

Scouts were sent out during the first weeks of March with no results. Mosby was very careful about picking his fights and saw no opportunities against the vigilant Yankees in the Vienna camp. An attempt to catch some of the Rangers using the dismounted tactics that worked so well in the fall proved fruitless.

With Col. Lowell away at Giesboro Point and the brigade under the command of Col. Lazelle, the disgruntled Major Thompson at Muddy Branch saw an opportunity. Still bitter over the minor responsibility he had been given within the regiment, his "banishment" to Muddy Branch with his battalion, and the implications that he had been behind the petition for the Californians to transfer out of the regiment, Thompson had no compunction about making life difficult for his superiors.

Thompson's first move came on the 8th of February, the day Lowell left for duties at the Cavalry Bureau. One of Lowell's last acts before leaving camp was to order the rotation of two companies out of the Muddy Branch camp and replacing them with two others from Vienna. Learning of the manpower shift Major Thompson made an appeal to his departmental commander, Maj. Gen. Augur, that the order be rescinded. A message soon reached the Vienna camp countermanding Lowell's order and adding that Thompson's command was not to be interfered with again "...*except through these Hd Qrs.*" Thompson had bypassed his regimental, brigade, and division commanders and gotten his way.[32]

Major Crowninshield responded by sending Capt. David DeMerritt out to Muddy Branch for a camp inspection. Sending a fellow Californian out to inspect Thompson was a nice touch by Crowninshield. Any negative results could not be blamed on the gulf between Massachusetts and California officers, as had been the case when Forbes and Holman had inspected back in November. When DeMerritt returned with the expected report of the poor operations at Muddy Branch, Crowninshield held it back waiting for Thompson to make the next move. The wait was not a long one.

On the 5th of March Crowninshield was directed, through Departmental Headquarters, to send the First Battalion to Muddy Branch to relieve the Third Battalion and that Thompson would remain, taking command of the Third. Crowninshield complied and sent the First Battalion away on the 8th of March, leaving the Vienna camp very quiet with the one remaining battalion doing the work of two. The First Battalion, companies B, D, E, and M, arrived at Muddy Branch the next day and Thompson put them in camp alongside the Third. Stating he did not have orders to release the Third for other duties he held them at Muddy Branch and for the first time, had more men under his direct control than did Crowninshield.[33]

On the 12th, Major Crowninshield

played his trump. In a dispatch forwarded, properly, through his brigade commander, he blasted Thompson's conduct.

> Sir
> I received on Monday March 8th an order to send the 1st Batt of this Regiment to Muddy Branch, to relieve the 3d Batt. of the Regt. at that place. I obeyed the order at once, but was much surprised to have a particular Battalion designated, as I have always supposed that the Comdg Officer of a Regt. would be allowed to designate the Batt or companies with which other portions of his regiment should be relieved. It can certainly make no difference to the Commanding General of the Department what particular companies are sent to Md. while it makes a great difference to the Regiment. It is well known here that Major Thompson has openly stated his intention of getting certain companies away from the Regiment, in defiance of the wishes of the Commanding Officer. It is respectfully submitted that at least the Comdg. Officer of a Regiment rather than a subordinate should guide the selections of detachments of his command. Unless this is the case it seems to me that a subordinate officer could by intriguing and false representations obtain the order for details which would greatly impair the efficiency of a Regt. and the authority of the Commanding Officer. I was very unwilling to send four good companies over to serve under Major D.W.C. Thompson, an officer of this Regt., who is continually endeavoring to create dissatisfaction among the enlisted men of the Regiment and who is totally lax in matters of discipline and drill and entirely ignorant of nearly all the other duties of a Cavalry officer. I believe that the efficiency of any companies sent to him will be materially lessened, as I hear that of those so long with him have already been. For confirmation of this I would respectfully refer to Col. C.R. Lowell, who formerly commanded this regiment and under whom Major Thompson served for some time, and to Capt. D.A. DeMerritt who lately inspected Major Thompson's command, by Col. Lowell's order. I would also respectfully submit that if Major Thompson is to be allowed to <u>interfere with the</u> details of this Regiment, the authority of the Comdg Officer — and the Esprit du Corps [*sic*] of the Regiment will be much impaired. It does not seem to me to be improper to make this remonstrance, and respectfully to request that any future interference [*sic*] by Major Thompson in the details or affairs of this Regiment be promptly discountenanced.

The next day the Third Battalion made the short trek from Maryland to the Vienna camp.[34]

The final chapter in Thompson's bid for control in the regiment was written on the 1st of March when Major Crowninshield's long-awaited promotion to lieutenant colonel was approved. Lt. Col. Henry Russell, who had never spent a day in the field with the regiment, was promoted to the colonelcy of the 5th Massachusetts Cavalry, leaving the spot open for Crowninshield's advancement. Aside from the raise in pay there was no change for the new lieutenant colonel; it was merely a change in title since he had been the commander of the regiment since Col. Lowell's appointment to brigade command. In celebration, the band serenaded before his tent that night.[35]

As was always the case after a fight, there was little time to dwell on the defeats or victories. Scouts were sent out at irregular intervals, sometimes mounted, occasionally on foot, in search of guerrillas and bushwhackers. For the several days that Major Thompson held the two battalions at Muddy Branch, the camp at Vienna was particularly hard-pressed to make all of the scout and picket commitments. The thin ranks of the 13th and 16th New York were also called upon for extra manpower.

On the 29th of February, after the men were mustered for pay by Major Forbes, a dismounted detachment from A and B Troops left on a scout under the command of Capt. Adams at 9 P.M. It began to snow after only an hour's march.

Camp of 2nd Massachusetts Cavalry, Vienna, Virginia, 1863. *Courtesy of Massachusetts Commandery Military Order of the Loyal Legion and the U.S.A.M.H.I.*

Pushing north to the Alexandria and Leesburg Pike, Capt. Adams turned on to the pike and headed west. After covering no more than five miles a halt was called and the men bedded down as best they could alongside the pike. Morning found them covered with three inches of fresh snow. Adams ordered the men into the trees about 300 yards from the road, and there they spent the day, shivering, waiting for rebels to pass by.

By evening Capt. Adams had had enough of the cold and led his men into the Union Church where fires were lit on piles of dirt spread on the floor. A comfortable night was had by all and in the morning a warm sun made a pleasant day for the two hour walk back to camp.[36]

Mail call on the 10th of March brought a special letter for Lt. Alvin Stone of Company M. Capt. Manning who had been captured at Dranesville managed to send a letter from Richmond stating that Manning's brother and the 55 other men captured were all doing fine with the exception of the seven wounded men. The same day Pvt. Frank Baker of Company A was returned to camp having deserted shortly after the trip from San Francisco. Apprehended after having joined a New York Infantry regiment, Frank was not destined to stay with the 2nd Massachusetts Cavalry. When the opportunity arose in June, he was gone again, this time for good.[37]

On the 17th, yet another detachment left for a scout through the country. Made up of 210 New Yorkers and 40 of the 2nd Massachusetts, this party came back to camp three days later with 13 captured rebels. Another on the 24th returned having seen no sign of the enemy.[38]

Occasionally some little incident

would happen in camp that would warrant conversation around the fire or maybe a diary entry. On the 22nd of March the surgeon of the 13th New York was shot by one of the pickets on an ugly evening of rain and snow. "He was dizzy headed at the time," recalled Dearborn. The weather seemed to dominate the talk. Day after day of rain and snow turned the company streets into a knee-deep morass.[39]

At the end of March, Col. Lowell returned from his duty at the Cavalry Depot and relieved Col. Lazelle of brigade command. Col. Lowell's presence was needed back with the brigade as the weather would soon break and the ubiquitous scouts for Mosby, which had never actually stopped, would be increased in frequency. April would prove a busy month.[40]

Thirty recruits joined the regiment on the 3rd of April and were given precious little time to settle into camp. The next morning a scout of 200 men, led by Major Frazier of the 13th New York, set off on a scout through western Fairfax County. Leaving Vienna late in the afternoon the column passed through Hunter's Mill and turned south for Chantilly. Here the column split, the New Yorkers pressing on for Centerville while the 2nd Massachusetts remained behind. It was an unusual move for Lowell to send the scout south of his own camp as most of the previous forays had been into the heart of Loudoun County to the west.[41]

By 4 P.M. the members of the 2nd Massachusetts that had remained at Chantilly were preparing for a cold night on the Stuart Farm. Private Dearborn recalled it the next day in his diary. "It was tough — dark, cold and wet — the worst night I have experienced for a long time. No fires to sit by and no chance to sleep." The weather had not improved by morning, the rain coming down so hard it took several tries before a small fire for coffee could be kindled. Despite being ordered to join the rest of the column at Centerville, the men of the 2nd, as well as their horses, took refuge in the Old Union Tavern. "...[A] desperate nightmare but the hardy soldiers wouldn't think of buffering the Storm King that howls without." The soaked column returned to camp at noon passing another scout headed on a raid up the Little River Turnpike toward Middleburg.[42]

The latest scout, made up of the able-bodied men of companies A and L, was more successful in its search for rebels. Led by the newly promoted Capt. John Phillips of Company C, the column rode hard and fast making the round trip to Middleburg and back in less than 24 hours. In Aldie the troopers captured ten of Mosby's men, some reportedly still in their beds. Several of the prisoners had been involved in the fight at Dranesville in February and their capture caused a good deal of satisfaction back in camp. But the give and take continued and two days later the Rangers captured a picket post of a sergeant and eight men of the 16th New York Cavalry, all supposedly asleep.[43]

A welcome break from raids and scouts was provided by the wedding of the regimental adjutant, 1st Lt. Charles M. Kinne. One of the original California Hundred, Kinne had enlisted as a private and had quickly been promoted to sergeant, then sergeant major. His commission as second lieutenant came about as a result of 1st Lt. McKendry being promoted to captain of Company G and 2nd Lt. John Sim being promoted to fill McKendry's spot. Within months Kinne was promoted to first lieutenant and given the vacant post of regimental adjutant.[44]

Though not a Harvard man or a member of the Boston elite, Kinne was accepted into the officers' clique and was "...as popular a man as there was in the whole Brigade." One of the other officer's wives was a bit of a matchmaker and started a correspondence between the 23-

year-old Kinne and the very attractive Miss Lizzie D'Arcey. They began exchanging letters in January, and in late February, when the officer's wife came to camp to visit, she was accompanied by Miss D'Arcey herself. By early April they had asked Chaplain Humphreys to read their vows.[45]

Monday the 11th of April at 10:15 in the morning, all the officers of the 2nd were in attendance at the wedding. The regimental band played and the couple exchanged vows and rings. The bride had earlier confided to the chaplain that she was afraid she would start laughing during the service. At the end of the ceremony she began to cry. Then Kinne began to cry. Then all of the officers began to cry. Lt. Col. Crowninshield, the highest-ranking officer at the service, pulled rank and being the first to offer his congratulations to the bride, gave her such a kiss that soon all the officers were wiping their eyes and getting in line to salute her. Decades later Humphreys recalled it as the best wedding he ever performed.[46]

In camp the horse of Pvt. Joshua Ross (A) threw him and leaped the abatis that surrounded the camp. Bugler Alfred Lee (A), Newburyport, a Massachusetts man who had enrolled in San Francisco to serve his home state, died of "brain fever." During a dress parade, Major Forbes was unsatisfied with Cpl. Henry Crum (A) and made him unpack and pack his saddle in front of the other men. Such conduct irked Dearborn who wrote, "Noble hearted Forbes. Who wouldn't growl to be under command of such an officer." Despite Dearborn's thoughts, Forbes was a popular officer who had built a solid reputation for being a fighter and leader.[47]

The camp at Vienna was situated along the line of the Loudoun and Hampshire Railroad. On the 17th, the engine Pickwick ran off the tracks and buried itself in the mud close to the abatis. No one was hurt, and by evening the engine was back on the track and the excitement over.[48]

Col. Lowell's return to duty with the brigade saw the already busy camp turn into a flurry of activity. On the 10th of April, the picket line was moved further out and now followed the line of Difficult Run Creek, about four miles out from the camp. The scouts and raids were now an everyday occurrence. But with all of the increased activity the Union plan of action still held a major and sometimes fatal flaw. The columns sent into Mosby's territory always followed the major roads while Mosby stuck to the smaller roads and paths. Back in October an article had been run in the *Daily Alta California* that expressed a desire to change this mode of operations. "The War Department has detailed us for the special purpose of clearing the surrounding country of the rebel guerrillas that infest it; if they expect us to accomplish this, by no means an easy task, they must let us fight the guerrillas our own way, either as we hunt Indians or at their own game of bushwhacking; but we never can catch them by traveling over the turnpikes, while perhaps at the very time the guerrillas are hid in the roadside, laughing at our folley [sic]."[49]

Most of the article, by Pvt. Thomas Merry of Company L, was a criticism of the leadership of Col. Lowell and was written at the height of the problems with Major Thompson. Nevertheless, it was a fact that sticking to the turnpikes was folly. It had proved disastrous to Capt. Reed, and had every potential for providing a new disaster. The tactic of marching dismounted men through the woods had been a good move and caught the Rangers off balance, but that same type of creative thinking had to be continued if success was to be expected.

On the morning of the 17th, Capt. Rumery led a small detachment on a scout to the west and heard of a large force of rebels in the vicinity of Dranesville. The column returned quickly to camp reporting to Col. Lowell at midnight. Rumery had discovered that Mosby was in the vicinity between Leesburg and Point of Rocks, collecting corn from local farmers. The rumors of large numbers of rebel troops were a ruse designed to keep small detachments away while the Rangers hid the corn. Hoping to catch the work in progress, Lowell had the entire brigade of 900 men turned out at dawn, rations cooked, and ready to march by 8 A.M. Wisely the column avoided the Pike and by smaller roads passed through Hunter's Mill, Frying Pan, and Farmwell to Leesburg. Arriving near nightfall Lowell found not the hundreds of rebels rumored but learned that only Mosby's C Company and a few recruits were in the area. There was a slight skirmish between the two forces before the rebels retreated to the west. One of Mosby's men was mortally wounded and 11 were captured. Lowell posted his men in and around town and spent a quiet night, the Rangers declining any further action. In the morning the column returned the way it had come with the exception of a dismounted squadron which circled behind Leesburg while the brigade was riding out the other side. Lowell had learned of a wedding party that was to be conducted in town and "...I sent 75 dismounted men to take part...." The party was over when the squadron arrived but some of the gray-clad guests remained and there was a sharp fight in the streets. Cpl. Charles Goodwin (H), Hudson, New York, was killed and three men slightly wounded, all of the casualties very probably shot by men in the rear ranks who began firing without orders. This unsuccessful bit of subterfuge complete, the squadron joined the main column on its return to Vienna.*[50]

The column returned to camp without event and was met there by the paymaster. The men drew their pay and the paymaster was treated to a serenade by the band. With the ink still wet on their pay slips, 50 men of Capt. Rumery's squadron saddled up and set out on an overnight scout. Rumery's men captured six Confederates, including a major and two other officers, who had been observing the brigade's pickets.[51]

The very next evening Mosby and 30 of his men struck at the pickets on duty at Hunter's Mill, some 2½ miles out from the Vienna Camp. The post was manned by 25 men of the 16th New York and were overrun by Mosby's dismounted men. "No resistance was made by the pickets, only three shots being fired," reported Lowell. Pvt. Corbett was even less kind: "...they ran as usual at the first fire." Nearly all of the force was captured, but in the darkness and confusion all but five managed to escape. Mosby sent the prisoners and some 18 to 20 captured horses back to Fauquier County in the charge of Lt. William Hunter while he and another Ranger went off on a scout.[52]

At reveille, Col. Lowell learned of the attack and with Major Forbes and 50 men set off in pursuit. Riding hard up the Little River Turnpike, Lowell overtook Hunter about ten miles away near Aldie. Hunter turned his small force and charged the Yankees but the forces were too unequal in size and the Confederates quickly retreated. Lt. Hunter was riding a fine gray horse he had captured the night before. During the skirmish the horse took a bullet,

---

Along for the ride, researching for his poem "The Raid to Aldie," was author Herman Melville. Humphreys, p. 24.

Opposite: Bugler Alfred Lee, Company A, 2nd Regiment, Massachusetts Volunteer Cavalry. *Courtesy of Richard K. Tibbals Collection, U.S.A.M.H.I.*

falling to the ground and pinning its rider. Lt. Hunter was captured and two other Rangers were wounded. Cpl. Bumgardner (A), San Francisco, slightly wounded in the arm, was the only Union casualty.[53]

Col. Lowell's report of the action is typical of his style with his superiors. He doesn't attempt to gloss over any of the details that mar the conduct of his command. His brigade got the worst of it in this action, and the fact that he captured an important member of Mosby's command did not compensate for his five captured troopers and the lost horses.[54]

C.C. Augur, commander of the XXII Corps and Department of Washington, rarely became involved with the details of the daily scouts of Lowell's cavalry brigade in Vienna. Lately Augur had been concerning himself with the calls for troops from his department to reenforce the Army of the Potomac. The overmanned heavy artillery regiments that garrisoned the forts ringing Washington were being issued rifles and being shipped to the front as infantry. With fewer men to work with, Augur was depending on those left under his command to accomplish more.

There was never any thought that Lowell's small brigade would be stripped from Augur as he had precious little cavalry within his corps. Actual cavalry under his command, other than Lowell's brigade, consisted of the 11th New York Cavalry in the District of Washington (most of it under the command of Major Thompson at Muddy Branch), one company of the 1st Michigan Cavalry assigned to the provost marshal, and two companies of the 1st Indiana Cavalry at Glymont Landing, Maryland. The large numbers of troopers at the cavalry remount depot, though geographically within his jurisdiction, were members of the Army of the Potomac and out of his reach.[55]

General Augur entrusted the cavalry operations to his division commander, Brig. Gen. Robert O. Tyler, a regular army officer and heavy artilleryman who would himself soon be sent to the Army of the Potomac to command his "heavies." Tyler had great trust in Lowell and assured Augur, "With Colonel Lowell in command of the cavalry I have no fear of trouble."[56]

The general in this case was referring to a raid about to be sent out that Gen. Augur had specifically directed. Acting on intelligence gathered from sources within Mosby's territory, the General designated individual houses to be searched for rebels and contraband goods destined to be smuggled across the Potomac. Tyler ordered Lowell to Leesburg then on to Paris at the foot of Ashby's Gap in the Blue Ridge, and several stops in between. Lowell was to be supported by Col. James McMahon's 164th New York Infantry.[57]

Reveille was blown at half-past four on the morning of the 28th of April and by 7 A.M. some 600 men of the brigade were in the saddle; 250 men of the 2nd Massachusetts and the balance from the 13th and 16th New York. Col. Lowell led the advance and avoiding the turnpike approached Leesburg "up the back way" arriving about noon. There were about a dozen Rangers in Leesburg at the time, most loitering around the hotel. The Yankee column was within 200 yards of the hotel before they were noticed by a group sitting on the verandah. The Rangers scattered, a few taking time to fire at the advancing Federals. In the gunfire one Confederate was killed, one wounded, and, though a few managed to escape (one hiding out in the Episcopal Church), the others were captured. The Yankees had swept in so fast that several of the captured were taken in the hotel bar.[58]

Lowell sustained no casualties and soon had his men searching the houses on Augur's list. Augur had indicated that a large amount of wool and tobacco were in Leesburg waiting to be smuggled into Maryland. Several hundred pounds of wool were confiscated and the regiment was able to supply themselves quite nicely with good southern tobacco, though the majority of the houses on the lists proved to be empty or impossible to find. A local granary allowed the men to give their horses a good feed before it was torched. The column then pushed on up the pike to Hamilton where it remained for the night.[59]

At 5 A.M. the men were split into two columns, Lowell leading the body of the troops across to Upperville, while Major Forbes took a detachment and continued up the pike to Snickersville. Lowell traveled through Upperville, Paris, Bloomfield and Rectortown, occasionally skirmishing with Mosby's men. Near Loughborough's Farm one of the 16th New York was killed while straggling away from the line of march. The column halted for the evening at Casey's Mills, near Upperville, where they met up with the infantry under Col. McMahon. Later that night, Forbes' detachment arrived in camp with half a dozen prisoners.[60]

One of the few casualties during the day was the luckless Capt. DeMerritt. Having survived the broken leg and temporary insanity, the officer now had the misfortune to shoot himself in the leg when reholstering his pistol. This wound would prove too much for him and by September he would be discharged for disability.[61]

The third day of the scout, April 30, Lowell let his troopers sleep in, not putting them on the road until 7 A.M. Accompanied by the infantry, the cavalry brigade proceeded on to Paris at the foot of Ashby's Gap, where some long-range skirmishing resulted in the death of one New Yorker and later, the capture of another. Once again these casualties were inflicted by Mosby's men against troopers who strayed away from the main column.[62]

Returning to Upperville, the infantry stayed at the previous night's camp while the cavalry pressed on to Green Garden Mills near Rectortown. Skirmishing broke out resulting in the killing of two rebels, the wounding of one, and the capture of two others. Here the 2nd Massachusetts took their first casualties of the raid. Sgt. Charles Clark (L), California, was killed in the gunfire that wounded Privates Daniel Boggs (L), David Ferrill (L), and Samuel Backus (L), all of California. Boggs, though severely wounded, would return to the regiment, but Ferrill's wound was worse, resulting in his discharge due to disability. Pvt. Backus recorded in his diary, "My left leg badly wounded." Maybe it didn't seem so bad the next day, for he never mentions the wound again. By dark the column had returned to the camp at Casey's Mills where the 164th New York was still encamped.[63]

As always, Lowell downplayed his report giving no more than dry facts and figures. The success of the raid did not escape Tyler who forwarded Lowell's report with the following endorsement: "I have the honor to commend to the favorable attention of the commanding general the activity and excellent conduct by Colonel Lowell and his command in the late scout. Colonel McMahon, who commanded the infantry, also deserves much credit." General Augur was just as pleased and said so in his endorsement when the report was forwarded to Army headquarters. "This is the third successful operation of Colonel Lowell within the last month, embracing in all a capture of about 50 of Mosby's men, between 30 and 40 horses and equipments, and a good deal of other property. I desire to commend in strong terms the zeal and ability displayed by Colonel Lowell in these various expeditions."[64]

As busy as April was, the first week of May was a brief lull, allowing the 2nd Massachusetts to catch their breath. "I write to assure you of my continued good health and not for the purpose of telling any news," Crowninshield wrote home. "Cause why. There is none to tell." Aside from the military funeral of Sgt. Clark and a few alarms from the pickets, there was little to put in diaries or letters home.[65]

It seemed every time there was a break in the action, Major Thompson took the opportunity to ruffle the feathers of Lowell and Crowninshield. This time he sent an order to the Vienna camp requiring the absent band members to return to their companies at Muddy Branch. Having recently added snare and bass drums as well as cymbals, the band was earning quite the reputation within the brigade. Obeying the orders of their battalion commander, five band members stowed their instruments and crossed the Potomac. Within a week Pvt. Corbett was able to record in his diary, "The band boys returned from Maryland, this PM, and now we are once more in full blast. Major Thompson failed in his attempts to break up the band."[66]

While the 2nd Massachusetts went about its business of scouts and pickets from the Vienna camp, there was constant activity around them as the Army of the Potomac made final preparations for the spring offensive. Troops marching back and forth across the Northern Virginia chessboard was hardly exceptional, but the passage of Gen. Burnside's IX Corps, 22,000 strong, was an event worth noting. Despite their hopes, though, the grand plans and movements did not include the 2nd Massachusetts Cavalry.[67]

Gen. Grant pushed the Army of the Potomac, 122,000 strong, across the Rapidan River on the 4th of May and into the area of second growth timber known as the Wilderness. Here General Lee met him with his 66,000 Confederates, utilizing the poor field conditions to his advantage. The fighting that began on the 5th, now known as the Overland Campaign, would continue on until the middle of June with the Army of the Potomac slowly moving southeast, stopping finally before Petersburg.[68]

During the first few days of the campaign, the 2nd Massachusetts sat quietly in camp, knowing something was afoot but not being involved or informed. On the 8th of May, Col. Lowell set out on a reconnaissance to the south, his orders to check the line of the Orange and Alexandria Railroad for rebel activity. Starting out at 3 P.M., the line of march led from the Vienna camp down the Manassas road to Fairfax Station and then along the line of the railroad. Stopping for the night along the right of way, they continued at first light and by noon were at Rappahannock Station. The beautiful country was scarred in all directions, evidence of the thousands who had been encamped here only days before. A few of the houses that had dotted the area before the war still stood, but the majority had been ripped down to supply wood for tents and campfires. It was an eerie scene, walking the horses through the deserted camps, the sound of the furious battle to the southeast occasionally being heard. There was no one to be seen, Rebel or Yankee.[69]

After the first days of fighting in the Wilderness, Gen. Grant ordered Gen. Burnside to direct all of his wounded to Rappahannock Station for transportation by rail up to Washington. Lowell's reconnaissance was to ensure the line of the Orange and Alexandria was free of the enemy and that the trains would be allowed to travel unimpeded. Within hours of the brigade leaving camp the plan to move the wounded was changed, with new provisions made to send them north via Fredericksburg. Lowell never learned of the change and continued on his scout as ordered, making camp the second night in the abandoned camp of the 50th New York Veteran Engineers. The next few days were spent traversing the stretch of track

Two photographs of Pvt. David Watson, Company M, 2nd Massachusetts Cavalry. *Courtesy of Mike Graswick.*

between the river and Catlett's Station, about ten miles to the north.[70]

Gen. Grant's losses in the Wilderness approached 17,500 amounting to nearly 15 percent of his total strength. Unlike his predecessors, Grant continued his offensive despite the staggering casualty figures. He could win a war of attrition but he had to be continually reenforced with soldiers—recruits as well as those transferred from quiet areas. On the 15th of May, Gen. R.O. Tyler was ordered to report with his entire division to the Army of the Potomac—the entire division with the exception of Lowell's brigade.[71]

The departure of the infantry and artillery meant little to the troopers at Vienna. Pickets and scouts continued as always and another raid set out on the 18th. One hundred sixty men of the 2nd Massachusetts led by Major Forbes took a tour of Loudoun County, passing through the Bull Run Mountains to Rectortown, north to Upperville at the foot of the Blue Ridge, then back to camp by way of Middleburg. Fifty-one hours, start to finish, with 40 hours in the saddle. The results were good if not spectacular: 11 prisoners and 30 horses, and a thorough search of what was thought to be Mosby's headquarters.[72]

Relaxing after the raid, Dearborn found time to catch up with a few letters, including one to his lost love. "May her life be long and her joys be many. May her path be strewn with flowers and her pillow soft as the downey fleece. Oh, Sue thy love as sweet as honey, and thy displeasure cruel as the grave. It is hard to be misunderstood by the one you love."[73]

An inspection by Lt. Col. Crowninshield awaited the men on the morning of the 23rd. The band received praises for "...being the cleanest and having the best looking horses...." The highlight of the day, however, was reserved for the men changing their Sharps Carbines for Spencer Repeating Carbines. The new weapons were awe-inspiring, holding seven .52-caliber rimfire bullets in a tubular magazine. All seven shots could be fired in under 30 seconds, making even a small force with the weapon formidable.[74]

The Orange and Alexandria Railroad, until lately the supply line of the Army of the Potomac, had become something of a burden. The army was now being supplied via Belle Plain on the Potomac River, some 12 miles east of Fredericksburg, and the railroad was no longer worth the effort required to keep it open. With Tyler's infantry gone, Mosby and White could break the line whenever and wherever they chose. On the 23rd the line was abandoned and Lowell was ordered to draw in his brigade closer to Washington, making his headquarters near Falls Church.[75]

The new camp was about a mile from the village, along the rails of the Loudoun and Hampshire Railroad as their former camp had been. The first night was spent in the open under a tremendous thunderstorm. An abatis was shortly erected and then the tents, but not the comfortable sibleys that had been home for the last year. The regiment pitched shelter tents, "...at least they are dignified by that title, the amount of cloth allowed each man is about five feet square, and by two joining stock and forming a partnership, enough is obtained to make a shelter for two men by driving stakes into the ground for the end, and making uprights of small trees with crotches in the end, using ridge poles of the same material and stretching cloth over the ridge poles a small A tent is formed about five feet wide and the same height, in which two men can live pretty comfortably as long as it does not rain too hard...."[76]

The next few days were scenes of constant activity in camp. Stables were built, troughs (latrines) dug, and those that could find boards made low bunks. One of the 13th New York died in camp and the band was there for the funeral. "When they attempted to lower the coffin, they found the grave was not large enough. The Major in command swore he would bury the man that dug the grave, if he could catch him." A few weeks later the band was preparing to play at the funeral of a soldier from the 16th New York who had accidentally shot himself. "...[J]ust before the funeral took place, a thunder storm came up, the lightning struck the coffin (which was setting outside the hospital), knocking it to pieces and throwing the body about 20 feet in a short time they got another coffin and we went on with the funeral."[77]

As the new camp was being settled the frequency of scouts was increased to a higher degree. A series of raids left Falls Church on May 29th, June 1st, and two on the 2nd. In the past the scouts would leave camp after the previous one had returned but now Lowell had them relieving the watch in the field. Major Forbes was rarely seen in camp those days, he or Captain Stone usually being in command of the patrols. These latest efforts, a combination of mounted and dismounted men, found little sign of guerrillas. Several civilians, suspected of horse thieving, bushwhacking, and spying were arrested and sent in to Washington.[78]

The routine of scouts and pickets was gratefully broken on the afternoon of the 8th of June. Three days' rations were prepared and within an hour 700 troopers were riding south. Several teams followed behind bearing enough rations for an additional three days. The excitement in the air was electrical, the men convinced that like the rest of Tyler's division, they were finally being called to join the Army of the Potomac. Marching for several hours, a halt for the evening was called at Bentsville.

The next morning they were joined by a column of 50 ambulances and it was then announced that the mission was to travel to the site of the battlefield in the Wilderness where some 300 wounded men were said to be in Rebel hands. Though disappointed they were not joining the army, they found the trip a change of scenery if nothing else. Two more days of travel saw the column halting for the evening on the banks of the Rappahannock River. Splashing across at the United States Ford the next morning, the men rode into the area so recently the scene of savage fighting. "On both sides of the plank-road upon which we were traveling, the woods were filled with newly made graves, and the entire Wilderness, ten miles long and four wide, was one vast graveyard."[79]

The scene affected Sgt. Maj. Robert Williams so much he described it in a letter home to his folks. "...[B]eside the road were a large number of the dead of both armies lying on top of the ground. You would also find a great many graves where some Friend had performed the last act of Human Friendship toward the fallen Hero. I saw in one small nook near the woods bodies lying on top of the ground so thickly that my curiosity led me to count them & there were (125) men killed and not buried on a piece of ground not so large as your garden."[80]

The Wilderness "...is covered with a small growth of trees from ten to twenty feet high, principally oak and pine, and the growth is very thick — in some places almost impassable. To render it still more impregnable, the rebels had constructed earthworks through its entire length, from an eighth to a quarter of a mile apart ... the wonder to me is not that so many lives were lost in the battle of the Wilderness, but that so many went through unscathed." At Parker's Store a small hospital was found attended by Confederate surgeons. There were numerous wounded rebels but only three Union soldiers, all too unfit to stand the trip north. A detachment pushed on to Locust Grove, the site of another hospital, where word was sent to Lowell that there were 40 to 45 wounded men, ready to be liberated and taken home.[81]

Reserving ten wagons for Locust Grove, the colonel sent the remaining wagons back across the ford. The wounded men were delighted to see their saviors, knowing that had they not arrived they would have all ended up in prison camps. Three men were found to be in too poor condition to travel and were given the unpleasant news that they would remain in the care of the Confederates. Mindless of their wounds and thinking only of home, they appealed to Col. Lowell to be taken no matter the risk. The rub was that there was no room for them. Lowell had sent away one ambulance too many, and the ten on hand were full and beginning to roll northward.[82]

Unable to leave the men, Chaplain Humphreys requested and received a detail of 48 men who alternated between riding and carrying the three men on stretchers. The trip was grueling. Dearborn recalled, "I helped carry the wounded as far as Chancellorsville. It was a hard case but it would have been harder to have left them behind."

Word came to Lowell of a force of Confederates that were approaching his column, and he responded by sending a detachment to drive the enemy back. Moving forward with the skirmishers, Pvt. James Watson saw the flash of the rifle shot that hit his horse, causing it to lunge, then collapse. James hit the ground with his right arm extended and his right leg stuck in the stirrup. The dying horse rolled over dislocating his right leg and pinning him to the ground while his comrades drove off the enemy. A surgeon popped the dislocated joint back into place and with nothing more than a swollen arm, Watson was able to mount another horse and continue the march.[83]

On the second day out one of the three stretcher cases died; a private from the 149th Pennsylvania, a husband and father of two in Philadelphia. He left a leg on the battlefield and now rested in a roadside field.[84]

The column of ambulances, with a strong escort, had reached Washington long before the stretcher detail arrived at the Falls Church camp. Chaplain Humphreys rode ahead and had the band turned out to welcome the two wounded men with the "Star Spangled Banner" and "Hail, Columbia." "The joy of the wounded captives whom we rescued may be imagined but cannot be described."[85]

A short break for the returning troopers was all too short, and within 24 hours another raid was passing through the abatis on the eternal search for Mosby and his men. Over the next few weeks a handful of enemy prisoners were taken but there was no real action to speak of. Crowninshield seemed quite bored in his letters home. On the 26th of June he mentioned idly that Mosby had acquired some artillery.[86]

Notes

1. Dearborn, *Diary*, Jan. 1, 1864.
2. Corbett, *Diary*, Oct. 7, 10, 1863, Jan. 10, 1864.
3. Dearborn, *Diary*, Jan. 2–14, 1864.
4. *Massachusetts Soldiers, Sailors, and Marines*, Vol. VI, pp. 228–328; Humphreys, *Field and Camp*, p. 390.
5. Dearborn, *Diary*, Jan. 12–14, 1864; Schouler, *Annual Report of the Adjutant General of Massachusetts for the Year Ending 1864*, p. 938.
6. Mortimer, *The California 100 and Battalion*, p. 29.
7. National Archives, Record Group No. 153, Special Orders No. 55, Court Martial Proceedings of William Ormsby, Nov. 14, 1863.
8. *Daily Alta California*, Mar. 22, 1864.
9. Mortimer, *The California 100 and Battalion*, p. 29.
10. National Archives, Record group 94,

Co. E Order book, General Order #10, Feb. 7, 1864.

11. *Daily Alta California*, Mar. 22, 1864.
12. Humphreys, *Field and Camp*, pp. 20–21; National Archives, Record Group 94, Co. E Order book, General Order #10, Feb. 7, 1864.
13. Corbett, *Diary*, Feb. 7, 1864; Humphreys, *Field and Camp*, p. 21; *Daily Alta California*, Mar. 22, 1864.
14. Emerson, *Life and Letters*, pp. 450–51; *Boston Journal*, Feb. 10, 1863.
15. Crowninshield, Feb. 2, 1864; Emerson, *Life and Letters*, p. 316; *Napa County Reporter*, Mar. 12, 1864.
16. *National Tribune*, Aug. 18, 1910.
17. Scott, *Partisan Life with Mosby*, p. 200; Williamson, *Mosby's Rangers*, p. 142.
18. Scott, *Partisan Life with Mosby*, p. 201; Williamson, *Mosby's Rangers*, p. 143.
19. *National Tribune*, Aug. 18, 1910.
20. Evans and Moyer, *Mosby's Confederacy*, p. 47; Williamson, *Mosby's Rangers*, 143; *The Boston Journal*, Feb. 24, 1864; *Daily Alta California*, Mar. 25, 1863.
21. Scott, *Partisan Life with Mosby*, p. 202.
22. Williamson, *Mosby's Rangers*, p. 144; *OR*, XXXIII, pp. 159–60.
23. Munson, *Reminiscences of a Mosby Guerrilla*, p. 86; *OR*, XXXIII, p. 160; *Boston Journal*, Feb. 24, 1864.
24. Russell, *The Memoirs of John S. Mosby*, pp. 270–71.
25. *National Tribune*, Aug. 18, 1910.
26. *OR*, XXXIII, pp. 159–160.
27. Roe, "In Rebel Prison: or, Experiences in Danville, Va.," *MOLLUS.*, Rhode Island, p. 273; *Massachusetts Soldiers, Sailors, and Marines*, Vol. 6, pp. 228–328; National Archives, Record Group 94, Co. B muster roll, Co. H muster roll, Dec. 31, 1863, to Feb. 29, 1864.
28. Corbett, *Diary*, Feb. 23, 1864; *OR*, LI, Pt. 1, p. 214; *Napa County Reporter*, Apr. 2, 1864.
29. Corbett, *Diary*, Feb. 25, 1864; Humphreys, *Field and Camp*, p. 392; Crowninshield, Feb. 27, 1864; *OR*, XXXIII, p. 159.
30. *Boston Herald*, Mar. 4, 1864; *Daily Alta California*, 26 Feb., 1864.
31. Corbett, *Diary*, Feb. 24, 1864; *OR*, LI, Pt. 1, p. 214.
32. National Archives, Record Group 94, Independent Cavalry Brigade, Dept. of Wash., Special Orders #14 and 15, Telegraph message dated Feb. 8, 1864.
33. National Archives, Record Group 94, Independent Cavalry Brigade, Dept. of Wash., Lacllotti to Lazelle, Letter dated Mar. 5, 1864.
34. National Archives, Record Group 94, Independent Cavalry Brigade, Dept. of Wash., Crowninshield to Lansing, Letter dated Mar. 12, 1864.
35. Crowninshield, Mar. 19, 1864.
36. Dearborn, *Diary*, Feb. 29–Mar. 2, 1864.
37. Corbett, *Diary*, Mar. 10, 1864; Dearborn, *Diary*, Mar. 10, 1864; *Massachusetts Soldiers, Sailors, and Marines*, Vol. VI, p. 231.
38. Corbett, *Diary*, Mar. 17, 1864; Dearborn, *Diary*, Mar. 24, 1864.
39. Dearborn, *Diary*, Mar. 27, 1864.
40. National Archives, Record Group 94, Military Service Record of Charles R. Lowell, Jr., Special Order No. 132.
41. Dearborn, *Diary*, Apr. 3, 1864; *OR*, XXXIII, p. 807.
42. Dearborn, *Diary*, April 4–6, 1864.
43. Corbett, *Diary*, April 10, 12, 1864.
44. Schouler, *Annual Report of the Adjutant General of Massachusetts for the Year Ending 1864*, pp. 940–45; *Massachusetts Soldiers, Sailors, and Marines*, Vol. VI, pp. 234, 235, 237.
45. Humphreys, *Field and Camp*, p. 394.
46. Corbett, *Diary*, Apr. 11, 1864; Humphreys, *Field and Camp*, pp. 395–96.
47. Dearborn, *Diary*, April 9, 12, 1864.
48. Dearborn, *Diary*, April 17, 1864.
49. *Daily Alta California*, Oct. 4, 1864.
50. Corbett, *Diary*, Apr. 18, 1864; Dearborn, *Diary*, April 18–19, 1864; Humphreys, *Field and Camp*, pp. 24–33; *OR*, XXXIII, pp. 306, 926.
51. Corbett, *Diary*, Apr. 21, 1864.
52. Corbett, *Diary*, Apr. 23, 1864; Scott, *Partisan Life with Mosby*, p. 217; *OR*, XXXIII, p. 308.
53. Corbett, *Diary*, April 23, 1864; Dearborn, *Diary*, April 23, 1864; Scott, *Partisan Life with Mosby*, pp. 212–13.
54. *OR*, XXXIII, p. 308.
55. *OR*, XXXIII, pp. 882, 888.
56. *OR*, XXXIII, p. 985.
57. *OR*, XXXIII, pp. 315, 985.
58. Dearborn, *Diary*, April 28, 1864; Wert, *Mosby's Rangers*, p. 159; Williamson, *Mosby's Rangers*, p. 156.
59. Dearborn, *Diary*, April 28, 1864; *OR*, XXXVII, Pt. 1, p. 363.
60. Dearborn, *Diary*, April 29, 1864.
61. Crowninshield, May 2, 1864; Dearborn, *Diary*, April 29, 1864; *Massachusetts Soldiers, Sailors, and Marines*, Vol. VI, p. 268; Na-

tional Archives, Record Group 94, Pension Record of David DeMerritt.

62. Dearborn, *Diary*, April 30, 1864; *OR*, XXXIII, p. 316.

63. Backus, *Diary*, April 30, 1864; Corbett, *Diary*, April 30, 1864; Dearborn, *Diary*, April 30, 1864; *Massachusetts Soldiers, Sailors, and Marines*, Vol. VI, pp. 303–309.

64. *OR*, XXXIII, pp. 315–16.

65. Crowninshield, May 5, 1864; Dearborn, *Diary*, May 2, 1864.

66. Corbett, *Diary*, May 7, 14, 1864.

67. Corbett, *Diary*, April 27, 1864.

68. Faust, *Encyclopedia*, p. 551.

69. *Daily Alta California*, July 15, 1864.

70. Crowninshield, May 15, 1864; Dearborn, *Diary*, May 9–12, 1864; *OR*, Vol. XXXVI, Pt. 1, pp. 269–72, 482–83, 512, 561.

71. Dearborn, *Diary*, May 14, 1864; Faust, *Encyclopedia*, pp. 823–825; *Boston Journal*, May 30, 1864.

72. Dearborn, *Diary*, May 18–20, 1864; *Boston Journal*, May 30, 1864.

73. Dearborn, *Diary*, May 22, 1864.

74. Dearborn, *Diary*, May 23, 1864.

75. Crowninshield, May 31, 1864; *Boston Journal*, May 30, 1864.

76. *Daily Alta California*, June 10, 1863.

77. Corbett, *Diary*, May 28, June 20, 1864.

78. Dearborn, *Diary*, May 29–June 2, 1864.

79. Humphreys, *Field and Camp*, pp. 51–53; Dearborn, *Diary*, June 9, 1864; *Daily Alta California*, July 15, 1864.

80. Williams to Parents, June 14, 1865, Misc. letters of Robert Henry Williams, Huntington Library, San Marino, Ca.

81. *Daily Alta California*, July 15, 1864.

82. Crowninshield, June 15, 1864.

83. Stanley, "From San Rafael to the Civil War and Back Again," *Marin County History*; National Archives, Pension Record of James Watson.

84. Dearborn, *Diary*, June 13, 1864; *Daily Alta California*, July 15, 1864.

85. Humphreys, *Field and Camp*, p. 58; *Daily Alta California*, July 15, 1864.

86. Crowninshield, June 26, 1864.

Chapter Eight

Jubal Early's Washington Raid

The 4th of July, 1864, was spent quietly in camp at Falls Church. There was some horse racing and jumping; on the whole, it was a rather peaceful day in camp. In the late afternoon Col. Lowell was informed of Gen. Jubal Early's advance down the Shenandoah valley and was ordered to send a scout to observe the gaps in the Blue Ridge. Early had been dispatched by Gen. Lee with 20,000 men to clear the Shenandoah of Federals, and, if practicable, invade Maryland, threaten Washington, and above all, draw troops away from Grant's army before Petersburg. In addition to observing the gaps, the Union scout was tasked with traveling through Leesburg at least twice in search of Mosby.[1]

At first light on the 5th, Major Forbes led 100 men of the 2nd Massachusetts and 50 from the 13th New York down the Little River Turnpike, through Aldie and on to Snicker's gap. By late in the afternoon Forbes had checked the gaps, and Leesburg and was confident there was no enemy on this side of the Blue Ridge. While at Leesburg, Forbes learned that Mosby had been conducting a raid near Point of Rocks but finding no sign of the enemy in the town, pushed on and camped south of Goose Creek.*[2]

Completing his raid at Point of Rocks, Mosby had a slight skirmish with the 8th Illinois Cavalry across the Potomac then headed south in the direction of Leesburg. Toward evening he learned of a detachment of cavalry seen in the vicinity of Aldie and Leesburg earlier in the day. Unsure of the size of the Yankee column, Mosby made camp to the west of Leesburg, his men sleeping lightly with reins at hand. Like his opponent he had 150 men.[3]

In the morning Forbes put his column back on the road, passing through Leesburg again before turning south toward Aldie. Mosby tailed the column through the morning, unsure of Forbes' intentions. When it became apparent that the Yankees would continue to Aldie before striking east for their camp, Mosby led his men off at an angle to reach the Little River Turnpike before the Yankees arrived. Striking

---

*Mosby was involved in cutting communication and supply lines near Harpers Ferry in preparation for Early's advance.

the Turnpike at Aldie, Forbes headed east for about a mile and a half and called the column to a halt for an hour's rest in the yard of the Skinner farm. The brick Mount Zion Church stood close by on the pike. Before allowing the men to rest the major posted pickets on the pike to the east and west of the farm.[4]

Mosby had struck the pike to the east near Arcola Post Office and prepared his men for a fight. The men were placed in a column of fours, and a single artillery piece (a 12 lb. howitzer) was placed at the top a low ridge along the road. A dozen skirmishers rode slowly down the pike in the direction of Forbes' men. As Mosby's men approached, the Federal pickets fired off a few shots and fell back in the direction of the Skinner farm. Hearing the firing of his advance guard, Forbes quickly called his men to arms, placing them in a double rank across the field and stretching over the pike. Capt. Goodwin Stone of Company L commanded the forward rank, 2nd Lt. Charles Amory of G Company the second. A third rank was forming behind the other two and all indications were that the Federals had deployed well and were ready to meet the charge. Then everything went wrong for Major Forbes and his men.[5]

The howitzer perched on the low ridge thundered, firing its only shot of the fight. The 2nd Massachusetts and 13th New York had never been under artillery fire and in hindsight the results were predictable. The shell was high and wide and missed the Yankee formation, but when it exploded the men and horses in the front rank "...were very much demoralized, and the solid formation of the line was completely broken...." Mosby's dozen skirmishers charged forward during this confusion and let down the rails of a fence that separated the field from the pike. With the fence down Mosby's column poured through, "...swooping down like Indians, yelling like fiends, discharging their pistols with fearful rapidity, and threatening to completely envelop our little band."[6]

Mosby extended his line to the left, hitting Forbes from the front and on the flank. For some of the Federals the shock was too much and they fled in a perfect rout. But not all fled. Forbes was well known to the Confederates as "Lowell's fighting Major" and there was still plenty of fight left in him. He called for the remainder of his men to fall back a few hundred yards to a wood at the right and rear of his position. Capt. Stone and Chaplain Humphreys yelled out to the men to reform in the woods, Forbes riding in front of them and waving his saber in an effort to inspire the men. Mosby saw his opportunity when the front rank of Federals began to fall back and ordered a charge all along his line. By this time the rear two squadrons of Federals were in flight and only the officers and the Californians of companies A and L attempted to rally with the major. Twice more the two companies rallied only to be pushed back in the direction of Mount Zion Church. Each time they stood, the remaining Northerners poured a terrific fire into the attackers, impressing one of the Confederates who later recalled, "[The Californians] fought as gallantly as men could fight." Conspicuous in the fighting was Sgt. William Hilliard (A), California, who distinguished himself in trying to rally the men.[7]

Forbes attempted one final stand, shouting to his men, "Now rally around your leader." He still carried his sword and when he saw the chance, slashed at Mosby himself. The sword would probably have killed the Rebel leader if not for the quick action of Capt. Tom Richards, who reached out and deflected the saber with his pistol causing it to sink deeply into his own shoulder. In a flash Mosby leveled his pistol at Forbes but miraculously missed his aim. Before he could fire again Forbes' horse was hit and fell, pinning the major to the ground, forcing his surrender. Seeing Forbes helpless on the ground, Lt. Amory charged forward to assist but was shot from the saddle. Forbes remained in Mosby's hands, an unusual beginning to a lifelong friendship.[8]

The remains of the Union force were now in flight northward on the Old Carolina Road. With Major Forbes down, the senior officer was Capt. Stone who, "...with great coolness and splendid pluck...," managed to rally a few men for a final volley. No sooner had his men fired than he lurched in the saddle with a bullet in his spine. Somehow Stone stayed in the saddle as his horse galloped off the field and into some woods. His horse eventually brought him back to the Falls Church camp, 14 miles away, but the wound was mortal and he died on the 18th of July.[9]

Their blood up, the victorious Rangers charged after the fleeing Yankees leaving the battlefield to the dead and wounded. The scene, which covered several acres, was particularly horrible considering the comparatively small size of the two forces. "The ground was strewn with guns, pistols, blankets and equipments of all kinds; dead and wounded were lying around; horses wounded and maddened with pain and fright, dashed wildly over the battleground, while others lay trembling, or rearing unable to stand."[10]

When Stone's horse carried him from the field, the only Union officer left on the

William H.J. Hilliard, Sgt. Company A, California Hundred. Later 2nd Lt. of Company L, 2nd Massachusetts Cavalry. *Courtesy of Vallejo Naval and Historical Museum.*

road was Chaplain Humphreys. Spurring his horse the chaplain caught up with some of the men and urged them to slow down before they exhausted their horses. Before they could respond a group of rebels appeared firing a volley that dropped one of the Yankees from the saddle. Pvt. Nathan Huestis of Company H, recalled a harrowing escape: "Then two rebs started after me, it was a race for life, and as their horses

were better than mine they soon came up with me. One of them, who was ahead, had the point of his sabre within four inches of my back, when our Chaplain rode up and shot him through the back; if ever I thanked God it was for that." The good chaplain, who did not mention this episode in his own memoirs, tried to make his load lighter by dropping his gauntlets, overcoat, and oat bag. One of the lead horses was played out and crashed to the ground, pinning its rider to the road. As the pursuing Confederates passed the trapped man, he was shot while vainly trying to surrender.[11]

Mosby and a dozen of his men were in hot pursuit of the fleeing Yankees, and for some reason were concentrating on capturing Chaplain Humphreys. Later the clergyman learned that the Confederates believed him to be "Yankee" Davis, the pro–Union civilian who frequently served as a guide for the 2nd Massachusetts. Davis rode a roan colored horse; the only other roan in the regiment, as luck would have it, was the "Parson's cob." But the horse had endurance and was steadily distancing itself from the pursuers.

Just as it seemed the chaplain was out of danger he had pangs of guilt for fleeing when the wounded and dying needed assistance. When the Confederates were out of sight he turned his horse sharply into the woods and waited patiently while the rebels passed and then gave up the chase. When darkness fell he set out back down the Old Carolina Road, walking his horse and softly calling out for any wounded men. The first he came across was the wounded Pvt. Owen Fox of Company H, still trapped under the body of his dead horse. Unable to find the wound in the dark, Humphreys nervously approached a nearby farmhouse for help.

Every farmer in the region was an ally of Mosby and there was real danger for a man alone in the area. Rebel or not the farmer had compassion and loaned Humphreys a lantern and blanket and helped him bring Fox into his home. The farmer's wife cared for the trooper as the chaplain set out looking for the man he'd seen shot from the saddle, still accompanied by the kindly farmer. The wounded man, a trooper from the 13th New York, was soon found and brought back to the farmhouse. The New Yorker was seriously wounded but would recover. Pvt. Fox died that night in terrible pain, crying out to Humphreys, "Chaplain, they shot me after I surrendered."[12]

During the night the chaplain's horse was stolen, a fact he learned when he ventured out to dig a grave for Fox. Humphreys was sweating at this unpleasant duty when a Confederate rode into the yard mounted on his missing roan. With a cocked pistol pointed at his head, the clergyman was forced down the road leaving the grave digging to the farmer. The Confederate soldier mocked his prisoner, singing rebel songs and ballads, and forcing him to pick up the pace in an attempt to overtake the prisoners with their 12-hour head start.[13]

As the day progressed the captor began to covet the chaplain's possessions; "…every now and then something I had about me excited my captor's propensities, and he would demand it with a gesture towards his pistol that could not be denied. Thus I was relieved in succession of my watch, my gold pencil, my steel spurs, my knife, my money, my photographs of friends at home, and at last he insisted on swapping hats with me. I had always prided myself on my shrewdness at a bargain, but I must confess that in this case

Opposite: Capt. Goodwin Stone, Company L, 2nd Massachusetts Cavalry. Died July 18, 1864, of wounds received July 6, 1864, at Aldie, Virginia. *Courtesy of U.S.A.M.H.I.*

Chaplain Charles A. Humphreys, 2nd Massachusetts Cavalry. Captured July 6, 1864, near Aldie, Virginia. *Courtesy of U.S.A.M.H.I.*

Mosby in the hope of being released to return to the wounded, he was rebuffed by the adjutant who answered, "No! You're a damned abolitionist preacher and you are going to suffer for it." Several days of marching, with little to eat, found them in a Lynchburg prison, actually a converted tobacco warehouse. For eight days the prisoners suffered under the most squalid conditions. On the sixth day, a Sunday, the chaplain gave a patriotic sermon that was overheard by the guards. For that crime he was placed in the guardhouse, where he stayed until all the prisoners were loaded on railroad cars for a tortuous six day journey to Macon, Georgia. At Macon the officers were taken to Camp Oglethorpe while the enlisted men traveled further down the line to Andersonville.[15]

For two weeks the officers suffered in the "Devil's Acre" until they were again put on the cars, this time bound for Charleston, South Carolina. The city of Charleston had been under bombardment by Union guns on Morris Island for several weeks. In an effort to halt the artillery the Confederates imprisoned some 300 Union officers, including Gen. George Stoneman, in the four-story brick Charleston Jail in the middle of the city, then notified the Union commander of their presence. This

the Virginia chivalry got the better of me."*[14]

Eventually Humphreys was able to join Major Forbes and the 53 other prisoners from the brigade. Asking to speak to

---

*The mild chaplain was still bitter over his treatment years later when he read that his captor had been praised for his act of heroism in capturing a prisoner and horse. "If it was an act of heroism to steal that horse from his hitch outside the house on a dark night, and then to drive before the muzzle of his pistol an unarmed Chaplain to prison, then we can only say that among guerrillas honors were easy." Humphreys, Field and Camp, p. 110.

desperate attempt at halting the bombardment failed and shells continued to rain down on Charleston, one every 15 minutes. "The prisoners constantly wear a forlorn and haggard look," reported one of the inmates, "owing in great measure to starvation and exposure to danger.... Constantly under fire by day and night ... many have become hopelessly insane while others have been incapacitated for all the duties of life hereafter, nothing but strong nerves and an inflexible will can save one under such circumstances." Maj. Gen. Foster, the commander of Union forces about Charleston, was furious and sent the following message to Maj. Gen. Samuel Jones, his counterpart in the city's defenses: "I must protest you placing defenseless prisoners of war in a position exposed to constant bombardment. It is an indefensible act of cruelty. The City of Charleston is a depot for military supplies. It contains not only arsenals but foundries and factories for the manufacture of munitions of war. Its wharves and the banks of the river on both sides are lined with hostile batteries. In its shipyards armed ironclads have been built and are building. To destroy these means of continuing the war is our plain object and duty. You seek to defeat this effort by means not known to honorable warfare — by placing unarmed and defenseless prisoners under fire. I have requested the President to place in my custody an equal number of prisoners of like grade, to be kept by me in positions exposed to the fire of your guns — so long as you continue a like course." Gen. Foster's plan was put into effect and soon the Confederates relented, moving the Union officers to another location, away from danger.[16]

After three weeks in Charleston Chaplain Humphreys, along with all other chaplains and surgeons, was selected for exchange. His messmates, Major Forbes and Lt. Amory, were both sick from the poor prison rations and polluted drinking water. Humphreys sold his boots to a guard using the money to buy food for his friends. His final act, before his release, was to strip and give them all his clothing to supplement their own ragged uniforms. On the 2nd of September he was released and within days was recuperating at Naushon, the island estate of John M. Forbes.[17]

Unknown to Major Forbes, letters and negotiations were in progress that would eventually result in his own release. Major F.P. Branch of the Confederate Army was a prisoner at Fort Pulaski, Georgia, and at the suggestion of some of Forbes' friends, requested that he be exchanged for Major Forbes at Charleston. For a time it appeared that Forbes would not be eligible for exchange, but rather, he would be singled out for confinement in the state penitentiary.[18]

Confederate officials had learned that Pvt. John H. Barnes of Mosby's battalion, who had been captured by the 1st D.C. Cavalry and 2nd Massachusetts in October 1863, had been sent to the Albany Penitentiary. Though the Confederate agent for exchange threatened the transfer, it did not come to pass. Nonetheless, during the last week of November Forbes was paroled and sent home to recover.[19]

Lt. Charles Amory was exchanged before Forbes but his wound at Zion Church and his sickness in southern prisons had broken his constitution for life. By mid–October he was dining in his father's home in Brookline with Chaplain Humphreys, an honored guest of the family. He eventually was well enough to return to the regiment for the closing campaigns and was there in the ranks during the Grand Review.[20]

When the word of the disaster at Mt. Zion Church reached the Falls Church camp, Lowell set off with 250 men and four ambulances to determine the extent of the defeat and gather up any wounded. After a year of sparring with Mosby and learning his tactics, there was no real thought that he could be pursued. Mosby had struck hard, as he had Capt. Reed in February, and was now far away, his men disbanded to wait for his next call.[21]

Though they had sparred and skirmished dozens of times, this was the third time in a year that Mosby's men and the 2nd Massachusetts had met with forces of comparatively equal size. Each time Mosby was able to take a decided advantage with a skillful use of terrain and surprise. Once again the colonel was forced to report he had been bested by his adversary: "I have only to report a perfect rout and a chase for five to seven miles." Lowell found 12 men dead on the field when he arrived, eight from his own regiment and four New Yorkers. The body of Owen Fox had been buried by the farmer on the Old Carolina Road, and he was not initially listed among the dead. The numbers of wounded and captured Lowell could only guess at, as those figures would change daily as stragglers wandered back to camp. Nine wounded and 38 captured was the final tally of the disastrous day at Mount Zion Church. Mosby reported a mere one killed and six wounded.*[22]

Among the dead was Pvt. John Johnson of Company I, a 21-year-old bricklayer from New York who had enlisted in the regiment 32 days before. Three other men from his company, Patrick Riordin, Charles Rollins, and Cornelius Tobin were found dead on the field, none of them having served more than 90 days. Cpl. Samuel Hanscom, of the California Hundred, was one of two westerners to die in the fight, the other being Corp. James McDonald, a 30-year-old miner from Company F. An English sailor, William Dumaresq, of Company K was the final name on the list of the day's killed in action. In the days to come, the list grew when Capt. Stone died from his wounds followed by Cpl. Bumgardner of the Hundred, who had been wounded twice before in skirmishes.[23]

Surprisingly, there was little blame placed upon any one individual for the defeat. The few people that felt Forbes' handling of the troops was the cause were definitely in the minority. Few officers have garnered so much praise after getting so thoroughly whipped. "Major Forbes, who was in command, fought gallantly, and was always in the thickest of the fight, encouraging and endeavoring to rally his men"; and, "Major Forbes, the bravest Federal officer we ever met"—these words from Mosby's men who had seen the major in action. Absent from the raid while sitting on a court-martial, Crowninshield expressed his worries in a letter home. "No one knows what has become of Major Forbes. I pray God he is safe, he is a man who would fight to the last & I fear he is killed." Finally, in his official report, Col. Lowell, rather than condemning Forbes, gave him additional praise. "The soldiers and citizens all speak in high terms of the gallantry of the officers; Major Forbes especially remained in the first field till every man had left it, emptied his revolver, and, in the second field, where Company A tried to stand, he disabled one man with his saber, and lunged through Col. Mosby's coat." In the days ahead, as the regiment's tempo reached a level as yet unseen, the talents of the "Fighting Major" would be sorely missed.[24]

The dead from the fight were buried on the field and the wounded brought back to the Falls Church camp. For the next two days the regiment sat by idly in camp as events to the north were becoming critical. Early's army had crossed the Potomac, brushing aside Union resistance in the Valley, and crossed the Potomac on the 5th

---

*A detailed list of casualties can be found in Appendix B.

and 6th at Shepherdstown. Now poised to sweep down from the northwest, Early had a once in lifetime opportunity to capture Washington. Ringed by massive fortifications, obstructions, and rifle pits, the defenses were an empty shell, the troops used to garrison the guns long since sent to Meade's Army of the Potomac. A swift march, in the style of "Stonewall" Jackson, and the capital would be his; but the capable Early was no Jackson.

Letting one day slip away, Early spent the 7th fruitlessly trying to find a way to crack the Federal position on Maryland Heights above Harpers Ferry. Frustrated in this attempt, he bypassed the pocket of resistance and pushed off to the east and the passes through South Mountain. Scratch forces of cavalry and militia attempted to slow the Confederate column, but it was hampered more effectively by the extreme heat and choking dust. Early's army had begun to straggle badly as it approached Frederick, where a small infantry force under Maj. Gen. Lew Wallace was preparing to challenge its advance. Severely outnumbered and without a prayer of victory, Wallace was reenforced at the 11th hour by troops of Brig. Gen. James Ricketts' 3rd Division of the VI Corps.[25]

Slow to see the danger presented by Early, Grant had finally ordered the VI and XIX Corps to the capital. With Ricketts' men swelling his numbers to near 8,000, Wallace, still badly outmanned, prepared a defensive position to the southeast of Frederick, along the east bank of the Monocacy River.[26]

Directly to the south of the two forces, still picketing their stretch of the Potomac, was Major Thompson's battalion at Muddy Branch. Not called upon to join Wallace's force, Thompson sent Capt. Eigenbrodt and Company E to picket the fords on the lower stretches of the Monocacy. Capt. Manning's Company M, led by Lt. Partridge, was posted on the Frederick Pike, to report any Confederate breakthrough and movement on Washington.[27]

The outcome of the battle of the Monacacy was inevitable, and by late afternoon the remains of Wallace's army was retreating in the direction of Baltimore. Although he failed to stop Early, Wallace was able to slow the advance for one critical day, giving time for the Union command to organize the city's defenses, and for the arrival of Grant's reenforcements. When news of the defeat reached department headquarters, Thompson was directed to fall back in the direction of Washington, but to stay parallel to the Confederate column and apprise Augur of Early's movements.[28]

Thompson drew in all of his pickets, loaded the camp gear on a canal boat, and set off on his mission. A fatigue party was organized to chop down trees and otherwise stall the Confederate advance, but other than hearing the booming of distant artillery, there was no hint of action in their quarter. It took Early all of the 10th to cross his artillery and supply trains over the Monacacy and get back on the route to Washington City. Light skirmishing occurred between his advance and Thompson's troopers, who slowly fell back while making reports of the enemy position.[29]

The bulk of the 2nd Massachusetts continued to sit idly in camp at Falls Church as events escalated across the Potomac. Finally, on the 10th of July, Lowell was directed to send one of his three regiments across to Gen. Augur, the other two staying behind in the event the Rebels made a move to the south of the city. Sensing an opportunity, Lowell requested permission, which was granted, to turn command of the brigade over to Col. Lazelle and accompany the 2nd Massachusetts across the river and on to Tennalytown.[30]

When Wallace retreated toward Baltimore, a small 60-man detachment of cavalry was cut off and compelled to fall back in the direction of Washington. Led by Capt. A. Levi Wells of the 18th Illinois Cavalry, they were eventually reenforced by a 500-man "brigade" under the command of Major William H. Fry of the 16th Pennsylvania Cavalry. Fry's command was an amalgam of dismounted and convalescent troopers from the Cavalry Depot, hurriedly mounted and sent to the front. Most of the troopers were strangers to each other; nearly every eastern cavalry regiment was represented in the body of horsemen. Fry led his small force northward, running into Early's advance north of Rockville where he skillfully sparred with the Confederates, forcing further delays as the rebels were compelled to deploy their forces against the threat. Repeating the scenario several times, Fry's force was eventually charged and driven back toward the defenses of Washington.[31]

July 11 dawned hot and hazy as Lowell trotted his command out on the Rockville Pike in search of the enemy, while Thompson's battalion was left to help man the rifle pits in front of Fort Stephens. Leading some 800 men (three squadrons of the 2nd Massachusetts and one of the 8th Illinois) out on the road to Rockville, the column came upon Fry's exhausted troopers. Adding the major's men to his force, Lowell pushed on up the road where he finally found the enemy in the vicinity of Old Tavern. About five miles out from Fort Reno, the Confederates were met and light skirmishing began, with Lowell's men slowly giving ground. Other squadrons of the 2nd Massachusetts sent out on the River Road and towards Brookville, likewise were compelled to gradually fall back on the line of fortifications. By midafternoon Lowell's cavalry had fallen back on the Union pickets, guarded by the massive emplaced guns.[32]

The Confederates brought up a small rifled cannon to support their infantry advance, but the 2nd Massachusetts was not shaken like their comrades had been at Mt. Zion Church the week before. The day spent on the picket line dragged slowly by, the men sparring lightly with the rebels, and watching the big guns in the fortifications send "flour barrels" at the enemy. "We were placed," recalled Pvt. Warren Cochran of Company F, "upon a kind of heavy skirmish line, where the rifle cannon shells came frequently into our midst. And the whining of small balls together with the general unsteadiness of things caused by the travel and explosion of the 100 lb. shells from our forts served to enliven our interests and keep us on duty without apparent fatigue."[33]

Pvt. Towle recalled the day on the front line. "Our squadron on being relieved from the skirmish line took a position on the main road back of a little rise just high enough to afford protection. Late in the afternoon a detachment of 90 infantry was ordered forward to relieve the dismounted cavalry on the skirmish line. They came marching up the road in close order with arms at right shoulder shift like militia on parade. They were very soldierly appearing until they reached the brow of the rise in front of us where they were first exposed to the confederate fire. None of them were hit, but the immediate result was that the command as a command, officers and all disappeared; and I often wondered, when, if ever, some of them stopped running. While there it was amusing to see civilians come out with their guns to get a shot at a reb, but none ventured beyond the brow of the hill."[34]

As the hot Monday wore on, the Confederate army continued to move forward and into positions around Silver Spring. Slowed to a crawl by the intense summer heat, some soldiers actually dying of sunstroke, Early had lost his race to take the northern capital. As his sharpshooters began to skirmish with the 14,000 clerks, convalescents, and militia manning the city defenses, Maj. Gen. Horatio G. Wright's veterans from the VI Corps and Brig. Gen. William Emory's Division of the XIX Corps bolstered the defenders with an extra 11,000 seasoned troops.[35]

Unsure of the numbers in the Union lines, Early continued to send forward skirmishers and sharpshooters, as his main body closed up and prepared for a possible assault. The fire on the skirmishing line heated up, and two men of the 2nd Massachusetts fell to enemy bullets. Pvt. John Dolan (D), Natick, Massachusetts, and Pvt. James McGrath (K), Worcester, were killed during the sporadic firing. Thomas Merry (L), California, took a bullet in the leg, but soon recovered and returned to duty. Night fell but the Confederates declined to make an assault, Early waiting for morning to make his final decision.[36]

Another hot morning presaged a hotter day. Shortly after dawn on the 12th, Lowell led two squadrons out on the River Road, between Forts Reno and Bayrd, to find the position of the Confederate right flank. Sending companies in several directions, he learned that Brig. Gen. John McCausland's cavalry brigade held the right along the Rockville Pike. Gathering in his patrols, Lowell dismounted three companies, dividing them between himself and Lt. Col. Crowninshield, and turned the Confederate flank, driving back the 14th Virginia Cavalry about one mile, "…the enemy throwing away arms, equipments, and retreating in great confusion." Confirming there was no enemy infantry in the area, Lowell held his new position for a few hours and then withdrew, followed closely by the enemy, to the Union infantry pickets. "Checked the enemy here and held him for the day notwithstanding they used their Artillery and sharpshooters. It was rather warm but the boys soon got used to their fire and took things cool." The tone in the diaries and letters of the regiment seems to indicate a metamorphosis. No longer opposed to guerrillas and bushwhackers that attacked from ambush, they were up against the Confederates' front-line troops and were actually enjoying themselves.[37]

Sometime during the day, Early learned of Grant's reenforcements and wisely chose to refrain from attacking. Though skirmishing continued throughout the day, the Confederate commander was resolved to retreat after nightfall. An interesting target for the sharpshooters appeared in the afternoon, when President Lincoln stood on the parapet of Fort Stephens to see the war firsthand. Gen. Wright convinced the president to take cover, but not before a surgeon standing next to Lincoln was struck by a bullet. Civil war legends persist that Lincoln retired only after someone yelled, "Get down you fool!" though few can agree who shouted the famous line. Perhaps it was the president's being shot at that spurred on Wright, but by dusk he had ordered a brigade forward to push back the troublesome sharpshooters. As night fell the Confederates quietly withdrew from their lines and began a retreat to Virginia.[38]

The lack of an enemy in the morning came as a shock to the Union command, which hastily sent out the cavalry to determine just where they were. Lowell, with 800 or so troopers, pressed up the Rockville Pike and by 10:15 had closed with the Rebel rear guard about half a mile from the small town of Rockville. Confederate stragglers scooped up by the advance were played out, complaining of having been "run to death," during the days of endless marching. Within 15 minutes, Capt. Rumery of Company D reported from the right of the Poolesville Road that he was observing enemy infantry columns. Lowell was on the flank of the retreating army, urging headquarters that "Any serious attempt against them with infantry must, I think, be made soon." The Union response was slow, and it would be late afternoon before Wright's divisions marched out past Fort Reno. An opportunity was passing and there was nothing Lowell could do but watch the cloud of dust marking the Confederate retreat, as he followed them closely moving to the west.[39]

Unable to attack the numerically superior Confederate rear guard, Lowell slowly followed the retreating column, entering Rockville at about 2 P.M. As a precaution, Fry's men were left on the high ground just outside of town, at the junction of the Washington and Baltimore roads. Stopping in front of the Montgomery House, Lowell dismounted and allowed the body of his troops to rest as he wrote out a quick report for Gen. Hardin. Lt. Col. Crowninshield, with two squadrons, was sent out on the Darnestown Road to keep a closer eye on the retreating column.[40]

The Confederate rearguard, a Virginia Cavalry Brigade under the command of Col. William "Mudwall" Jackson (a cousin of the famous "Stonewall") was becoming hard pressed to keep the Federal advance at bay. The Confederate cavalry was exhausted after an aborted raid to free the prisoners at Point Lookout, an expedition that had led them east of the capital on a man- and horse-breaking ride. When Gen. Early learned how close the Federals were on his heels he ordered Brig. Gen. Bradley T. Johnson and his famous "Maryland Line" to push back the Yankees and gain some breathing room. Lowell was so effective in his pursuit that Johnson later wrote, "The Second Massachusetts Cavalry hung upon our rear and made it very uncomfortable for us generally."[41]

Taking up a defensive position along a small stream, Jackson's troops waited for the Federal advance in a long double line of skirmishers with Johnson's mounted squadrons behind. Crowninshield, thinking he was still pushing an exhausted rear guard detachment, was rapidly approaching two brigades strung out in fighting formation.[42]

"As we advanced," recalled Pvt. George Towle, "to a fringe of pine timber which grew so close that our horses could not pass through, ... numbers 1, 2 and 3 of each set of fours, of who I was one, was left to hold the horses. Beyond the fringe of pines was low ground overgrown with high grass and weeds through which there were ditches, and while our dismounted skirmish line was crossing that the confederates deployed a very strong double line of infantry skirmishers which flanked our line for a long distance at either end, and the confederate line pushed rapidly forward. The force was altogether too much for ours and our line commenced a hasty retreat and many were unable to escape."[43]

Caught unexpected by Jackson's men, Crowninshield's troops, already retreating, were stampeded when Johnson's Marylanders charged through Mudwall's line and into the fleeing Yankees. "The dust in the road was so thick that it was almost impossible to there distinguish friend from foe." The dust, along with the tall grass and ditches, provided a haven and escape route for several of the men, while several others were immediately taken prisoner. The horse holders made a break for the road and with their riderless horses kicking up more dust, made a circuitous ride around Rockville to safety. The bulk of the detachment fell back on Rockville in a rout.[44]

Writing his report on the porch of the Montgomery House, Lowell heard the firing but before he could give any orders Crowninshield's retreating men ran smack into his column resting in the road. The first few ranks melted away in the rush, and the dust and confusion nearly caused the entire force to panic. With the crush of men and horses blocking the road and effectively preventing a counterchage to stem the tide, Lowell needed an organized defense but there was no time. "But Colonel Lowell was not a man to give up the day."[45]

Clutching his hat in his hand, Lowell shouted, "Dismount! and let your horses go!" there being no time or spare men to hold them. Letting a horse go in battle was not a natural act for a cavalryman, and it was a sign of the utter trust the men had gained in him that they instantly obeyed. Forming a hasty line across the road, "He waited till the enemy came near, fired one volley at short range,— it checked the rush; another,— it stopped it. Then Lowell, on foot, ran out before them, waving his hat, and they ran forward firing, and the rout was averted."[46]

For a brief time the tide was turned, and the Confederates retreated back through the dust, seeking refuge in backyards and side streets. Lowell's troops pushed nearly to the edge of town before the superior numbers of the enemy forced an orderly withdrawal out of Rockville to Major Fry's position at the crossroads. Several men from Crowninshield's shattered squadrons who had escaped the rebel onslaught were captured as the enemy surged forward again, cutting off escape.[47]

"On turning, I observed that all had fled from our part of the field except one Corpl. of my acquaintance, and I urged him to try for escape. We passed over an open block and into the town through a withering shower of shot, and I found seclusion in a garden from where I was driven in the enchanted land." The heat and dust of the day soon overcame Pvt. Cochran of Company A who was forced out of hiding to find a drink. "In seeking water I lost my liberty and soon learned that more than fifty of my Regt. had been so unfortunate as myself."[48]

Passing through Rockville, Johnson sent his men to the south in an effort to flank Lowell out of his position. "But, neither Lowell's Californians nor the stubborn Fry would break." Fry's troops responded by charging headlong into the Confederates, briefly taking Johnson prisoner. Lowell's position on the high ground was good but could not be held for long against a determined attack. Falling back again, this time about two miles outside of Rockville, Lowell took a strong position that Johnson declined to test. Feeling he had followed Early's orders, Johnson was content to take his men back to Rockville. From start to finish the affair lasted barely 20 minutes.[49]

As always, Lowell's report was far from sugarcoated; nor did it bulge with excuses. "My regiment in the town, I fear was mostly enveloped by the enemy and were very severely whipped." At first glance it appears Lowell definitely got the worst of it, but considering he had one scratch regiment against two brigades, it was nothing short of a miracle his command was not wiped out. He reported 30 casualties that afternoon, but, unusually, he was far from the actual tally. One man dead on the field, 28 wounded (three mortally), and 32 captured for a total of 61 casualties. The numbers go up when six deserters from Company G are factored in. The Confederate dead and wounded are unknown, but a captain and 37 privates were captured, indicating the casualties on each side were probably fairly equal.*[50]

By midafternoon Lowell's position was stable and he was ordered to Maj. Gen. Wright's headquarters at Tennalytown to give a thorough report of the day's events, as well as to pass on the location of the rebel army. The infantry had finally left the Washington defenses, and with Major Thompson's battalion in the lead, began the pursuit of Early.[51]

---

*A detailed list of the casualties can be found in Appendix C.

In command while Lowell was with Wright, Crowninshield kept a close eye on the Confederates remaining in Rockville and endeavored to find ammunition for his men as well as forage and water for the horses which had gone through the day with neither. Through the night stragglers from the fight returned to camp, lessening the days losses and increasing the numbers for the next day's pursuit.[52]

In the morning Lowell sent scouts to the north towards Brookville and Middleburg, confirming that Early had headed for the fords of the Potomac and back to Virginia. Passing through the now deserted Rockville, Lowell once again closed with Johnson's command outside Poolesville. The skirmish that lasted for an hour and a half had none of the intensity as the fight the day before. His 800 troopers still without infantry support, Lowell saw no point in a useless spilling of blood. By the time the VI Corps finally arrived, Early had gotten his troops across the Potomac by way of Conrads and Edwards ferries.[53]

Notes

1. Dearborn, *Diary*, July 4, 1864; Humphreys, *Field and Camp*, pp. 93–94.
2. *OR*, XXXVII, Pt. 1, pp. 358–59.
3. Williamson, *Mosby's Rangers*, p. 186.
4. Scott, *Partisan Life with Mosby*, pp. 246–47.
5. Humphreys, *Field and Camp*, p. 96; *OR*, Vol. XXXVII, Pt. 1, p. 359.
6. Humphreys, *Field and Camp*, p. 96; Orton, *Record of California Men in the War of the Rebellion, 1861 to 1867*, p. 850; *OR*, XXXVII, Pt. 1, pp. 359–60.
7. Munson, *Reminiscences of a Mosby Guerrilla*, p. 96; Scott, *Partisan Life with Mosby*, p. 248; Williamson, *Mosby's Rangers*, p. 187; *OR*, XXXVII, Pt. 1, p. 359; *Boston Herald*, July 12, 1864.
8. Crawford, *Mosby and His Men*, p. 227; Emerson, *Life and Letters*, p. 454; Humphreys, *Field and Camp*, pp. 98–99.
9. Humphreys, *Field and Camp*, p. 100.
10. Williamson, *Mosby's Rangers*, p. 188.
11. Humphreys, *Field and Camp*, p. 101; National Archives, Record Group 94, Pension Record of Nathan Huestis.
12. Humphreys, *Field and Camp*, pp. 105–06.
13. Humphreys, *Field and Camp*, pp. 107–110.
14. Humphreys, *Field and Camp*, p. 111.
15. Humphreys, *Field and Camp*, pp. 113–32.
16. Humphreys, *Field and Camp*, pp. 127–38; Speer, *Portals to Hell*, p. 214; *OR*, VII, pp. 826–27, 874–76, 1007.
17. Humphreys, *Field and Camp*, pp. 142–43.
18. *OR*, VII, pp. 867–69.
19. *OR*, VII, pp. 792–93.
20. Humphreys, *Field and Camp*, pp. 148, 407.
21. *OR*, XXXVII, Pt. 1, pp. 358–60.
22. Schouler, *Annual Report of the Adjutant General of Massachusetts for the Year Ending 1864*, p. 947; Russell, *Memoirs of Col. John S. Mosby*, p. 276; *OR*, XXXVII, Pt. 1, pp. 358–60; *New York Tribune*, July 11, 1864.
23. *Massachusetts Soldiers, Sailors, and Marines*, Vol. VI, pp. 228–328.
24. Crawford, *Mosby and His Men*, p. 227; Crowninshield, July 7, 1864; Williamson, *Mosby's Rangers*, p. 187; *OR*, XXXVII, Pt. 1, pp. 358–60.
25. Cooling, *Jubal Early's Raid on Washington*, pp. 38–43, 53–61.
26. Cooling, *Jubal Early's Raid on Washington*, pp. 53–57; Early, *Jubal Early's Memoirs*, p. 387.
27. *OR*, XXXVII, Pt. 1, p. 143.
28. *OR*, XXXVII, Pt. 1, p. 142.
29. Cooling, *Jubal Early's Raid on Washington*, p. 102; *OR*, XXXVII, Pt. 1, p. 143.
30. *OR*, XXXVII, Pt. 1, p. 170.
31. Cooling, *Jubal Early's Raid on Washington*, p. 102; Fitzpatrick, "Jubal Early and the Californians," *Civil War Times Illustrated*, May 1998, p. 53.
32. Emerson, *Life and Letters*, p. 321–22; *OR*, XXXVII, Pt. 1, pp. 239–240, 249.
33. Cochran, *A True Story of the Civil War 1861–1865*, p. 13; Emerson, *Life and Letters*, p. 321.
34. Towle, *Recollections*, p. 30.
35. Cooling, *Jubal Early's Raid on Washington*, p. 121.
36. Cooling, *Jubal Early's Raid on Washington*, pp. 114, 123, 126; *Massachusetts Soldiers,*

Sailors, and Marines, Vol. VI, pp. 228–328; National Archives, Record Group 94, Pension Record of Thomas Merry.

37. Dearborn, *Diary*, July 12, 1864; *OR*, XXXVII, Pt. 1, pp. 237, 240, 250.

38. Bowen, *Yankee from Olympus*, p. 194; Cooling, *Jubal Early's Raid on Washington*, pp. 142–45.

39. Cooling, *Jubal Early's Raid on Washington*, pp. 182–83; *OR*, XXXVII, Pt. 1, pp. 251, 276.

40. Fitzpatrick, "Jubal Early and the Californians," *Civil War Times Illustrated*, May 1998, p. 55; *OR*, XXXVII, Pt. 1, p. 252.

41. Backus, "Californians in the Field," *MOLLUS.*, p. 12; Cooling, *Jubal Early's Raid on Washington*, pp. 157–76, 183; Humphreys, *Field and Camp*, p. 149.

42. Fitzpatrick, "Jubal Early and the Californians," *Civil War Times Illustrated*, May 1998, p. 56.

43. Towle, *Recollections*, pp. 13–14.

44. Fitzpatrick, "Jubal Early and the Californians," *Civil War Times Illustrated*, May 1998, p. 56; Towle, *Recollections*, p. 14; *OR*, XXXVII, Pt. 1, pp. 260, 280.

45. Higginson, "Lowell," p. 318; Humphreys, *Field and Camp*, p. 150.

46. Cochran, *A True Story of the Civil War 1861–1865*, p. 4; Emerson, *Life and Letters*, pp. 40–41; Humphreys, *Field and Camp*, p. 150.

47. Cochran, *A True Story of the Civil War 1861–1865*, p. 4; Fitzpatrick, "Jubal Early and the Californians," *Civil War Times Illustrated*, May 1998, pp. 57–60; *OR*, XXXVII, Pt. 1, p. 252.

48. Cochran, *A True Story of the Civil War 1861–1865*, p. 4.

49. Fitzpatrick, "Jubal Early and the Californians," *Civil War Times Illustrated*, May 1998, pp. 60–61.

50. *Massachusetts Soldiers, Sailors, and Marines*, Vol. VI, pp. 228–328; *OR*, XXXVII, Pt. 1, pp. 252, 280.

51. *OR*, XXXVII, Pt. 1, pp. 278, 287.

52. *OR*, XXXVII, Pt. 1, p. 282.

53. Dearborn, *Diary*, July 14, 1864; *OR*, XXXVII, Pt. 1, p. 252.

Chapter Nine

The Shenandoah Valley

With the retreat of Early's army back to the Old Dominion and the marshaling of Federal forces for a pursuit, the 2nd Massachusetts Cavalry entered a new chapter in its history and left behind a year of picketing and raiding against Mosby. Although they would face Mosby and his Rangers again, no longer would they be tied to the defenses of Washington or the Independent Cavalry Brigade of the XXII Corps. Command of the brigade would soon pass officially to Col. Lazelle of the 16th New York Cavalry who had been in nominal command since Lowell led his regiment north into Maryland.

The first two weeks following the fight at Rockville were spent marching and countermarching across the northern Virginia countryside. Crossing the Potomac on the 15th of July, 1864, at Kelly's Ford, it once again seemed that Lowell's command was the only one involved in the pursuit. Wright's VI Corps and part of the XIX Corps under Brig. Gen. Emory had not reached Poolesville until late on the 14th, long after Early had escaped across the river. For the next two days Wright did little more than consolidate his straggling command. An order on the 15th to send Lowell two regiments and a rifled battery from the VI Corps appears to have been disregarded in the reorganization of troops around Poolesville. Lowell would have to make do with the 2nd Massachusetts Cavalry and the "Provisional Brigade" he'd led since the 11th.[1]

From Kelly's Ford Lowell traveled to an elevation overlooking White's Ford where his troops confirmed the location of Early's columns. "At dusk they gave us a salute of 8 guns. One horse was killed and ten men wounded."* This volley constituted the day's action, Lowell withdrawing to Harrison's Island for the night. In the morning, July 16th, the northern cavalry recrossed into Maryland, rode to White's Ford, and led the VI Corps in an uncontested crossing of the Potomac. For the next few days the regiment slowly followed up Early's retreat into the Shenandoah Valley through Snicker's Gap.[2]

The Union Army of West Virginia, under Gen. David Hunter entered the picture when it came out of the Alleghenies and threatened Early from the west. Fighting between the two forces compelled Early to withdraw up the Valley, prompting Wright to believe, "...the object of the

---

None of the wounded were from the 2nd Massachusetts Cavalry.

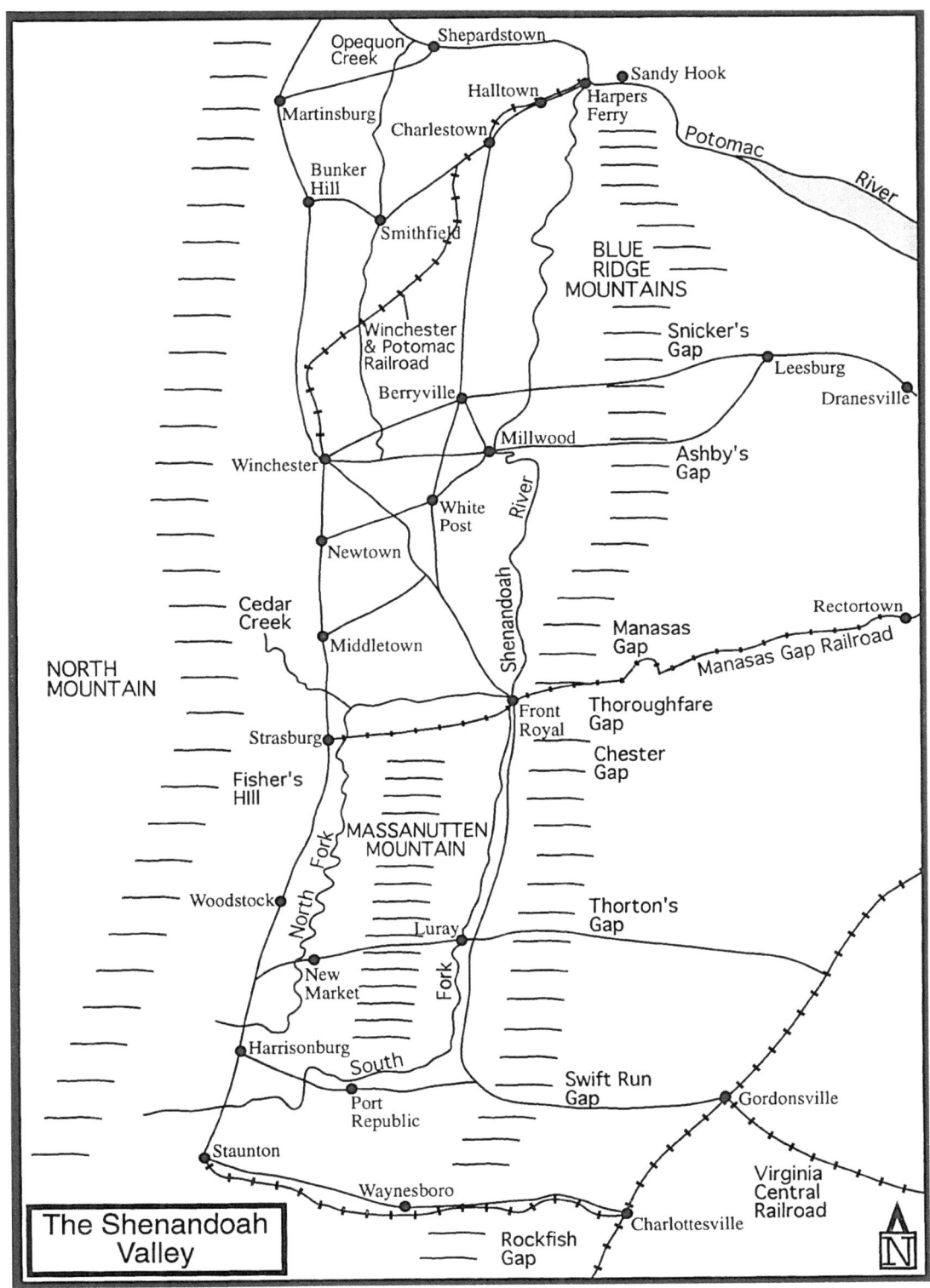

expedition to be accomplished." Just when it appeared that a sizable force was in position to challenge Early, Wright chose to break off the pursuit and return to the Washington fortifications. On the 21st, the 2nd Massachusetts Cavalry was posted to cover the right flank of the VI Corps as it about faced and marched back to the capital, leaving the fate of the Valley in the hands of Hunter. The 23rd found the regiment back in their old camp at Fall's Church and Major Thompson's battalion back at Muddy Branch. It would prove to be a short stay.[3]

When Early learned of Wright's return to Washington he reversed his army, swept aside Hunter's inferior force, and again dispatched troops into Maryland. Wright once more led the VI and XIX Corps out of Washington in pursuit of the Rebel invaders. As Early's intention at the start of his campaign had been to draw forces away from Petersburg and keep them from assisting Grant, it is obvious that at this point he had greatly succeeded. Early on the morning of the 26th, Lowell was summoned and the 2nd Massachusetts Cavalry placed at the head of the pursuing column. By 4:30 P.M. the advance had reached Rockville where a halt was called and the infantry came up. Thompson's battalion at Muddy Branch was relieved by the 8th Illinois Cavalry and joined the regiment that evening.[4]

On the 27th of July, as the infantry advanced to Monocacy, the cavalry under Lowell was sent to watch the fords of the Potomac to ensure Early's main body was not making another dash on the capital. For the next several days it was the same story all over again — march and countermarch, with the exception of Thompson with 600 men who remained in Poolesville. The week was best summed up in a letter by Lt. Col. Crowninshield to his mother.

> Hd. Qrs. Monocacy River Md.
> Aug 2nd 1864
>
> My Dear Mammy
> A little over a week ago I wrote to you from Falls Church saying that I would write you again & favor you with a longer letter the next day. That night at two o'clock I got orders to report with my Regt. to Maj. Gen. Wright. Since that time we have done hard marching but no fighting. We have been in Shepardstown Va. & South Mountain pass where I was in a fight two years ago & in fact we have been almost everywhere except where we ought to have been. Gen. Hunter who now commands all the forces seems to do exactly what he ought not to do. Instead of being in Winchester Va. now as he ought to be we are on the Monocacy & leave Maryland & Pennsylvania open to the Rebel cavalry. Hunter has men enough to defeat the rebel cavalry but he has been using them up by hard & useless marches & has thus far invariably marched in the wrong direction. I am disgusted & I think that the officers & men of the army feel that they have not been properly handled. We ought to have fought the enemy just beyond Snicker's Gap & I thought of course we were going to, but instead of that we marched for Washington & the general said that the Rebels were in full retreat for Richmond. We all knew that that was not so & we felt that if we pushed on we could fight Gen. Early & probably recapture most of his plunder. Three days ago we might have fought the Rebels at Martinsburg but a little cavalry raid into Pennsylvania recalled all our army into Maryland & caused long & hard marches with no result.* Such melancholy imbecility on the part of our leaders is disgusting. What we will do I don't know & I don't much care. I am not normally desponding but if all our armies are managed as badly as this one is I don't think the war will ever end.[5]

The cavalry raid was the infamous Chambersburg raid where Early's cavalry, failing to receive a demanded ransom, burned a majority of the town to the ground.

During the hard marching, Major Thompson's "battalion" of 600 men continued to scout the fords near Poolesville. On the 30th a detachment of the 8th Illinois Cavalry was overwhelmed by a company of Mosby's men at Cheeks Ford, and in his report of the fight, Major J.M. White claimed that Thompson had been within supporting distance. Though it was not a true statement (the guilty party was a Lt. Van Ness of the 3rd New Jersey Cavalry), when Maj. Gen. Augur saw the report he ordered White to confirm that Thompson had indeed failed to support him. Though the confusion was quickly cleared up and everyone made assurances that Thompson had not acted improperly, this event appears to have affected Thompson greatly, and coupled with all the previous problems within the regiment, he had had enough. A week later he submitted the following through channels.

> Cavalry Camp near
> Halltown Va. Aug 9th 1864
>
> Lt. Col. Caspar Crowninshield
> Comdg 2d Ms Cav
>
> Colonel
> I have the honor to tender my resignation as Major in the 2d Ms Cavalry and request that it be honorably accepted. I respectfully submit the following reasons for the same. Some eighteen months since I raised in the State of California a Battalion of four companies of cavalry and came east with them in the expectation that it would be an independent command and a representative force from my state in the war. The State of Massachusetts paid the transportation of this Battalion from California for which the number of men in it were credited to her quota, but it was not the wish or intention of those who raised the Battalion to have it lose it's [sic] state identity or be merged in any other organization. On the arrival of the Battalion east it was assigned to the 2d Ms Cavalry and has been with it since, and has to a great extent lost it's [sic] identity as a representative force from California, much to my disappointment and regret. This unfortunate arrangement has produced such an unpleasant state of feeling between myself and the superior officers of the Regiment that it is not my wish, and I do not think it is my duty to remain in it longer. I believe that I can render much better and more satisfactory service to Government and the cause of the Union in some other position. I have been constantly in the service for more than eighteen months without any loss of time from leave or absence or sickness, and on this account I respectfully request that this resignation be accepted to take place on the 31st of this month so as to give me time to settle my accounts with the Government which I am prepared to do and turn over all property in my charge.
>
> I am Colonel Most Respt Yours
> D W C Thompson
> Maj 2d Ms Cav

Later that day the letter made its way to Gen. Sheridan where it was accepted, and Major Thompson's military service came to a close.[6]

It was indeed a loss to the service. Major Thompson had done well under fire, had done commendable service at the Muddy Branch outpost, and was always ready to step in on behalf of the Californians. His one flaw was his inability to get along with Lowell and Crowninshield. Despite his claims there never was any agreement, implied or otherwise, that the Californians would be an independent command. This was quite obvious even before he formed the battalion and the Hundred arrived in Boston and was attached to the 2nd Massachusetts Cavalry. Major Thompson returned to California where he maintained his contacts within the military, and eventually rose to major general commanding the State Militia.[7]

Through the years Confederate armies had ranged up and down the Shenandoah Valley, drawing sustenance from its fertile fields and farms, and using the Blue Ridge Mountains, which border its eastern side, as a screen to hide their movements.

Early's raid on Washington and the follow-up raid on Chambersburg made it clear to Gen. Grant that this avenue of invasion, not to mention the area's capacity to provide food and forage, must be finally and decisively cut off. Other Union commanders had come to the same conclusion but none of the generals had been equal to their Confederate counterparts. Now the right man for the job was at hand in Maj. Gen. Philip H. Sheridan, commander of the cavalry of the Army of the Potomac. Five foot four and knobby headed, Sheridan was a relentless fighter, something the Valley had yet to see in a northern general. On the 6th of August Gen. Grant appointed Sheridan to the command of the Army of the Shenandoah.

Sheridan's new army consisted of Wright's VI corps, two divisions of the XIX corps under Maj. Gen. William Emory, and Maj. Gen. George Crook's two divisions of the Army of West Virginia. Twelve batteries of artillery comprised his second arm. When he left the Army of the Potomac, Sheridan brought two divisions of cavalry which he combined with the one division from the Army of West Virginia into a corps commanded by Maj. Gen. Alfred Torbert. During the inevitable reorganization, the 2nd Massachusetts Cavalry was assigned to the Third Brigade of Brig. Gen. Wesley Merritt's First Division. Command of the Third Brigade, consisting of the 2nd Massachusetts, 22 Pennsylvania, 1st Maryland, and a detachment of the

Maj. Gen. Philip H. Sheridan. *Courtesy of U.S.A.M.H.I.*

14th Pennsylvania, was given to Col. Lowell. No more independent duty and boredom, the 2nd Massachusetts Cavalry was finally part of the first team.[8]

> Halltown, Aug 9, 1864
>
> I've been ever so busy lately; I've hardly had time to sleep or think, except Sunday, when I slept all day, having been up all night before. I am to have the 3d Brigade, — 1st Division in the new Cavalry Corps, — nothing very stunning, I fear, but good enough for a beginner. General Merritt has the Division. Everything is chaos here, but under Sheridan is rapidly assuming shape. It was a lucky inspiration of Grant's or Lincoln's to make a Middle Military Division and put him in command of it; it redeems Lincoln's character and secures him my vote, if I have one.
>
> It *is exhilarating* to see so many cavalry about and to see things going *right* again.[9]

Reveille blew the next morning at half past two in the camp of the 2nd Massachusetts Cavalry. A general advance was ordered for 5 A.M. with Crowninshield's regiment posted on the extreme right. It was an easy march, Lowell's brigade having the smallest distance to cover, and by afternoon Sheridan was holding a line from Summit Point (Lowell) to White Post, with his infantry centered near Berryville. To prevent being flanked, Early's army had moved south with the Federals, and now presented a defensive position along Opequon Creek, in a posture to cover Winchester. The 2nd Massachusetts Cavalry got into a skirmish with the butternuts opposite their position, capturing 18 and losing two in turn, one of them Sgt. John Fletcher of the California Hundred. This sharp little fight inaugurated 21 straight days of action for the 2nd Massachusetts.[10]

Up at 3 A.M. the next morning, the regiment "…moved out at sunrise on an empty stomach. The boys are not too pleased with this." Two days before the men had been issued rations for four days and had, as was the custom, promptly eaten all the food. Advancing on Winchester, the 2nd had some minor skirmishing with some Confederate cavalry, taking five prisoners and driving some 200 rebels out of the town. Sheridan was attempting to pick a fight with Early who refused to be drawn out but chose to retreat slowly up the valley.*[11]

The morning of the 12th dawned clear and hot, presaging another blistering day. Sheridan again moved his army to the south, vainly attempting to round Early's right flank. Crowninshield's regiment passed through Newtown and Middletown and finally caught up with the enemy along Cedar Creek. "Had a smart skirmish with them in the afternoon." Fighting lasted through the day with infantry finally relieving the 2nd Massachusetts at sundown. Pvt. John Thompson (B), Boston, a member of the regimental band, took a glancing bullet on the knee, a painful wound but not enough to keep him out of action for long. The Confederates facing them did not stand up so well, losing 17 prisoners to Lowell's command. During the course of the day Early's army slowly continued its move up the valley, finally calling a halt at Fisher's Hill.[12]

Setting up camp in an open field north of Cedar Creek, the 2nd Massachusetts enjoyed a few comparatively quiet days. There was sporadic fighting on the picket line, but no casualties other than Pvt. Amos Ryley (M), a 25-year-old sailor from Mystic Bridge, Connecticut, who was captured and spent the next six months in a rebel prison camp. Pvt. John Winship arrived with the regiment's mail and all the

---

*The Shenandoah River runs north through the valley toward the Potomac River, thus making a southerly movement "up."

men quickly scribbled letters for his return trip.[13]

Learning that Early had been reenforced by two divisions of infantry as well as some cavalry and artillery, Sheridan chose to withdraw his forces to a defensive position around Halltown, two miles south of Harpers Ferry. In retreating, Sheridan put into effect an order by Gen. Grant: "...it is desirable that nothing should be left to invite the enemy to return. Take all provisions, forage, and stock wanted for the use of your command; such as cannot be consumed, destroy."[14]

"Left Cedar Creek 9 a.m.," Dearborn recorded on the 17th of August, "and moved toward Winchester. Burned all hay along the Valley and drove away the stock." Lowell wrote his wife, "I had the right rear with orders from Grant to drive in every horse, mule, ox, or cow, and burn all grain and forage, — a miserable duty which continued till Winchester." Within a mile of Winchester, Gen. Torbert made a stand against the pursuing rebels with Wilson's division of cavalry, Lowell's brigade, and a small brigade of infantry. Engaged only briefly at the beginning of the fight, the 2nd Massachusetts Cavalry lost seven men captured. The first six were Pvt. Thomas Kelley (B), a Boston bounty jumper who had recently been court-martialed and returned to the regiment, Pvt. Patrick Burke (G), Springfield, one of the "old men" of the troop at 41, William White (K), Norridgewock, Maine, and privates Charles Dealing(L), San Francisco, and Michael Kelly (L) and Daniel McDonald (L), both of Boston. Last was Pvt. William Harmon (K), an 18 year old from St. John, New Brunswick, who mustered into the regiment in mid–June. Not much on patriotism, young William soon tired of prison life and enlisted in Company F of the 1st Foreign Battalion, Confederate States Army.[15]

The morning of the 18th was quiet with an occasional welcome rain falling on the parched troops. At half past three in the afternoon the Confederates began shelling the 2nd's new position near Opequon Creek. "Shot and shell flew pretty thick for a while," Pvt. Corbett of Company A recorded, "but we soon silenced them. The fight lasted a hour, when the rebels retreated." Falling back a mile after the fight, the 2nd spent a quiet night, grateful for having a day with no casualties.[16]

Picketing was the order of the day on the 19th. There were a few scattering shots between skirmishers as Crowninshield's men held the line between Lowell's brigade and Wilson's division. Rations had run out again and apples constituted the day's bill of fare, but another mail delivered by Winship made many forget their growling stomachs. The next morning three days' rations were issued, and so after a good feed the men were more than ready when the rebels made a sortie against the picket line. Pvt. Ezra Rumery (L), San Francisco, was wounded and the Confederate charge handily repulsed.[17]

A much stronger attempt was prepared by the Confederates for the next morning. At half past ten, "...the enemy advanced and the firing commenced.... We held our position till 2 P.M. at which time we were compelled to fall back amid the howling of shells and hissing of bullets. It was terrific and we did our duty well."[18]

"There were two Shells burst within six feet of my Horses heels but both escaped injury," Sgt. Maj. Williams assured his parents. "I was of course obliged to be where there was the most danger for I must keep up with the Colonel & He was always in front when we were moving toward the enemy & in the rear when moving from there were several solid shot & shell passed between us when not more than 20 ft. apart, but we were lucky."[19]

The enemy line was from the division

of Confederate Gen. Robert Rodes who inflicted 250 Federal casualties before the fighting ceased; seven were from the 2nd Massachusetts Cavalry. Pvt. John O'Leary (M), Roxbury, stopped a rebel bullet and died on the field. Wounded were privates Alonzo Grout (A), Lowell; John Ward (A), Boston; Charles Boyle (D), Boston; John Boynton (D), Manchester; Daniel McDougal (L), San Francisco; and Corp. Patrick O'Neil (K), unknown.[20]

By 5 A.M. on the 22nd, the regiment passed through Charlestown with the rebels following closely behind. Rear guard skirmishing continued, the Federals slowly giving ground as the day advanced. About a mile outside of Charlestown, "The enemy came up to our rear at this place and heavy skirmishing was kept up the rest of the distance — our Batterys shelling them from favorable position." The only casualty for the 2nd Massachusetts was Capt. John Phillips (C), Boston, who was shot in the arm by a guerrilla. It was a nasty wound, and the captain would be forced to take a discharge in March.[21]

Finally a halt was called and Sheridan's forces encamped around Halltown, the same town they had been in when action had commenced two weeks prior. Picketing and skirmishing continued on the 23rd as the 2nd Massachusetts Cavalry and a portion of the 2nd Pennsylvania Cavalry went out to reconnoiter and found part of the Confederate army strongly posted just north of Charlestown. On the afternoon of the 24th, "...our forces made a dash on the enemy line and succeeded in capturing several prisoners." During the action Lowell's horse "Billy," a loan from John M. Forbes, took a bullet through the neck: "...it will not hurt him at all, however, — will add to his value in Mr. Forbes eyes at least a thousand dollars." Back on the 19th his mount "Ruskh," a very tall sorrel, had taken a ball in the fore leg; three days later "Dick," the imprisoned Major Forbes' horse, was crippled with a shot to the off hind leg. The following weeks would be very hard on the colonel's mounts.[22]

Thirteen Confederates were taken back to the Union line, Crowninshield's only casualty being Corp. Patrick Leonard (K). A 33-year-old shoemaker from Ireland, Leonard had served 14 months in the 4th New York Cavalry, deserting New Year's Day, 1863. Taking a year off from the war he enlisted in the 2nd Massachusetts Cavalry on the 13th of January and was soon promoted to corporal. During the action of the 24th a Rebel bullet passed through his left calf, taking a large portion of the muscle with it. Leonard would spend the next 40 years on crutches. That evening Lowell's brigade was reenforced by the 25th New York Cavalry, a brand-new regiment which had been mounted only seven days before. Easily the largest regiment in the brigade, its untested troopers had to be trained under fire. Lowell confessed, "...I have my hands full."[23]

The morning of the 25th dawned fine and pleasant and an un-official cease-fire was agreed upon between the two picket lines. For five hours, "...the boys traded papers, coffee, and tobacco with the Rebels." Later in the afternoon a squadron was sent out on another reconnaissance of the Rebel lines. Led by the popular Capt. Eigenbrodt of Company E, the force captured four prisoners but at the terrible price of the death of the captain. A native of Germany, the former Supervisor of Alameda County had recruited Company E, the "California Cossacks," many of the recruits coming from near his home in Alvarado. Elevated to battalion commander when Major Thompson resigned, Capt. Eigenbrodt was shot out of the saddle in a charge against the enemy posted behind breastworks. "Thus was lost to the battalion one of its bravest and best loved officers, and to California one of its most patriotic and valuable citizens."[24]

The following day the 2nd Massachusetts Cavalry was just itching for a fight, though some started the morning by once again trading newspapers across the picket line. Hardly a shot was fired during another "fine and pleasant" day, as Pvt. Dearborn faithfully recorded in his diary. In the late afternoon yet another reconnaissance was called for and Col. Lowell joined the 2nd Massachusetts Cavalry on the foray. Sheridan and his staff rode into camp just before Lowell led the four companies out and took an advantageous position to observe. "One afternoon," Pvt. Towle of Company A recalled, "part of our regiment under command of Colonel Lowell rode on through the timber to the left of the infantry and reached a position opposite the extreme right of the confederate skirmish line, which extended beyond our own infantry skirmish line. Between the timber in which we were and the confederate skirmish line was a distance of I would judge three or four hundred yards, all of which was open. Col. Lowell formed his command in single rank facing the enemy and then moved slowly out of the timber and shortly after reaching the open ground gave orders to charge as foragers, that is in open order, on the enemy's picket line in our front. That was done, and before the confederates had time to re-load after discharging their first shot we were on top of them and swept off a section of the picket line."[25]

"Lowell led an attack against the advance of the enemy's infantry," Pvt. Samuel Backus remembered, "and charged up a rail fence, behind which they were intrenched, and while he and a few of his men held them there — he himself actually whacking their leveled muskets with his saber — the rest tore down the barrier, and then they all charged again...." As Lowell jumped the remains of the rail fence Sheridan turned to his orderly and remarked, "Lowell is a brave man." Also conspicuous was Lt. Col. Crowninshield whose actions led Surgeon DeWolf to write, "His heart was steel that day, and always is in a fight — God bless him and protect him!" Among the 74 captured were the lieutenant colonel, three captains, and 69 men of the 15th South Carolina Infantry. "We took about as many prisoners," Crowninshield wrote, "as we had men engaged & everyone said the Regt. did splendidly, we have no reporter with us & so you will probably see no mention of it in the papers."*[26]

Pvt. Towle recalled that as the prisoners were being led to the rear, "...the confederates pushed forward a battery and commenced shelling our men, among whom of course were the confederate prisoners. There was a corn field to one side of the open ground and some of the confederates had succeeded in escaping into that. After the prisoners had been taken some distance to the rear Col. Lowell, as he stood facing the confederate line, saw two confederates come out of the edge of the corn field and start back to their own lines. I was his orderly that day and he ordered me to go after them and bring them in. I soon overtook them, faced them about and started for our lines. They were so out of breath that they could not move quickly. As we moved the wind from an exploded shell which struck the ground right at my horse's heels blew my cap off and the ground which it threw up covered me with sand and dirt and filled the interstices between my saddletree and my horse's back with sand. My first impression was that my horse's rump had been cut off." Miraculously both horse and rider were unhurt and Towle soon had the two men back with the other prisoners, drawn up in a line in

---

*Lt. Col. Crowninshield was correct about the fight not reaching the papers. Col. Lowell refused to allow newspaper correspondents in his camp. Emerson, Life and Letters, p. 70.

camp where they, "...were much chagrined when they learned that they had been captured by Massachusetts troops, a feeling which will be readily understood by those familiar with conditions at that time." Pvt. Dearborn spoke to a few of the prisoners: "The Rebs estimate their losses in K[illed], W[ounded], M[issing] to be 300. They say they never saw such cav. fighting before."[27]

But, as always, the day's successes were not gained without loss. First lieutenant Charles Meader, originally a sergeant in Company M but now commanding the California Hundred, was clubbed to death with a musket butt in hand to hand fighting, "Too brave to retreat and too proud to surrender." Falling nearby was Pvt. James Ackerman (A), Ukiah, California. Wounded were Henry Schrow (A), San Francisco, who was hit in the head by a rifle butt, fracturing his skull and putting him out of the war, and Pvt. Charles Dean (H), a 19-year-old farmer from Charlestown, who was struck by a ball in the right arm, breaking the bone above the elbow and crippling the limb for life. Refusing a discharge, Dean was transferred in February to the Veteran Reserve Corps.[28]

On the 27th, Early began to draw his troops back to a position near Bunker Hill. Noting the lines were empty in front of them, Lowell took the 2nd Massachusetts Cavalry out to determine the enemy's new position. "Came up with their rear guard just beyond Charlestown. There being only two squadrons of us they drew out a heavy skirmish line and pressed us back to town. Co. K charged their line but being overpowered by them forced to retire...." Skirmishing went on through the day. "Brought in the bodies of Lt. Meader and Ackerman and buried them with military honors. Capt. Eigenbrodt's grave was also found, his body will be embalmed and sent home." Describing the day to Effie, Lowell wrote, "...if I had a little more pluck, I think I might have sent you a battle flag, but Caspar [Crowninshield] thinks it more likely *I* should have gone to Richmond." Lowell did not lose a horse that day, but while reconnoitering with the colonel of the 22nd Pennsylvania Cavalry, he had his bridle reins shot off close to his hand.[29]

Two men from Company K were killed in the failed charge: Pvt. John Marden, Portsmouth, New Hampshire, and Cpl. Thomas Martin. Though not a member of the California 100 or Battalion, Martin claimed California as his residence when enlisting in Massachusetts back in January '63. Pvt. Patrick Gavin, Millbury, also of Company K, was captured but was lucky enough to be paroled less than six weeks later. Sgt. George Bishop (E), Philadelphia, took a crippling wound and was soon given a medical discharge.[30]

The next day was quite confusing for both officers and men, no one really sure whether Early was actually retreating or just feinting. The 2nd Massachusetts broke camp at 10 A.M. and moved to a new bivouac on the other side of Charlestown. Skirmishing continued, the lines changing back and forth through the day, but only one member of the regiment became a casualty. Cpl. John O'Connell (F), San Francisco, a 24-year-old former sailor who had served in the 2nd California Volunteers under the alias Michael Walsh, was severely wounded near Summit Point, but would recover and serve with his company through the end of the war.[31]

On moving camp to Summit Point on the 29th, Pvt. Corbett recorded in his diary, "When we got there we found that we were nearly surrounded by rebels here. We employed a little strategy by bringing out the fife and drums of the Band and playing so as to make the Rebels think that we had a force of Infantry with us." His next day's entry continued, "Our strategy last evening was completely successful as we captured several prisoners during the night. The first thing they asked when they got into camp, 'Where is your Infantry?' Our own pickets when they heard the drums thought they were being reenforced. A good joke on the rebs." Later in the afternoon the enemy charged the brigade picket line, killing two men of the 2nd Maryland Cavalry, and slightly wounding Capt. William Rumery of Company D, the only casualty for the 2nd Massachusetts Cavalry.[32]

For nearly a week the 2nd Massachusetts Cavalry was involved in little more than an occasional exchange of picket fire. Sheridan and Early continued to spar and probe, each looking for an opening, but unwilling to risk all without a definite advantage. The political situation in the North, especially with the upcoming presidential election, put Sheridan in a tenuous position. Naturally aggressive in battle, he could not, Lincoln could not, afford a setback in the Valley. A defeat was unthinkable, and a passive defense was unacceptable. Early mistook this policy of caution as one of excessive timidity on Sheridan's part. Col. Lowell held a different opinion of his new commander and put it in words to his wife. "By the way, I like Sheridan immensely. Whether he succeeds or fails, he is the first General I have seen who puts as much heart and time and thought into his work as if he were doing it for his own exclusive profit. He works like a mill-owner or an iron-master, *not* like a soldier, — never sleeps, never worries, is never cross, but isn't afraid to come down on a man who deserves it." The commanding general also had a growing respect for the young Col. Lowell, having seen him in action for the better part of a month.[33]

On the 8th of September the Third Brigade was broken up and Lowell was placed in command of the tough brigade of regular U.S. Cavalry. Special Orders No. 103, of the First Division, removed the 1st New York Dragoons from the brigade and placed the 2nd Massachusetts Cavalry in its place. Previously commanded by brigadier generals John Buford and Wesley Merritt, the unit was designated the Reserve Brigade, and consisted of the 1st, 2nd, 5th and 6th U.S. Cavalry.*[34]

This new assignment of Lowell's is noteworthy for it was based solely on his growing reputation within the army. Prior to August he had been virtually unknown, though Sheridan was undoubtedly aware of his reorganization of the Cavalry Depot back in March, and had certainly heard of his performance against Mosby. But very few had seen the little colonel in action. Maj. Gen. Emory, commanding the XIX Corps, had been his colonel when Lowell was still a captain in the 6th U.S. Cavalry. Brig. Gen. George Custer, commanding Merritt's First Brigade, had been a fellow captain when both were on McClellan's staff. Both had seen Lowell under fire and had a high respect for his abilities.[35]

"I have stepped into a rather trying position now," Charles wrote Josephine, "the regular Brigade is hard to run; there are many prides and prejudices, — and then, too, much more is expected from an officer commanding it, than from one commanding a little patched-up affair like my last command. However, I shan't worry at all, but shall try to do what I can. I don't think I now care at all about being a Brigadier-General. I am *perfectly* satisfied to be a Colonel, If I can always have a brigade to command; — that's modest isn't it?"[36]

From the 8th to the 18th of September the regiment kept its camp near Summit Point, picketing on the left of the cavalry line and in front of the VI Corps. Though there was near constant skirmish-

---

The 6th Pennsylvania Cavalry, assigned to the Brigade, was immediately ordered to Pleasant Valley for muster out.

ing, little of note happened until the 13th when Sheridan sent a division of VI Corps and two brigades of cavalry to develop the enemy near a crossing of Opequon Creek. The enemy was found in force on the west side of the creek and the 2nd Massachusetts Cavalry was busy fighting and skirmishing through the day.[37]

Early in the fight the skirmish line of the 2nd Massachusetts was overrun and captured by the Confederates, prompting a counterbharge that recaptured the men and made prisoners of their former captors. An officer and 11 men of Gen. John B. Gordon's division were taken by the 2nd Massachusetts. Surgeon Oscar DeWolf recalled, "...while making a reconnaissance across the Opequon Creek, the enemy were found strongly posted behind a fence and could not be flanked. General Sheridan said they must be moved and Lieutenants Crocker and Thompson ... begged permission to do it — and they did it."[38]

During another part of the action Company A was sent to find another ford further up the creek. This ford too was heavily defended, so a sergeant and two men were sent off in search of yet another, the company drawn up close to the bank of the stream to wait. Pvt. Towle recalled the scene. "The South [west] bank of the creek was occupied by a few confederate sharpshooters and we were within easy range. The result was that nearly every shot they fired either a man or horse of our Company was hit. The sharp-shooters were bunched close together, and as we stood there was a branch of a tree that came between me and their position, for which I was not unthankful. While returning from there, Dearborn, who was in the set of fours next behind me, was shot through the right temple, and at about the same time my horse was wounded. Dearborn fell off his horse when he was shot, but his horse kept its place in the ranks. So soon as we halted I hastily transferred my equipment to Dearborn's horse. I have never been able to regard that maneuver as anything but the result of crass stupidity. The Company neither in advancing or in retreating fired a shot, nor did it in the slightest aid in the discovery of a ford. All the Company did was sit on their horses, like bumps on logs, and serve as targets for the confederate sharpshooters. Dearborn was in every sense of the word a fine man and a good soldier."[39]

The fight was the costliest to the 2nd Massachusetts of any since entering the Valley. Pvt. Valorous Dearborn (A), San Francisco, died on the field; Winfield Wilburn (I) of Friendship, Maine, was wounded and died that evening, as did Alexander Logan (D), an 18-year-old Massachusetts bootmaker. John Shiffer (F) one of the miners from California, died of his wounds on the 19th, followed by William Colgan (C), Roxbury, on the 28th who slowly bled to death after a bullet clipped an artery in his left leg. Also wounded was Richard Fleet (C), Fall River; Edward McKnight (D), Ashland, who lost his left arm after a bullet struck his elbow; George Morse (D), Ashland; John McLaughlin (G), Concord, New Hampshire; and Joseph McClease (I), Boston. George Sewall (F) another miner from the Golden State, was captured and died four months later in Andersonville.[40]

The next day, cold and stormy, the 2nd Massachusetts Cavalry moved camp to the rear of the brigade headquarters where they were issued rations and mail was passed out. Gen. Custer came by the camp where he "...complimented the 2nd Massachusetts Cavalry on the splendid charge that they made yesterday by saying that it was the best Cavalry charge he [had] ever seen made."[41]

The stalemate in the Valley finally took a nod to Sheridan's corner with two very important events. First, on the 16th, Sheridan learned of the depletion of Early's force by the return of Maj. Gen. Anderson and his men to Lee's army. Secondly, the near constant cavalry reconnaissances revealed that Early had widely scattered his forces in an attempt to break the union railroad near Martinsburg.[42]

An impatient War Department had been pressuring Grant to get Sheridan moving in the Valley. Rather than send orders to Washington through the War Department, which was in the habit of modifying them, Grant chose to meet Sheridan in person, arriving in Charlestown on the 17th. Grant carried with him a plan for dealing with Early's army, but when Sheridan briefed him on the situation and his own plan to attack the Confederates, Grant chose to keep his own plan in his pocket and ordered Sheridan to, "Go in."[43]

Unfortunately for Sheridan, Early learned of Grant's presence in the Valley and rightly came to the conclusion it meant imminent action on the part of the Yankees. Quickly concentrating his forces outside Winchester, he was not in the vulnerable position Sheridan supposed him to be. Sheridan's plan, based on the assumption that Early's force was still scattered, was to send the cavalry divisions of Merritt and Averell to the north of Winchester to watch for a concentration of the enemy, while the infantry made its way through Berryville Canyon, led by Wilson's cavalry division, and attacked the enemy east of the town. A bold plan, but one with a potentially fatal flaw: if anything went wrong on the march the infantry could easily become bottled up in the narrow canyon.[44]

"Boots and saddles sounded this morning at 1 o'clock," Pvt. Corbett recalled of the 19th of September. By 2 A.M. Merritt's division was in motion, followed within an hour by the columns of Sheridan's infantry. The 2nd Massachusetts Cavalry, along with the rest of the Reserve Brigade, was tasked with forcing Seivers Ford, while Custer's First Brigade did the same to the north at Lockes Ford. "…[W]e commenced the fight at daylight by crossing the Opequon & we fought from that time until dark."[45]

The Confederates put up a stiff resistance, but Lowell's brigade soon completed the crossing, driving the enemy back in the direction of Winchester. The cavalry held their gains, steadily pushing and probing, while the infantry began their assault to the south. Though the real action was now in the hands of the foot soldiers, the cavalry had plenty to keep them busy on their own front.[46]

Pvt. Towle recorded how his morning went on the banks of the Opequon. "Where this [the crossing] had been done the confederates fell back on their reserve which was in some timber at the top of a long hill. The slope was entirely open. Where we were it was wooded. Immediately in front was an open and very steep descent to the foot of that long open slope. At the edge of the wood the skirmish line, composed of men from one of the regiments of U.S. regulars then attached to our brigade, had stalled. We were deployed as skirmishers in their rear and ordered forward. We rode right through their line. The confederates, apparently in challenge, had placed a battle flag at the top of the long slope in front of their position; as much as to say 'if you damn yankees want that flag come and get it.' Our regiment from our position, and one of Custer's from his, made a charge up the hill toward that flag. I shall never forget the ceaseless sing of minié balls as we rode up the long slope. My then constant wonder was how it was possible that anything as big as a mosquito could escape. Strangely few were hurt. Neither regiment succeeded in capturing that flag at that time; instead they swung off into the timber to the right and near the confederate reserve."[47]

To the east of Winchester Sheridan's infantry attack had bogged down when his

Guidon of Company M (formerly Company C while in California), 2nd Massachusetts Cavalry. *Courtesy of Michael K. Sorenson.*

columns became jammed in the narrow Berryville Canyon. Forced to deploy his troops piecemeal as they made their way out of the defile, Sheridan was ably countered at every step by Early's veterans. Finally, in the late afternoon, Sheridan's superior numbers became too much and the Confederate lines began to buckle. With the scent of victory in the air, the cavalry began to mass for one of the most stunning scenes of the war, long remembered by all who saw it.[48]

Col. James H. Kidd of the 6th Michigan Cavalry (Custer's Third Brigade), later recalled the epic scene. "The Union cavalrymen were now all mounted. The Michigan brigade (Custer's) was on the left of the turnpike; to its left, the brigades of Devin and Lowell; on the right, Averell's division of two brigades—five brigades in all—each brigade in line of squadron columns, double ranks. This made a front of more than half a mile, three lines deep, of mounted men. That is to say, it was more than half a mile from Averell's right to Merritt's left. At almost the same moment of time, the entire line emerged from the woods into the sunlight. A more enlivening and imposing spectacle never was seen. Guidons fluttered and sabers glistened. Officers vied with their men in gallantry and zeal. Even the horses seemed to catch the inspiration of their riders. Then a left half wheel began the grand flanking movement which broke Early's left flank and won the battle."[49]

During the confusion of the charge the 2nd Massachusetts Cavalry was divided, one battalion charging with Lowell and the rest of the brigade, the other two following Crowninshield, slightly to the right of Devin's brigade. "On they came," wrote Crowninshield, "6 or 7 thousand men with sabers drawn & shouting like demons. It was a splendid fight. I never shall forget it. We rode completely over the Rebel cavalry ... they have not stopped running yet." Pvt. Towle recalled the "...confederate cavalry and infantry, speedily retreating in quick and bad order. Infantry dead and wounded were all around. During the day Colonel Lowell's command captured three pieces of artillery, and Custer's command, as usual, captured a number of battle flags."[50]

The 2nd Massachusetts Cavalry ended the day with 13 casualties, a remarkable figure considering the amount of action they had been in. The only man killed was Pvt. George Emerson (I), a 21-year-old New Hampshire farmer. Two officers were wounded, 1st Lt. Edward Thompson (F) and 1st Lt. Josiah Baldwin (L), both original members of the California Battalion. Thompson's wound was slight and he was not out of the saddle for long. Not so with Lt. Baldwin who took a ball in the lower right thigh, which passed through, permanently destroying the tendons and muscle attached to the knee. The leg did not have to be amputated, but was forever lame, forcing his discharge in May. Also wounded were privates John Porter (C) of St. John, New Brunswick; David Gregory (C) of Wales; Edward Chadwick (F), a Nantucket sailor; George Dehaven (F), a 26-year-old Sherborn painter; Charles Granville (K) a Lynfield, Massachusetts, shoemaker; and John Felch (L), of San Francisco. Felch was horribly wounded by a bullet that "...passed through the lower jaw breaking the jaw bone and carrying away the lower lip and causing the loss of eight teeth." Disfigured for life, Felch would never eat solid food again. Captured in the fight was Pvt. Henry McAlistar (C) of Princeton, Iowa; 18-year-old Charles Bosworth (C), Greenwich, who had enlisted only two months before; Corp. Charles Nystrom (L), San Francisco; and 2nd Lt. Wesley Howe (M), also from the Golden State.[51]

"By the time it was dusk," wrote Pvt. Towle, "Early's forces were in full retreat and we went into camp near Winchester feeling very jubilant indeed. That evening general Custer flaunted his captured flags before Colonel Lowell and inquired why he had none to show. Lowell's reply was 'Oh, flags do not hurt anybody, why don't you capture some artillery.'"[52]

Following Early the next morning, Sheridan found his adversary drawn up at Fisher's Hill, near Strasburg, 21 miles south of Winchester. The "Gibraltar" of the valley was flanked by Massanutten on the east, Little North Mountain on the west, and Tumbling Run along its base; it was a position of great natural strength. Hoping to flank Early out of the position on the 22nd, Sheridan sent Merritt's and Wilson's divisions of cavalry, under the command of Gen. Torbert, around the northern end of Massanutten Mountain and down the Luray Valley where they would then cross the mountain at New Market Gap, thus blocking Early's retreat. "At a place called Snake Hill," wrote Crowninshield, "we found the Rebel Cavalry strongly entrenched, we attacked but could not carry the position." The bullets were still flying as Pvt. James Corbett made his daily diary entry. "The fighting is mostly with artillery shot and shell are flying around loose and we are all hungry and ugly, no rations yet."[53]

While the cavalry was stalemated in the Luray Valley, Sheridan successfully drove Early from Fisher's Hill, completing his Winchester victory and forcing the Confederates to retreat south. If all had gone as planned the Rebel army would have been trapped, but Gen. Torbert had botched his assignment and once more Early escaped to fight again. In the early hours of the 23rd the cavalry pulled out of their positions in the Luray Valley and moved northward to regroup before trying another time. Leading the mounted columns was the lengthy ambulance train of the two divisions. As the train approached Front Royal, at the head of the valley, it was spotted by 120 of Mosby's Rangers under the command of Capt. Sam Chapman. Operating in the Shenandoah with orders to disrupt Sheridan's communications, the raiders thought they had come across a lightly escorted wagon train, ripe for the taking.[54]

Splitting his force to take the wagons from front and rear, Chapman discovered too late that the wagons were followed by endless columns of mounted Yankees. Before he could put a halt to the attack, his forward detachment pitched into the front of the train, shooting drivers and scattering the escort. The response was immediate. The 1st and 2nd U.S. Cavalry and the 2nd Massachusetts Cavalry charged the Rangers who characteristically scattered in all directions, every man for himself. "We pitched in to them," Pvt. Corbett recalled, "driving them to the mountains killing seventeen and taking four prisoners.... I had the pleasure of capturing one of them myself." Capt. Moses Harris of the 1st U.S. Cavalry recalled, "A number of Mosby's men were killed and some ten or twelve taken prisoner." Crowninshield wrote home that 14 had been killed or captured; Lowell stated in his official report that 13 died; Merritt, in his account, claimed 18. Confederate accounts testify that none of their men died on the field and though a few were wounded, all but six escaped into the woods. Rebel versions also list some 15 to 20 Yankees killed in the fight. It is important to consider Lowell's claim of 13 killed, for in all of his previous reports he had *never* padded his numbers or failed to report a setback.[55]

The 2nd U.S. Cavalry, leading the charge, had one man mortally wounded, Lt. Charles McMaster. The 2nd Massachusetts Cavalry took no casualties. After the dust had cleared the wounded McMaster was found in the road, where he told his companions he had been shot after he surrendered, a charge that Rangers vehemently denied for years after.*[56]

The scene quickly became ugly as men of the 2nd U.S. shouted for vengeance. Every trooper in blue was aware of the depredations of the "bushwhackers," and with their blood up led away and shot four of the prisoners. Gen. Torbert questioned the remaining two men as to Mosby's whereabouts, but when they remained silent he directed the provost marshal to hang them. Shortly thereafter the two men were strung up with a placard on one stating, "This will be the fate of Mosby and all his men."[57]

Having faced the Rangers for a full year and knowing better than any present the gallantry and villainy of their foe, the 2nd Massachusetts Cavalry looked upon the incident with regret and embarrassment. Lowell did not mention the killings in his official report but in a letter to Effie confided, "I was sorry enough the other day that my Brigade should have had a part in the hanging and shooting of some of Mosby's men...." Crowninshield echoed the feeling to his mother: "I am glad my Regt. had nothing to do with this."[58]

The two divisions spent the night in Front Royal, and in the morning again moved against the Confederate position in the Luray Valley. Finding that the rebels

---

*The charges were certainly easy for the 2nd Massachusetts Cavalry to believe, at least two men having been similarly shot down by Mosby's men in the past year.

had pulled out, the Federals pursued. "Met the Rebels two miles from Luray," wrote Corbett. "Drove them out of their rifle pits and through the town capturing 150 prisoners." Crowninshield wrote of the affair, "...we utterly routed the Rebel Cavalry." When the dust cleared and the ranks reformed, Pvt. Philip Baybutt was holding the battle flag of the 6th Virginia Cavalry. In his postwar recollections, Pvt. Towle wrote, "In riding after the confederates through the woods one of our men saw on a bush about half of a confederate flag that had been torn from its staff which he seized as he rode by and put in his pocket." Crowninshield, Lowell, and Gen. Merritt all reported that the flag (the whole flag) had been captured in the charge, and Congress agreed, bestowing the Medal of Honor on Pvt. Baybutt on the 19th of October. Baybutt, a 25-year-old Englishman, had enlisted in February and soon been assigned to Company A. Towle, an original member of the California Hundred, was possibly being resentful towards this foreign recruit when he penned his recollections. The narrative of the Company A muster roll as well as the report of the Massachusetts Adjutant General both confirm that a Rebel battle flag had been captured, not a piece of one.[59]

That evening the regiment camped near the head of the Luray Valley at a spot abundant with roasting ears and "...quite a large band of sheep, the slaughter of which consumed nearly as much ammunition as we had used earlier in the day." The mutton and corn went down well, it had been a full week since any rations had been issued.[60]

The following morning, the 25th, the Union cavalry finally made its way through New Market Gap, too late to cut off the Confederate retreat, and linked up with Sheridan in the village of New Market. Sheridan was making a rapid pursuit of Early who was fleeing up the Valley as fast as he could. Pausing long enough to pass out four days' rations, the 2nd Massachusetts pushed on another ten miles south, camping just outside of Harrisonburg. A very rare day with no fighting and no casualties.[61]

Reveille was sounded at 2 A.M. and by five the regiment was once more headed south. Lowell's Brigade was detached from Merritt and sent with Wilson's Third Division to press on to Staunton. Scores of wounded were found in Harrisonburg, and through the day more prisoners, cattle, and stores were added to the day's haul. The day ended in the suburbs of Staunton, a town Corbett considered "...very pretty, one of the finest places that I have seen in the Confederacy." Staunton was not only picturesque, it was a major supply depot for the Valley, situated on the line of the Virginia Central Railroad. Aroused at 4 A.M., the 2nd Massachusetts spent 12 solid hours destroying the railroad, depot, Confederate commissary and quartermaster stores, as well as a large boot and shoe factory.[62]

At 4 P.M. the columns headed east along the line of the railroad in the direction of Waynesboro. One of the last buildings destroyed in Staunton was a tobacco warehouse, each of the troopers taking a box of the product apiece. "There was an oversupply secured and a good deal of exchange when it was found that one had better tobacco than another; in which case the poorer would be discarded en masse. The result was that the road from Staunton to Waynesboro was for some distance pretty well paved with tobacco."[63]

At Waynesboro the important railroad bridge over the South River was destroyed as well as more Rebel stores. After a full day of burning the men were hot and tired, and many took advantage of a nearby millpond to take a cooling swim. Lowell's Brigade was thrown forward, across the river, where it picketed the approach to

Rockfish Gap in the Blue Ridge. It was here that Early stopped running. At 5 P.M., without the slightest warning, the Confederate cavalry brigade of Brig. Gen. William Wickham hit the exposed Reserve Brigade, front and flank, with a battery of artillery in support. Lowell was forced back across the river and into line with Wilson's Division, but not before some hard fighting on the east bank. Pvt. Corbett made his daily diary entry during the heat of the fight, quite possibly thinking it might be his only chance. "Musket Balls and Shells flying around quite lively. The rebels are flanking us and whipping us at the same time. The fighting is getting quite hot." A rebel shell struck Lt. Col. Crowninshield's horse, "Old Jim," killing the animal and narrowly missing the rider's right leg.[64]

The Confederates were pressing hard and Capt. George Bliss, 1st Rhode Island Cavalry, remembered, "Looking again toward the enemy, I saw Colonel Charles Russell Lowell, who had been in command of the picket line, riding toward us with his horse in a walk—the last man to fall back before the advance of the enemy. The Confederate bullets were whistling about him, and frequent puffs of dust in the road showed where they struck right and left of the brave soldier." Lowell ordered Bliss's company, as well as a portion of the 3rd New Jersey Cavalry, to advance with sabres and slow the Rebel advance. "Give a cheer, boys, and go at them," Lowell yelled when they wavered. Bliss led the charge which temporarily halted the Confederates and resulted in his own capture.[65]

Capt. Moses Harris of the 1st U.S. Cavalry recalled that "...in spite of all our efforts we were steadily forced back into the little village of Waynesboro, where we were assailed by what was more formidable than the enemy's bullets—the tongues of the women. The variety of epithets in their vocabulary was truly astounding, and when their supply of these was exhausted they did not hesitate to resort to missiles of a more tangible nature with which they pelted us from the windows of their houses. The remainder of the Confederate force, infantry, cavalry, and artillery, coming to the assistance of the women, we were ignominiously expelled from the town, and the enemy, as though the object of his tremendous attack had been accomplished, appeared for the time contented with his achievement."[66]

Regrouping in Waynesboro, the Reserve Brigade was nearly flanked by a column of infantry that had approached in the dark. Gen. Torbert, who had given orders for Wilson's division to return to Staunton, was conferring with his staff when a Confederate volley lit up the darkness in a rare night attack. Luckily the cavalry chief was unscathed. The enemy had nearly enveloped the Reserve Brigade when Lowell, using the only road left open, extracted his command and began the march to Staunton, serving as rear guard during the long and confusing night. He later wrote of the affair, "...what was left of Early's army came in upon our left flank and came near doing us a mischief, but we got away in the dark...."[67]

The running fight was a costly one for the 2nd Massachusetts. Killed on the field was 35-year-old William Hurley (I), Salem; John Burns (L), California; and Corp. Edward Kingsley (L) a 28-year-old hatter, also from the Golden State. Among the wounded were Henry Crum (A), San Francisco, who, when his horse was shot from under him, fell under a wagon which rolled over him crushing his right leg; Thomas O'Laughlin (C), Boston; Corp. John Good (G), a 20-year-old Boston sailor; Patrick Cavenaugh (I), Charlestown; Patrick Kelly (I), Boston; James P. Hunter (L), California; and James P. Wilburn (M), Sebastapol, California, who was hit so badly in the arm it had to be amputated. Captured were Patrick Shay (C),

Springfield; Nathan Haskall (D), Peru, Massachusetts; and Franklin Schellinger (F) of Trenton, New Jersey, who, while at the prison pen in Salisbury, North Carolina, joined Co. D, 2nd Regiment, Foreign Legion Confederate States Infantry. Corneille Shea (I), a 27-year-old teacher from New York City, refused the same offer and died two months later at Salisbury.[68]

The only officers on the casualty list were 2nd Lt. Henry F. Woodman (I) who took a severe wound to the knee, and 1st Lt. Charles Kinne who took a slight wound from a spent ball. Both officers had begun the war as privates in the California Hundred.[69]

Capt. Harris summed up the trip to Waynesboro: "Although this expedition might not have been considered a brilliant success, it was felt by the Reserve Brigade that its whole duty had been well and courageously performed, and that it had no cause for self reproach or chagrin at its result.[70]

Notes

1. Cooling, *Jubal Early's Raid on Washington*, pp. 187–88; *OR*, XXXVII, Pt. 1, p. 339.
2. Dearborn, *Diary*, July 16–19, 1864; *OR*, XXXVII, Pt. 1., pp. 398, 406–407.
3. Cooling, *Jubal Early's Raid on Washington*, p. 203; Orton, *Records of California Troops in the War of the Rebellion 1861 to 1867*, p. 850; *OR*, XXXVII, Pt. 1, pp. 369, 412.
4. Cooling, *Jubal Early's Raid on Washington*, pp. 378–79; *OR*, XXXVII, Pt. 1, pp. 449, 457–58.
5. Crowninshield, Aug 2, 1864; *OR*, XXXVII, Pt. 1, p.474.
6. *OR*, XXXVII, Pt. 1, pp. 529, 563; National Archives, Record Group 94, Service Record of D.W.C. Thompson.
7. Thompson, "California in the Rebellion," California Commandry, *MOLLUS.*, pp. 129–141.
8. Wert, *From Winchester to Cedar Creek*, pp. 18–22; *OR*, XLIII, Pt. 1, p. 422.
9. Emerson, *Life and Letters*, p. 322.
10. Corbett, *Diary*, Aug. 10, 1864; Orton, *Records of California Men in the War of the Rebellion 1861–1867*, p. 855; *OR*, XLIII, Pt. 1, p. 486.
11. Dearborn, *Diary*, Aug. 11, 1864.
12. Corbett, *Diary*, Aug. 12, 1864; Dearborn, *Diary*, Aug. 12, 1864; Wert, *From Winchester to Cedar Creek*, p. 31; *Massachusetts Soldiers, Sailors, and Marines*, Vol. VI, p. 245.
13. Corbett, *Diary*, Aug. 13, 1864; Dearborn, *Diary*, Aug. 13, 1864; *OR*, XLIII, Pt. 1, p. 486.
14. *OR*, XLIII, Pt. 1, p. 697–98.
15. Dearborn, *Diary*, Aug. 17, 1864; Emerson, *Life and Letters*, p. 324; *Massachusetts Soldiers, Sailors, and Marines*, Vol. VI, pp. 228–328.
16. Corbett, *Diary*, Aug. 18, 1864.
17. Dearborn, *Diary*, Aug. 19, 1864; *Massachusetts Soldiers, Sailors, and Marines*, Vol. VI, p. 308.
18. Dearborn, *Diary*, Aug. 21, 1864.
19. Williams to Parents, Letter dated Aug. 26, 1864, Misc. letters of Robert Henry Williams, Huntington Library, San Marino, Ca.
20. Dearborn, *Diary*, Aug. 21, 1864; Wert, *From Winchester to Cedar Creek*, p. 35; *Massachusetts Soldiers, Sailors, and Marines*, Vol. VI, pp. 228–328.
21. Corbett, *Diary*, Aug. 22, 1864; Emerson, *Life and Letters*, p. 329; *Massachusetts Soldiers, Sailors, and Marines*, Vol. VI, p. 251.
22. Emerson, *Life and Letters*, pp. 325–26.
23. Emerson, *Life and Letters*, p. 329; *Massachusetts Soldiers, Sailors, and Marines*, Vol. VI, p. 299.
24. Orton, *Records of California Men in the War of the Rebellion 1861–1867*, p. 851; *Oakland Tribune*, Jan 22, 1956.
25. Dearborn, *Diary*, Aug. 26, 1864; Emerson, *Life and Letters*, p. 49; Towle, *Recollections*, p. 15.
26. Backus, "Californians in the Field," *MOLLUS.*, California Commandry, p. 13; Crowninshield, Sept. 8, 1864; Emerson, *Life and Letters*, p. 52.
27. Dearborn, *Diary*, Aug. 26, 1864; Towle, *Recollections*, p. 15.
28. Orton, *Records of California Men in the War of the Rebellion 1861–1867*, p. 851; *Massachusetts Soldiers, Sailors and Marines*, Vol. VI, pp. 228–328; National Archives, Record Group 94, Pension Records of Charles Dean and Henry Schrow.
29. Dearborn, *Diary*, Aug. 27, 1864; Corbett, *Diary*, Aug. 27, 1864; Emerson, *Life and*

Letters, p. 330; Wert, *From Winchester to Cedar Creek*, p. 38.

30. *Massachusetts Soldiers, Sailors, and Marines*, Vol. VI, pp. 228–328.

31. Dearborn, *Diary,* Aug. 28, 1864; Orton, *Records of California Men in the War of the Rebellion 1861–1867,* p. 862; *Massachusetts Soldiers, Sailors, and Marines,* Vol. VI, p. 271.

32. Corbett, *Diary,* Aug. 29–30, 1864; Crowninshield, Sept. 8, 1864; Emerson, *Life and Letters,* pp. 330–31; *OR,* XLIII, Pt. 1, p. 962.

33. Emerson, *Life and Letters,* p. 336.

34. Emerson, *Life and Letters,* p. 54; *OR,* XLIII, Pt. 1, p. 490.

35. Emerson, *Life and Letters,* p. 21; Sears, *George B. McClellan: The Young Napoleon,* p. 237.

36. Emerson, *Life and Letters,* pp. 337–338.

37. *OR,* XLIII, Pt. 1, p. 490.

38. Emerson, *Life and Letters,* p. 53.

39. Corbett, *Diary,* Sept. 13, 1864; Towle, *Recollections,* p. 18; *Massachusetts Soldiers, Sailors, and Marines,* Vol. VI, p. 232.

40. *Massachusetts, Soldiers, Sailors, and Marines,* Vol. VI, pp. 228–328; *The Medical and Surgical History of the Civil War,* Vol. X, p. 740, Vol. XI, p. 44.

41. Corbett, *Diary,* Sept. 14, 1864.

42. Sheridan, *Civil War Memoirs,* pp. 240–41.

43. Grant, *Personal Memoirs of U.S. Grant,* pp. 474–75; Wert, *From Winchester to Cedar Creek,* p. 43.

44. Sheridan, *Civil War Memoirs,* pp. 242–43.

45. Corbett, *Diary,* Sept. 19, 1864; *OR,* XLIII, Pt. 1, p. 490.

46. *OR,* XLIII, Pt. 1, p. 490.

47. Towle, *Recollections,* p. 19.

48. Faust, *Encyclopedia,* p. 835.

49. Kidd, *A Cavalryman with Custer,* pp. 284–85.

50. Crowninshield, Oct. 2, 1864; Towle, *Recollections,* p. 19; *OR,* XLIII, Pt. 1, p. 490.

51. *Massachusetts, Soldiers, Sailors, and Marines,* Vol. VI, pp. 228–328; *The Medical and Surgical History of the Civil War,* Vol. VIII, pp. 47–49; National Archives, Record Group 94, Pension Records of Josiah Baldwin and John Felch.

52. Towle, *Recollections,* p. 19.

53. Corbett, *Diary,* Sept. 22, 1864; Crowninshield, Oct. 2, 1864; Wert, *Winchester to Cedar Creek,* p. 109.

54. Wert, *Mosby's Rangers,* pp. 211–213; Williamson, *Mosby's Rangers,* p. 239.

55. Corbett, *Diary,* Sept. 23, 1864; Harris, "With the Reserve Brigade," *Journal of the United States Cavalry Association,* Vol. III, no. 10, p. 238; Wert, *Mosby's Rangers,* p. 213; Williamson, *Mosby's Rangers,* p. 240; *OR,* XLIII, Pt. 1, pp. 441, 490.

56. Harris, "With the Reserve Brigade," *Journal of the United States Cavalry Association,* Vol. III, No. 10, p. 238; Williamson, *Mosby's Rangers,* p. 240.

57. Wert, *Mosby's Rangers,* pp. 214–215.

58. Emerson, *Life and Letters,* p. 353.

59. Corbett, *Diary,* Sept. 22, 1864; Crowninshield, Oct. 2, 1864; Schouler, *Annual Report of the Adjutant General of Massachusetts for the Year Ending 1864,* p. 949; Towle, *Diary,* p. 20; *OR,* XLIII, Pt. 1, p. 441; National Archives, Record group 94, Service and Pension records of Philip A. Baybutt, Company A muster roll August 31–October 31, 1864.

60. Towle, *Diary,* p. 21.

61. Corbett, *Diary,* Sept. 25, 1864; *OR,* XLIII, Pt. 1, p. 491.

62. Corbett, *Diary,* Sept. 26, 1864; *OR,* Vol. XLIII, Pt. 1, p. 491; Schouler, *Annual Report of the Adjutant General of Massachusetts for the Year Ending 1864,* p. 949.

63. Towle, *Diary,* p. 21.

64. Corbett, *Diary,* Sept. 28, 1864; Crowninshield, Oct. 2, 1864; *OR,* XLIII, Pt. 1, p. 491.

65. Bliss, "The Cavalry Affair at Waynesboro," *Southern Historical Society Papers,* Vol. XIII, pp. 427–430.

66. Harris, "With the Reserve Brigade," *Journal of the United States Cavalry Association,* Vol. III, No. 10, p. 240.

67. Corbett, *Diary,* Sept. 28, 1864; Crowninshield, Oct. 2, 1864; Emerson, *Life and Letters,* p. 351.

68. *Massachusetts Soldiers, Sailors, and Marines,* Vol. VI, pp. 228–328; National Archive, Record Group 94, Pension Record of Henry Crum.

69. Emerson, *Life and Letters,* p. 352.

70. Harris, "With the Reserve Brigade," *Journal of the United States Cavalry Association,* Vol III, No. 10, p. 242.

Chapter Ten

"So strong a love for country"

By late afternoon on the 30th of September, 1864, the cavalry rejoined the infantry at Mt. Crawford some 18 miles south of Staunton. Here the 2nd Massachusetts Cavalry gratefully set up camp, welcomed 65 new recruits to the ranks, and rested its played out horses. For several days the regiment was able to rest, involved in little more than picketing and the occasional movement of the camp over short distances.[1]

On the 4th of October the 2nd Massachusetts, along with the rest of Sheridan's army, began a slow retrograde movement down the Valley. Grant's order to lay waste to the region was once again put into effect and the torch was set to the upper Valley. "Last night the heavens were lit up for miles with the glare of burning buildings, houses, and barns...." For four days the regiment assisted in the destruction. "Matches were issued to the Regt. with orders to burn everything in the shape of forage that could be found, as I write, hundreds of barns and houses can be seen burning."[2]

It was an ugly duty, hard on officers as well as the men. Pvt. Towle noted that by the final day, Lt. Col. Crowninshield was uncharacteristically drunk on applejack as he ordered the men off to drive in some stock. One of the animals driven in was a cow, the only one left at a small farm of two barefoot women. Col. Lowell reluctantly ordered the cow driven off, one of the girls following along pleading with him to let her take the animal home. When the colonel refused she straightened up, fire and hate in her eyes, and said to Lowell, "Take her god damn you and go to hell with her!" Ugly duty indeed for such a gentle, philosophical man.[3]

Three years of war had finally begun to wear down Charlie Lowell and it began to show in his letters home to Effie. Beginning with a letter on the 28th of September he wrote, "I used to look forward to things somehow — now I don't look forward, but all the old pleasures of looking forward seems to be stirred in with things as they come along. I can't explain what I mean, but the difference is immense." A few days later he wrote, "I do wish this war was over!... Never mind. I'm doing all I can to end it"; followed soon after by, "We are expecting another brush with their cavalry today, as we are ordered to advance again. *I should like to have Sunday's quiet.*" Finally in an undated October letter he wrote, "…I don't want to be shot till I've had a chance to come home. I have no idea that I shall be hit, but I want so much not to now, that it sometimes frightens me." The rest he needed and craved would never come.[4]

After his defeat at Fisher's Hill, Early had requested Gen. Lee to send him more cavalry, to which Lee responded by dispatching the "Laurel Brigade" under Brig. Gen. Thomas L. Rosser. After weeks of setbacks the arrival of the horsemen boosted the morale of the citizens and soldiers, and Rosser quickly became known as the "Savior of the Valley." Wasting no time, Rosser arrived in the valley on the 5th of October and the next day began harassing the Union rear guard.[5]

The harassment turned into a sharp fight on the 8th when Rosser pressed so hard against Custer that Lowell turned the Reserve Brigade to assist him. While the colonel deployed the Regulars, the 2nd Massachusetts Cavalry, the only compact body of troops in sight, came under fire of a Confederate battery. Crowninshield quickly moved his troops to a less exposed position, but not before they nervously watched a solid shot strike the ground directly in front of them and ricochet uncomfortably close over their heads.[6]

In command of the 2nd Massachusetts skirmish line was 1st Lt. Henry Alvord, who, having just returned from Provost duty in the Washington garrison, had not been under fire for months. Young Henry, 20 years old, did well that day. "I was ordered by Colonel Lowell to take command of the line in the immediate front of the enemy, and remained there gradually driving them until darkness closed the engagement. Bullets struck all around me thickly — one glancing on a rock in front of my horse bounded up so that I caught it in my hand." During this skirmishing Col. Lowell lost his 12th horse of the campaign, and another bullet struck the pommel of his saddle and glanced through his coat. Near dark Lowell ordered the skirmish line forward. "We were then substantially out of ammunition and when ordered to advance that fact was reported to Col. Lowell. His reply was 'That makes no difference; advance.' That we did, and the confederates gave way."[7]

Pvt. James Collins (C), Boston, died of his wounds two weeks later. Pvt. Michael Lynch (C), Marlboro, Massachusetts, and John Hardy (D), Temple, Maine, both took wounds but neither was severe.[8]

The aggressive action by the supposedly whipped Rebels irritated Sheridan. "As we proceeded," Sheridan recalled, "the Confederates gained confidence, probably on account of the reputation with which its new commander had been heralded, and on the third day's march had the temerity to annoy my rear guard considerably. Tired of these annoyances, I concluded to open the enemy's eyes in earnest, so that night I told Torbert I expected him either to give Rosser a drubbing next morning or get whipped himself.…"[9]

On the morning of the 9th of October, Merritt deployed his brigades across the Valley Pike just north of Woodstock. Lowell's Reserve Brigade was on the left, Devin in the center, and Kidd's on the right. Gen. Custer (having recently replaced Wilson, who had been sent to command Sherman's cavalry) placed his division across the Back Road three miles to the west. Sheridan watched these deployments from the crest of Round Top Mountain.[10]

Rosser had placed his brigades in position on both roads to resist the Federal advance, and indeed held them in check for about two hours. In an effort to break the stalemate, Merritt ordered Lowell to charge his brigade against the center of the enemy line. The colonel placed the 1st U.S. Cavalry in a column of fours followed behind by the 5th U.S. Cavalry. The 2nd Massachusetts Cavalry took a position on either flank, also in columns of fours. The charge was ordered and the Confederate line evaporated before them. At nearly the same time, Custer, on the Back Road, made a flanking movement against the forces arrayed against him with similar results. In the center, connecting the two divisions, Kidd's Michigan Brigade charged, sending the Confederates reeling. The result of these three charges was staggering. Across the entire front Confederate resistance collapsed, soldiers, horse artillery, supply wagons, all streaming to the rear as fast as they could go. The rout was complete, turning into a horse race by the Northern cavalry in an attempt to take prizes. "On a little rise to the left of the road," wrote Pvt. Towle, "on the outskirts of Woodstock there were three pieces of Confederate artillery which we captured shotted; their support having stampeded; the men at the guns had not fired them. At that time our horses were very much worn down, many of them so weak that they would stagger as they walked. As we continued after the Confederates those having the best horses found themselves in the lead, and when we reached the confederate wagon train, about nine miles from where the fight started, there were only nine of us together." The chase continued for 26 miles, finally stopping near New Market where the remnants of the Rebel cavalry found protection with the infantry.[11]

The fight, known as Tom's Brook by both sides and the "Woodstock Races" by the victors, was the worst battering the Confederate cavalry took during the war. The 2nd Massachusetts finished the day having captured four pieces of artillery, two forges, five wagons and several prisoners, at a cost of six wounded. Pvt. Lawson Lawrence(C), Gloucester, Rhode Island, died of his wounds on the 22nd of October in Baltimore. Also wounded were Cornelius Conners (D), Salem; William Morris (E), of San Francisco, who had been captured at Coyle's Tavern and paroled in April; and Sgt. Elhanam Wakefield (F) and Osborn Ayer (L), both also from San Francisco. All but Morris were eventually discharged for their wounds. The only officer wounded was 1st Lt. Samuel F. Tucker, a former private in Company L, who was hit in the right hand, for which he later drew a pension. Sgt. Charles Benjamin (A), San Francisco, was thrown from his horse during the wild ride, injuring his back severely, an injury later attributed as the cause of a crippling spinal disease. Total Union casualties for the day's successes were nine killed and 48 wounded. The movement down the Valley continued the next morning.[12]

A new camp was established on the 10th along the northern bank of twisting Cedar Creek. Four days' rations were issued, and the men had the first opportunity in a long time to wash themselves and their clothes. "It's just noon," Lowell wrote, "and we have gone into camp for the day in a lovely green field with plenty of forage, and lots of rails to burn, — and I've just had a bath, soaped from head to heel. It's still cold (frost and ice this A.M. as I had to lie out with nothing but an overcoat, but it's splendid October and very exhilarating."[13]

The rest continued for two days, briefly interrupted on the 12th when, for some inexplicable reason, Lowell ordered the 2nd Massachusetts and the rest of the brigade out to drill, the first they had done since June. It was probably to break in some new recruits, but the drill was quickly stopped when noticed by Gen. Merritt who wanted the men resting.[14]

The following day the regiment was witness to a lively artillery duel. The Confederates had begun shelling the camps of the XIX corps and then turned their aim on the Union guns that had responded with counter battery fire. Two brigades of Union infantry advanced and were routed by a Confederate division. Lowell's troopers were mounted and held in reserve through the fight, but were never called on while the infantry extricated themselves from a tight spot. Twenty-seven-year-old Edward Seagrave (L) of San Francisco was wounded while waiting in ranks.[15]

The fight on the 13th was an attempt by Early to discover Sheridan's intentions. Having dispatched the VI Corps northward where it would eventually be sent to Grant, Sheridan's weakened force was probed by Early to discover whether it would hold the line or give ground. It was obvious that Sheridan intended on resisting any Confederate advances and called for the return of the VI Corps. Early was once again successful in keeping troops from the Petersburg front.[16]

Sheridan was summoned to Washington on the 14th to meet with Secretary Stanton and Chief of Staff Halleck about future Union activities in the Valley. Ensuring that Early was back in his Fisher's Hill encampment, and that his own troops were safely bivouacked around Middletown, Sheridan left his army for the conference. Anticipating a transfer of troops, he took Merritt's division of cavalry with him.[17]

"Marched all night until half past one this morning," recorded Corbett, "when we encamped near Front Royal. Reveille sounded at half past three. Started on the back track at 6." The return of Merritt's division to Middletown was prompted by an intercepted Confederate message: "Lieutenant-General Early: Be ready to move as soon as my forces join you and we will crush Sheridan. LONGSTREET." It was a ruse, as Sheridan suspected, but just to play it safe the cavalry was soon sent clip-clopping back up the pike. A successful bit of subterfuge on Early's part, but one that would prove fatal to his forces in the days to come.[18]

The 2nd Massachusetts Cavalry, along with the rest of the First Division, went into camp on the far right of the Union line, about a mile and a half west of Middletown. The army's three infantry corps were encamped along the steep banks of Cedar Creek, the VIII Corps on the left, XIX in the center, and the VI on the right. Custer's cavalry division was on the extreme right with Merritt between him and the infantry.[19]

Knowing full well that Sheridan was planning on sending some of his troops to reenforce the Army of the Potomac, Early approved a bold plan that would place his supposedly whipped army on the Union left flank, and attack in one final do or die battle. The plan was a good one and on the evening of the 18th/19th Early's men quietly left their Fisher's Hill camps and moved undetected to a position just south of the Union VIII Corps. At dawn he would put it all on the line, believing his 17,000 could surprise and defeat 30,000 unsuspecting Yankees. Sheridan, returning from his Washington conference, spent the night in Winchester, 20 miles to the north.[20]

Reveille was held for the 2nd Massachusetts Cavalry at half past three on the morning of the 19th of October, the men grunting and complaining in the cool misty air. Col. Lowell had received orders to take the Reserve Brigade on a reconnaissance across Cedar Creek at first light, and had the men in the saddle and moving by 4 A.M. As Lowell's men were riding out of camp, Gen. Rosser, with two brigades of Rebel cavalry, splashed across the creek and engaged the pickets of Col. James Kidd's First Brigade. Quickly roused from sleep, Kidd moved his brigade up to support his skirmishers, while Lowell was ordered to halt and, if needed, support Kidd's Michiganders.[21]

Rosser's orders from Early were to "occupy" the Federal cavalry, and he was content to skirmish with Kidd while his artillery fired in support. The Reserve Brigade, waiting patiently in ranks, was noticed by the rebel artillerymen who quickly had them targeted. "We drew up behind a little hill," recalled Pvt. Towle, "but the battery soon secured a good range with the result our position was far from comfortable. As we were there drawn up a solid shot struck the horse of the man next me in the breast, going completely through. The horse dropped instantly, and I shall never forget the peculiar look of surprise on the soldiers face as he stood astraddle his fallen horse."[22]

Lowell, conferring with Kidd, could clearly hear the sound of battle on the left of the Union line. Early's infantry attack on the Federal left flank had been a complete surprise, and he was now pushing hard against the routed VIII Corps and the embattled XIX. Sheridan, hearing the artillery from Winchester, began the 20-mile ride to his army, a ride which would take hours but would forever be immortalized in prose and folklore.[23]

As the morning progressed and the Union left continued to fall back, the cavalry stood idle to the right, awaiting orders. Finally, Gen. Horatio Wright, commanding in Sheridan's absence, ordered Torbert to send Merritt's and Custer's divisions to bolster the crumbling Union left. Waiting and wondering, Lowell and Kidd could only speculate what was happening to the southeast. Telling Kidd he would soon return, Lowell appeared to be about to go in search of orders, when, according to Kidd, he decided to head to the sound of the fighting without orders. "I said to him: 'Colonel, what would you do if you were in my place?' 'I think you ought to go too,' he replied and, presently, turning in his saddle, continued: 'Yes, I will take the responsibility to give you the order,' whereat, the two brigades took up the march toward the point where the battle, judging from the sound, seemed to be in progress. It was into the thickest of the fight that he led the way, Michigan willingly following."[24]

The ride to the left brought the two brigades to a ridge that they continued to follow to the east and just north of the town of Middletown. To the south of the ridge the troopers could see the panorama of the entire battlefield, with the Confederates massed on the ridge to the south. They were a sight to behold, walking their horses across the VI Corps' front as if on dress parade, in full view of the enemy. "On coming out into the open, near where we had been in camp, we saw the whole country in front of us, and for some distance to the south, covered with our straggling infantry. In some cases there would be a division flag with perhaps 50 men with it; but usually a soldier was walking by himself. There was some officers trying to stop the retreat. When a soldier was ordered to halt he would stop and face about, but immediately the officer had ridden to halt another soldier the first would turn around and leisurely continue his march to the rear."[25]

The stragglers were from the VIII and XIX Corps which had been driven back by Early's assault and were now in full retreat. The VI Corps held steady on the right and checked the gray tide, slowly giving ground to a position north of Middletown. Brig. Gen. William Dwight of the 1st Division, VI Corps, watched in admiration as the two brigades of cavalry rode by. "They moved past me, that splendid cavalry; if they reached the Pike, I felt secure. Lowell got by me before I could speak, but I looked after him for a long distance. Exquisitely mounted, the picture of a soldier, erect, confident, defiant, he moved at the head of the finest body of cavalry that to-day scorns the earth it treads."[26]

Pvt. Charles Atmore, Company A, California Hundred, 2nd Massachusetts Cavalry. Captured July 6, 1864, Aldie, Virginia. Died September 26, 1864, Andersonville, Georgia. *Courtesy of Vallejo Naval and Historical Museum.*

called on the nearby brigade of Col. Alpheus Moore (First Brigade, Second Division) to advance and occupy a stone wall that abutted the road. "He protested that his men had great objections to fighting dismounted, and declined to accede to my request." To Devin's relief the Reserve Brigade arrived, Lowell quickly ordering his men to dismount and take up the position behind the wall. "For a time all remained quiet in our front, but soon the enemy's skirmishers began to be heard from, and it was only necessary for a head to be shown above the wall to attract a score of bullets."[27]

At this point in the fight Early had been so successful that the entire Northern line arrayed against him consisted of no more than a single division of the VI Corps and Torbert's cavalry. When all that stood between Early and a smashing victory was one final push, he inexplicably paused. Later claiming that his soldiers "...had been up all night and were much jaded," he believed they were too exhausted and disorganized for further offensive action and so "I determined, therefore to try and hold what had been gained, and orders were given for carrying off the captured and abandoned artillery, small arms and wagons." The move, taken so close to victory, invited defeat, for near that time Phil Sheridan arrived on the field, his presence electrifying his troops. Divisions of the VIII and XIX Corps which had been routed and scattered, reorganized during

While en route to the left of the line, orders finally came from Merritt to continue the march and to take up a position on the east side of the Valley Pike. Devin's brigade, earlier used to stem the flow of the retreating VIII Corps, was already in line when Lowell arrived, his right firmly anchored to the Pike. Hotly pressed and fearing his left flank was vulnerable, Devin the lull, convincing Sheridan that not only could he resist Early, he could counterattack and drive the Confederates back across Cedar Creek. Shouting orders to reorganize his lines, Sheridan sent a messenger to Lowell, whose position along the stone wall put him in closest contact with the enemy, asking if he could hold on there. Lowell's simple answer; he could.[28]

As if to disprove Lowell's confidence, a demonstration was made against his line, succeeding in taking a barn that opened his men to enfilading fire on the right. In response he ordered a countercharge. Lines were quickly formed, Lowell and Capt. Eugene Baker, commanding the 1st U.S. Cavalry, recklessly riding back and forth in front of the men to inspire them. "This courageous example," recalled Sgt. Moses Harris, "at the critical moment, inspired the little force anew with the determination not to disappoint the faith which had been staked upon their soldierly courage and conduct." Up and over the stone wall, the dismounted cavalry charged at the veteran infantry who met them with a hail of bullets. Down went Capt. Rufus Smith of the California Hundred, followed moments later by 1st Lt. Henry Kuhls, both severely wounded, Smith mortally. A sharp fight ensued with several casualties on both sides, the Southern infantry eventually giving way and falling back. Merritt, watching from the rear, swelled with pride. "Never did troops fight more elegantly than at this time. Not a soldier shirked his duty, not a soldier who did not conduct himself like a hero."[29]

Returning to the shelter of the stone wall, another Confederate advance soon threatened their position. First lieutenant Henry Crocker of Company E (who had recently distinguished himself at Locke's Ford) saw an opportunity and quickly presented it to Lt. Col. Crowninshield. "About this time a body of the enemy was seen to emerge from the woods and advance upon our front. My mind was immediately set upon checking those fellows, so I rode up to Colonel Crowninshield and asked permission to charge them." Asking for two companies, Crocker proposed to clear them out or not come back. This charge would be mounted.[30]

"I hurried back to my company and told the boys, very much to their satisfaction, of the work before us. We waited until we knew the advancing force could give us but one volley before we could reach them, and I gave the command: 'Forward! Trot! Gallop! Charge!' and away we went with sabres flashing in the sunlight. The expected volley was received, saddles were emptied and horses went down, but on we went. In less time than it takes to tell we were among them, their line was broken and we demanded their surrender. Many ran back into the woods where we could plainly see the enemy in force, but did not fire upon us for fear of hitting their own men. We brought back fourteen prisoners on the run."*[31]

With the bullets flying thickly it was almost inevitable that Crocker would be hit. A Confederate minié ball entered inches below his left knee, passing through the flesh of his calf, just grazing the bone on the way. "In the heat of our charge I had felt a dull, throbbing pain in my left leg, and knew that I had been wounded, but that did not prevent me from stopping, on our return, to pick up Lt. McIntosh, whose horse had been killed and who was loosening the cinch from his saddle." Mounting behind, McIntosh and Crocker raced back to the safety of the Union lines.

---

*From these prisoners it was learned that Longstreet had not joined Early, information Sheridan claimed was vital to his decision to counterattack. Humphreys, Field and Camp, p. 176; Sheridan, Civil War Memoirs, p. 279.

Thirty-two years later Henry Crocker, now a freight agent with a stiff left leg, would be presented the Medal of Honor.[32]

Minutes later the Confederates made a third attempt to gain the Union line, this time striving to set up a barricade of fence rails that extended beyond Lowell's left, but the fire from the massed Spencers quickly drove back this foray. During this last fight, while riding nearly to the stone wall, the 13th and final horse of the campaign was shot out from under the colonel, and the bullet that carried his name finally found him. Riding with Col. Smith H. Hustings of the 5th Michigan Cavalry (Kidd's Brigade), Lowell was struck full in the chest, reeling, but somehow staying in the saddle. Hustings, helping him off the dying horse, opened his coat and searched for the wound where Lowell, unable to speak, was pointing. Rather than finding a gaping wound, the two men found a distorted lead bullet, probably a ricochet off the stonewall that had nearly spent its force when it slammed into Charley. Hustings pocketed the bullet and breathed a premature sigh of relief; the wound was serious and most probably mortal. One of Lowell's tubercular scarred lungs had collapsed and he was bleeding internally, the blood already flecking his lips, and the color abandoning his face. Before returning to his own regiment, Hustings helped Lowell's aides carry him back from the firing line, where they attempted to make him comfortable, covering him with an overcoat and building a small embankment for protection. Attempting to reassure the men, Lowell, hardly able to whisper, smiled and told them, "It is only my poor lung." Hearing that the colonel was down, Gen. Torbert rode up to check on the brigade commander. Seeing him laid out, coughing blood and barely able to speak, he urged Lowell to head for the rear, which the stricken officer steadfastly refused to do. Torbert consented to his remaining, the battle having subsided to skirmish and artillery fire.[33]

Early, believing he had won the day, stopped the assault, and waited for the Yankees to yield the field. Sheridan, having earlier made up his mind to counterattack, took full advantage of the lull by placing his reorganized divisions in position for the thrust. Changes to the cavalry deployments were made, Custer's division returning to the right of the line.[34]

A few minutes before 4 P.M. Sheridan advanced. Heralded by as many as 200 bugles, the infantry stepped off in a solid blue wall, both flanks covered by Torbert's mounted troopers. With assistance Lowell mounted his horse, drew his sabre, and whispered commands to his aides. Adrenaline coursing through his veins and color returning to his face, Charley spurred his horse and charged his brigade against a battery immediately to their front. "We moved up over the hill in regimental front...," remembered Towle. "As we advanced I was near to the right of our regiment and Charlie Benjamin was next on my right. We each at the same time saw what looked much like a soldier's cap coming through the air, to escape which he dodged to the right and I to the left, and cannon shot or shell, for such it was, the wind of which was plainly felt, passing between us. I never saw our regiment act with more coolness or steadiness when on a dress parade than it did at that time."[35]

Luck was with Pvt. Towle, but it had finally turned its back on Charles Lowell. A bullet, thought to come from the second floor of the nearby Blinke House, passed through his body from shoulder to shoulder, severing the spinal cord and tumbling him backwards off his horse. The charge continued right up to the mouth of the guns, but unable to crack the Confederate line, was driven back. "We charged all most [sic] up to the wall but we could not carry it," related Crowninshield. "The fire was perfectly fearful, grape & canister & musket balls came into us in perfect showers, we were driven back with considerable loss. How any of us escaped I don't see, but thank God who spared me." Lowell was scooped up by his men, and though he was paralyzed from the shoulders down, pleaded with them to carry him along behind the next charge.[36]

"Old Badgers" McKendry was thrust into command of the 2nd Massachusetts Cavalry as Caspar Crowninshield took Lowell's place at the head of the brigade. Like Devin and Kidd, he quickly realigned his troops and a second charge was made against the battery and its infantry support. Under the command of Brig. Gen. Gabriel C. Wharton, the Confederate infantry was fighting for its life, and again the charge was repulsed.[37]

Once again Merritt's division retreated, reformed and pressed forward a third and final time. "I never expected to succeed or get out alive," confided Crowninshield, "the enemy's fire was terrific. Compared with it Ball's Bluff was child's play. But I saw our infantry charging on the right and I charged and said, 'God, just take my soul!'" Early's line cracked and then shattered. "When the whole Cavalry Corps burst upon the line with a 'yell' it was too much for them. They could not stand it. At first they wavered then broke, than ran, and the day for them was lost."[38]

The 2nd Massachusetts Cavalry joined in the pursuit of the beaten Confederates, following them to Mt. Crawford, then falling back to camp at Woodstock. "That night I had picket duty," told Pvt. Towle, "and as I rode out to my post saw on the ground what looked like a horse's nosebag. Reaching over I picked it up only to find that it was a boot with a piece of a man's leg in it." It had been a long and difficult day for the regiment, and evening provided a chance to take stock of the day's casualties.[39]

Dead was Capt. Rufus W. Smith (A), a 30-year-old native of Maine and former captain of the "Light Guard" of San Francisco. First lieutenant of Company F, Smith had commanded the company during De-Merritt's insanity, and was promoted to captain of the California Hundred after the death of Capt. Reed. "No member of the battalion had a higher reputation for courage, gallantry and daring." To a friend who had recently visited him in camp he had remarked that he would "...either wear the eagle on his shoulder or perish on the battlefield." Also killed were Pvt. William Walton (D), St. Louis; Cpl. Asa Davis (E), San Francisco; Sgt. Alvin Russel (E), San Francisco; Pvt. Stephen Green (F), Stoughton, Massachusetts; Pvt. Stephen Weisberger (F), San Francisco; and 1st Sgt. Merrill C. Beal (M), San Francisco.[40]

First lieutenant Henry Crocker (E) would walk with a limp for the rest of his life and would be out of action till the closing days of the war. In December he would be promoted to captain of Company F. First Lieutenant Henry Kuhls (L), San Francisco, who had started the war as a sergeant, was severely wounded but mended quickly and was back on duty for his December promotion to captain of Company K. Also on the wounded list were Sgt. Willam Henry Harrison Hussey (A), San Francisco, the acting second lieutenant for the company, who took a disabling wound to the left shoulder; Frank Libby (A), California, who was nearly blinded by the concussion of a bursting artillery shell; Pvt. Stephen Cole (D), Ashland, Massachusetts; Timothy Sullivan (D), Watertown, who took a gunshot wound to the scalp that was later attributed as the cause of his severe epilepsy; Sgt. Charles Roberts (F), the California trooper who had kept such a meticulous diary in 1863, who took a slight gunshot wound to the right thigh; Pvt. Jeffery Cornnell (H), Boston; Pvt. Carl

Redmann (H) of Germany who would die of his wounds two weeks later in Winchester; Jared Sparhawk (L), San Francisco; and Pvt. Thomas A. Burke (K), South Danvers, who deserted from a Baltimore hospital rather than face another day like October 19th. Numbers for the 2nd Massachusetts Cavalry were seven killed and 18 wounded, of which two would die of their wounds.[41]

At the top of the list of the day's casualties was Col. Lowell. During the pursuit of the Confederate army, Charles had been taken to an old house in Middletown that was serving as a makeshift hospital. Oscar De Wolf, the surgeon of the 2nd Massachusetts Cavalry attended to Lowell and related his final hours. "There were four or five that night in the room. Lowell lay on the table, shot through from shoulder to shoulder; the ball had cut the spinal cord on the way. Of course, below this he was completely paralyzed. Four others were lying desperately wounded on the floor. One young officer was in great pain. Lowell spent much of his ebbing strength helping him through the straits of death. 'I have always been able to count on you, you were always brave. Now you must meet this as you have the other trials — be steady — I count on you.' When he heard the groans of the Rebel wounded that were bought into the yard, he sent me away to look after them. As the night wore on and his strength failed, I said: 'Colonel, you must write to your wife.' He answered that he was not able, but I said it could be managed; so putting a scrap of paper on a piece

Col. Charles Lowell and his wife Josephine Shaw Lowell. Vienna, Virginia. *Courtesy of U.S.A.M.H.I.*

of board, I held his arm above him, putting a pencil between his fingers, and holding the hand against the paper, told him I thought he would find that he could use his fingers. And thus he wrote a word or two of farewell to her."[42]

Two lines were all he could manage to write, relying on DeWolf to dictate his final orders and requests. He wanted his pistol to be given to Caspar Crowninshield, commenting, "I was very fond of him." A note of congratulations was sent out to Col. Gansevoort of the 13th New York Cavalry for his recent victory over Mosby. Several pieces of business concerning the brigade were dealt with to ensure all would be in order for its new commander.[43]

As morning approached he became quieter, but was fully conscious to the end which came near 8 A.M. on the 20th, 11 days short of his first wedding anniversary. Charlie Lowell was 29. The news of his death came as a staggering blow not only to his men, but all the way up the chain to Sheridan himself. In their words:

Col. Charles R. Lowell, Jr. Died October 20, 1864, of wounds received October 19, 1864, at the battle of Cedar Creek, Virginia. *Courtesy of U.S.A.M.H.I.*

Pvt. George Towle (A): "His death was a great loss, and I have no doubt that the subsequent history of his command was much changed by his death. Notwithstanding the wide distance that separates a private from his Colonel I have always felt his death as a distinct personal loss."[44]

Pvt. Samuel Backus (L): "Colonel Lowell was one of the most brilliant officers in the service. The movements of his thoughts were like flashes of lightning."[45]

Pvt. Thomas H. Merry (L): "It was here that our brave Colonel, commanding the brigade, was shot while gallantly leading a charge, and died soon after." [This was written 12 years after the war by the same Thomas Merry who was so critical of Lowell in the California papers during the months spent fighting Mosby.][46]

Chaplain Humphreys: "I need hardly say that Charles Russell Lowell was the most brilliant officer I ever met."[47]

Lt. Col. Crowninshield: "Colonel Lowell died like a hero & he certainly was one of the bravest of the brave.... No hero of old was more fearless than he. It makes me sad to think of his poor wife, she is to be confined in a month."*[48]

Amos A. Lawrence: "Few men have combined so many talents, and accomplishments, so much learning and so much

---

*On the 30th of November, Josephine gave birth to a daughter, Carlotta Russell Lowell.

Charles Lowell monument, Middletown, Virginia. *Author's collection.*

Mt. Auburn Cemetery, Boston. *Courtesy of Larry Rogers.*

virtue, with so strong a love for country."⁴⁹

Brig. Gen. George A. Custer: "We all shed tears when we knew we had lost him. It is the greatest loss the Cavalry Corps has ever suffered."⁵⁰

Brig. Gen. Wesley Merritt: "His fall cast a gloom on the entire command. No one in the field appreciated his worth more than his division commander. Young in years, he died too early for his country, leaving a brilliant record for future generations, ending a career which gave bright promise of yet greater usefulness and glory."⁵¹

Maj. Gen. Alfred Torbert: "Thus the service lost one of its most gallant and accomplished soldiers. He was the *beau ideal* of a cavalry officer."⁵²

Maj. Gen. Philip H. Sheridan: "I do not think there was a quality which I could have added to Lowell. He was the perfection of a man and a soldier."⁵³

Sheridan (in a letter to John M. Forbes): "I watched him closely during the campaign, and had he survived that day at Cedar Creek, it was my intention to have more fully recognized his gallantry and genius by obtaining for him promotion in rank, and a command which would have enlarged his usefulness and given more scope to his remarkable abilities as a leader of men."⁵⁴

Sheridan (in a letter to Josephine Shaw Lowell): "Had General Lowell lived, it is my firm belief that he would have commanded all my cavalry and would have done better with it than I could have done."⁵⁵

Capt. George B. Sanford: "He commanded the respect of all who knew him, and in his brigade was regarded with the warmest admiration and affection. A few days after the battle, I had the pleasure of carrying to Gen. Merritt his brevet as Major General of volunteers, and of being the first to congratulate him on its receipt. Lowell's commission as Brigadier General had come in the same mail, too late, and I well remember Merritt's emphatic remark, when I told him of it: 'I would gladly give up *this* if he could only take *that*.'"⁵⁶

Several accounts of Lowell's death include either the deathbed or posthumous awarding of his brigadier's star by Sheridan. A nice little story but not true. Sheridan had recommended Lowell's promotion weeks before, "...for gallant and meritorious services at the Battles of Winchester and Fisher's Hill." Dated for the 19th of September, his commission was issued and signed on the 19th of October, 1864.⁵⁷

Charles Lowell's funeral was held at Harvard on Friday, the 28th of October, at the College Chapel.

Edward Waldo Emerson wrote: "I remember, one rainy day when the sudden gusts blew the yellow leaves in showers from the College elms, hearing the beautiful notes of Pleyel's Hymn, which was the tune to which soldiers were borne to burial, played by the band as the procession came, bearing Charles Lowell's body from his mother's house to the College Chapel; and seeing the coffin, wrapped in the flag, carried to the altar by soldiers; and how

Lt. Henry Alvord, Company K., 2nd Massachusetts Cavalry. Later captain of Company I. *Courtesy of U.S.A.M.H.I.*

strangely in contrast with the new blue overcoats and fresh white and red bunting were the campaign-soiled cap and gauntlets, the worn hilt and battered scabbard of the sword that lay on the coffin."[58]

First lieutenant Henry Alvord was detailed to accompany Lowell's body home for burial. Devastated by his colonel's death, he wrote the following during his return to the regiment: "I must confess that for the first time in my soldiers life I do not want to rejoin the command. In spite of my endeavors to keep cheerful I am 'blue' all the time. Leaving a happy home to enter the army, I led an easy life therein and finally with Colonel Lowell I found a true and very dear friend and almost a second home — an army home where I was as contented as I possibly could be. But now he is gone I feel alone again — like a stranger in a strange land. I have lost my dearest friend and my 'army home' is broken up. I loved, I honored and admired — I almost worshipped him, and now he is no longer at Head Quarters with the command. I feel there is no longer any interest there for me."[59]

Notes

1. Corbett, *Diary*, Sept. 30, 1864; *OR*, XLIII, Pt. 1, p. 491.
2. Corbett, *Diary*, Oct. 4–5, 1864; Sheridan, *Civil War Memoirs*, p. 264.
3. Towle, *Recollections*, p. 22.
4. Emerson, *Life and Letters*, pp. 351–57.
5. Sheridan, *Civil War Memoirs*, p. 265; Wert, *From Winchester to Cedar Creek*, pp. 160–61.
6. Towle, *Recollections*, p. 22; *OR*, XLIII, Pt. 1, p. 491.
7. Sherman, "A New England Boy in the Civil War," *New England Quarterly*, v. (1932), p. 332; Towle, *Recollections*, p. 22.
8. *Massachusetts Soldiers, Sailors, and Marines*, Vol. VI, pp. 238–328.
9. Sheridan, *Civil War Memoirs*, p. 265; Wert, *From Winchester to Cedar Creek*, pp. 160–61.
10. Kidd, *A Cavalryman with Custer*, p. 294; Sheridan, *Civil War Memoirs*, p. 266; *OR*, XLIII, Pt. 1, p. 492.
11. Kidd, *A Cavalryman with Custer*, p. 294; Towle, *Recollections*, p. 22; Wert, *From Winchester to Cedar Creek*, pp. 161–64; *OR*, XLIII, Pt. 1, p. 492.
12. Orton, *Records of California Men in the War of the Rebellion 1861–1867*, pp. 854–70; *Massachusetts's Soldiers, Sailors and Marines*, Vol. VI, pp. 228–328; National Archives, Record Group 94, Pension Record of Charles Benjamin.
13. Corbett, *Diary*, Oct. 11, 1864; Emerson, *Life and Letters*, pp. 355–56.
14. Corbett, *Diary*, Oct. 12, 1864; Emerson, *Life and Letters*, p. 358.
15. Corbett, *Diary*, Oct. 13–14, 1864; Harris, "With the Reserve Brigade," *Journal of the United States Cavalry Association*, Vol. III, No. 11, p. 363; *Massachusetts Soldiers, Sailors, and Marines*, Vol. VI, p. 308.
16. Early, *Jubal Early's Memoirs*, p. 437.
17. Sheridan, *Civil War Memoirs*, pp. 269–70; Wert, *From Winchester to Cedar Creek*, pp. 168–170.
18. Corbett, *Diary*, Oct. 16, 1864; Sheridan, *Civil War Memoirs*, pp. 269–70.
19. Corbett, *Diary*, Oct. 18, 1864; Wert, *From Winchester to Cedar Creek*, pp. 170–71.
20. Early, *Jubal Early's Memoirs*, pp. 439–43; Sheridan, *Civil War Memoirs*, p. 272.
21. Corbett, *Diary*, Oct. 19, 1864; Kidd, *A Cavalryman with Custer*, p. 303; Wert, *From Winchester to Cedar Creek*, p. 213.
22. Towle, *Recollections*, p. 23; Wert, *From Winchester to Cedar Creek*, p. 213.
23. Kidd, *A Cavalryman with Custer*, p. 303; Sheridan, *Civil War Memoirs*, p. 273; *OR*, XLIII, Pt. 1, p. 449.
24. Kidd, *A Cavalryman with Custer*, pp. 303–04; *OR*, XLIII, Pt. 1, pp. 443, 449.
25. Kidd, *A Cavalryman with Custer*, p. 304; Towle, *Recollections*, p. 23.
26. Emerson, *Life and Letters*, p. 63; Kidd, *A Cavalryman with Custer*, p. 303.
27. Harris, "With the Reserve Brigade," *Journal of the United States Cavalry Association*, Vol. III, No. 10, p. 366; Kidd, *A Cavalryman with Custer*, p. 306; *OR*, XLIII, Pt. 1, pp. 478, 492.
28. Early, *Jubal Early's Memoirs*, pp. 447–48; Sheridan, *Civil War Memoirs*, pp. 276–78.
29. Backus, "Californians in the Field," *MOLLUS.*, California Commandry, p. 17; Corbett, *Diary*, Oct. 19, 1864; Harris, "With the Re-

serve Brigade," *Journal of the United States Cavalry Association*, Vol. III, No. 10, p 367; Orton, *Records of California Men in the War of the Rebellion 1861–1867*, p. 851; *OR*, XLIII, Pt. 1, p. 450.

30. Tibbals, "Thirty Years Later," *Civil War Times Illustrated*, April 1986, Vol. XXV, No. 2, pp. 39–40.

31. Tibbals, "Thirty Years Later," *Civil War Times Illustrated*, April 1986, Vol. XXV, No. 2, p. 40.

32. Tibbals, "Thirty Years Later," *Civil War Times Illustrated*, April 1986, Vol. XXV, No. 2, p. 39; National Archives, Pension Record of Henry Crocker.

33. Emerson, *Life and Letters*, p. 64; Greenslet, *The Lowells and Their Seven Worlds*, p. 258; Higginson, "Lowell," p. 325; *OR*, XLIII, Pt. 1, pp. 450–51.

34. Sheridan, *Civil War Memoirs*, p. 278; *OR*, XLIII, Pt. 1, p. 434.

35. Emerson, *Life and Letters*, p. 31; Humphreys, *Field and Camp*, p. 180; Kidd, *A Cavalryman with Custer*, p. 311; Towle, *Recollections*, p. 24; Wert, *From Winchester to Cedar Creek*, p. 230.

36. Crowninshield, Oct. 21, 1864; Emerson, *Life and Letters*, p. 31; Greenslet, *The Lowells and Their Seven Worlds*, p. 258; Humphreys, *Field and Camp*, p. 180; Lewis, *The Guns of Cedar Creek*, p. 287.

37. Emerson, *Life and Letters*, pp. 65–66.

38. Corbett, *Diary*, Oct. 19, 1864; Crowninshield, Oct. 21, 1864.

39. Towle, *Recollections*, p. 24.

40. *Massachusetts Soldiers, Sailors, and Marines*, pp. 228–328; *Daily Alta California*, Oct. 30, 1864.

41. *Massachusetts Soldiers, Sailors, and Marines*, Vol. VI, pp. 228–328; *The Medical and Surgical History of the Civil War*, Vol. VII, p. 119; National Archives, Record Group 94, Pension Records of Frank Libby, Charles Roberts.

42. Emerson, *Life and Letters*, p. 66; Greenslet, *The Lowells and Their Seven Worlds*, pp. 258–59; Higginson, "Lowell," p. 326.

43. Crowninshield, Oct. 21, 1864; Emerson, *Life and Letters*, p. 66.

44. Towle, *Recollections*, p. 24.

45. Backus, "Californians in the Field," *MOLLUS.*, California Commandry, p. 17.

46. *National Tribune*, May 12, 1887.

47. Humphreys, *Life and Letters*, p. 181.

48. Crowninshield, Oct. 21, 1864.

49. Lawrence, *Life of A. Amos Lawrence with Extracts from His Diary and Correspondence*, p. 199.

50. Higginson, "Lowell," p. 327.

51. *OR*, XLIII, Pt. 1, p. 450–51.

52. *OR*, XLIII, Pt. 1, p. 434.

53. Perry, *Life and Letters of Henry Lee Higginson*, p. 232.

54. Hughes, *Letters and Recollections of John Murray Forbes*, Vol. 2, p. 114.

55. Greenslet, *The Lowells and Their Seven Worlds*, p. 259.

56. Hagemann, *Fighting Rebels and Redskins, Experiences in Army Life of Colonel George B. Sanford 1861–1892*, pp. 297–98.

57. Humphreys, *Field and Camp*, p. 188; Schouler, *Annual Report of the Adjutant General of Massachusetts for the Year Ending 1864*, p. 952.

58. Emerson, *Life and Letters*, p. 68.

59. Sherman, "A New England Boy in the Civil War," *New England Quarterly*, v. (1932), pp. 332–33.

Chapter Eleven

"Let them know there is a God in Israel"

Early's army was a beaten foe, halting in New Market where it stopped to assess the damage and plan for another day. In the future it would make occasional forays against the Yankees, but would never again pose a serious threat. Returning to the site of the battle on the 21st, the 2nd Massachusetts Cavalry went into camp some four miles south of Middletown. The days turned cold and the men huddled around fires, talking, resting, and drinking coffee. One evening the men noticed Pvt. John Hunter (A) "...slowly revolving himself in front of the fire. After noticing the movement for sometime one of the boys asked him why he was doing that, to which he replied that he was 'trying to keep them damn gray backs on the move.'" The regiment camped on "...the brow of a hill where the wind has full sweep at us from all parts...," and where the men grumbled about the lack of warm army blankets while they shivered at night under the only ones available — their saddle blankets. A move to a grove on the 28th cut the chill wind and improved the troopers' morale.[1]

On the 24th Chaplain Humphreys returned from captivity, noting in his diary how different the regiment appeared and the absence of so many men and officers. The men warmly welcomed him back and he quickly returned to his old duties as if he had never been away. Picketing and foraging accounted for the men's time, activities that kept them vigilant, especially after the capture of four men on the 28th. Privates John Thompson (B), Boston, Charles Foote (F), California, Nathan Fordham (L), California, and Lewis Weeks (L), Jefferson, Maine, were all taken while out foraging.[2]

Construction parties began work on restoring the Harpers Ferry and Winchester Railroad, and on the 3rd of November the Reserve Brigade was ordered to Charlestown to protect the workers. Every few days, as the work progressed, the regiment moved south, camping at Charlestown, Halltown, Summit Point, Wadesville, and Stevenson Station. There was little to keep the troopers occupied other than an occasional foray by Mosby's men. The Rangers, who had been at the center of the 2nd Massachusetts Cavalry's world a year ago, now hardly rated a mention in letter or diary. "Guerrillas still lay around our pick-

Pvt. George Holt, Company A, California Hundred, 2nd Massachusetts Cavalry. *Courtesy of Vallejo Naval and Historical Museum.*

ets," Corbett recorded on Nov. 9, "and attack a wagon train once in a while, but do not make much by their operations."[3]

Election day came on the 8th but the regiment was unable to cast their ballots. For fun the men held a mock election and reelected Lincoln in a landslide victory. There were 349 men in camp that evening, and 238 voted for the president, the other 111 opting for George McClellan. "But five votes for McClellan by Californians, none in Co. A Cal 100," bragged Corbett. The country voted along the same lines as the 2nd Massachusetts, and the president, buoyed by Sheridan's recent victory, was swept into a second term.[4]

Promotions, brought on by the death of Col. Lowell, were made official on the 10th of November, when commissions arrived for Lt. Col. Crowninshield and Capt. McKendry. Caspar, still commanding the brigade, wore the eagles of a full colonel, while "Old Badgers," leading the regiment, tacked on a major's oak leaves. (Major Will Forbes, recovering from his imprisonment, was promoted to lieutenant colonel.) The band serenaded that night to congratulate the two officers. A few days later the band serenaded Lt. Josiah Baldwin (A), who had been severely wounded in the right knee at Winchester. He was convalescing nine weeks after the injury in a nearby home, still unable to be transferred to a Northern hospital.[5]

Mosby continued to strike at the edges of the Union army in the Valley, occasionally taking wagons and prisoners. On one of the raids two of Little Phil's staff were killed and the wrath of Sheridan descended on that area east of the Blue Ridge Mountains known as Mosby's Confederacy. In a letter to Chief of Staff Henry Halleck, Sheridan stated, "I will soon commence work on Mosby. Heretofore I have made no attempt to break him up as I would have employed ten men to his one, and for the reason that I have made a scape-goat of him for the destruction of private rights. Now there is going to be an intense hatred of him in that portion of the valley which is nearly a desert. I will soon commence on Loudoun County, and let them know there is a God in Israel." Tasked with carrying out this duty was Merritt and his First Division of cavalry, to whom Sheridan directed, "To clear the county of these parties that are bringing destruction down upon the innocent, as well as their guilty supporters, by their cowardly acts, you will consume and destroy all forage and subsistence, burn all barns and mills and their contents, and drive off all stock in the region...."[6]

Rising at 3 A.M. on the morning of the 29th, the Reserve Brigade was soon crossing the Blue Ridge at Snicker's Gap, while the First and Second brigades crossed to the south at Ashby's Gap. Crowninshield left the 2nd U.S. and 30 men of the 2nd Massachusetts to hold the gap while the remainder of the brigade descended the grade to begin the task at hand. Chaplain Humphreys stood in the gap gazing down at the farms and fields that would soon be torched. "The necessity of destruction is one of the many dark phases of the war. As we descended the eastern slope of the Blue Ridge, nothing could be more beautiful than that garden of Virginia flanked on the further side by the Bull Run mountains."[7]

The chaplain had been in prison when the regiment had participated in the burning of the upper Valley in early October. Seeing the lit torches and destruction led him to record, "This was the most unpleasant task we were ever compelled to undertake. It was heart-piercing to hear the shrieks of women and children, and to see even men crying and beating their breasts, supplicating for mercy on bended knees, begging that at least one cow — an only support — might be left. But no mercy was allowed. It was a terrible retribution on the county that had for three years supported and lodged the guerrilla bands and sent them out to plunder and murder."[8]

Sheridan's orders were followed to the letter, and by raid's end, four days later, Loudoun County was a barren wasteland. The Reserve Brigade alone reported the capture of 87 horses, 474 head of cattle, and 100 sheep. Destroyed were 230 barns, eight mills, one distillery, 10,000 tons of hay, and 25,000 bushels of grain. Crowninshield estimated the total value of all goods captured and destroyed reached $411,620.[9]

Appalled by the destruction, Chaplain Humphreys was able to justify at least one of the animals driven off. "In this expedition I got even with the Confederacy on the score of horses, and made up for the one the guerrillas had taken from me when I was captured in July, by securing a young but very fine animal, tall and graceful, and with a very dainty step, as if dancing to music, and she carried me to the end of the war."[10]

Try as they might, Mosby's men were rarely able to strike at the 3,000 horsemen engaged in the burning. Merritt planned well and left few opportunities for the Rangers to pounce on small bodies of Yankees, always protected as they were by armed and ready troopers. There were Union casualties, but during the four days of the raid the 2nd Massachusetts Cavalry remained unscathed.[11]

Returning to their Kernstown camp on the 3rd of December, the horsemen found Sheridan's army reduced by the transfer of the three divisions of VI Corps to the Petersburg front. Anticipating a move to winter quarters, the men began to build huts and stockade tents to ward off the cold nights. Pvt. Towle and a friend took a quartermaster's wagon to one of the abandoned VI Corps camps and took down a log hut which they moved and reconstructed at their own camp. Complete with fireplace and mud chimney, Towle sold the cabin to some new recruits for $50. "That was my first sale of real estate and a fortunate sale it was, because within two or three weeks after that we broke camp."¹²

As the days grew shorter they grew steadily colder. Pvt. Corbett noted the falling temperatures and the first snow of winter which left eight inches across the countryside. "This has been the coldest day of the season, everybody is suffering especially our poor horses, as they have no stables." As if to make up for the poor weather, rations improved and the men enjoyed potatoes and soft bread, the first they'd tasted since June.¹³

On the 15th of December, Col. Crowninshield was relieved of brigade command by Brig. Gen. Alfred Gibbs, a West Pointer and Mexican War veteran. Gibbs, who had commanded the brigade briefly prior to Col. Lowell, was a solid officer and would periodically share command of the brigade with Crowninshield while one or the other was on leave or special assignment. Crowninshield gratefully went home on leave within hours of Gibbs taking command, and was still absent when the regiment departed for its last action of the year.¹⁴

For several months Grant had been urging Sheridan to strike across the Blue Ridge Mountains and cut the Virginia Central Railroad in the vicinity of Gordonsville. The line was vital to Lee's supply of his army at Petersburg. The need to break the rail line was great, but the timing of the raid could not have been worse due to the weather. "The winter as a whole was exceptionally severe for Virginia, snow falling frequently, and the mercury sinking sometimes to zero." Rightly predicting the hardship of the raid, Pvt. Corbett conspired to have the band left behind.¹⁵

"This morning (Dec. 19th) I went to Major McKendry and asked that the Band might be excused from going on this raid, he refused. So I went back and mounted the boys on the poorest horses we could find in the Regt, then reported to him that the horses were not fit for the trip. We were drawn up in line on the right of the Regt. McKendry came out and looked at the horses and excused us from going, but he was awful mad and hated to do it, but we didn't care how mad he was so that we got clear of going." The 15 members of the band slightly brought down the total number of troopers in the raid, but the brigade was strengthened by the addition of the men of the 1st Rhode Island Cavalry.¹⁶

Reveille was held at 4:15 A.M. on the 19th, "...a cold, dismal, rainy morning." Torbert led the Divisions of Merritt and Powell toward Chester Gap, while Custer's Division advanced on Staunton to occupy the remnants of Early's army. The 2nd Massachusetts Cavalry, near the end of the column, was halfway through the gap when the halt was called for the night. "A bleaker camp could not be imagined. It was excruciating at the climax of this inclement season to be perched on top of a pass in the Blue Ridge and to face the icy blasts as they sucked and swirled through the narrow gorge." The men huddled under blanket, as close to the fires as possible, the painful wind preventing all but the hardiest from having a few hours' fitful sleep.¹⁷

Reveille at 5 A.M. was followed by a quick descent of the eastern slope where the air was marginally warmer but free of the bitter wind. A day's march covered 35 miles and they passed through Sandy Hook, Gaines Crossroads, Flint, and Sperryville, stopping near Woodville where a warmer camp allowed the men their needed sleep. Up at 4:30 the troopers found their blankets covered with four inches of fresh snow.¹⁸

Unknown to Torbert, Custer was being attacked in his camps near Staunton by the remnants of Rosser's cavalry. Surprising the sleeping Yankees, Rosser managed to drive Custer's superior numbers back in confusion, successfully removing him from the picture for the remainder of the raid. Custer's move to occupy Early was an absolute failure, and allowed the Confederates to board the railroad cars and be in front of Gordonsville before Torbert's arrival.[19]

Another day in the saddle and the suffering of men and horses became acute. "...much of the road was covered with ice which made it difficult for horses that were not sharp shod to keep their feet. It was not unusual to see a dozen horses down at a time." On the 23rd the column forded the Rapidan River, breaking through the thick ice before crossing.[20]

Once across the river a reconnaissance was made in the direction of Gordonsville. Prisoners and two pieces of artillery were taken and it was learned that Early had arrived in force, his numbers strengthened by reinforcements from Petersburg. Any possibility of breaking the Virginia Central was now dashed and Torbert reluctantly ordered the return to the Valley.[21]

The cold became even more intense on Christmas Eve as the long column torturously made its way along the frozen road. "On this day we passed hundreds of horses worn out by the toilsome march and left dead by the side of the road; and we kept passing dismounted men who could not keep up with the column, some of them with boots worn through and a few barefoot and leaving tracks of blood in the frozen crust." Camp was made at 9 P.M., the men cold, tired, and hungry. Rations had run out and what little there was had been foraged from nearby farms.[22]

In the saddle before first light, the men wished each other Christmas greetings, all hoping for a merrier Christmas the next year. Foragers were sent out in several directions as the main column pushed on to the north and forded the North Fork of the Rappahannock. One group came across some Confederate stores and destroyed 150,000 Sharps carbine cartridges, 1,000,000 percussion caps, 200 muskets, and 90 blankets.[23]

A few of the 2nd Massachusetts Cavalry entered a home, surprising one of Mosby's men, who had returned home for Christmas dinner in "...a fine new gray uniform, very fine boots, and ... a blue neck tie." The foragers took the prisoner, the roast turkey, and several salted hams. "From there we rode to the next house, about one half mile away, and there found another turkey ready for the oven, which with some large blankets we took also."[24]

The turkeys helped the hunger pains but did little to warm the men as the temperature continued to fall. "Our sufferings this day from the cold were very severe. Our feet were almost frozen, encased as they were in wet and frozen boots, and dangling in the frosty air. There is not sufficient exercise in the slow motion of a cavalry column to send the warm blood away down to the feet. Our only relief was a partial one when the column halted — in stamping upon the ground."[25]

Continuing north on the 26th, the column passed through Warrenton, New Baltimore, Georgetown, and White Plains. A stop at Sulphur Springs allowed the men to drink the supposedly rejuvenating water at the now destroyed resort. None claimed any renewing of youth and the march continued.[26]

The next day, December 27th, the column reached Middleburg and turned west for the Blue Ridge Mountains. Crossing through Ashby's Gap and passing into the Valley, the 2nd Massachusetts Cavalry came across a herd of sheep and thoughts of a mutton supper entered the men's heads. "The Shenandoah was too deep for the sheep to ford, so as we came along each would grab a sheep and ferry it across. After we had crossed there was a short halt, and many soldiers, in preparation for their evening meal, slaughtered a sheep. In many cases before they had time to dress the sheep they were ordered to move. Two soldiers would then take their sheep between them and dress it as they rode along. There were cows in the drove and that night I was fortunate in finding one that could stand to be milked. We then proceeded to a point a short distance south of Winchester where we went into camp for the winter."[27]

Official orders to go into winter quarters came on the 4th of January and the men busied themselves constructing huts and stables. Col. Crowninshield returned on the 5th, assuming command of the brigade; Gen. Gibbs was called to lead the division while Gen. Merritt was on furlough.[28]

There was little to disturb the routine of winter quarters. Picket duty, stable guard, chimney building, card playing and letter writing were the norm. On the 12th, McKendry was out with 200 men on a reconnaissance to Strasburg and Fisher's Hill. Not a Rebel was to be found.[29]

The First Cavalry Division went through a grand review on the 17th, the reviewing officers being generals Torbert, Merritt, Crook, and Gibbs. Of all the regiments in line, the 2nd Massachusetts Cavalry was singled out as the finest looking on the field, though Crowninshield confessed, "The men are at present too ragged & dirty & poor (not having been paid for 8 months) to make a very fine appearance." Reviews became a diversion for the next few weeks as the brigade was paraded on the 30th and the entire cavalry corps on the 31st. The final review was conducted by Sheridan himself, along with the celebrated Union spy and honorary major, Pauline Cushman.[30]

The reviews were more than just show. Sheridan was preparing the corps for the campaign that would drive the remnants of the Confederate army forever from the Shenandoah Valley. With orders from Grant to destroy the Virginia Central Railroad and the James River Canal, Sheridan was then to press on and join Gen. William T. Sherman's army in North Carolina. Five days' rations were issued on the evening of February 26, a day of cold, continuous rain. The next day Sgt. Corbett noted, "Reveille sounded this morning at 3 o'clock, broke camp at 5, camped this evening near Woodstock. I have no idea where we are going."[31]

A reorganization of forces before the march left the 2nd Massachusetts Cavalry in Gibbs' Reserve Brigade, along with the 6th U.S., 6th Pennsylvania Cavalry, and the 1st Rhode Island Cavalry. At the head of the corps was Maj. Gen. Wesley Merritt, Sheridan having sacked Torbert for his failures at Luray Valley and Gordonsville. The rain on the 27th continued on the 28th, swelling the streams and turning the roads into rivers of mud. By the 1st of March the column had entered Staunton which Early had hastily abandoned, and moved on to Waynesboro. It was here on the 2nd that Custer's division rode Early to ground and routed his 1,500 defenders. Nearly the entire force was captured, Early managing to escape into the Blue Ridge, his once proud army of 14,000 reduced to a mere corporal's guard.[32]

The following morning (March 3rd) the division continued the march in the direction of Charlottesville while the Reserve Brigade lagged behind to destroy the iron rail road bridge over the north fork of the South River, as well as all Confederate stores captured during the previous day's action. Gibbs reported the destruction of, "1 light steel 3-inch ordnance limber and caisson; also 100 wagons, forges, battery, and ammunition wagons; threw ammunition into the river; also a large quantity of muskets, small ammunition and other ordnance stores." The bridge was dealt with by burning ties at intervals, allowing the bonfires to twist and warp the iron, effectively destroying it. For good measure powder was placed on the remains and ignited. Before the bridge was fired the 1st Rhode Island Cavalry was detached with two other regiments to escort the prisoners back to Winchester. Along with this column went the dismounted troopers whose horses had given out during the week.[33]

The rain continued to fall, an omen of things to come, for as the rain fell, conditions on the road deteriorated. "...[T]he rain had been pouring in torrents through these days," wrote Chaplain Humphreys, "and the roads were bad beyond description, and horses and men could hardly be recognized for the mud which covered them. As the horses by their tramping kneaded out water from the clayey mud, and as each successive rank of fours naturally stepped in the hollows made by the rank in front of it, the mud soon lay in ridges a foot and a half to two feet high like heavy beams across the road, and the horses who were unfortunate enough to be at the end of the moving column had to step very high and with great labor over these barriers, soon exhausting themselves." George Towle recorded his memories as well: "There was practically no bottom to that road, in the hollows would be many mortar beds, often belly deep, while in the sloping portions of the road would be tramped into ridges extending across the road as high as a horse could step over. If a horse fell in one of these mortar beds he would be left as he fell, and often be buried alive by the mud kicked over him by the horses following.... On the march it was a frequent occurrence for a horse to step on the heel of the one ahead, the result of which would be that the next morning the horse would be a cripple. In such a case the soldier would proceed afoot. The crippled horses were shot by the rear guard each morning."[34]

Slogging into Charlottesville on the 5th, Sheridan called a halt to allow the Reserve Brigade and wagons to catch up with the column. Seven days' rations were issued to each man, and, to quicken the pace, all of the supply wagons and tents were burned. The troopers were far from idle as the wagons slowly made their way to Charlottesville. Details were sent down the line of the Virginia Central Railroad being destroyed for 15 miles in either direction. "The rails were pried loose from the ties, the ties placed in piles, the rails balanced over the piles of ties and the ties set on fire. As the ties burned the rails would bend. Sometimes a rail that was red hot in the middle would be taken and twisted around a tree. Forage for the horses was also found as well as chickens, pork, wine and apple-jack."[35]

Having efficiently broken both the railroad and James River Canal, Sheridan was now free to strike off to the southeast for his union with Gen. Sherman. The swollen James River, completely unfordable, presented a barrier to putting this plan into action. A bridge at Duguidsville was burned by Confederates just as the Yankee troopers dashed up to capture it. "Being thus unable to cross until the river should fall, and knowing that it was impracticable to join General Sherman, and useless to adhere to my alternative to return to Winchester, I now decided to destroy more thoroughly the James River Canal and the Virginia Central Railroad and then join General Grant in front of Petersburg. I was master of the whole country north of the James as far down as Goochland; here the destruction of these arteries of supply could be easily compassed, and feeling the war was nearing its end, I desired my cavalry to be in at the death."[36]

"On the 6th marched without transportation to Scottsville, twenty-one miles; worked till midnight destroying James

River Canal, locks, boats with subsistence stores, and bridges." The march continued, each day resulting in more destruction of the southern infrastructure. In his official report Gen. Gibbs detailed his burning and destruction each day of factories, mills, bridges, warehouses, storehouses, and canal locks. For three days the command traversed the area between New Market and Columbia at the mouth of the Rivanna River. The rain continued.[37]

The morning of the 12th the columns turned to the northeast, leaving the James and striking out for the Virginia Central Railroad at Tolerville. Reaching the village on the 13th, Devin turned his division to the east, destroying the rail line for the 15 miles to Frederick Hall station. The day was spent burning cross ties and cars, and bending rails. After 12 hours of work, the men were back in the saddle for six more hours of riding before resting for the night.[38]

Twenty-seven miles were covered on the 14th with the 2nd Massachusetts Cavalry in the advance. At Hanover Junction the march followed the line south to Taylorsville where a halt was called and details were sent out to burn bridges. The targets were the railroad bridges where the Virginia Central and Richmond and Fredericksburg crossed the South Anna and Little rivers. Tasked with destroying the Virginia Central crossing of the South Anna, the 2nd Massachusetts Cavalry and the 5th U.S. arrived at the same spot that Crowninshield and his First Battalion had first seen the elephant back in June of '63.[39]

"There was," recalled Pvt. Towle, "a small body of confederates there, as there

Pvt. Henry Mazy, Company A, California Hundred, 2nd Massachusetts Cavalry. *Courtesy of Vallejo Naval and Historical Museum.*

had been when we first visited that bridge more than a year earlier, but they offered no opposition, although their fortifications were much stronger than when we were first there." Col. Crowninshield wrote, "One day near the South Anna River my advance guard had a skirmish or rather made a charge on almost 100 Rebs who ran and abandoned a fort which contained 3 pieces of heavy artillery loaded & ready to be fired but the Rebs were very much demoralized." Men of the 2nd Massachusetts turned the guns (3 three-inch ordnance rifles) and fired the cannon at the retreating Confederates. The bridge was once again destroyed and the advance returned to Taylorsville with their captured cannon.[40]

Justly concerned with Sheridan's presence only 15 miles north of Richmond, Gen. Lee dispatched troops to check the Federal movement. Unable to advance further, Sheridan turned his divisions to the north and marched to Chesterfield Station just over the North Anna River. Here, near the end of the grueling raid, the sun broke through, warming the men and drying the roads. Striking out to the southeast the column passed through Mangohick Church, Aylett's, and King William Courthouse. On the 18th, Sheridan's two divisions reached White House Landing where they found food and forage sent to them by Gen. Grant.[41]

The raid over, a few of the dismounted men were able to get new horses or mules to replace those lost during the march. Some accounts state one horse in four did not complete the march; the 2nd Massachusetts Cavalry lost fully one third. The dismounted troopers were sent on to City Point, Virginia, Grant's supply depot on the James River, where they waited for fresh mounts. New clothes were issued to some, the others making do by washing old uniforms and themselves in the chilly water of the Pamunky River. Mail, unknown to the men for three weeks, finally caught up with them; but above all, for seven days the men were able to rest. As the war entered its final days, they would need that rest.[42]

Notes

1. Corbett, *Diary*, Oct. 23–28, 1864; Towle, *Recollections*, p. 26.
2. Humphreys, *Field and Camp*, p. 411; *Massachusetts Soldiers, Sailors, and Marines*, Vol. VI, pp. 228–328.
3. Corbett, *Diary*, Nov. 9, 1864; *OR*, XLIII, Pt. 1, p. 96.
4. Corbett, *Diary*, Nov. 8, 1864; Humphreys, *Field and Camp*, p. 416.
5. Corbett, *Diary*, Nov. 10, 11, 21, 1864.
6. Sheridan, *Civil War Memoirs*, pp. 286–87; *OR*, XLIII, Pt. 1, pp. 55–56, 671–72.
7. Corbett, *Diary*, Nov. 29, 1864; Humphreys, *Field and Camp*, p. 191.
8. Humphreys, *Field and Camp*, p. 192.
9. Stackpole, *Sheridan in the Shenandoah*, p. 379; *OR*, XLIII, Pt. 1, p. 673.
10. Humphreys, *Field and Camp*, p. 192.
11. Wert, *Mosby's Rangers*, p. 263.
12. Corbett, *Diary*, Dec. 3, 1864; Stackpole, *Sheridan in the Shenandoah*, p. 380; Towle, *Recollections*, p. 27.
13. Corbett, *Diary*, Dec. 9–15, 1864; Humphreys, *Field and Camp*, p. 419.
14. Humphreys, *Field and Camp*, p. 419; Sifakis, *Who Was Who in the Civil War*, p. 246; *OR*, XLIII, Pt. 1, p. 97.
15. Humphreys, *Field and Camp*, p. 195; Stackpole, *Sheridan in the Shenandoah*, p. 380.
16. Corbett, *Diary*, Dec. 7, 19, 1864.
17. Humphreys, *Field and Camp*, p. 195; Sheridan, *Civil War Memoirs*, p. 287; *OR*, XLIII, Pt. 1, p. 97.
18. *OR*, XLIII, Pt. 1, p. 97; *Official Military Atlas of the Civil War*, Plate 74.
19. Early, *Jubal Early's Memoirs*, pp. 457–58; Sheridan, *Civil War Memoirs*, pp. 287–88.
20. Mortimer, *The California 100 and Battalion*, p. 43; Towle, *Recollections*, p. 26; *OR*, XLIII, Pt. 1, p. 97.
21. Humphreys, *Field and Camp*, p. 198; Sheridan, *Civil War Memoirs*, p. 288; *OR*, XLIII, Pt. 1, p. 97.
22. Humphreys, *Field and Camp*, pp. 200–201; Towle, *Recollections*, p. 26.
23. Humphreys, *Field and Camp*, p. 201; *OR*, XLIII, Pt. 1, p. 97.
24. Towle, *Recollections*, p. 26.
25. Humphreys, *Field and Camp*, pp. 201–02.
26. Humphreys, *Field and Camp*, p. 202; *OR*, XLIII, Pt. 1, p. 97.
27. Towle, *Recollections*, p. 26; *OR*, XLIII, Pt. 1, p. 97.
28. Corbett, *Diary*, Jan. 4–5, 1865; Crowninshield, Jan. 11, 1865; *OR*, XLIII, Pt. 1, p. 98.
29. *OR*, XLVI, Pt. 1, p. 125.

30. Corbett, *Diary*, Jan. 17–31, 1865; Crowninshield, Jan. 19, 1865.

31. Corbett, *Diary*, Feb. 27, 1865; Sheridan, *Civil War Memoirs*, p. 293.

32. Corbett, *Diary*, Mar. 2, 1865; Sheridan, *Civil War Memoirs*, pp. 293–95; *OR*, XLVI, Pt. 1, p. 500; Starr, *The Union Cavalry in the Civil War*, Vol. 2, p. 366.

33. Corbett, *Diary*, Mar. 3, 1865; Humphreys, *Field and Camp*, pp. 207–08; *OR*, XLVI, Pt. 1, pp. 490, 500. Starr, *The Union Cavalry in the Civil War*, vol. 3, p. 376.

34. Humphreys, *Field and Camp*, p. 208; Towle, *Recollections*, p. 28. Starr, *The Union Cavalry in the Civil War*, vol. 3, p. 376.

35. Humphreys, *Field and Camp*, p. 208; Diary of Frederick Quant, Mar. 5, 1865: hereafter cited as Quant, *Diary*; *OR*, XLVI, Pt. 1, p. 500; Towle, *Recollections*, p. 28.

36. Sheridan, *Civil War Memoirs*, pp. 296–97.

37. *Atlas to Accompany the OR*, plate 74; *OR*, XLVI, Pt. 1, pp. 490–92, 500.

38. Corbett, *Diary*, Mar. 13–14; *OR*, XLVI, Pt. 1, pp. 492, 500.

39. *OR*, XLVI, Pt. 1, pp. 492, 500–01.

40. Corbett, *Diary*, Mar. 14, 1864; Humphreys, *Field and Camp*, p. 215; *OR*, XLVI, Pt. 1, pp. 492, 500–01, 981; Quant, *Diary*, Mar. 14, 1864; Towle, *Recollections*, p. 28.

41. *OR*, XLVI, Pt. 1, p. 501.

42. Backus "Californians in the Field," *MOLLUS*., California Commandry; Quant, *Diary*, Mar. 18–25, 1865.

Chapter Twelve

Appomattox

Reveille at daylight on the 25th of March, 1865, called out all able bodied men of the regiment. Roll call that morning found only 85 men fit for duty. The entire Reserve Brigade, 1st, 5th and 6th U.S. Cavalry, and 2nd Massachusetts, could field only 437 men. Camp was broken and an easy day's march brought them to King Charles Courthouse for the night's halt. In the saddle again by dawn, the regiment reached the James River where they crossed at Deep Bottom Bridge. "We crossed on pontoons. President Lincoln passed up the river on the boat 'Ocean Queen' as we were getting ready to cross.* We [the band] played him several patriotic airs, which he acknowledged by waving his hat. We marched about two miles then camped in the woods."[1]

Breaking camp at 7 A.M. the morning of the 27th, the troopers crossed the Appomattox River at Broadway Landing, going into camp within three miles of Petersburg. The campsite was inside the massive earthworks the Army of the Potomac had thrown up to the east and south of the city, and the 2nd Massachusetts spent the next day listening to the constant artillery and picket fire. Five days' rations were issued indicating another move the next morning.

Since June 1864 Gen. Grant had held Gen. Lee in check by a siege of the city of Petersburg. Earthworks stretched from the northeast of Richmond to the southwest of Petersburg. The key to ending the siege was to close off the roads and railroads that supplied Lee's troops with the food and ammunition needed to carry on the struggle. For months Grant had been slowly extending his left toward the vital Southside railroad, forcing Lee to move his flank as well and thereby stretching his already thin lines even more. On the 28th of March, Grant ordered Sheridan to move his cavalry to the left and, supported by V Corps, break the Southside railroad as well as the final rail link, the Danville railroad. As Sheridan had been a department commander when he led the raid from Winchester, Grant made his cavalry a separate corps, not attaching it to the Army of the Potomac under General Meade. Sheridan answered only to Grant.[2]

Breaking camp at dawn on the 28th, the 2nd Massachusetts joined the column

---

*Lincoln's boat was the *River Queen*, though on this occasion he was with Grant and Sheridan on the *Mary Martin*.

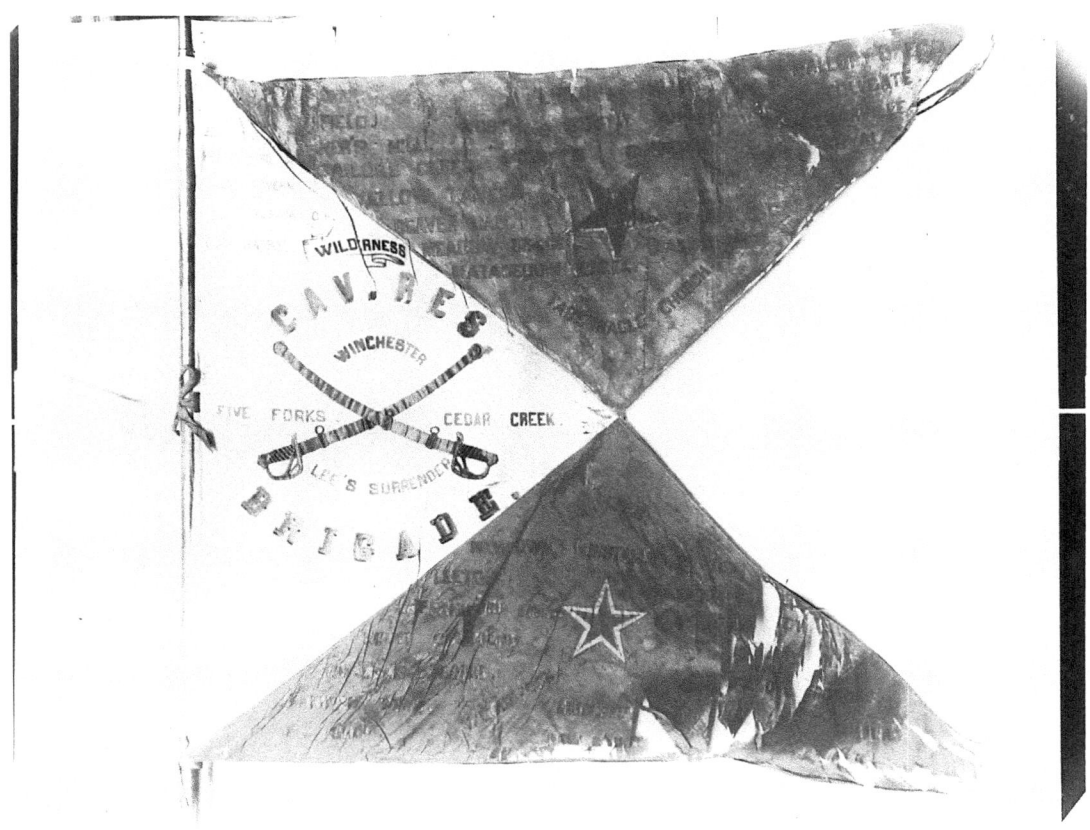

Guidon of the Cavalry Reserve Brigade. *Courtesy of United States Military Academy, West Point Museum.*

of cavalry that headed due west, crossing the Weldon Railroad and Hatcher's Run, before making camp two miles from Dinwiddie Courthouse. "Dinwiddie Court House," wrote Sheridan, "though a most important point in the campaign, was far from attractive in feature, being made up of a half-dozen unsightly houses, a ramshackle tavern propped up on two sides with pine poles, and the weatherbeaten building that gave official name to the crossroads." While here, Sheridan received new orders from Grant to abandon the raid on the rail line and to concentrate on turning Lee's right.[3]

Up again at dawn, the 2nd Massachusetts had the advance of Gen. Devin's division as it pressed forward to probe the enemy near the crossroads known as Five Forks. Traveling on the Plank Road, Crowninshield's troopers met with the enemy vedettes just past Dinwiddie Courthouse and skirmishing began. The Confederate pickets were driven back to their main line, the cavalry of Gen. Fitz Hugh Lee. Fighting began in earnest and lasted till dark.[4]

Rain fell throughout the day as the two forces skirmished and fought over a piece of swampy ground. The Reserve Brigade was reenforced by Devin's First and Second Brigades and the line held steady through the day. In the afternoon Crowninshield attempted a charge but was thrown back with minor losses. As the 2nd Massachusetts returned to its lines Capt.

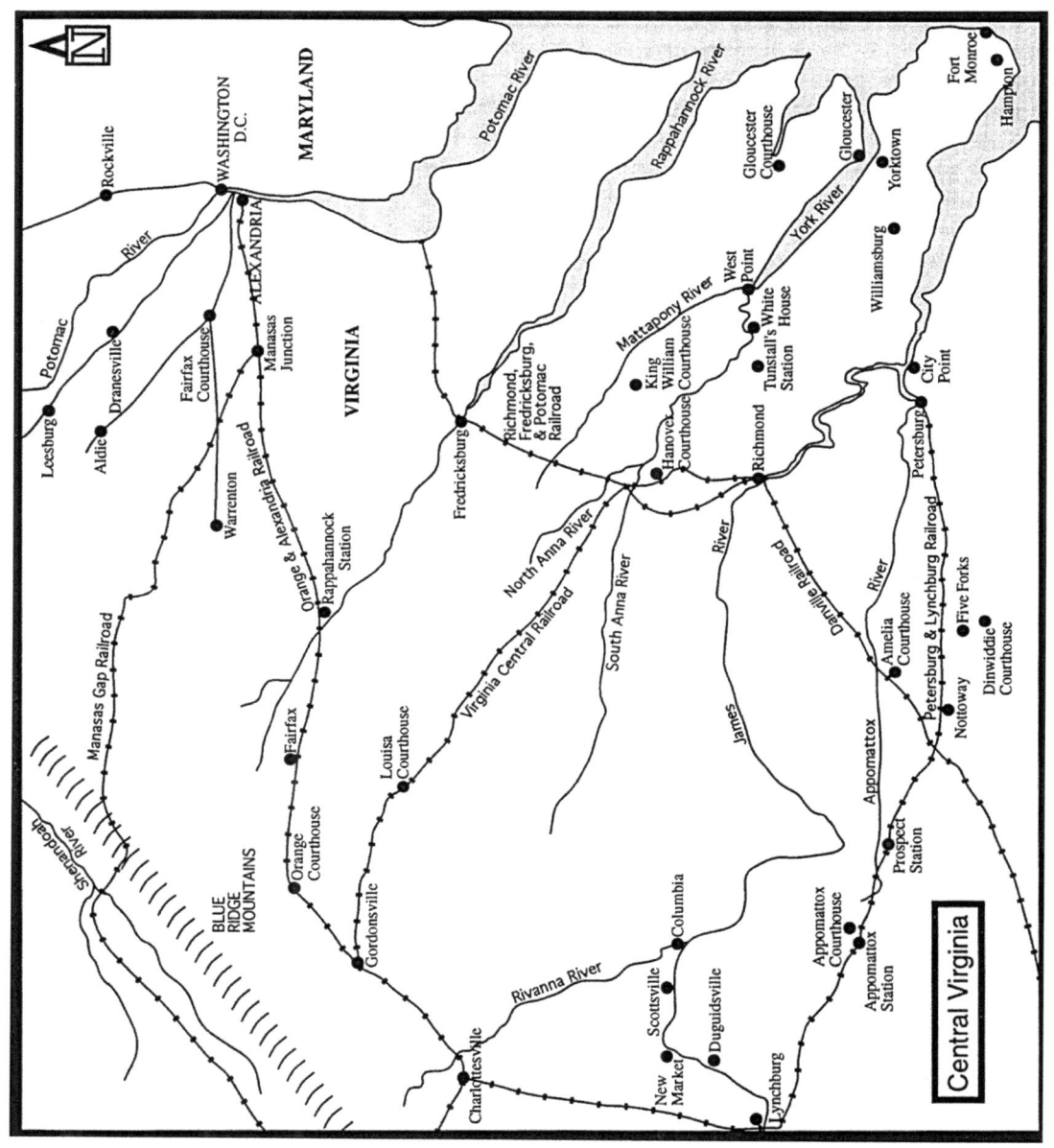

Henry Kuhls (K), "...an enthusiastic, hot blooded German," defiantly turned his horse back toward the enemy. The Confederates declined to fire on the one-man charge and merely took him prisoner as he pierced their lines. Kuhls, who, prior to his commission, had been an enlisted man in Adam's Company L of the California Battalion, would be paroled within the week. Also captured were Pvt. Henry Peel (K), Boston, and wounded was Cpl. William Moore (E), Gardiner, Pennsylvania, who had been shot before in action against Mosby in July '63. As night fell, the Reserve Brigade was pulled back and put in a position south of Dinwiddie Court House near Stony Creek.[5]

Gen. Lee had noted the movements designed to turn his right flank, and to counter the move had dispatched Fitz Hugh Lee's cavalry, and the infantry division of Gen. George Pickett. Pickett moved further to the west than Sheridan, and by the morning of the 31st stood poised to fall on the Union left.

Moving at dawn, the Yankee cavalry was within three miles of Dinwiddie Court House when the Confederates attacked from the west. Pickett's division was successful, driving back Sheridan's troopers, who fell back slowly, contesting every inch of ground. The 2nd Massachusetts fought doggedly, the men dismounted due to the heavily wooded terrain. In the late afternoon, when the situation looked the worst, Custer's division arrived to stem the Confederate advance. While his men formed ranks to the right of the 2nd Massachusetts, Custer ordered his band to play behind Crowninshield's troopers and soon the strains of "Garry Owen" were heard in the woods. "The regiment hastily threw up breastworks of rails from behind which they met the enemy's charge with a terrible fire from their carbines, which most effectively checked their advance."[6]

Casualties in the 2nd Massachusetts Cavalry were remarkably light given the heavy fighting and rough terrain. Killed was 1st Lt. Lewis Munger (F), San Francisco. "This promising young officer enlisted in California, and had been promoted to First Lieutenant for faithful service and distinguished bravery."[7]

Wounded were 1st Lt. Edward Thompson (B), San Francisco, a former enlisted man of Company F and now an aide to brigade commander Gen. Gibbs; Pvt. Timothy Tucker (M), Salem, wounded through the lungs; and 1st Lt. Augustus L. Papanti (D), Boston. Papanti, the acting captain of Company D and the son of one of the prominent dancing masters of Boston, was seriously wounded, ironically, in the left foot and just below the right knee. Papanti recovered and in later years ran one of the most fashionable dancing schools in Boston. Several more were wounded and captured but the records are unfortunately vague about who the men were. Captured, very briefly, was Sgt. Sam Corbett.

"While on a foraging expedition this afternoon I was captured and taken into an Earth work. I was on my horse and was led by a Rebel sergt. as soon as they got me inside the works, they let go the horse. I at once made a break for liberty. My horse jumped over the breastwork and across the ditch outside, but the worst part of the ride was down a fearfully steep hill. Just as I was about halfway down it, my right stirrup strap tore from the saddle. This threw me, but being a good rider I hung on with my left foot and succeeded in getting back into the saddle, but wrenched my side painfully." Corbett eluded the pursuit, returning to camp with two broken ribs which he bound in place with a carbine strap.[8]

Sheridan had held the line against Pickett and Lee; in order to prevail, though, he would need the muscle of infantry. Grant ordered Maj. Gen. G.K. Warren's V Corps to the right of Sheridan for a morning attack on the 1st of April.

Falling back briefly for ammunition and forage, the 2nd Massachusetts Cavalry went into camp near the courthouse at midnight. Reveille blew at 3 A.M. and the fighting resumed at dawn. Through the day the cavalry, fighting dismounted, drove the Confederates back, the Rebels finally taking refuge in their earthworks around Five Forks in the early afternoon. For three hours the cavalrymen waited on line while the infantry slowly made their way into position. The fighting became so sparse that several Confederates joked that the fighting was through for the day — "...only an April fool!" At 4:30 P.M., Warren's infantry finally attacked the Confederate left while the cavalry hammered again on the right. Within half an hour the Confederate line was crushed. The 2nd Massachusetts went up and over the earthworks capturing prisoners and equipment at a furious rate. At day's end, thousands of Confederate prisoners were in Union lines and Robert E. Lee's right flank had been decisively turned.*[9]

Five men of the 2nd Massachusetts Cavalry fell during the day's fighting, including Cpl. Charles Thayer (F), San Francisco, the last man in the regiment to be killed in battle. Wounded were Sgt. Arthur Parker (D), Ashland; 1st Sgt. Thomas Ferguson (H), Boston; and 18-year-old Pvt. Charles Field (L), Leverett. Pvt. James Smith (B), who had enlisted in Norfolk, Virginia, in late September '64, was captured but released within days.[10]

"I have just time to write a few lines," Crowninshield wrote to his mother on the 2nd, "to let you know that I am all right so far. We have been fighting for three days & yesterday we were very successful, we fought on foot & with the 5th Corps & captured a long line of breastworks & took many guns & several thousand prisoners. The infantry are on our right & are fighting desperately but with what success I can't yet say but I think everything is going on well."[11]

The fighting on the right was a general advance by Grant's armies against the Petersburg defenses. The cavalry, on the far left, pitched into the remnants of Pickett's division and by early morning had "...cut the South Side railroad at 9 a.m. Our Brigade was the first on the road." The vital rail line gone, his right flank turned, and his entire front crumbling, Robert E. Lee ordered the evacuation of Petersburg and Richmond, leading his army to the west where he hoped to evade Grant and link up with Gen. Joseph Johnston's Confederate army in North Carolina. The regiment spent most of the day tearing up a ten-mile section of the railroad, but by early evening had rejoined the pursuit and closed with the enemy's rear guard by 9:00 P.M.[12]

The Confederate retreat continued on the 3rd, the 2nd Massachusetts passing scores of abandoned wagons, caissons, and forges, which they paused to burn as they went by. At dark the regiment went into camp, Corbett noting in his diary, "The Rebels are right ahead and doing their best to get out of the way."[13]

Early the next morning news of the surrender of Richmond reached the men and they cheered themselves hoarse. President Lincoln, with a small escort of sailors, was touring the captured Confederate capital, and was later provided with a carriage and a larger escort of mounted men. Earlier that morning, at the remount camp at City Point, Privates James Watson and Samuel Backus, both of the California Hundred, were issued new uniforms and attached to the presidential escort of 25 mounted men. James was astounded at

---

*Historians and eyewitnesses claim the number of prisoners to range from 2,400 to 5,200 out of a force of 9,000.

the sight of the fire-gutted buildings and debris-littered streets.[14]

Pvt. George Towle, also at City Point, was impressed by the staggering number of enemy prisoners passing through on their way to northern prison camps. "There were a large number of negroes working for the quartermaster at City Point, and as these prisoners were going onboard the transports the negroes gathered along the line on the lookout for any one they knew. Occasionally a negro would see his old master or some one he knew in the line, whereupon in the most respectful manor [sic] imaginable he would address him and make inquiries regarding the folks at home; following which he would retire behind piles of hay and laugh his head off; apparently at the changed conditions, he being free and his old master being in bondage."[15]

Gen. Lee called a halt on the 4th and sent out wagons in all directions to bring in food for his starving army. Little was found and a vital day was wasted. Sheridan used the time to close on the enemy where he hoped to cause Lee to turn in defense where he could be overwhelmed. The 2nd Massachusetts Cavalry passed more abandoned Confederate supplies, taking the time to bury several cannon, marking the spot with wooden headstones. In the evening the regiment welcomed back to their ranks Lt. Col. Forbes. Captured and imprisoned, "Lowell's Fighting Major" had been released in December but details with his parole prevented his return till the present. Promoted to the number two spot in the regiment after Lowell's death, Forbes, who was far from fully recovered from the effects of his imprisonment, was pleased to be back now that the end seemed near.[16]

On the afternoon of the 5th, Gen. Lee resumed his retreat while Grant massed his troops in an expected attack on Amelia Courthouse. The attack was canceled when it was learned that Lee was on the move again, and the pursuit was resumed. The 2nd Massachusetts Cavalry spent the day in the saddle, finally going into camp near the village of Burksville.[17]

The morning of the 6th, the men were issued five days rations of coffee and sugar and by 7:00 A.M. were once more in the saddle. Lee's columns were marching as quickly as possible when, unwittingly, a gap formed in his line, a gap that was soon filled by Union cavalry. Lee's rearguard was trapped between cavalry in front and infantry in the rear, precipitating a desperate fight across Sailor's Creek. "We have been fighting them all day and are whipping them badly," Corbett wrote in midfight. The Confederates fought back with fury, holding back the infantry and throwing back Custer's cavalry in two bloody assaults. The Reserve Brigade strengthened Custer's line for a third charge that was successful and sealed off the gap in Lee's line. As Merritt's cavalry held the Confederates, Grant sent the II and VI corps in to finish off the rebels. "The Confederates thus cut off, fought like fiends."[18]

The fight was an absolute disaster for Lee's army. Over 8,000 Confederates were captured including six generals. Fully one fourth of Lee's army was gone, prompting him to utter, "My God! Has the army been dissolved?" The 2nd Massachusetts pursued remnants of Gen. Richard Anderson's shattered division until nightfall, then slept in the road with reins held in their fists. They were awakened briefly by a crash of artillery, but quickly fell back to sleep as the enemy battery withdrew.[19]

Reveille sounded at 4:00 A.M. and Grant's pursuit continued, the 2nd Massachusetts riding all day with little more than a light skirmish toward evening. That night Sheridan marshaled all of his forces, including VI Corps of infantry, and gave orders for the morning's rapid march on Appomattox Station.

Gathering together at Prospect Station,

the cavalry pushed hard and arrived at Appomattox Station ahead of the Confederate advance, capturing four trains loaded with supplies for Lee's men. Turning to the east Sheridan deployed his cavalry and pushed back the Confederate advance guard in the direction of the main body. "The Rebels seem to be demoralized and do not fight with the usual vigor and well they may be for we have kept them going for the last two weeks." At 2:00 A.M. the halt was called. It was the 9th of April.

"The first streak of daylight lighting up the horizon was the signal for the ball to open and it did with a will. We had nothing to oppose Lee but cavalry and nobly did they do their work. We fought them dismounted, they tried hard to break our line and poured in the shot and shell with their musketry until the air seemed full of it." Artillery fire poured down on the cavalrymen, one shell burying itself in the ground between Col. Crowninshield and Lt. Burlingham, luckily not exploding. The Confederates were massing for a breakout when the solid columns of the XXIV Corps were observed filing in behind the cavalry.[20]

Postwar photograph of Francis Lowder (left), Company H, 2nd Massachusetts Cavalry. With him are his son Robert F. Lowder (standing), grandson Robert E. Lowder, and great-grandson George Lowder. *Photograph courtesy of James D. Lowder.*

Preparations were made for an advance, the troopers mounting their horses, ready for the charge. Before the advance could be signaled a flag of truce was raised and brought into the Union line. "We all dismounted," recalled Chaplain Humphreys, "and such a scene of handshaking and embracing I have never elsewhere witnessed. Some tossed their hats and cheered; some rolled on the ground, yelling like Indians; some sobbed like children, only with exuberance of joy. The wild cheers that ran along the line told the story from rank to rank, and an audible wave of joy swept through the whole army. The long and anxious war was over."[21]

That afternoon the terms of surrender were signed in the nearby farmhouse of Wilmer McLean and later that evening the regimental band was sent to Sheridan's headquarters where they played for Grant, Sheridan, Meade, and a host of others. The regiment camped a mile from the courthouse in the woods near the Martin House.[22]

The formal surrender of the Army of Northern Virginia would take place on the 12th of April, but the 2nd Massachusetts was not destined to see this final chapter. At 7:00 A.M. on the 10th, camp was struck and the cavalry began a retrograde movement through Prospect Station, Burkesville, Farmville, to Nottoway Station. "We are marching slim and easy, being in no particular hurry, and giving the horses a chance to rest. Everything is quiet on Sabbath day at home no firing and none of the music of war that we have been accustomed to for so long a time. The silence seems oppressive." Good-byes were said to Chaplain Humphreys, who, feeling the need to begin his ministry, talked about his situation with Gen. Sheridan and handed in his resignation on the 14th of April.[23]

The regiment remained at Nottoway Station, some 25 miles west of Petersburg, till the 19th, moving again on that date to the outskirts of Petersburg itself. It was at Nottoway Station that the regiment learned of the death of President Lincoln. "Every man in the army feels as though he has lost a friend," wrote Corbett. Pvt. John Winship (A) was in Washington on regimental business and saw "…the whole city draped in mourning, every house store shop and office is shrouded in crape & cambrick." Not leaving till the day after the funeral, Winship wrote to his fiancée, Miss Sarah Hyde, describing the scene. "I didn leave washington till the after the muneral [funeral] and went to see the President as he lay in State in the capitol the day after the funeral he looked very natural and was in the richest coffin I ever saw. There was more people at the funeral than I ever saw together at one time before … the prosession blocked the street from one side to the other and was one hour and fifty mints in passing the treasury building besids the masses that flocked on the side streets the roofs of the houses on boath sides of the street was covered with eager spectaters and every window and doar was crowded with heads."[24]

The regiment, reduced in size during the spring campaign, began to grow as men returned from remount camps, hospitals, special duties, and enemy prison camps. Capt. William Manning (L), captured as a first lieutenant at Dranesville, returned to the regiment with 1st. Lt. Charles Amory (G), who had been imprisoned with Forbes and Humphreys in Charleston, South Carolina. With them they brought 150 enlisted men who had been remounted and equipped at City Point. Still weak and unable to bear the hardships of camp life, Lt. Col. Forbes resigned his commission and returned to his father's estate at Naushon. William Forbes soon recovered and married the daughter of Ralph Waldo Emerson before plunging into the world of business. He would become the president of the American Bell Telephone Company during its early years, and passed away in 1897.[25]

Camp life was easy and uneventful, the men enjoying the rest but naturally beginning to ask the question: What happens now? The regiment had mustered in its companies between January and May 1863 and as it was a three-year regiment, still had a significant amount of time to serve. Speculation about early discharges, garrison duty in the south, or active operations in the Trans-Mississippi theater were the hot topics at the camp fires. Rumors soared on the evening of April 23 when rations were issued along with the orders to march at daylight.

Surrender negotiations between Gen. Sherman and Gen. Johnston had broken down in North Carolina and a resumption of hostilities between the two armies seemed imminent. In the saddle by 6 A.M. on the 24th, Sheridan's cavalry was sent south to ensure the swift end to any renewed fighting. Four days of marching

U.S. flag presented to veterans of the California Hundred and California Battalion by Major D.W.C. Thompson at the end of the war. *Courtesy of the California State Capitol Museum.*

found the 2nd Massachusetts Cavalry just above the North Carolina border near the town of South Boston. It was here that news of Johnston's surrender was received and the column turned about for the return to Petersburg.[26]

"The next morning," wrote Pvt. Towle, "we started for our return to the North and frequently met straggling confederates on their way home. I have never felt more sympathy for any one than I did for those men. Before the war it was a common Southern boast that one Southerner was a equal in fighting ability of five Northerners and with that belief firmly fixed they entered into the contest. Now they were returning to their homes under the necessity of there confessing to their sweethearts and wives that they had been defeated by those whose fighting ability they had been taught to despise; not only that, but all that they had, had been risked and lost on the result of their enterprise. A more sorrowful homecoming is hard to imagine."[27]

After a leisurely march back to Petersburg, the regiment went back into camp on the 3rd of May about a mile north of the city. Rations and forage were in abundance as well as peanuts, pies and cakes sold by the "Feminine Gender" of Petersburg. "I should judge by the taste of them that they were made from the flesh of our abandoned horses!" A week of easy living preceded the next march, this time to the capital.

Leaving Petersburg on the 10th of May, the regiment moved north in daily marches. Rising late and camping early, even the slow pace ate up the miles and by the 16th they were pleasantly situated at Camp Wyndham on the banks of the Potomac. Marching through Falls Church earlier in the day had been a treat when all of the townsfolk had come out to greet and wave at their old friends from the 2nd Massachusetts Cavalry. The new campsite was in the woods and quite comfortable despite the rain that had begun on the 19th and drenched them for three days.[28]

Reveille at 4 this A.M.," wrote Corbett on the 23rd, "all of the boys looking their very best, all of our mules were exchanged for horses & we all have on new clothes." A grand review of the armies of the United States was to be conducted through the streets of Washington — Meade's army on the 23rd, followed the next day by Sherman's men. The day was beautiful, the rain having stopped, and, just to be on the safe side, a fire engine doused the streets to settle any dust.[29]

Leading the parade was Gen. Meade and his staff, followed by the Cavalry Corps led by Maj. Gen. Merritt.* First came Custer's Third Division, followed by Maj. Gen. Henry Davies' Second, with the First Division of Thomas Devin bringing up the rear. Behind the mounted troopers came the horse artillery brigade which preceded the endless ranks of infantry. The next to the last regiment in the procession of cavalry was the 2nd Massachusetts.[30]

"We passed by the old capitol buildings, and as we turned toward Pennsylvania Avenue there were canvases stretched from building to building across the street on which different legends were printed. There had been a great deal of discussion in our company as to whether the government would furnish transportation back to San Francisco, and one of the first legends we encountered was one reading 'The only debt we can never repay; the debt we owe to our victorious union defenders!' On reading that [Cpl. Frederick] Hall, who rode next to me, turned and said 'there, didn't I tell you they wouldn't give us our

---

*Sheridan had been called west where Confederates were still active and tensions were building with the French in Mexico. Starr, The Union Cavalry in the Civil War, Vol. 2, p. 500.

transportation!' When we formed in company front I found myself on the extreme left next the curb and it was not long before I received a number of bouquets; one of which I stuck in my scabbard and handed the others to other soldiers. I never felt so nervous on entering that parade. We passed down the entire length of Pennsylvania Avenue and up past the Treasury building and in front of the White House where the President and reviewing officers were stationed." Capt. Henry Alvord, commanding the Third Battalion, recorded that as the 2nd Massachusetts passed the review stand, "Grant remarked, 'That is the best looking of all the cavalry brigades—*they are soldiers!*'"[31]

After the review the regiment returned to their camp in Bladensburg, Maryland, some coming back the next day to watch as Sherman's army paraded. For the remainder of the week the regiment sat in camp. "The regiment now numbers 1300 men 300 of them have never been mounted. They are recruits who enlisted before the war ended. Poor fellows they will have no chance to meet grim visaged war face to face but will have all the glory of being in the Union Army."[32]

On the 29th of May, camp was broken and the regiment marched through Washington and Alexandria and into camp at Cloud's Mill, Fairfax County, Virginia. The camp was a pleasant one, situated in the woods alongside the Orange and Alexandria Railroad. Once again the men had little to do in camp but wait and wonder what was going to happen next. There were constant talk and rumors among the Californians about transportation home, but no answers. On the 1st of June, all of the prisoners of war in parole camps as well as the officers and men unfit for duty were mustered out of the service. On the 10th, 2nd Lt. Huntington Wolcott (I), Boston, died of "camp fever," the last officer in the regiment to die in uniform. A mere 19 years old, young Huntington was the great grandson of Oliver Wolcott, a signer of the Declaration of Independence.[33]

Regimental band, 2nd Massachusetts Cavalry. *Courtesy of U.S.A.M.H.I.*

"This evening we played for Col. Crowninshield," Corbett noted in his diary on the 20th of June, "as he has resigned and will leave tomorrow. We hate to lose him as he is the best liked officer in the Regt." That day Crowninshield prepared a farewell letter which was read to the troopers.

> Head Qrs 2d Mass Cav Vols
> June 20, 1865
>
> Soldiers of the 2d Massachusetts Cavalry my resignation having ben accepted I must bid you Farewell.
>
> We have served together for over 2 years and the trial of those years will never be forgotten. The friends we have lost and the Glorious Victories in which we have participated will live in our memories forever.
>
> For the high reputation which this Regiment has obtained for Gallantry in the Field and Soldiers conduct in Camp, I thank you. I feel justly proud of our Regiment.
>
> There is no stain upon our record and hereafter we can proudly boast that we belonged to the 2d Mass Cavalry and fought under Sheridan.
>
> By Order of
> C. Crowninshield
> Col. 2d Mass. Cav.[34]

Crowninshield departed for Boston the next day, leaving command of the regiment to Major McKendry. A few days later, by General Order No. 65, Caspar Crowninshield was "...to be Brig. General, U.S. Volunteers, by brevet, for gallant and meritorious services during the war, to date from Mar 13, 1865." One of his last actions before resigning was the ordering of a special flag for the Californians. He paid for it out of his own pocket, a final gesture to what he knew from the very beginning was the backbone of the regiment. The flag was of dark blue silk with the Seal of the State of California in the center, surrounded by the names of 23 of the general engagements the regiment fought in.[35]

Five days later, the 25th, Gen. Gibbs left for duty in Texas and the Reserve Brigade was broken up. The proud brigade that had fought under John Buford, Wesley Merritt, Alfred Gibbs, Charles Lowell, and Caspar Crowninshield was no more. The regular regiments accompanied Gibbs west, while the 2nd Massachusetts Cavalry moved camp to Fairfax Courthouse to await their muster out. Here the chief concern was decent food, for half the rations issued were routinely discarded being unfit to eat. It was widely speculated that the Government was trying to use up all of its store of rations, no matter what their condition.[36]

Rumors about further service were finally laid to rest on the 8th of July when the muster out rolls were received from Washington. By the 19th of July, the rolls were completed and that evening the 2nd Massachusetts Cavalry was mustered out of the service of the United States. Honorary promotions were handed out in abundance: "Old Badgers" McKendry to colonel as well as dozens of others including several sergeants to second lieutenant. However, these were honorary, and all of the men were mustered out at their previous ranks. "We are now brevet citizens," Corbett wrote, "and will remain so until we doff the blue uniform."[37]

On the 20th, widely recognized as the final date of service for the regiment, the men formed ranks and marched the five miles to Vienna. The horses had been turned in the week before so the men had no option but to move on foot under a blistering summer sun. The heat became too much for many and several dropped out along the way including Pvt. Stephen Cole (D), Ashton, who was still recovering from a bullet wound in the right shoulder taken at Cedar Creek. While marching he fell further and further behind, finally dropping in the dust along the side of the road. His brother Orton, also of Company D, stayed with him but was unable to re-

Flag designed by Col. Caspar Crowninshield and presented to the Californians at the end of the war. *Courtesy of the California State Capitol Museum.*

to Providence, Rhode Island, and a final train north to Readville, Massachusetts, brought the regiment to their old barracks at Camp Meigs.

From the first day back in the Bay State it was noted how very poor the food was. Rations were thrown out rather than eaten and food was purchased from local vendors. The men, especially the California Hundred, noted the difference in treatment they were receiving as compared to the heady days of January '63 when Boston threw open their doors for the West

vive him until a thunderstorm drenched them in the late afternoon. Never the same afterwards, his family blamed the sunstroke for his death in 1886.[38]

Boarding freight cars in Vienna on the 22nd, the regiment passed through Washington on the way to Philadelphia. The weather was still extremely hot and the men were packed into the cars so tightly that only a few could lie down at a time. Towle admitted that, "...shortly after the train was in motion we used the butts of our carbines as battering rams and knocked off about two feet of the four sides of the cars so that we might have more air. There were about 40 cars in the train and we must have supplied enough kindling wood to last the people along that track for a long time."[39]

A stop in Philadelphia for breakfast at the Union Volunteer Rooms and then across the Delaware River for another waiting train. This train, packed as heavily as the last, was of better construction and try as they might, the soldiers were unable to ventilate it. A steamer from New York City

Capt. Archibald McKendry, Company A, 2nd Regiment, Massachusetts Volunteer Cavalry. *Courtesy of Massachusetts Commandery Military Order of the Loyal Legion and the U.S. Army Military History Institute.*

Coast soldiers. "Needless to say we were not given a reception at Faneuil Hall as we had been on our first arrival there, nor did any of the ladies of Charleston enter our camp for any purpose, nor were we the subject of any attention of any character whatever."[40]

The cruelest blow of all, however, came when the Californians were told that neither the Commonwealth of Massachusetts nor the Federal Government would provide for their transportation home. A lawyer was retained and finally in November Washington consented to pay for the fare for any that wished to return to San Francisco. However, this was still August and though many of the men wished to stay on the east coast, those wanting to return to the Golden State would be forced to pay for the tickets themselves.

On the 3rd of August, 1865, the 2nd Massachusetts Volunteer Cavalry Regiment, 883 men strong, was paid off and officially disbanded. Of the 502 Californians who made up the original California Hundred and Battalion, only 182 were still there at the end. The missing men can be accounted for by adding up the number of promotions out of the regiment, discharges for disability (sickness and wounds), paroled prisoners, and those who died on the field or of their wounds, or in Southern prisons. During the course of the war the regiment lost eight officers and 82 enlisted men killed and mortally wounded, and three officers and 138 enlisted men by disease.

There was no fanfare on the 3rd, no final speeches or parades. No mention was made in any of the newspapers. They had served for two and a half years on average and now it was over. The men simply left camp, alone or in small groups, returning to their old lives or embarking on new ones. It was over.

Notes

1. Backus, "Californians in the Field," *MOLLUS.*, California Commandry, p. 19; Corbett, *Diary*, Mar. 25–26, 1865; Quant, *Diary*, Mar. 25–26, 1865.
2. Faust, *Encyclopedia*, p.578; Sheridan, *Civil War Memoirs*, p. 307.
3. Sheridan, *Civil War Memoirs*, p. 311.
4. *OR*, XLVI, p. 128.
5. *Massachusetts Soldiers, Sailors, and Marines*, Vol. 6, pp. 238–328; *OR*, XLVI, p. 1128.
6. Schouler, *Annual Report of the Adjutant General of Massachusetts for the Year Ending 1865*, p. 634.
7. Orton, *Record of California Troops in the War of the Rebellion 1861–1867*, p. 852.
8. Corbett, *Diary*, Mar. 31, 1865; National Archives, Record group 94, Pension Record for Samuel Corbett.
9. Corbett, *Diary*, Apr. 2, 1865; Quant, *Diary*, Apr. 1, 1865; Trudeau, *Out of the Storm*, p. 28.
10. *Massachusetts Soldiers, Sailors, and Marines*, Vol. VI, pp. 238–328.
11. Crowninshield, Apr. 2, 1865.
12. Corbett, *Diary*, Apr. 2, 1865; Schouler, *Annual Report of the Adjutant General of Massachusetts for Year Ending 1865*, p. 635.
13. Corbett, *Diary*, Apr. 3, 1865.
14. Ashcroft, "From San Rafael to the Civil War and Back Again," *Marin Independent Journal*; Backus, *Diary*, Apr. 4, 1865.
15. Towle, *Recollections*, p. 29.
16. Corbett, *Diary*, Apr. 7, 1865.
17. Corbett, *Diary*, Apr. 5, 1865.
18. Corbett, *Diary*, Apr. 6, 1865; Humphreys, *Field and Camp*, pp. 269–73.
19. Trudeau, *Out of the Storm*, p. 114.
20. Corbett, *Diary*, Apr. 9, 1865; Crowninshield, Apr. 14, 1865; Schouler, *Annual Report of the Adjutant General of Massachusetts for the Year Ending 1865*, p. 636.
21. Humphreys, *Field and Camp*, p. 289.
22. Corbett, *Diary*, Apr. 9, 1865; Quant, *Diary*, Apr. 9, 1865; *OR*, XLVI, Pt. 1, p. 1129.
23. Corbett, *Diary*, Apr. 11, 1865; Humphreys, *Field and Camp*, p. 293.
24. Schouler, *Annual Report of the Adjutant General of Massachusetts for the Year Ending 1865*, p. 637; John Winship to Sarah A. Hyde, Apr. 18, 23, 1865, John Winship Letters, Bentley Historical Library, University of Michigan.
25. Emerson, *Life and Letters*, p. 393;

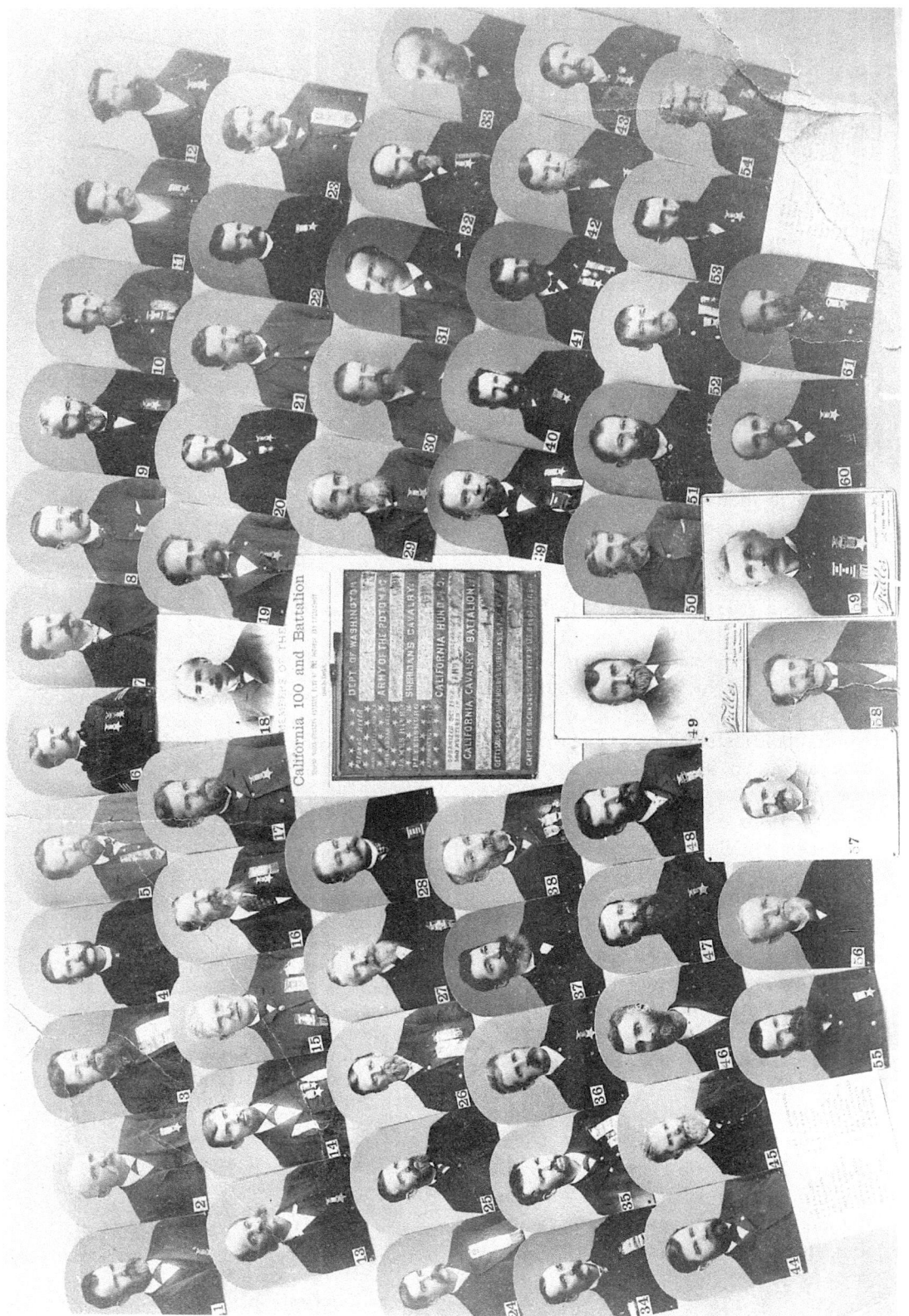

Schouler, *Annual Report of the Adjutant General of Massachusetts for the Year Ending 1865*, p. 637.

26. Corbett, *Diary*, Apr. 24–29, 1865; Quant, *Diary*, Apr. 24–29, 1865.

27. Towle, *Recollections*, p. 30.

28. Corbett, *Diary*, May 10–21, 1865.

29. Trudeau, *End of the Storm*, p. 317.

30. Corbett, *Diary*, May 23, 1864; *OR*, XLVI, Pt. 2, p. 1191.

31. Sherman, "A New England Boy in the Civil War," *New England Quarterly*, v. (1932), p. 31; Towle, *Recollections*, p. 31.

32. Corbett, *Diary*, May 27, 1865.

33. Corbett, *Diary*, May 29–30, 1865; Schouler, *Annual Report of the Adjutant General of Massachusetts for the Year Ending 1865*, p. 638; Towle, *Recollections*, p. 31; *Army and Navy Journal*, Vol. II, p. 718.

34. Corbett, *Diary*, June 20, 1865; National Archives, Record Group 94, 2nd Massachusetts Cavalry, Regimental Letters Box.

35. Crowninshield, June 5, 1865.

36. Corbett, *Diary*, June 25–30, 1865.

37. Corbett, *Diary*, July 19, 1865; National Archives, Record Group 94, 2nd Massachusetts Cavalry, Regimental Letters Box.

38. National Archives, Record Group 94, Pension Record of Stephen Cole.

39. Corbett, *Diary*, July 22–24, 1865; Towle, *Recollections*, p. 31.

40. Towle, *Recollections*, p. 32.

Opposite: Photographs of the California Hunded and Battalion taken during reunion in San Francisco. American flag in center was presented to the veterans by Major D.W.C. Thompson. Pictured are: 1. Sylvanus H. Shaw (E); 2. Samuel I. Beebee (L); 3. Cyrus F. Demsey (A); 4. Thomas D. Barnsted (A); 5. Henry H. Wyatt (E); 6. George E. Baldwin (L); 7. Solon D. Kimbal (L); 8. Harry W. Mortimer (E); 9. Frederick J. Quant (A); 10. Stephen F. Landis (F); 11. Luman A. Manchester (E); 12. John Fletcher (A); 13. Benjamin F. Rawson (F); 14. Leonard F. Smith (E); 15. Ebenezer Spencer (L); 16. Jared L. Sparrowhawk (L); 17. William H. McNeil (A); 18. Isaac S. Warner (M); 19. James P. Wilburn (M); 20. Alfred A. McLean (L); 21. Samuel S. Smith (A); 22. Henry M. Goodrich (M); 23. James Watson (A); 24. Adelbert S. Sheldon (E); 25. Robert A. Campbell (E); 26. Francis E. Barron (L); 27. Edward F. Seagraves (L); 28. Charles E. Benjamin (A); 29. Abel A. Withrow (M); 30. Daniel K. McDougal (L); 31. Samuel F. Tucker (L); 32. Thomas L. Rogers (E); 33. George W. Towle (A); 34. Abraham Loane (A); 35. William F. Wilcox (M); 36. George M. Lee (M); 37. Charles Roberts (F); 38. Zabdiel B. Adams (L); 39. James L. Wheat (A); 40. Samuel W. Backus (L); 41. Charles M. Jenkins (E); 42. Warren L. McEwen (E); 43. Edward Straub (E); 44. Eugene F. Loud (L); 45. Jackson Cossell (F); 46. Henry Miles (M); 47. Edwin W. Woodward (A); 48. William A. Robinson (A); 49. Ezra G. Rumery (L); 50. Josiah A. Baldwin (L); 51. Isaac R. McIntosh (A); 52. George I. Holt (A); 53. John T. Campbell (E); 54. James Bard (L); 55. William Starr (E); 56. Abner T. Mallory (E); 57. William C. Manning (L); 58. De Witt Clinton Thompson; 59. Charles M. Kinne (A); 60. Jonathan Merriam (A); 61. Henry Schrow (A). *Courtesy of California Section, Photograph Collection, California State Library.*

Epilogue

On a chilly October morning Samuel Corbett stood by the rail of the steamer *Colorado* and watched the city of San Francisco draw closer. Near him was Fred Quant and John Fletcher, like him ex-members of the California Hundred. It was nearly three years earlier that a similar steamer had taken them in the opposite direction, their futures unknown. They were not the first to arrive home — George Towle had in September — and others were soon to follow.

Adjusting to civilian life was not as easy as they had expected. Corbett found he could not sleep in a bed, often waking on the floor unsure how he arrived there. Many continued to suffer the effects of their wounds or struggled with ravaging disease. Empty sleeves, crutches, limps, and weakened bodies were a badge they all wore in one form or another.

The flags they had carried throughout the war came home with them and were turned over to the Adjutant General of the State; the Bear Flag guidon of the California Hundred, the American flag given to the company by Abbie Lord in Boston, and the blue silk flag listing the battles, a present from Col. Crowninshield. The flags would be brought out from time to time, for parades or reunions. Each time the numbers of the men would be fewer, the old heads a little grayer. Eventually, inevitably, they were all gone, with nothing more to show the world their accomplishments than a few tattered diaries, collections of old letters, and some photographs of men in blue uniforms, some with a curious brass badge on their caps: "CAL 100."

> I left camp for good yesterday P.M. and arrived at Sister Lizzie's last evening — I have once more put on a Citizen's Suit of clothes and feel like a free man — No more reveille turning out at 3 A.M. in the cold and wet cooking a breakfast of Pork Hardtack and coffee, No more standing picket to be shot at by Rebel guerrillas. No more rolling up in wet blankets, to take a roll in the mud to sleep — No more standing in line of Battle with Bullets and Shells Singing their sweet Songs in our ears, putting many of us to sleep with their gentle lullaby, the Soundest Sleep ere known to Mortal Man — No more shall my ears listen to the loud roar of artillery or the pop-pop of the musketry. In all probability I shall never live to see another Army fighting in this country — I am glad that I have had this experience. I am glad that I was so fortunate as to be one of the defenders of this Grand Republic.
> — Samuel J. Corbett
> August 6, 1865

Appendix A

Casualties at the Battle of Dranesville, Virginia, February 22, 1864

Killed (by company)

Capt. J. Sewall Reed (A), San Francisco
William Downey (B), Boston.
James Miles (B), Brookline.
Richard Powers (B), Roxbury.
Stephen Spooner (B), Ashland.
Byron Grover (E), San Francisco.
Abraham Waters (K), Medford.
Henry Dexter (M), Barton, Vermont.
George Ferrier (M), Metz, Indiana.
James McCammon (M), Warren, Illinois.

Wounded

John Hayden (B), Boston, died of his wounds February 29, 1864, at Vienna, Virginia.
James O'Halloran (B), Watertown, recovered and returned to duty.
William Wyatt (E), Strongsville, Ohio, recovered and returned to duty.
Joseph Spofford (H), Gloucester, recovered and returned to duty.
John Locke (M), Milo, Maine, recovered and returned to duty.
Joseph Seccin (M), Hungary, recovered and returned to duty.
Charles Thomas (M), Nantucket, transferred to the 187th Company, First Battalion, Veteran Reserve Corps.

Captured

David Dennison (B), Canton, paroled November 17, 1864.
George Duley (B), Ashland, died October 4, 1864, as a prisoner of war at Andersonville.
Samuel Goodman (B), Boston, died August 17, 1864, as a prisoner of war at Andersonville.
Arthur Hyde (B), Boston, died August 19, 1864, as a prisoner of war at Andersonville.
William Jackson (B), Brooklyn, N.Y., died September 10, 1864, as a prisoner of war at Andersonville.
Thomas Kelley (B), Boston, paroled April 22, 1865, mustered out July 19, 1865.
Joseph Kemp (B), Roxbury, while confined at Andersonville Joseph enlisted in the 10th Tennessee Infantry, and was captured in arms against the U.S. at Egypt Station, Mississipi, on the 28th of December, 1865. Taken to the Alton Military Prison he was allowed to enlist in the 5th U.S. Volunteers.
Thomas Kice (B), Boston, died on May 3, 1865, as a prisoner of war at Andersonville.
Philip McDonald (B), Boston, died April 8, 1864, as a prisoner of war at Andersonville.
John McGuire (B), Hopkinton, paroled December 16, 1864, returned to duty.
Ephraim Pinney (B), Stafford, Ct., released April 29, 1865, mustered out June 9, 1865, at Boston.
Charles Rich (B), Boston, died May 22, 1865, as a prisoner of war at Andersonville.

Sgt. George Sanborn (B), Boston, died September 7, 1864, as a prisoner of war at Andersonville.

Michael Scott (B), Boston, died September 1, 1864, as a prisoner of war at Andersonville.

Cushman Stevenson (B), Boston, died October 7, 1864, as a prisoner of war at Andersonville.

John Witter (B), Boston, paroled November 25, 1864.

John Cain (E), New York City, released April 30, 1865.

Josiah Crawford (E), Dexter, Maine, released April 28, 1865.

Jackson Fisher (E), Emmitsburg, Maryland, died April 9, 1864, as a prisoner of war at Andersonville.

Corp. William Millican (E), Tennessee, died August 29, 1864, as a prisoner of war at Andersonville.

Judson Mossman (E), Rockland, Maine, paroled November 26, 1864, returned to duty.

John Osts (E), Rochester, New York, released April 30, 1865.

Frank Paris (E), Quebec, Canada, died August 11, 1864, as a prisoner of war at Andersonville.

John Spaulding (E), Somerset County, Maine, died June 19, 1864, as a prisoner of war at Andersonville.

Corp. Levi Turner (E), Charlestown, paroled October 18, 1864, returned to duty.

George Wilcox (E), Jackson County, Michigan, released Apr 22, 1865.

Arthur Worster (E), Sonoma, California, paroled November 1864. Arthur died of disease on May 17, 1865, while on furlough from a Baltimore hospital.

Andrew Carver (G), N. Carver, died August 29, 1864, as a prisoner of war at Andersonville.

William Henderson (H), Roxbury, died October 29, 1864, as a prisoner of war at Millen, Georgia.

Corp. Jesse Hunt (I), Worcester, died November 18, 1864, as a prisoner of war at Savannah, Georgia.

1st Lt. William Manning (L), California, paroled February 7, 1865, returned to duty.

Newman Barnes (M), Chester, died June 7, 1864, as a prisoner of war at Andersonville.

William Bell (M), San Francisco, died September 7, 1864, as a prisoner of war at Andersonville.

Joseph Burke (M), Ireland, died July 4, 1864, as a prisoner of war at Andersonville.

Alvin Coffin (M), Bridgewater, died August 11, 1864, as a prisoner of war at Andersonville.

Jarius Dexter (M), Lowell, died July 27, 1864, as a prisoner of war at Andersonville.

David Folger (M), Nantucket, released November 19, 1864, returned to duty.

Henry Goodrich (M), Jerseyville, Illinois, escaped from prison, mustered out June 22, 1865, at Washington, D.C.

Herman Gozzens (M), New York, wounded in the arm, died in September 1864, as a prisoner of war at Savannah, Georgia.

Patrick Hackett (M), New York, died September 7, 1864, as a prisoner of war at Andersonville.

Cpl. Jacob Halstead (M), San Francisco, died March 25, 1864, as a prisoner of war at Andersonville.

Edward Hamblin (M), Dedham, died June 8, 1864, as a prisoner of war at Savannah, Georgia.

John Harty (M), Guysboro, Nova Scotia, died April 27, 1864, as a prisoner of war at Andersonville.

Francis Hewes (M), Charelstown, paroled March 27, 1865, returned to duty.

Charles Holden (M), Lowell, paroled (date not shown), and transferred to the 72nd Company, Second Battalion, Veteran Reserve Corps.

John Jones (M), Wales, Great Britain, died April 18, 1864, as a prisoner of war at Andersonville.

David Knapp (M), Canada East, died April 14, 1864, as a prisoner of war at Andersonville.

Cpl. William Lawrence (M), Santa Clara, California. William escaped from the prison pen at Danville, Virginia, as described by Pvt. Alfred Roe of the 9th New York Heavy Artillery: "The only escapes from our prison were effected by two men, one a member of the Second Massachusetts Cavalry, though he was a Californian, who let themselves down into a sink, wrenched off the grate leading into the narrow sewer, and at the imminent peril of suffocation, through indescribable filth, made their way out to the river and eventual liberty." After his ordeal, William returned to duty.

George Lee (M), San Jose, California, released April 28, 1865.

Capt. George Manning (M), California, wounded in the left leg by a shotgun, paroled from Libbey Prison, Richmond, Virginia (date not shown), and discharged May 15, 1865.

James Munroe (M), S. Seekonk, died August 20, 1864, as a prisoner of war at Andersonville.

Edward Price (M), Dills City, Oregon, died June 15, 1864, as a prisoner of war at Andersonville.

Anthony Simmonson (M), Hollidaysburg, Pennsylvania, wounded in the battle, died August 26, 1864, as a prisoner of war at Andersonville.

Thomas Stevens (M), England, died July 3, 1864, as a prisoner of war at Andersonville.

Archibald Taylor (M), Dutch Flat, California, died in September 1864, as a prisoner of war at Savannah, Georgia.

Uriah Weymouth (M), Lowell, died August 15, 1864, as a prisoner of war at Andersonville.

Massachusetts Soldiers, Sailors, and Marines, Vol. VI, pp. 228–328.

MOLLUS., Rhode Island.

Records of California Men in the War of the Rebellion, pp. 854–870.

National Archives, Record Group 94, various service and pension records.

Daily Alta California.

Appendix B

Casualties at the Battle of Mt. Zion Church, July 6, 1864

Killed (by company)

Corp. Samuel Hanscom (A), San Francisco.
Corp. James McDonald (F), California.
Charles Oeldraiher (G), Boston.
Owen Fox (H), East Braintree.
John Johnson (I), Canajoharie, New York.
Patrick Riordan (I), Marlboro.
Charles Rollins (I), Stanstead, Canada East.
Cornelius Tobin (I), Marlboro.
William Dumaresq (K), Jersey Island, England.

Wounded

Corp. William Bumgardner (A), San Francisco, died of his wounds in a farmhouse in Aldie, Virginia, July 22, 1864. Reinterred after the war at Arlington National Cemetery.
William Hillard (A), California, took a gunshot wound to the right shoulder which ran under the skin, across his ribs, and lodged near the backbone. He recovered and returned to duty.
Benjamin Beeth (F), California, discharged for disability on June 7, 1865.
James Logsden (F), California, recovered and returned to duty.
William Thomas (G), Brooklyn, New York, deserted from a hospital in Alexandria, Virginia.
George Wentworth (G), Jamaica Plain, took a sabre cut on the scalp, transferred to 239th Company, First Battalion, V.R.C.
Henry Wentworth (G), Jamaica Plain, recovered and returned to duty.
Capt. Goodwin Stone (K), Newburyport, died of his wounds at Aldie, Virginia, on July 18, 1864.
John Clark (L), California, recovered and returned to duty.

Captured (Partial Listing)

Charles Atmore (A), Boston, died September 26, 1864, a prisoner of war at Andersonville.
Charles Benjamin (A), San Francisco, was wounded in the left leg during the fight but managed to escape, spending three days in a swamp before making it to Union lines. He recovered from his wound and returned to duty.
Abraham Loane (A), San Francisco, released April 28, 1865, mustered out at Readville on June 5, 1865.
John Loring (A), Boston, released April 28, 1865, mustered out at Boston on June 5, 1865.
Freeman Perkins (A), Boston, paroled May 5, 1865, mustered out in Boston July 15, 1865.
Benjamin Thaxter (D), Boston, paroled in December, 1864, and died January 15, 1865, of disease in Annapolis, Maryland.
Corp. Joseph Bradford (F), California, wounded during the battle, died August 22, 1864, a prisoner of war at Andersonville.
John Nottage (F), Ashland, died September 30, 1864, a prisoner of war at Andersonville.

George Parker (F), N. Bridgewater, paroled December 3, 1864, and returned to duty.

Patrick Sullivan (F), Boston, paroled March 10, 1865, and returned to duty.

Edward Walker (G), Chelsea, released April 22, 1865.

Daniel Dougherty (H), Marlboro, paroled March 10, 1865, mustered out in Readville on June 10, 1865.

Daniel Doyle (H), Marlboro, died March 12, 1865, a prisoner of war at Danville, Virginia.

Dennis Doyle (H), Marlboro, paroled (date not shown).

John McGowan (H), Georgetown, paroled December 1, 1864, returned to duty.

Cornelius Sline (H), Salem, paroled December 1, 1864, returned to duty.

William Wheeler (H), Hopkinton, sent to prison at Millen, Georgia. No further record.

John Lyons (I), Lowell, no further record.

John Coleman (K), Randolph, released May 1, 1865, and mustered out in Boston on July 12, 1865.

John Kelley (K), Jersey City, New Jersey, paroled February 1865, at Goldsboro, North Carolina, discharged June 17, 1865 at Annapolis, Maryland.

Patrick Matthews (K), Cambridge, released April 22, 1865, mustered out on June 5, 1865.

James Rand (K), Lowell, escaped from prison near Charleston, South Carolina, returned to duty.

John Pratt (L), Boston, paroled November 15, 1864, returned to duty.

Massachusetts Soldiers, Sailors, and Marines, Vol. VI, pp. 228–328.

Records of California Men in the War of the Rebellion, pp. 854–870.

National Archives, Record Group 94, various service and pension records.

The Medical and Surgical History of the Civil War, Vol. VII.

Appendix C

Casualties at the Battle of Rockville, July 13, 1864

Charles A. Backus (K), Nantucket, killed on the field, the only man of the regiment to die that day.

Wounded (by company)

Henry Allen (A), San Francisco, took a bullet near the left knee joint while carrying orders for Col. Lowell. He died on the 16th of August at Mt. Pleasant Hospital, Maryland, "...through neglect of surgeon."

John Scott (A), Boston, deserted from the hospital in Washington, D.C.

Stephen Griffin (B), Boston, received a sabre cut on his scalp and right ear, recovered and returned to duty.

John McNeff (C), Ware, recovered and returned to duty.

Sgt. William Minot(C), Massachusetts, shot through both thighs by a single bullet. He was discharged for disability in July 1865.

Charles P. Relmond (C), Richmond, Virginia, transferred to the Eighth Company, Second Battalion, Veteran Reserve Corps (VRC).

Joseph Wallace (C), discharged for disability in June 1865.

John Gillespie (D), Melrose, died of his wounds on July 20th, 1864, in Washington, D.C.

Charles D. Hart (D), Ashland, transferred to Company C, 19th V.R.C.

Corp. Frank Hill (D), unknown, recovered and returned to duty.

George Johnson (D), South Boston, discharged for disability in May 1865.

Leonard Smith (E), San Francisco, was shot in the head during the fighting. His horse spooked, fell and rolled on him, resulting in a broken hip. While lying in the road a Confederate hit him in the back of the head with a sabre, while another shot him, the bullet striking his arm. Leonard survived, recovered, and returned to duty.

Charles Curtis (F), California, discharged for his wounds March 8, 1865.

James Hill (F), San Francisco, took a bullet that passed completely through his chest. He recovered and returned to duty.

Benjamin Kercheval (F), San Francisco, was shot in the left thigh. Recovered and returned to duty.

William Ray (F), Nantucket, discharged for disability in June 1865.

Corp. John Bayley (H), Boston, discharged for disability in May 1865.

William Curry (H), Boston, recovered and returned to duty.

Corp. Henry Hodson (H), Halifax, Nova Scotia, recovered and returned to duty.

Francis Lowder, (H), County Kerry, Ireland, was hit by a bullet which fractured his skull; another pierced his left thigh. Francis was discharged for disability in February 1865.

Sgt. Joseph Spofford (H), Gloucester, discharged for disability in July 1865. Joseph had also been wounded at Dranseville, February 22, 1864.

Alexander Tupper (H), Gloucester, discharged for disability in May 1865.

John May (I), Boston, recovered and returned to duty.

Edward Kelley (I), Boston, transferred to the Third Company, Second Battalion, V.R.C.

George Nicholson, Jr. (K), Nantucket, discharged for disability in May 1865.

Joseph Stone (K), Connecticut, was shot in the back of his left shoulder and then knocked off his horse by a rifle butt. He fell against a fence post, breaking three ribs. Joseph recovered and returned to duty.

Corp. George Carr (L), San Francisco, died of his wounds on October 21, 1864.

Abram Barenson (M), Salem, recovered and returned to duty. Abram was wounded again, by accident, at Winchester, Virginia, September, 1864.

Captured

Michael Carr (A), Lawrence, paroled March 4, 1865, and deserted May 28, 1865.

Joseph Collins (A), Pensacola, Florida, paroled February 22, 1865, and deserted May 28, 1865.

George Goulding (A), San Francisco, captured when his horse fell and pinned him to the ground. He was confined at Danville, Virginia, where he contracted scurvy. Paroled on February 22, 1864, he returned to duty.

James Howlett (A), Chelsea, paroled February 22, 1865, and discharged for disability May 27, 1865.

Jonathon Merrian (A), San Francisco, exchanged March 2, 1865, and discharged from hospital in Readville, Massachusetts, June 13, 1865.

David Moulton (A), Portsmouth, New Hampshire, paroled February 22, 1865, and returned for duty.

Cornelius Murphy (A), N. Cambridge, paroled and discharged for disability on August 18, 1865.

Henry Tubbs (A), San Francisco, paroled February 22, 1865, and returned for duty on the 21st of May, 1865.

Sgt. William Anthony (C), San Francisco, a former member of the California Hundred, sent to Prison No. 1, Danville, Virginia. He was placed in a temporary hospital shed with 17 others (including John Connealy [C]) of which only four survived. Reduced to a skeleton from "bloody flux," he survived and was paroled October 18, 1864. In May 1888, William Anthony committed suicide.

John Connealy (C), Marlboro, was captured within ten feet of Sgt. Anthony. Held in Prison No. 1, Danville, Virginia, and paroled on October 18, 1864.

John Glasscot (C), Buffalo, New York, died December 12, 1864, as a prisoner of war in Danville, Virginia.

Carl Haglan (C), Sweden, paroled February 22, 1865, and returned to duty.

Bernard Kelley (C), Northampton, paroled February 22, 1865, and discharged for disability on June 1, 1865.

George Pack (C), Boston, died February 12, 1865, as a prisoner of war in Danville, Virginia.

John Peterson (C), Boston, paroled October 17, 1864.

John Slemp (C), Boston, paroled February 22, 1865, and returned to duty.

Warren Cochran (F), Russian River, California. Cut off from the regiment, Warren hid in a yard until captured while searching for water. Imprisoned at Danville, Virginia, he escaped on January 31, 1865, was recaptured near Mt. Airy, North Carolina, escaped again, and walked to the Union lines at Knoxville, Tennessee.

Jackson Cossell (F), California, paroled February 22, 1865, and returned to duty.

Corp. Joseph Johnson (F), California, paroled October 17, 1864, and returned to duty.

Francis Smith (F), Hopkinton, died February 1, 1865, as a prisoner of war at Danville, Virginia.

Daniel Case (H), Middleton, died December 21, 1864, as a prisoner of war at Salisbury, North Carolina.

Sgt. Frank Downes (H), Boston, paroled February 22, 1865, and returned to duty.

William Green (H), Middleton, paroled February 19, 1865, and discharged July 14, 1865 at Readville, Massachusetts.

James McKay (H), St. John, New Brunswick, paroled February 22, 1865, and returned to duty.

Owen McLean (H), S. Boston, paroled February 22, 1865, and returned to duty.

Samuel Moore (H), Wayland, paroled February 22, 1865, and returned to duty.

James Pardridge (H), Harvard, paroled February 23, 1865, and returned to duty.

Robert Bampton (I), Roxbury, released February 21, 1865, and mustered out July 14, 1865, at Readville, Massachusetts.

Milo Fisher (I), Theresa, New York, released March 13, 1865, and mustered out June 12, 1865, at Annapolis, Maryland.

John Hughes (I), Nova Scotia, paroled February 22, 1865.
Corp. William Pingle (L), California, paroled February 23, 1865, but died of disease on April 15, 1865.

Deserted

Thomas Adams (G), Boston.
Joseph Carr (G), Philadelphia, Pennsylvania.
John Hackett (G), Stanstead, Canada East.
William Hubbard (G), Stanstead, Canada East.
William Leupold (G), New York City.
Peter Schmitt (G), New York City.

Massachusetts Soldiers, Sailors, and Marines, Vol. VI, pp. 228–328.
Records of California Men in the War of the Rebellion, pp. 854–870.
National Archives, Record Group 94, various service and pension records.
The Medical and Surgical History of the Civil War, Vol. VII.

Bibliography

Unpublished Sources

Gerry Chase Private Collection.
  Valorus Dearborn Diary.

The Huntington, San Marino, California.
  Charles Roberts Diary.
  Letters of Robert H. Williams.

LaPorte County Historical Museum, LaPorte, Indiana.
  A True Story of the Civil War by Warren Cochran.

Lydia Lucas Private Collection.
  California 100 and Battalion by Harry W. Mortimer.

Mace, Joann Beer, *Massachusetts Cavalry from California 1862–1865*. Masters Thesis, 1967.

Massachusetts Historical Society, Boston, Massachusetts.
  Caspar Crowninshield letters, Crowninshield-Magnus Papers.
  A. A. Lawrence Papers.

Massachusetts State Archives at Columbia Point, Boston, Ma.
  Executive Letters Collection.
  Letters Official Collection.

Minnesota Historical Society, St. Paul, Minnesota.
  Jesse A. and Luman P. Washburn Papers.
  Samuel Bond Journal.

National Archives, Washington, D.C.
  Records of the Adjutant General's Office 1780s–1917 (Record Group 94).

University of California, The Bancroft Library, Berkeley, California.
  Samuel James Corbett Papers.
  Frederick J. Quant Diary.
  Some Personal Recollections of George Washington Towle.
  Autobiography of Wells Wallace West, West and Benson Family Papers.

University of Michigan, Bentley Historical Library, Ann Arbor, Michigan.
  John Winship Letters.

Newspapers

Boston Herald
Boston Journal
Boston Post
Boston *Randolph Transcript and Norfolk Advertiser*
Boston *Saturday Evening Express*
Boston *Saturday Evening Gazette*
Dedham Gazette
Marin Independent Journal
Napa County Reporter
Napa County *Register*
National Tribune
New York Times
Oakland Tribune
Pacific Echo
Sacramento Daily Union
Sacramento *Evening Bulletin*
San Francisco *Daily Alta California*

Published Sources

Alvord, Henry E. "Early's Attack upon Washington." *Military Order of the Loyal Legion of the United States*. War Papers No. 26, District of Columbia. 1897.

———. "A New England Boy in the Civil War," edited by Caroline B. Sherman. *New England Quarterly*. V (1932).

Ashcroft, Lionel. "From San Rafael to the Civil War and Back Again." *Marin Independent Journal*.

Backus, Samuel W. "Californians in the Field: Historical Sketch of the Organization and Services of the 'California Hundred' and 'Battalion' 2d Massachusetts Cavalry." *Military Order of the Loyal Legion of the United States*. War Papers No. 4. California Commandry. 1889.

Bartol, Cyrus Augustus. *The Purchase of Blood: A Tribute to Brig. Gen. Charles Russell Lowell, Jr., Spoken in the West Church, October 30, 1864*. Boston: John Wilson and Son, 1864.

Bingham, Col. Robert. "North Carolinians at South Anna Bridge." *Confederate Veteran*, vol. XXXIV.

Bliss, George N. "The Cavalry Affair at Waynesboro." *Southern Historical Society Papers*, vol. XIII. Richmond, Va.: Broadfoot Publishing Company, Morningside Bookshop, 1990.

Bonny, Orrin H. and Lorraine. *Battledrums and Geysers: The Life and Journals of Lt. Gustaves Cheyney Doane, Soldier and Explorer of the Yellowstone and Snake River Regions*. Chicago: The Swallow Press, 1970.

Bowen, James L. *Massachusetts in the War 1861–1865*. Springfield, Mass.: Clark W. Bryan, 1889.

Coddington, Edwin B. *The Gettysburg Campaign: A Study in Command*. New York: Charles Scribner's Sons, 1968.

Cooling, B. Franklin. *Jubal Early's Raid on Washington, 1864*. Baltimore: Nautical & Aviation Publishing Company of America, 1989.

Crawford, J. Marshall. *Mosby and His Men*. New York: Carleton, 1867.

Crowninshield, Benjamin W. *A History of the First Regiment of Massachusetts Cavalry Volunteers*. Boston and New York: Houghton Mifflin, 1891.

Devine, Judge W.A. "Defense of the South Anna Bridge." *Confederate Veteran*, vol. XL.

Divine, John E. *35th Battalion Virginia Cavalry (Whites)*. Lynchburg, Va.: H.E. Howard, 1985.

Duncan, Russell. *Blue-Eyed Child of Fortune: The Civil War Letters of Robert Gould Shaw*. Athens: University of Georgia Press, 1992.

Early, Jubal A. *Jubal Early's Memoirs*. Baltimore: Nautical & Aviation Publishing Company of America, 1989.

Emerson, Edward Waldo. *Life and Letters of Charles Russell Lowell*. Boston: Houghton Mifflin, 1907.

Emilio, Luis F. *A Brave Black Regiment*. New York: DaCapo Press, 1995.

Evans, Thomas J., and James M. Moyer. *Mosby's Confederacy*. Shippensburg, Pa.: White Mane, 1991.

Farwell, Byron. *Ball's Bluff*. McLean, Va.: EPM Publications, 1990.

Faust, Patricia L., Ed. *Historical Times Illustrated Encyclopedia of the Civil War*. New York: Harper & Row, 1986.

Ferguson, David L. *Cleopatra's Barge: The Croninshield Story*. Boston: Little, Brown, 1976.

Fisher, Kenneth. "The Union's Bear Flag Defenders." *America's Civil War*, January 1990.

Fitzpatrick, Michael F. "Jubal Early and the Californians." *Civil War Times Illustrated*, vol. XXXVII, No. 2, May 1998.

Greenslet, Ferris. *The Lowells and Their Seven Worlds*. Boston: Houghton Mifflin, 1946.

Hagemann, E.R., ed. *Fighting Rebels and Redskins, Experiences in Army Life of Colonel George Sanford 1861–1892*. Norman: University of Oklahoma Press, 1969.

Harris, Moses. "With the Reserve Brigade." *Journal of the United States Cavalry Association*, vol. III. Leavenworth, Kans.: Press of Ketcheson & Reeves, 1890.

Harrison, Noel. "The Sojourn of the Second Massachusetts Cavalry in Vienna." *Northern Virginia Heritage*, June 1985.

Higginson, Henry L. "Charles Russell Lowell." *Harvard Memorial Biographies*. Cambridge: Sever and Francis, 1866.

Higginson, Thomas Wentworth. *Massachusetts in the Army and Navy During the War of 1861–1865*. Boston: Wright & Potter, State Printers, 1896.

Hughes, Sarah F. *Letters and Recollections of John Murray Forbes*. 2 vols. Boston and New York: Houghton Mifflin, 1899.

Humphreys, Charles A. *In Field, Camp, Hospital and Prison in the Civil War 1863–1865*. Boston: George H. Ellis, 1918.

Hunt, Aurora. *The Army of the Pacific.* Glendale, Calif.: The Arthur H. Clark, 1951.

Jones, Virgil Carrington. *Gray Ghosts and Rebel Raiders.* McLean, Va.: EPM Publications, 1984

_____. *Ranger Mosby.* McLean, Va.: EPM Publications, 1972.

Kidd, James H. *A Cavalryman with Custer.* Reprint Edition. New York: Bantam, 1991.

Kirsch, Robert, and William Murphy. *West of the West.* New York: Dutton, 1967.

Langellier, Philip, and Wayne Colwell. "Cavaliers from California." *Gateway Heritage.* Missouri Historical Society, vol. V, no. 3, Winter 1984-85.

Lavender, David. *California: A Bicentennial History.* New York: W.W. Norton, 1976.

Lawrence, William. *Life of Amos A. Lawrence with Extracts from His Diary and Correspondence.* Boston and New York: Houghton Mifflin, 1899.

Lewis, Thomas A. *The Guns of Cedar Creek.* Reprint Edition. New York: Dell, 1980.

Longacre, Edward G. *The Cavalry at Gettysburg.* Lincoln and London: University of Nebraska Press, 1993.

Massachusetts. Adjutant General's Office. *Massachusetts Soldiers, Sailors, and Marines in the Great Civil War,* vol.VI. Norwood, Mass.: Norwood Press, 1931.

The Medical and Surgical History of the Civil War. Wilmington, N.C.: Broadfoot Publishing Co. and Morningside Bookshop, 1991.

Melville, Herman. "The Scout toward Aldie." *Selected Poems of Herman Melville.* Warren, Robert P., ed. New York: Barnes & Noble, 1998.

Milano, Anthony J. "The Story of the 2d and 20th Massachusetts Volunteer Infantry Regiments from 1861 through 1863 as Told by the Letters of Their Officers." *Civil War,* vol. XIII.

Morison, John Hopkins. *Dying for Our Country: A Sermon on the Death of Captain J. Sewell Reed and Rev. Thomas Starr King, Preached in the First Congregational Church in Milton, March 13, 1864.* Boston: John Wilson and Son, 1864.

Mosby, John S. *The Memoirs of John S. Mosby.* Edited by Charles Wells Russell. Boston: Little, Brown, 1917.

Munson, John W. *Reminiscences of a Mosby Guerilla.* Reprint Edition. Washington, D.C.: Zenger, 1983.

Nagel, Paul C. *Descent from Glory, Four Generations of the John Adams Family.* New York: Oxford University Press, 1983.

Orton, Richard S. *Record of California Men in the War of the Rebellion 1861–1867.* Sacramento: J.D. Young, 1890.

Parker, Hershel. "Herman Melville." *American History Illustrated,* vol. XXVI, no. 4, Sep/Oct 1991.

Peace, A.S. "Fighting Against Great Odds." *Confederate Veteran,* vol. XXXIV.

Roe, Alfred S. "In a Rebel Prison: Or, Experiences in Danville, Va." *Military Order of the Loyal Legion of the United States.* Providence, Rhode Island: Published by the Society, 1891.

Schouler, William. *Annual Report of the Adjutant General of Massachusetts for the Year Ending December, 1863.* Boston: Wright & Potter, 1864.

_____. *Annual Report of the Adjutant General of Massachusetts for the Year Ending December, 1864.* Boston: Wright & Potter, 1865.

_____. *Annual Report of the Adjutant General of Massachusetts for the Year Ending December, 1865.* Boston: Wright & Potter, 1866.

Scott, Maj. John. *Partisan Life with Col. John S. Mosby.* New York: Harper & Brothers, 1867.

Sears, Stephen W. *George B. McClellan: The Young Napoleon.* New York: Tecknon & Fields, 1988.

Sheridan, Philip, H. *Civil War Memoirs.* Reprint edition. New York: Bantam Books, 1991.

Siepel, Kevin H. *Rebel: The Life and Times of John Singleton Mosby.* New York: St. Martin's Press, 1983.

Sifakis, Stewart. *Who Was Who in the Civil War.* New York: Facts on File, 1988.

Speer, Lonnie R. *Portals to Hell.* Mechanicsburg, Pa.: Stackpole, 1997.

Sperry, Bliss. *Life and Letters of Henry Lee Higginson.* Boston: Atlantic Monthly Press, 1921.

Stackpole, Edward J. *Sheridan in the Shenandoah.* Harrisburg, Pa.: Stackpole, 1992.

Starr, Stephen Z. *The Union Cavalry in the Civil War.* 3 vol. Baton Rouge and London: Louisiana State University Press, 1981.

Stuntz, Connie P., and Mayo S. Stuntz. *This Was Vienna, Virginia.* Vienna, Va.: Constance Pendelton Stuntz and Mayo Sturdevant Stuntz, 1987.

Thompson, DeWitt C. "California in the Rebellion." *Military Order of the Loyal Legion of the United States.* California Commandry.

Tibbals, Richard K. "Thirty Years Later." *Civil War Times Illustrated*, vol. XXV, no. 2, April 1986.

Trudeau, Noah B. *Out of the Storm: The End of the Civil War April–June 1865.* Baton Rouge: Louisiana State University Press, 1994.

U.S. War Department. *Atlas to Accompany the Official Records of the Union and Confederate Armies.* Reprint Edition. Gettysburg, Pa.: The National Historical Society, 1974.

_____. *The War of the Rebellion: Official Records of the Union and Confederate Armies.* 128 vols. Washington, D.C.: U.S. Government Printing Office, 1880–1901.

Van Diver, Frank E. *Jubal's Raid.* New York: McGraw-Hill, 1960.

Warner, Ezra J. *Generals in Blue.* Baton Rouge: Louisiana State University Press, 1964.

Wert, Jeffry D. *From Winchester to Cedar Creek.* Carlisle, Pa.: South Mountain Press, 1987.

_____. *Mosby's Rangers.* New York: Simon & Schuster, 1990.

Williamson, James J. *Mosby's Rangers.* New York: Kenyon, 1896.

Index

Ackerman, James 149
Adams, John Quincy, Jr. 48
Adams, Zebdiel B. 38, 76, 92, 110, 111, 201
Alabama, C.S.S. 41
Aldie, Va. 47, 71, 73, 77, 83, 95, 103, 112, 125, 126, 129, 130, 206
Allen, Elizabeth 48
Allen, Henry 208
Alvord, Henry 56, 57, 102, 162, 173, 174, 196
America 48
Ames Co. 10
Amory, Charles 126, 127, 131, 193
Anderson, Richard H. 151, 191
Andersonville, Ga. 31, 130, 151, 203–206
Andrew, John A. 7, 9, 12, 17, 30, 31, 34, 36, 37, 47, 69, 86, 91, 97
Anthony, William 209
Antietam, Battle of 9, 10, 15, 27
Appomattox Station 191, 192
Armstrong, Hugh 24
Army of Northern Virginia 58, 73, 193
Army of the Cumberland 47
Army of the Potomac 9, 13, 15, 57, 58, 72, 75, 76, 118, 120, 133, 144, 163, 186
Army of the Shenandoah 144
Army of West Virginia 144
Ashby's Gap 73, 75, 116, 117, 178, 180
Assembly Hall 20, 22, 23
Atmore, Charles 206
Auger, Christopher C. 93, 97, 104, 109, 116, 117, 133, 143
Averell, William 56, 152, 153
Ayr Hill, Va. 93, 94

Baaron, Francis 201
Backus, Charles 208
Backus, Samuel 81, 117, 148, 170, 190, 201
Baker, Edward C. 26, 27
Baker, Eugene 166
Baker, Frank 111
Baker, Lafayette C. 91, 97, 98
Baldwin, George 201
Baldwin, Josiah 154, 177, 201
Balke, Charles 35
Ball, Warren 47
Ball's Bluff, battle of 27, 48, 168
Baltic 85
Baltimore, Md. 12, 13
Bampton, James 209
Banks, Nathaniel P. 47, 57
Bard, James 78, 201
Barenson, Abram 208
Barnes, John H. 131
Barnes, Newman 204
Barnes, Walter S. 74
Barnstead, Thomas 50, 53, 60, 82, 96, 201
Baybutt, Philip 156
Bayley, John 208
Beach, Nathan 84
Beal, Merrill C. 168
Beauregard, P.G.T. 75
Beebee, Samuel 201
Beeth, Benjamin 206
Bell, William 204
Benjamin, Charles 167, 201, 206
Berryville, Va. 145, 152, 153
Billy Gooding's Tavern 3, 84, 86, 162
Bingham, Robert 60
Binns, Charlie 95, 96
Bishop, George 149

Bladensburg, Md. 13, 196
Blagden, George 76
Bliss, George 157
Bluxone, Isaac 40
Boggs, Daniel 117
Bond, Samuel 25
Boston Journal 50, 53, 85
Bosworth, Charles 154
Boyle, Charles 147
Boynton, John 147
Bradford, Joseph 206
Branch, F.P. 131
Brickley, Richard 74
Briggs, Charles 25, 26, 32, 51, 55
Buford, John 56, 150, 197
Bull Run, First and Second Battle of, 10, 13, 75, 77
Bumgardner, William 116, 132, 206
Burdick, Joseph B. 25n, 60, 61
Burke, Joseph 204
Burke, Patrick 146
Burke, Thomas 169
Burlingham, Henry 24, 192
Burlington and Missouri Railroad 12
Burnap, Oscar 98
Burns, John 157
Burnside, Ambrose E. 15, 51, 56, 118
Busteed, Richard 50, 51, 53, 55

Cabot, Louis 47, 102
Cain, John 84, 204
California Battalion 34, 40, 42, 45, 64, 73, 78, 79, 81, 92, 96, 106, 143, 149, 154, 189, 194, 199
California Cossacks 38, 147
California Column 5, 6

Index

California Hundred 22–25, 29, 31, 32, 36, 37, 39, 40, 45, 57, 58, 60, 65, 76, 77, 79, 81, 83, 87, 90, 108, 127, 132, 143, 145, 149, 158, 166, 168, 177, 183, 190, 194, 198, 199, 202
California Rangers 23
California troops: 6; 1st Infantry 5, 40; 1st Light Dragoons 20, 22, 25; 1st Regiment California Militia 23; 2nd Cavalry 5, 38, 39, 149; 3rd Infantry 27; 5th Infantry 5; 9th Infantry 23; Black Hussars 25; Citizens Dragoons 20; Eureka Light Horse Guards 20; Light Guards 25, 168; Old California Guard 25; Oakland Home Guard 38; Vallejo Rifles 25
Cameron, Simon 13
Camp Brightwood 68, 69, 71, 73, 74
Camp California 55
Camp Gilpin 51
Camp Grimshaw 50
Camp Meigs 31, 43, 64, 65, 69, 198
Camp Oglethorpe 129
Camp West 55
Camp Wyndham 195
Campbell, John 201
Campbell, Robert 201
Canby, E.R.S. 5
Carleton, James H. 5, 6
Carr, George 209
Carr, Michael 209
Carver, Andrew 204
Case, Daniel 209
Casey, Silas 67, 68
Cavenaugh, Patrick 157
Cedar Creek, Va. 145, 146, 162, 163, 166, 170, 173
Centerville, Va. 76–78, 81, 83, 84, 87, 89, 92, 112
Chadwick, Edward 154
Chancellorsville, Battle of 57
Chaplin, William 6
Chapman, Samuel 85, 155
Chapman, William 105
Charleston, S.C. 129, 130
Charlestown, Va. 147, 149, 176
Charlottsville, Va. 181, 182
City of Albany 59
City Point, Va. 184, 190, 191, 193
Clark, Charles 117, 118
Clark, John 206
Cleopatra's Barge 48
Cochran, Warren 134, 137, 209
Coffin, Alvin 204
Cold Harbor, Battle of 27
Cole, Orton 197
Cole, Stephen 168, 197
Coleman, John 207
Colgan, William 151
Collins, James 161

Collins, Joseph 209
Commodore Jones 62
Confederate troops: 1st Foreign Battalion 146; 2nd Foreign Legion 158
Connealy, John 209
Connecticut, U.S.S. 41, 43
Conner, P. Edward 27, 28
Conners, Cornelius 162
Constitution 40
Cooke, Philip St. George 13
Cooper, Seth 98
Corbett, Samuel 50, 55, 60, 101, 114, 118, 146, 149, 152, 154–157, 163, 177, 179, 181, 189, 190, 195, 197, 202
Cornnell, Jeffery 168
Cossell, Jackson 201, 209
Coyle's Tavern see Billy Gooding's Tavern
Crawford, Josiah 204
Crocker, Henry H. 38, 151, 166, 167, 168
Crook, George 144, 181
Crowninshield, Ben 61
Crowninshield, Benjamin W. 48
Crowninshield, Caspar 29, 45, 47–53, 55–61, 64, 83, 85–88, 90, 92, 93, 97, 102, 104, 106, 108–110, 113, 118, 120, 122, 132, 135–138, 142, 143, 145–149, 154–157, 160, 161, 166–168, 170, 177–179, 181, 183, 187, 190, 192, 197, 198, 202
Crowninshield, Fanny 48
Crowninshield, George 48
Crowninshield, Jacob 48
Crum, Henry 113, 157
Cunnigham, William 77
Curry, William 208
Curtin, Andrew G. 27
Curtis, Charles 208
Curtis, James F. 6
Cushman, Pauline 181
Cushman, Stevenson 204
Custer, George A. 150–154, 161–164, 167, 173, 179–181, 189, 191, 195

Dabney, Louis 102, 103, 105
Daily Alta California 6, 21–23, 37, 40, 65, 67, 96, 97, 113
D'Arcey, Lizzie 113
Davies, Henry 195
Davis, Alexander "Yankee" 95, 129
Davis, Asa 168
Davis, Hasbrook 58
Davis, Jefferson 25
Davis, P.A. 61
Dealing, Charles 146
Dean, Charles 149
Dearborn, Valorus 95, 96, 101, 112, 113, 120, 122, 146, 148, 149, 151

DeForest, William 74
Dehaven, George 154
Delaware troops: 12th Cavalry 59; 4th Infantry 50, 55
DeMerritt, David A. 39–43, 69, 83, 85, 86, 92, 109, 110, 117, 168
Demsey, Cyrus 85, 201
Dennison, David 203
Devin, Thomas C. 153, 154, 161, 165, 168, 183, 187, 195
Dew, Francis 31*n*
DeWolf, Oscar 89, 102, 148, 151, 169, 170
Dexter, Henry 203
Dexter, Jarius 204
Dinwiddie Courthouse, Va. 187, 189, 190
District of Columbia troops: 1st Cavalry 91, 94, 97, 98
Dix, John 50, 55, 58, 59, 61
Doane, Gustaves "Cheney" 81, 82
Dolan, John 135
Dougherty, Daniel 207
Downes, Frank 209
Downey, William 203
Doyle, Daniel 207
Doyle, Dennis 207
Dranesville, Va. 22, 83, 99, 104–106, 109, 111, 112, 114, 193, 203
Duley, Charles 31
Duley, Eastman 31
Duley, George 31, 203
Dumaresq, William 132, 206
Dwight, William 164

Early, Jubal 125, 133–136, 138, 140, 142, 144–146, 149–157, 161, 163–168, 176, 179–181
Eby, James H. 54
Eigenbrodt, Charles S. 38, 76, 92, 94, 98, 133, 147, 149
Ellet, Richard S. 60
Ellis John S. 39
Ellsworth Rifles 25
Elzey, Arnold 54
Emerson, Edward Waldo 173
Emerson, George 154
Emerson, Ralph Waldo 193
Emory, William H. 13, 135, 140, 144, 150
Express 50

Fairfax Courthouse, Va. 71, 77, 82, 93, 94, 197
Falls Church, Va. 82, 120–122, 125, 127, 131–133, 142, 195
Felch, John 154
Ferguson, Thomas 190
Ferrier, George 203
Ferrill, David 117
Field, Charles 190
Fillebrown, Henry H. 20
Fisher, Jackson 204
Fisher, Milo 209

Index

Fisher's Hill, Va. 145, 154, 161, 163, 173, 181
Five Forks, Va. 187, 190
Fleet, Richard 151
Fletcher, John 145, 201, 202
Folger, David 204
Foote, Charles 176
Forbes, John Murray 8–13, 15–17, 29, 30, 37, 45, 47, 131, 147, 173
Forbes, Mary 45
Forbes, William H. 11, 29, 45, 47, 64, 76, 86–88, 93, 97, 102, 109, 110, 113, 114, 117, 120, 121, 125–127, 130–132, 147, 177, 191
Fordham, Nathan 176
Fort Bayard 135
Fort Ethan Allen 81
Fort Keyes 50, 51
Fort Magruder 14, 55
Fort Monroe 13, 47, 50, 55, 60
Fort Norfolk 60
Fort Pulaski 131
Fort Reno 135, 136
Fort Stephens 68, 134, 135
Fort Sumter 9
Fort Yuma 5
Foster, John G. 131
Foster, Robert S. 61
Fox, Owen 129, 132, 206
Freemont, John C. 57
French, William 72
Fries, Henry 101
Front Royal, Va. 155, 163
Fry, William 134, 136, 137
Frying Pan, Va. 114

Ganesvoort, Henry S. 81, 170
Garrity, Thomas 74
Gavin, Patrick 149
Getty, George 61
Gettysburg, Pa. 27, 72, 73
Gibbs, Alfred 179, 181, 183, 189, 197
Giesboro Point 73, 104, 109
Gillespie, John 208
Glasscot, John 209
Gloucester Point, Va. 50, 51, 53, 54–57, 62, 64, 68, 83, 90
Godwin, D.J. 53
Golden Age 25, 26
Good, John 157
Goodman, Samuel 203
Goodrich, Henry 201, 204
Goodwin, Charles 114
Gordon, John B. 151
Gordonsville, Va. 179, 180, 181
Goulding, George 209
Gozzens, Herman 204
Grant, Ulysses S. 118, 120, 125, 133, 135, 142, 144–146, 152, 160, 163, 179, 181, 182, 184, 186, 187, 189, 190–192, 196
Granville, Charles 154
Green, Stephen 168
Green, William 209

Gregg, David 75, 76
Gregory, David 154
Griffin, Stephen 208
Grimshaw, Arthur H. 50
Grout, Alonzo 147
Grover, Byron 203

Hackett, Patrick 204
Haggerty, Annie 64
Haglan, Carl 209
Hall, Frederick 195
Halleck, Henry W. 27, 28, 36, 37, 47, 72, 92, 163, 177
Halltown, Va. 38, 143, 145–147, 176
Halstead, Jacob 204
Hamblin, Edward 204
Hanover Courthouse, Va. 14
Hanscom, Samuel 132, 206
Hanson, Peter 85
Hardin, Martin D. 136
Hardy, John 161
Hargrove, Taswell L. 59
Harmon, William 146
Harpers Ferry 72, 133, 146, 176
Harris, Moses 155, 157, 158, 166
Harrison's Landing, Va. 15
Harrover, Robert 94
Hart, Charles 208
Harty, John 204
Harvard 10, 13, 86, 87, 97, 103, 112, 173
Haskall, Nathan 158
Hawkins, James 74
Hayden, John 108, 203
Hayford, James 85
Heintzelman, Samuel P. 67, 68, 72, 73
Henderson, William 204
Hero 59
Hewes, Francis 204
Hicks, Thomas H. 13
Higginson, Henry Lee 12, 15, 16, 30
Hill, Daniel Harvey 62
Hill, Frank 208
Hill, James 208
Hilliard, William 126, 127, 206
Hodson, Henry 208
Holden, Charles 204
Holman, George F. 50, 51, 97, 109
Holmes, Oliver Wendell, Jr. 48
Holt, George 177, 201
Hood, John Bell 54
Hooker, Joseph 17, 55–58, 72
Howe, Wesley 154
Howlett, James 209
Huestis, Nathan 127
Hughs, John 210
Hull, Chauncey 78
Humphreys, Charles A. 86, 87, 89, 94, 101, 103, 108, 112, 122, 127, 129–131, 170, 176, 178, 182, 192, 193
Hunt, Jesse 204

Hunter, David 140, 142
Hunter, James P. 157
Hunter, John 176
Hunter, William 114, 116
Hurley, John 85
Hurley, William 157
Hussey, William H.H. 27, 168
Hustings, Smith H. 167
Hyde, Arthur 203
Hyde, Sarah 193

Illinois troops: 8th Cavalry 125, 134, 142, 143; 12th Cavalry 58, 59; 18th Cavalry 134
Indiana troops: 1st Cavalry 116
Irving, Henry P. 74

Jackson, Dr. James 11
Jackson, Thomas J. 69, 133, 136
Jackson, William 136, 203
Jefferson 48
Jefferson, Thomas 48
Jenkins, Charles 84, 85, 201
Jessup, M. 6
Johnson, Bradley T. 136–138
Johnson, George 208
Johnson, John 132, 206
Johnson, Joseph 209
Johnson, William 31*n*
Johnston, Joseph E. 190, 193, 194
Jones, John 204
Jones, Samuel 131
Joy, Maurice 74

Kamehameha II 48
Keefe, Michael 89
Kelley, Bernard 209
Kelley, Edward 209
Kelley, John 207
Kelley, Thomas 146, 203
Kelly, Michael 146
Kelly, Patrick 157
Kemp, Joseph 106, 203
Kenebec 50
Kercheval, Benjamin 208
Keyes, Erasmus B. 50, 51, 55, 56, 58
Kice, Thomas 203
Kidd, James H. 153, 161–164, 167, 168
Kimbal, Solon D. 201
King, Rufus 75, 77, 85
King, Thomas Starr 23, 40
Kingsley, Edward 157
Kinne, Charles Mason 112, 158, 201
Knapp, David 204
Kuhls, Henry 166, 168, 189

La Gloriette Pass, Battle of 5
Landis, Stephen 201
Laurel Brigade, 161
Lawrence, Amos A., Jr. 8, 9, 16, 17, 29, 34, 53, 97, 170
Lawrence, Lawson 162

Lawrence, William 106, 204
Lazelle, Henry 81, 104, 109, 112, 133, 140
Lee, Alfred 113, 114,
Lee, Fitz Hugh 187, 189
Lee, George 201, 204
Lee, Henry 8
Lee, Robert E. 9, 56–58, 61, 73, 82, 118, 125, 152, 161, 184, 186, 187, 189, 190–192
Lee, W.H.F. 61
Leesburg, Va. 27, 71, 74, 82, 83, 89, 104, 105, 109, 114, 116, 125
Lenter, William 6
Leonard, Patrick 147
Libby, Frank 168
Lincoln, Abraham 6, 10, 12, 16, 27, 31n, 69, 104, 135, 145, 150, 177, 186, 190, 193
Little, Hazen D. 78
Liverpool 9
Loane, Abraham 88, 201, 206
Locke, John 203
Logan, Alexander 151
Logsden, James 206
Longstreet, James 54, 163
Lord, Abbie 32, 108, 202
Loring, John 206
Los Angeles, Ca. 5
Loud, Eugene 201
Lowder, Francis 192, 208
Lowell, Anna 15
Lowell, Anna Cabot Jackson 10
Lowell, Carlotta Russell 170n
Lowell, the Rev. Charles 10
Lowell, Charles Russell, Jr. 9–17, 29–31, 36, 37, 45, 48, 56, 58, 64, 65, 67, 68, 71–79, 81–83, 85–88, 90–99, 102, 104, 109, 110, 112–114, 116–118, 120–122, 125, 132–138, 140, 142, 143, 145–149, 152–157, 160–174, 177, 179, 191, 197, 208
Lowell, Charles R., Sr. 10, 11
Lowell, James Jackson 14, 48
Lowell, James Russell 10, 13
Lowell, Josephine Shaw 30, 64, 68, 75, 79, 86, 87, 94, 149, 150, 160, 169, 170, 172, 173
Luray Valley 154–156, 181
Lynch, Michael 161
Lynch, William 31n
Lyons, John 207

McAlistar, Henry 154
McCammon, James 203
McCarty, John 84, 86
McCausland, John 135
McClease, Joseph 151
McClellan, George B. 9, 13, 15–17, 51, 150, 177
McDonald, Daniel 146
McDonald, James 132, 206
McDonald, Philip 203
McDougal, Daniel 147, 201

McEwen, Warren 201
McGowan, John 207
McGrath, James 135
McGuire, John 203
McIntosh, Isaac 166, 201
McKay, James 209
McKendry, Archibald 23, 65, 112, 168, 177, 179, 181, 197, 198
McKinney, John 84
McKnight, Edward 151
McLaughlin, John 151
McLean, Alfred 64, 201
McLean, Owen 209
McLean, Wilmer 192
McMahon, James 116, 117
McMaster, Charles 155
McNeff, John 208
McNeil, William 201
Madison, James 48
Mail Steam Ship Co. 7
Mallory, Abner 201
Manchester, Luman 201
Manker, William 85
Manning, George 38, 106, 111, 133, 204
Manning, William C. 73, 77, 78, 103, 106, 111, 193, 201, 204
Marden, John 149
Martin, Thomas 149
Mary Martin 186n
Maryland troops (Union): 1st Cavalry 144; 2nd Cavalry 150
Marysville, Calif. 6
Mason, Charles 94
Massachusetts troops: 7th Artillery 61; 1st Cavalry 16, 45; 4th Cavalry 102; 5th Cavalry 45, 90, 101, 110; 2ndInfantry 45; 6th Infantry 12; 13th Infantry 31; 16th Infantry 31; 20th Infantry 15, 46, 48; 53rd Infantry 32; 54th Infantry 8, 30, 65, 69, 90; Light Dragoons (militia) 33; National Lancers (militia) 33
Matthews, Patrick 207
May, John 209
Mazy, Henry 183
Meade, George G. 73, 93, 133, 186, 192, 195
Meader, Charles E. 101, 149
Melville, Herman 114n
Merriam, Jonathan 201, 209
Merritt, Gilbert 64
Merritt, Wesley 144, 145, 150, 152–156, 161–166, 168, 173, 178, 179, 181, 191, 195, 197
Merry, Thomas H. 65, 67, 96, 97, 113, 135, 170
Michigan troops: 1st Cavalry 116; 5th Cavalry 167; 6th Cavalry 71
Middleburg, Va. 71, 99, 104, 112, 120, 138, 180
Middletown, Va. 145, 163, 164, 169, 171, 176
Miles, Henry 201

Miles, James 203
Millen, Ga. 204
Millican, William 204
Minot, William 208
Mississippi Marine Brigade 61
Monroe, James 48
Moore, Alpheus 165
Moore, Samuel 209
Moore, William 74, 189
Morris, William 85, 162
Morse, George 151
Mortimer, Harry W. 103, 201
Mosby, John S. 69–71, 76–78, 81–86, 89, 92–96, 99, 103–106, 109, 112–114, 116, 117, 120, 122, 125–127, 129, 131, 132, 140, 150, 155, 170, 176–178, 180, 189
Moulton, David 209
Mt. Savage Iron Works, Md. 12, 13
Mt. Zion Church, Va. 96, 126, 131, 132, 134
Mountjoy, Richard 105
Muddy Branch, Md. 89, 90, 92, 96, 97, 109, 110, 116, 118, 133, 142, 143
Munger, Lewis 189
Munroe, James 205
Munson, John W. 106
Murphey, Cornelius 209

New Orleans, La. 11, 12
New Jersey troops: 1st Cavalry 73; 3rd Cavalry 143, 157
New York Tribune 85
New York troops: 2nd Cavalry 59; 4th Cavalry 147; 5th Cavalry 71; 6th Cavalry 75; 11th Cavalry 92, 97, 116; 13th Cavalry 81, 85, 89, 98, 103, 108–110, 112, 116, 120, 125, 126, 129, 170; 16th Cavalry 81, 82, 96, 98, 103–105, 108–110, 112, 114, 116, 117, 121, 140; 25th Cavalry 147; 1st Dragoons 150; 9th Heavy Artillery 106, 204; 164th Infantry 116, 117; 50th Veteran Engineers 118
Nicholson, George 209
Norcross, Daniel 24
Norcross, John 74
North Carolina troops: 44th Infantry 59, 60
Nottage, John 206
Nye, J.W. 41
Nystrom, Charles 154

Ocean Queen 26, 32, 41, 42
O'Connell, John (Michael Walsh) 149
Oeldraiher, Charles 206
O'Halloran, James 203
O'Laughlin, Thomas 157
O'Leary, John 147
O'Neil, Patrick 147

Index

Orange and Alexandria Railroad 56, 75, 95, 118, 120, 196
Ormsby, William "Pony" 102–104
Osts, John 204
Owen, John 85

Pack, George 209
Panama 6, 26, 41, 42
Papanti, Augustus 189
Paris, Frank 204
Paris, Va. 73, 75, 117
Parker, Arthur 190
Parker, George 207
Partridge, Benjamin F. 133
Partridge, James 209
Payne, Norman B. 42
Payson, Charles 52, 102
Peel, Henry 189
Pendergast, William 31n
Peninsula campaign 9, 13–16, 51
Pennsylvania troops: 1st California/71st Infantry 26, 27; 2nd Cavalry 147; 5th Cavalry 55; 6th Cavalry 150n, 181; 8th Cavalry 85; 11th Cavalry 59, 60; 14th Cavalry 145; 16th Cavalry; 22nd Cavalry 144, 149; 149th Infantry 122; Reserve Corps 72
Perkins, Freeman 206
Petersburg, Va. 142, 163, 178, 179, 182, 186, 190, 193, 194
Peterson, John 209
Pettigrew, James J. 59
Phillips, John 112, 147
Pichacho Pass, Az., Skirmish at 5, 6
Pickett, George 54, 58, 59, 189, 190
Pingle, William 210
Pinney, Ephraim 203
Pioneer Guard 40
Platts Hall 23, 39, 40
Pleasonton, Alfred 71, 73
Poolesville, Md. 72, 73, 142, 143
Pope, John 10, 77
Porter, John 154
Powell, William H. 179
Powers, Richard 106, 203
Pratt, John 207
Price, Edward 205

Quant, Frederick 201, 202

Rand, James 207
Rankin, Ira P. 7, 8, 20, 36, 37, 47, 97
Rawson, Benjamin 201
Ray, William 208
Readville, Mass. 31, 35, 50, 56, 64, 90, 198, 206, 209
Redmann, Carl 169
Reed, James Sewall 7, 8, 20, 22, 23, 25, 31–34, 48, 55, 57, 58, 60, 83, 87, 89, 90, 92, 93, 101, 104–106, 108, 113, 132, 168, 203
Relmond, Charles P. 208

Renard, Peter 78
Rhode Island troops: 1st Cavalry 157, 179, 181, 182; 5th Infantry 30
Rice, Charles E. 88, 102
Rich, Charles 203
Richards, John T. 60, 102
Richards, Tom 126
Ricketts, James 133
Riley, Daniel 31n
Riley, Sylvester 31n
Ringold, George 23
Riordan, Patrick 132, 206
River Queen 186n
Robbins, Frank 14
Roberts, Charles 41, 69, 78, 82, 83, 168, 201
Robinson, William 201
Rockville, Md. 134, 135, 137, 138, 142, 208
Rodes, Robert E. 75, 147
Roe, Alfred 106, 204
Rogers, Thomas 201
Rollins, Charles 132, 206
Rosecrans, William 47
Ross, Joshua 113
Rosser, Thomas L. 161, 163, 164, 179
Rummery, Ezra 146, 201
Rummery, William M. 60, 87, 95, 96, 113, 114, 135, 150
Russell, Alvin 168
Russell, Henry S. 29, 30, 45, 64, 86, 90, 101, 102, 110
Ryley, Amos 145

Sailor's Creek, Va. 191
San Francisco, Calif. 5, 7, 8, 20, 22, 24–27, 35, 36, 39–42, 65, 67, 91, 108, 111, 113, 116, 154, 157, 162, 163, 168, 189, 190, 195, 202, 203, 206, 208, 209
San Jacinto, U.S.S. 41
Sanborn, George 204
Sanford, George B. 173
Savannah, Ga. 204, 205
Schellinger, Franklin 158
Schrow, Henry 149, 201
Scott, John 208
Scott, Michael 204
Scott's 900 (11th New York Cavalry) 92, 97
Seagrave, Edward 163, 201
Seanel, David 6
Seccin, Joseph 203
Sedgwick, John 15
Seven Days battle 14
Sewall, George 151
Seward, William H. 55
Shaw, Robert G. 29, 30, 48, 64, 76
Shaw, Sylvanus 201
Shay, Patrick 157
Shea, Cornelius 158
Sheldon, Adelbert 201
Sheridan, Philip H. 143–148,
150–156, 160, 161, 163–167, 170, 173, 177, 178, 181, 182, 184, 186, 187, 189, 191–193, 195n, 197
Sherman, William T. 181, 182, 193, 195, 196
Shiffer, John 151
Short, William 84
Sibley, Henry H. 5, 6
Siegel, Franz 57
Sierra Nevada 40
Sim, John W. 60, 112
Simmonson, Anthony 205
Slemp, John 209
Sline, Cornelius 207
Slocum, Henry W. 72
Slough, John P. 72
Smith, Francis 209
Smith, James 190
Smith, John 74
Smith, Leonard 201, 208
Smith, Norman 84
Smith, Roswell 74
Smith, Rufus 42, 76, 166, 168
Smith, Samuel 201
Smith, William F. 50
Sonora 42
South Anna River, Va., skirmish at 59–61, 183
South Carolina troops: Washington Artillery 72; 15th Infantry 148
Sparhawk (Sparrowhawk), Jared 169, 201
Spaulding, John 204
Spear, Samuel P. 59–61
Spencer, Ebenezer 201
Spofford, Joseph 203, 206
Spooner, Stephen 106, 203
Stanford, Leland 37
Stanton, Edwin M. 6–8, 17, 37, 47, 68, 85, 91, 98, 104, 163
Starr, William 201
Staunton, Va. 156, 160, 181
Stevens, Thomas 205
Stevenson, J.D. 6
Stone, Alvin 42, 111
Stone, Charles P. 13, 27
Stone, Goodwin 53, 77, 87, 102, 121, 126, 127, 129, 132, 206
Stone, Joseph 209
Stoneman, George 14, 56, 85, 130
Stoughton, Edwin 71
Strasburg, Va. 154, 181
Straub, Edward 201
Stuart, James E.B. 69–71, 73, 75, 82, 85, 105
Sullivan, Eugene 6
Sullivan, Patrick 207
Sullivan, Timothy 168
Summit Point, Va. 145, 149, 150, 176
Sumner, Charles 12, 13
Sumner, Edwin V. 15
Swan 56

Taylor, Archibald 205
Taylor, C.L. 22
Tennessee troops: 10th Infantry 106, 203
Tenny, William C. 48
Terry, David (Daniel) 74
Texas 5, 6, 23, 47
Thaxter, Benjamin 206
Thayer, Charles 190
Thomas, Charles 203
Thomas, William 206
Thompson, DeWitt Clinton 36, 37, 41, 47, 64, 67, 83, 89–92, 96–98, 109, 110, 113, 116, 118, 133, 137, 142, 143, 147, 194, 201
Thompson, Edward 151, 154, 189
Thompson, John 145, 176
Thompson, Marion Brown 37
Tobin, Cornelius 132, 206
Tom's Brook, Va. 162
Torbert, Alfred T.A. 144, 146, 154, 155, 157, 161, 164, 165, 167, 173, 179–181
Towle, George 20, 22, 26, 32, 35, 36, 51, 62, 81, 87, 88, 99, 134, 136, 148, 151, 152, 154, 156, 160, 162, 164, 167, 168, 170, 178, 182, 183, 191, 195, 198, 201, 202
Townsend, Hiram, 40
Tracy, Patrick 10
Trent 41
Trenton Iron Co. 11
Tubbs, Henry, 36, 209
Tucker, Samuel 162, 201
Tucker, Timothy 189
Tupper, Alexander 208
Turner, Levi 84, 204
Turner, Tom 84
Tuscon, Az. 5
Tyler, Robert O. 108, 116, 117, 120, 121

Union Army Corps: II Corps 15, 191; III Corps 14; IV Corps 14, 50; V Corps 186, 189, 190; VI Corps 133, 135, 138, 140, 142, 144, 150, 151, 163–165, 178, 191; VIII Corps 163–165; IX Corps 118; XI Corps 50, 57; XII Corps 72; XIX Corps 133, 135, 140, 142, 144, 150, 163–165; XXII Corps 67, 93, 116, 140; XXIV Corps 192

United States Regular Troops 6, 12, 13; 3rd Artillery 5, 72; 1st Cavalry 150, 155, 162, 166, 186; 2nd Cavalry 150, 155, 178; 3rd Cavalry 13; 5th Cavalry 150, 162, 183, 186; 6th Cavalry 9, 11, 13–16, 150, 181, 186; 5th Infantry 203; 8th Infantry 106; 9th Infantry 39
Upperville, Va. 72, 117, 120

Valverde, Battle of, 5
Van Vleet, DeWitt, 74
Varnum, Joseph 84
Vennum, Hiram 74
Vermont troops: Vermont Infantry Brigade 71
Verrick, George 84
Vienna, Va. 82, 93, 94, 97, 98, 103, 106, 108–114, 116, 118, 120, 197, 198, 203
Virginia Central Railroad 58, 59, 156, 179–183
Virginia troops: 1st Cavalry 69; 4th Cavalry 99; 6th Cavalry 75, 156; 8th Cavalry 99; 12th Cavalry 99; 14th Cavalry 135; 35th Cavalry battalion 70, 89, 92; 43rd Cavalry Battalion; 9th Infantry 54
Von Borcke, Heros 105
Von Kronensheldt, Johannes Kaspar Richter 48
Von Massow, Robert 105
Von Voaast, James 39

Wakefield, Elhanam 162
Walker, Edward 207
Wallace, Joseph 208
Wallace, Lew 133
Walton, William 168
Ward, John 147
Warner, Isaac 201
Warren, Gouverneur K. 189, 190
Warrenton, Va. 75
Washburne, E.H. 23
Washburne, Francis 47, 51, 52, 57, 87, 98, 102
Waters, Abraham 203
Watson, David 119
Watson, James 24, 25, 122, 190, 201
Waynesboro, Va. 156–158, 181

Weeks, Lewis 176
Weisberger, Stephen 168
Welch, Horace B. 42
Wells, Levi 134
Wentworth, George 206
Wentworth, Henry 206
West, Wells 95, 96
Weymouth, Uriah 205
Wharton, Gabriel C. 168
Wheat, James 24, 201
Wheeler, William 207
White, Elijah V. 83, 89, 93, 120
White, J.M. 143
White, William 146
White House, Va. 59, 61, 62, 184
White Post, Va. 145
Wickham, William 157
Wilburn, James P. 157, 201
Wilburn, Winfield 151
Wilcox, George 204
Wilcox, William 201
Wilderness, Battle of the 120, 121
Williams, Benjamin T. 97
Williams, Frank 89, 94, 105
Williams, Robert 121, 146
Williamsburg, Va. 14, 55, 56
Wilson, James 146, 152, 156, 157, 161
Wilson, Peter H. 96
Winchester, Va. 142, 145, 146, 152, 154, 163, 164, 169, 173, 176, 177, 181, 182, 208
Winship, John 145, 193
Wise, Henry 61
Withrow, Abel 201
Witter, John 204
Wolcott, Huntington 196
Wolcott, Oliver 196
Woodman, Henry 158
Woodstock, Va. 161, 162, 168, 181
Woodward, Edwin 201
Worster, Arthur 204
Wright, George 23, 37
Wright, Horatio G. 134–138, 140, 142, 144, 164
Wyatt, Henry 201
Wyatt, William 203
Wyndham, Percy 71, 73

Yorktown, Va. 14, 50, 55–57

www.ingramcontent.com/pod-product-compliance
Ingram Content Group UK Ltd.
Pitfield, Milton Keynes, MK11 3LW, UK
UKHW050702160426
5217IPUK00038B/1864